THE
BROTHERS

THE BROTHERS

◆

The Saatchi & Saatchi Story

◆

I V A N   F A L L O N

CONTEMPORARY
BOOKS
CHICAGO

Library of Congress Cataloging-in-Publication Data

Fallon, Ivan.
  The brothers : the Saatchi & Saatchi story/ Ivan Fallon.
    p.   cm.
  ISBN 0-8092-4310-5
    1. Saatchi & Saatchi—History.   2. Advertising agencies—History.
  I. Title.
  HF6181.S23F35   1989
  338.7'616591—dc20   89-37680
                                                                    CIP

For Sue, Tania, Lara, and Padraic Robert

Published by Contemporary Books, Inc.
180 North Michigan Avenue, Chicago, Illinois 60601
Manufactured in the United States of America
International Standard Book Number: 0-8092-4310-5

Published simultaneously in Canada by Beaverbooks, Ltd.
195 Allstate Parkway, Valleywood Business Park
Markham, Ontario L3R 4T8 Canada

CONTENTS

ACKNOWLEDGMENTS

The original idea for this book came from Richard Cohen of Century Hutchinson, who also talked me into doing it, while Frank Delaney proposed me as the author. The Saatchi brothers themselves, Maurice and Charles, were far from enthusiastic when first I broached it; they had received many approaches from other would-be biographers and had brusquely refused to cooperate in the slightest. In the end I told Maurice that despite his reluctance, I would go ahead anyway—unless he and Charles were so opposed that they would cut off all contact with their family, employees, and friends. I was keenly aware that had they wanted to they could have closed off so many avenues that it would not have been possible to write this book, and in any case I needed access to *them*. At that stage I had known Maurice for about ten years and as a financial journalist had followed closely—and often written about—the affairs of Saatchi & Saatchi. But Charles was for me—as for almost everyone else—a distant, brooding presence, seldom seen and even less often pinned down for a discussion of anything, least of all his family background and personal life. It had long been accepted that he did not give interviews; even many of his own staff had never glimpsed him. Conversely—and many would say deliberately—his desire for privacy had the effect of making everything he did highly news-worthy. Yet remarkably little, as I was to discover, was known about either of the brothers, and what little there was was often wrong—even their birthplace and original nationality.

Eventually they consented to give me a kind of qualified access and agreed they would not obstruct me in talking to anyone I wanted to. Having made that promise, Maurice in particular was generous with his own time. I had access, when I wanted it, to anyone inside Saatchi & Saatchi anywhere in the world with no conditions imposed upon my interviews other than the standard one that the Saatchis insist on for all journalists before they allow any employee to be interviewed: they must not be quoted directly, although the information given can be used and attributed indirectly. I found it a small price to pay, particularly as in those circumstances Saatchi staff members were much more prepared to speak their minds and add to the flow of anecdotes that every Saatchi employee has collected about the brothers. Charles proved particularly reluctant to talk about his art collection, but he pointed me to people who could explain his philosophy on the subject—and I had little trouble getting his critics in the art world to air their views. One of my more interesting experiences, after the book was finished, was to be taken by Charles on a tour of his gallery, but even then he didn't much like explaining the art.

As my research progressed, I found there was a well-worn path to the doors of most of those I approached for interviews. In the past most of these people had respected the brothers' keen desire to stay out of the public spotlight, and those doors had remained firmly closed. Often even those who had quarreled with the brothers still checked with either Maurice or Charles before they would agree to see me; but nobody I approached refused to talk to me, and invariably they were frank, open—and often critical. The brothers must have wondered from a distance what I was discovering but never tried to control where I went, who I saw, or what I learned. Nor did they make any attempt to gain or exercise any influence over what I wrote about them. I showed them an early draft of the manuscript, as indeed I showed it to several others who were centrally involved, including Tim Bell. As a result I made a number of changes, but more by way of elaboration than anything else. I was told by others that the brothers were distressed by some of the material in this book, but they never asked for anything to be removed and their courtesy to me never wavered. When the book finally appeared in Britain, I sent them both early copies and on publication day received a present in return: my own book, but neatly reversed on me. The same dust jacket had been used (goodness knows where they got it from), but the words *The Brothers* had been changed to *Fallon* and they had substituted *The Rise & Rise of Saatchi & Saatchi* [the subtitle of the British edition] with the flatteringly exaggerated *The Rise & Rise of Britain's Top Newspaper Editor, by C. & M. Saatchi*. Inside was the handwritten inscription: "Greetings from the Bazaar (or is it the Bizarre!). Much love, Charles and Maurice." My comment that they had, from their Middle East background, generations of the bazaar bred into them must have stung. They must have had other objections, too, but they never voiced them, at least not to me. It was the first time I had been subjected to the full impact of the legendary Saatchi charm—and, like most others, I found it disarming.

This book is a revised and expanded version of the book that appeared in Britain in 1988. It is based on more than one hundred interviews in London and New York with most of the people the brothers have ever had any close contact with in business, the arts, politics, or other areas of their lives. I have been very fortunate in that for many of these people, contact with the Saatchis was a memorable event, often the high point of their lives, and their recollection of it has usually been keen. The time scale is also short enough for memories still to be reasonably fresh; most of the central characters are around the same age as the brothers—early to mid-forties—and because Saatchi & Saatchi only came into existence in 1970, the main events are fairly recent. A number of people I interviewed more than once, and some up to half a dozen times. Where possible I have quoted them on the record, but often people talked more freely off the record, and I have respected that. Where I quote a conversation, I have always tried to check it with both sides.

I am especially grateful to Naim Dangoor for his invaluable help and guidance on the history of Iraqi Jews; to Barry Day for his advice both on political advertising and on the American advertising industry; to all those who gave me their time, particularly Tim Bell, who could not have enjoyed reliving some of the events described; to Jeremy Sinclair, Michael Dobbs, Martin Sorrell, Brian Basham, Frank Lowe, Milt Gossett, Carl Spielvogel, and many others; and to Lindsay Masters and Christine Barker, who besides submitting to interviews also allowed me access to the Thatcher campaign library.

Among those I interviewed were: Terry Bannister, Christine Barker, Brian Basham, Tim Bell, Edward Booth-Clibborn, Frankie Cadwell, John Chiene, Sir Robert Clark, Professor Percy Cohen, Ron Collins, Ross Cramer, Charles Crane, Nick Crean, Geoff Culmer, Naim Dangoor, Herman Davies, David Davis, Barry Day, Michael Dobbs, Rodney Fitch, Kenneth Gill, Milt Gossett, Michael Green, James Gulliver, Josephine Hart, John Hegarty, Robert Heller, Michael Heseltine, Keith Hopkins, Lord King of Wartnaby, Fred Krantz, Jennifer Laing, Frank Lowe, Sir Kit McMahon, Chris Martin, Rick Martindale, Lindsay Masters, Marisa Masters, Simon Mellor, Victor Millar, Bill Muirhead, Sean O'Connor, Greg Ostroff, Cecil Parkinson, Sir Gordon Reece, Norman Rosenthal, David Saatchi, Doris Saatchi, Nick Serota, Stella Shamoon, Robert Shulman, Alan Siegel, Anthony Simonds-Gooding, Jeremy Sinclair, Violette Shamash, Martin Sorell, Carl Spielvogel, David Sylvester, Norman Tebbit, Alan Tilby, Vanni Treves, Marina Vaizey, Michael Wahl, Roy Warman, Ed Wax, Brian Wolfson, and Lord Young of Graffham.

In addition, there were a number of people who talked to me on the basis that their names would not be mentioned but to whom I am also grateful. I have also quoted from some of the many articles and other material that has been written on the Saatchis and on the events related here, notably in the trade press.

A special note of thanks must go to Richard Cohen, the best editor an author can have; to Lynden Stafford, who meticulously copyedited the manuscript; and to Vivienne Schuster, my agent. Special thanks are also due to Laurence Good for his research and hard work, to his father, John, and to my daughter, Tania. But above all I have to thank my wife, Sue, who put even more hours into this book than I did, not only on research and interviews but in every other aspect of the book as well.

THE
BROTHERS

INTRODUCTION

Robert E. Jacoby is a short man—5 feet, 4½ inches tall—Napoleonic, cigar-smoking, elfin-featured, with a penchant for military heroes (Rommel and Patton). He ran the world's third largest advertising business, Ted Bates, with an autocratic and often intimidating style that inevitably encouraged the dictator image. One former employee described him as "Stalinesque but without the compassion"; others compared him to Franco. He was different from most advertising executives. A cum-laude economics graduate from Princeton, he had worked as an economics analyst for Shell Oil before moving to Madison Avenue, where he learned his trade at the knees of two of the great figures of the age: Ted Bates himself, a former vice president of Benton & Bowles who took the Colgate Palmolive account and struck out on his own; and Bates's legendary copywriter, Rosser Reeve, who developed the very simple but highly effective advertising philosophy that came to be known as the Unique Selling Proposition (or USP)—that every advertisement should offer an unusual or "unique" benefit to the consumer. Reeves's book, *Reality in Advertising*, was required reading for all aspiring adpeople in the 1960s, and a generation of Americans tuned in to the Bates campaigns for the United States Navy ("It's not just a job, it's an adventure") or for Mars' M&Ms ("Melt in your mouth—not in your hand") or for Prudential ("Get a piece of the Rock").

In 1974, the year Ted Bates died, Jacoby took over as chief executive and for a dozen years presided over one of the most financially successful advertising agencies in America. He expanded the business through an aggressive series of mergers, each time increasing the profit margins, which led to growing criticism that Bates cared too much about the bottom line and not enough about the ads it made possible.

In the spring of 1986 Jacoby was no longer looking for agencies to buy. He was in his late fifties, a hard-drinking, notorious womanizer, with less and less interest in running the business. He was now looking to sell Bates but not just to anyone. Jacoby was concentrating all his considerable energies and bargaining skills into what would be his last and greatest deal, one that would, if it came off, make him the richest man in the history of advertising. That spring the takeover spree that had rolled through corporate America in the Reagan years had arrived on Madison Avenue. On April 28 Allen Rosenshine, chairman of BBDO International, announced the first megamerger in advertising history: BBDO, the sixth-largest American agency, was merging with Needham Harper Worldwide (number sixteen) and Doyle Dane Bernbach (number twelve) to create a group with annual billings of $5 billion. "We are the biggest," boasted Rosenshine, before adding, presciently, as it turned out, "but maybe only for five minutes."

The first week in May witnessed impossible, absurd rumors in the industry. Ogilvy & Mather was to team up with Interpublic to form a colossus that would make even Rosenshine's new group, now called Omnicon, look small. J. Walter Thompson and Young and Rubicam were to merge. Bates was linked with any one of a dozen agencies as Jacoby let it be known he wanted a buyer. And everywhere the footprints of the predator Madison Avenue feared most were to be found: Saatchi & Saatchi had trawled the length and breadth of the American advertising industry, holding talks here, making offers there, getting increasingly desperate to make the jump to what its founder brothers, Charles and Maurice Saatchi, wanted more than anything: to become the world's number-one advertising business.

The Saatchis had achieved some success. In the four years since they had bought their first New York agency, Compton Advertising, the Saatchis had added two more: Dancer Fitzgerald Sample and Backer & Spielvogel. But they had failed to get Doyle Dane Bernbach despite a cash offer of $30 a share, and half a dozen other tentative talks had led to nothing.

But for eighteen months they had been holding talks with Ted Bates, which several times had come close to agreement, only to break down as they argued over payment terms. The trade press and the industry knew all about the talks—and that both sides were also talking to just about every potential partner on Madison Avenue. Reports in the trade press that spring referred to a probable price tag on Bates in the range of $250 to $300 million, the maximum that most analysts believed the agency, owned by its employee-shareholders, was worth. Jacoby had set his targets higher than that, however: he wanted $500 million, which would make it the biggest deal ever done in the industry. At that price he had plenty of willing sellers among his own staff, nearly one hundred of whom would become millionaires. Jacoby himself would do better: he would get more than $100 million, a huge sum by any standard but undreamed of in the agency business, where salaries were high but capital small. It would also make him a pariah in his own industry, a person widely condemned as a figure of greed who opened the way for the British invasion of Madison Avenue.

Back in London Charles and Maurice Saatchi were running out of options. They were aware that Jacoby was cleverly playing with them and were furious at the way he trampled over all the careful rules they liked to set when they made takeovers, particularly an "earn out" agreement whereby they paid half of the bid price down and the rest over several years, depending on profits. But Jacoby knew how much the Saatchis wanted a major deal, knew the options open to them better than they did, and saw, as the windows of opportunity closed, that they had to go for Bates—or risk being shut out of the top three advertising businesses where they had publicly vowed to be.

The final deal took less than a week to negotiate. Jacoby sent the Saatchis a single sheet of paper setting out his bid terms. He knew they had the money, raised through the London stock market just weeks before. It was now or never, he told them—and the price was $500 million. Maurice Saatchi came back with a final offer: $400 million now, $50 million payable in 1988. In the City of London, he explained, the view was that Bates was worth $450 million at most—and even that was extracting a handsome premium. Jacoby had a way around it. He rang Maurice. He had a proposal that he said "will make it easy for both of us." He would borrow $57 million from the banks, and once the acquisition had gone through, the Saatchis would assume the loan. In London, the Saatchis could announce they had paid $450 million, but in fact the Bates shareholders would be getting $507 million.

Maurice talked it over with Charles, then rang back. They would do it. "Great," said Jacoby. "Send all your monkeys over. We'll do it here this time." Six months earlier he had turned up in London with documents all ready to sign only to find the Saatchis had set new conditions.

The deal was finally signed just after seven o'clock on the evening of May 8, 1986. It was midnight in London when Maurice Saatchi got the call to say it was finally done. Jubilantly he broke out the champagne. Saatchi & Saatchi now had billings of $7.5 billion worldwide, half as big again as Rosenshine's merged Omnicon group. Less than sixteen years after he and his brother founded their agency in a tiny office in London's Soho district, they had become the biggest in the world.

Neither Charles nor Maurice Saatchi had an inkling that night that with Bates they had bought more than size. They had also bought problems and controversy on a scale they had never encountered before. Over the next two years there would be times when they wished they had never heard of Ted Bates—or of Robert E. Jacoby.

1
ERE BABYLON WAS DUST

In the summer of 1985 Michael Wahl, founder and proprietor of one of America's largest sales-promotion companies, was approached by a New York investment banker. Would he be interested in selling his business to Saatchi & Saatchi? "No," said Wahl. "I don't want to sell out to the Japanese." In one of London's more select clubs, a Conservative member of Parliament leaned across the lunch table. "Why does the prime minister surround herself with all these foreigners—these Italian advertising chaps, for instance?" Many similar stories abound. Sometimes the Saatchi brothers are thought to be Italian, sometimes American; the satirical magazine *Private Eye* refers to them simply as "the Corsican Brothers." On occasion people who work for them wonder if they exist at all. In May 1987 when the executives of a Saatchi subsidiary, Rumrill-Hoyt, located in Rochester, had a housewarming party for their new headquarters, they posed for pictures beside full-size cardboard cutouts of the brothers. It was probably the closest anyone in that office would ever get to their bosses.

Considering that they are household names in business circles around the world, Charles and Maurice Saatchi are probably surrounded by more myths and misconceptions than any other businessmen. In Britain for years it was fashionable to talk about their being "Italian ice-cream salesmen," oiling the wheels for the smooth running of the Conservative party machine. They were the two boys who had changed Margaret Thatcher's voice and hairstyle, whose slick advertising and promotion had put her on Downing Street—and continued to guide her every move. They were upstarts with overgrand ambitions who would soon meet their nemesis. They were destroying the values and craft of Madison Avenue, or what was left of it, with their limitless hunger for size, power, and money. Yet who were they really? Where did they come from? In a world of ambitious business executives and corporate predators, what singled them out from the pack?

By the time they had become the biggest advertising agents in the world's history, the Saatchis were correctly identified in most newspaper and magazine profiles as being of Iraqi Jewish background. But invariably, the articles reported that their father emigrated from Iraq to Britain "before the War" or even "during the War," inferring that the boys were born in Britain after he arrived. The only previous book written about them describes their family background in a single sentence: they are "the middle two of four sons of an Iraqi Jewish businessman settled in North London." Articles repeat the same anecdotes about them, attempting to stereotype two men not easily stereotyped. They have accomplished an extraordinary public sleight of hand by getting their names known around the globe, yet keeping their personal lives private. They have not encouraged the myths that have sprung up, but neither have they sought to correct them, being happy to let the mystery grow and deepen. Even those who have worked for them for years know little about their private lives. Everyone with a television set in the free world has seen their advertisements; everyone in the advertising world knows the legend. Few know the real story.

Charles Nathan Saatchi, second son of Nathan and Daisy Saatchi, was born in Baghdad in 1943 into a large family household containing literally dozens of aunts, grandparents, cousins, and servants. Nathan was a prosperous textile merchant, importing cotton and woolen goods from Europe, who shared a huge house, which had several wings, with his brother, who was also his business partner. An extended and close family living in some prosperity and even luxury was not atypical of other Iraqi Jewish families at the time.

Charles's elder brother, David, had been born in 1937, and with the arrival of a second child, Nathan decided it was time to move. Perhaps he had fallen out with his brother; perhaps Nathan had become more westernized because of his frequent travels, but around 1943 he moved out of the old family home and bought a house for himself in the suburbs. There too there were servants and helpers, and by Western standards it remained a large household. It was there in 1946 that Maurice Nathan Saatchi was born.

Between the births of Nathan's second and third sons, the political climate in Iraq changed dramatically. In midwar, when Charles was born, it was relatively peaceful, although only two years before, on April 18, 1941, Rashid Ali al-Gaylani, an Arab nationalist with pro-German sympathies, had formed a new government that included elements notorious for their Nazi connections and their anti-Jewish sentiment. A month later, with Rommel's troops advancing toward Egypt, Rashid Ali declared war on Britain: so began the harassment of a community that had prospered and multiplied around Baghdad from Babylonian times. In the 1920s and 1930s over 50 percent of the trade and finance of Iraq had been in Jewish hands. Now events were in train that were to cause the second exile of the oldest community in the Jewish diaspora and end twenty-five centuries of continuous sojourn in a land fundamentally important for the culture and teachings of the Jewish religion. Rashid Ali's government did not last long—it fled at the end of May when British troops approached the outskirts of Baghdad. But in the aftermath, with British troops still waiting to enter, demobilized Iraqi soldiers turned on the Jewish community, killing between 170 and 180 people and wounding many others.

When Tobruk fell to the Germans, the news was greeted with open jubilation in nationalist circles in Baghdad. The overthrow of Rashid Ali and the battle of Alamein at the end of 1942 caused the nationalist feeling to abate again, and by 1943 there was little overt sign of the trauma that lay only a few years away. The latter years of World War II were actually a time of considerable growth in the Iraqi economy. "Trade flourished, prices increased by the day, with profit margins increasing accordingly, and there was much activity in the financial sphere," wrote Nissim Rejwan, a former Iraqi journalist, in his book *The Jews of Iraq*. The Jews, of course, were dominant in all these areas of business, and few sensed the disaster that lay ahead. "The Jews, at least those of the older generation, virtually forgot the trauma of 1941 and became fully occupied with their daily pursuits," stated Rejwan.

The Saatchi family was not one of the very wealthy who built their castles and fine houses along the banks of the Tigris River, which flows through the heart of the city, but it was well-to-do nonetheless. Literally translated, *Sa'atchi* means "watchmaker" or, more properly, "watch dealer"—there has never been a watchmaking industry in Iraq. The first part of the name means "watch" in Arabic, and the ending is the Turkish adjectival possessive expression common in Iraqi and used in connection with a number of other crafts. It is still used and is still, as it has always been, colloquial and not proper Arabic. The family has long forgotten the origin of the name, if it ever knew it, but Nathan believes it goes back to his forebears in Vienna; others in the family suggest it may be Venetian. They are almost certainly wrong. In Iraq today many people are called Sa'atchi or Saati because they deal in watches; among them are (or were) Jewish, Christian, and Muslim families. With the decreasing influence of the Turkish language in Iraq in the 1930s and 1940s, many families who did not like the Turkish ending used "Saati" instead of "Saatchi."

Nathan himself was born in Baghdad, as was his father, so for generations the family had lived in that city. In Nathan's day there were few records of marriages and births, and those that existed were either destroyed during the Ottoman Empire or later with the exit of the Jewish population after World War II.

Other Baghdad emigrants associate the Saatchis with a watch and jewelry business, but there is no evidence of this. Violette Shamash, for instance, who grew up with Daisy Saatchi, recalls a watch emporium on the main street of Baghdad that was called Saatchi and was where everyone went for watches. But she too seems to be mistaken in believing it was owned by Nathan's family. Certainly by the time the boys were born, his business was mainly in buying goods in Europe and exporting them to Iraq, Lebanon, Syria, and other parts of the Middle East. Contemporary pictures of Baghdad at the time show a uniform mass of unpainted two-story houses nestling on both banks of the river, often flooded when the river burst its banks. The center, where Nathan (pronounced Nat-*than*) Saatchi and his brother ran their business, was full of busy, palm-lined thoroughfares, already jammed with cars, trucks, and buses.

For centuries Baghdad was along the meeting point of the routes of southwest Asia, the nodal point of the caravan trails between East and West. It commanded the two waterways of the Tigris and Euphrates, close to the upward limit of navigation on the Tigris, which in Baghdad was crossed by a single bridge of boats. An airport was finished before the war, but a railway linking Baghdad to the Bosporus was only completed in 1940. Even before that, however, it had become noticeably westernized. In 1947, the year the Saatchis left Baghdad, one observer who knew it well mourned, "The traveler who wishes to see a purely Eastern city will not find it in Baghdad except in the byways and in a few of the old mosques which remain."

Some older quarters still preserved their purely oriental character, but during the twentieth century changes had taken place in the city itself that had altered it out of recognition. Some of the main roads had been straightened and a macadam surface laid down so that most of the city had been opened up to motor traffic. There was a telephone and taxi service, and a modern water system had at last replaced the old canals and insanitary methods of drawing water from the Tigris. Two of David Saatchi's lasting memories are of the icemen delivering ice to the Saatchi refrigerators and the habit of sleeping for a couple of hours in the afternoons, traditional in many hot climates.

The population in 1938 was 400,000, according to most estimates, having doubled in twenty years. Inside the town some of the old covered bazaars still survived, but by the time Charles Saatchi was born Western-style stores were common.

Nathan Saatchi is a short, slight man who, like most middle-class Jews of Iraq, is well educated. The predominant foreign culture in Iraq was French, but the British had been in and out of the area since 1917 and had left their mark too. Many educated Baghdad Jews speak up to five languages, including English and French, but the main one is Iraqi Arabic, with English taught as the second language. Nathan, like all his contemporaries, went through the age-old ritual of using a matchmaker when it came to finding his wife: the story is related of how he was told to walk past the window of a certain house at a certain time, and there would be a pretty girl standing there. Daisy Ezer (many Baghdad Jews were given foreign, usually French or English, names at this time) had been to the Alliance School for Girls, an institution sponsored by the French government, and came from a similar middle-class background. She was seventeen when they married in 1936; Nathan was twelve years older.

Nathan and Daisy had grown up in a Jewish community that saw little of the pogroms or anti-Semitism that their Ashkenazi brethren lived through in Eastern Europe at the time. When the British entered Baghdad in 1917, the Jews constituted the largest single group in the population—80,000 out of 202,000. The rest were Sunnis, Shi'ites, Turks, Christians, and Kurds, and for the most part they lived in reasonable harmony. The Jews were by far the wealthiest and best educated, and they had a worldwide network of business contacts, much of it with fellow Baghdad Jews who had moved on over the years to India, England (the Sassoons had come from Baghdad), and the Far East (the Kadooris of Hong Kong also originated in Baghdad). Under centuries of Ottoman rule the Jews were given "protected minority" status, and more recently they had become full citizens, enjoying equal rights with their Muslim neighbors. To the horror of the Jewish population, the British, after World War I, proposed setting up indigenous governments in Syria and Mesopotamia, as Iraq was then called. In 1921 the Jews asked for British citizenship but were refused, and they watched uneasily as Amir Faisal, the son of Sharaf Hussein ibn 'Ali, who had led the Arab revolt against the Ottoman sultan, was brought from Mecca at the insistence of Colonel T. E. Lawrence ("Lawrence of Arabia") to take over the Kingdom of Iraq, the first Arab country to attain independence from the British.

For a time, however, they continued to thrive. One Baghdad Jew, Sassoon Heskel, even became finance minister, while another was a justice of the supreme court; in the new parliament of 1925 five of the thirty-two deputies were Jews. From the mid-1930s, coinciding with the rise of Nazism in Europe, the position began to change, but there was still little sign that 2,500 years of history were drawing to a close.

Few Jews of the generation of Charles and Maurice Saatchi have anything more than a superficial knowledge of the culture they left behind, yet the generation of Nathan and Daisy was steeped in it. Hebrew associations with Iraq go back to the time when Abraham, the very first Hebrew (*Abraham* means "from the other side," meaning he had come from the other side of the Euphrates River), set out from southern Iraq to Canaan to form a new nation, which he was convinced was destined to bring the knowledge of God to the world. Twelve centuries later, in 597 B.C., King Yehoyachin and many of the leading citizens of Judah were brought as slaves to Babylon, the site of which is close to modern Baghdad. Eleven years later, in 586 B.C., one of the major events of Jewish history occurred.

The Babylonian king, King Nebuchadnezzar, razed Jerusalem but contrary to the legends neither killed nor enslaved all of its inhabitants.

What he did do was take the entire aristocracy of the Jews into exile in Babylon. They were craftsmen, physicians, and priests—practically all the skilled and educated people in the population. Only poor peasants remained in the war-ravaged valleys of the Judean hills. From this deportation most historians date the final fashioning of the Jewish religion. "Out of the crucible of exile and affliction, Judah emerged, purged and purified, into a new people—the Jews," wrote Rabbi Isidore Epstein. "Spreading quickly throughout the earth, the Jews carried wherever they settled a new message—Judaism. Shaped and nurtured by a faith which was impervious to change of circumstance and environment, Judaism in captivity not only survived but also developed a dynamic which in turn was destined to captivate the world."

The Jews had always regarded Babylonia as the cradle of their civilization, the place of the Tower of Babel, Noah, the Garden of Eden, and the origin of many of their beliefs. The Babylonians spoke a language very similar to the Hebrew of the Jews, and in some cities of Babylon it was identical. Far from being treated harshly, the Jews in Babylon were given fruit trees and vineyards, lands and houses, and were even allowed to keep what gold and jewels they brought from Jerusalem. According to the Jewish historian Naim Dangoor, they "gradually took the position of colonists rather than of captives." When the Persian king Cyrus the Great captured Babylon and tried to repatriate the Jews, only 40,000 returned to Jerusalem. Another 80,000, encouraged by the Persians, stayed and prospered in the rich land by the waters of Babylon, though still, according to the psalm, weeping when they remembered Zion.

Dangoor, whose grandfather was the chief rabbi of Baghdad, points out that the Jews of Baghdad number among their ancestry such significant figures as Joshua the High Priest, Ezra the Scribe, Nehemiah the Prophet, and the great Rabbi Hillel, a gentle philosopher and teacher whose most famous and lasting saying was: "If I am not for myself, who will be for me? And if I am only for myself, what am I? And if not now, when?" It is a line curiously evocative of the Saatchi philosophy.

At one time Babylonian Jewry totaled a million and may have constituted the largest part of the Jewish population. It produced one of the great jewels of Jewish history: the Babylonian Talmud, written between the second and fifth centuries B.C. It also gave the Jews something else—their love of commerce. In Israel the Jews had been an essentially agricultural race: peasants, settlers, cattle breeders, and traders. To survive and retain their culture, they had to change. Writes Nissim Rejwan: "It was in Babylonia that the occupations of merchant, trader, financier and banker were introduced to Jewry—professions which continue to be favourites with Jews up to our own day."

Despite this background, when Charles Saatchi was four and his brother Maurice only a baby, Nathan and Daisy decided to abandon their life in Iraq and leave with whatever they could take. They were the forerunners of what became a huge exodus. Within a few years they were followed by some 120,000 Jews, leaving only 15,000 behind. After mass executions of Jews in 1969, the others followed, leaving just a few hundred elderly Jews in Baghdad today. As the *Jerusalem Post* declared in 1986: "No other exodus in Jewish history, except the exodus from Egypt, was comparable in terms of its drama and spontaneity to the story of the Iraqi Jews."

Trouble for the Jews of Iraq started a few months after the end of World War II. Major events were happening in the Arab world that would sweep them up. The League of Arab Nations had been created with the principal aim of preventing the creation of a Jewish state in Palestine, and in Iraq the official attitude toward the Jews underwent a change. Measures were taken to reduce the number of Jews in the civil service; restrictions were imposed on the teaching of Hebrew; all contacts with Palestine were prohibited; and Jews were forced to take on Muslim partners in their businesses. Jews found it increasingly difficult to gain admittance to state schools and universities. Government ministers talked darkly about political Zionism "poisoning the atmosphere." Jews were forbidden to buy land. At the beginning of 1947 a new regulation required that any Jew leaving the country had to deposit a guarantee of £1,500 regardless of the purpose of travel. Jews were no longer accepted into government schools.

In 1946 Nathan Saatchi went to London, bought a couple of cotton and wool mills, and began looking for a house. He toyed with the idea of living in Canada or the United States, but he liked London. An uncle had gone to Britain in the 1930s, but they were not close, and essentially Nathan was proposing to put down roots in a strange land that he hardly knew. Both he and Daisy spoke English, but with a distinctive Middle Eastern accent. He was away for the best part of a year and missed the birth of Maurice.

The Iraqi economy was in one of its worst recessions, partly the result of the huge inflation of the war years, and the Saatchi family business suffered badly. Nathan was no longer leaving very much behind. In 1947 he and his family sold the business, and he, Daisy, and their three children set off for England. Jews who left after 1949 had their assets confiscated, but Nathan was probably able to take a certain amount with him. Among the emigrants from Iraq at the time, stories abound of gold coins smuggled out inside tubes of toothpaste and diamond earrings stuffed down socks. "My father, who came out about the same time as the Saatchis, brought what he could easily carry in his pockets, which was nothing really," says one Sephardic Jew. "He had a big business in Baghdad, but he arrived in England with the equivalent of just a decent year's salary. My mother still moans about the jewelry she left behind. They all do."

Nathan anticipated disaster by a couple of years. With Maurice in Daisy's arms, the family caught a train to Lebanon, then a boat to Marseilles, and another boat from there to England. The trip took three months. Daisy had been far more reluctant than Nathan to leave, but for her generation there was no question of a wife not going with her husband.

They settled in a house in Ossulton Way, on the edge of Hampstead Golf Club, one of the more select parts of North London. For a few years it was a lonely existence. They had exchanged a warm, friendly, large house for a home that by British standards was big but that was no longer peopled by an extended family and servants. The climate was cold, and the boys soon discovered that they couldn't even buy chocolate: London was still in the grip of postwar rationing. Many of the Saatchi friends and callers were fellow exiles from Baghdad who began pouring into London in the late 1940s, but at home now, on Nathan's orders, only English was spoken. Even a request for food had to be made in English, or it was not answered. David, age ten, spoke only Arabic, so he was sent to boarding school in Brighton to learn English ways as fast as he could. Within a few years he was wearing cavalry-twill trousers and sports jackets and playing English cricket and soccer; his English, if not grammatically perfect, was at least spoken with a good English accent.

The richer Iraqi Jews of the day mostly went either to the United States or to Britain. The poorer ones on the whole went to Israel to become the butt of another kind of prejudice: the Ashkenazi Jews, mostly refugees from Germany and Eastern Europe, looked down on these more traditional, less Westernized people. It was a strange prejudice. As Stephen Birmingham writes in his book, *Our Crowd*, which describes the Jewish banking families of New York: "In the unwritten hierarchy of world Jewry, the Sephardim are considered, and consider themselves, the most noble of all Jews because as a culture, they claim the longest unbroken history of unity and suffering."

However, the Sephardic Jews who set up the great banking houses in New York—the Nathans, Hendrickses, Cardozos, Baruchs, Lazaruses, and the rest—had mostly arrived after a journey that had begun several centuries before in Spain, where they had been expelled, coincidentally, the same year Columbus discovered America. The Sephardim who now arrived in the new state of Israel or journeyed farther to the United States and Britain were not, on the whole, westernized, although there had been a tradition in the 1920s and 1930s for the richer families to send their children to English schools to be educated. The Saatchi boys were soon to pick up English ways, but for their parents it was much more difficult to adjust.

It did not take Nathan long to build up his business again, and by the time a fourth son, Philip, was born in June 1953, the Saatchi family was in a position to move again, this time to a large home on Hampstead

Lane, Highgate, today one of the most expensive and sought-after areas of London. One old family friend from their Baghdad days recalls visiting them in 1961, and the Saatchis already had what she described as a "lovely home with seven bedrooms." In fact, it had even more than that.

All four boys grew up tall and strong—each is six feet tall or more, towering over the slight Nathan. Like most Jewish families, the Saatchis observed their religion, and for years afterward colleagues of Charles and Maurice can remember them leaving business meetings to be at their parents' home on a Friday night.

As they prospered, both Nathan and Daisy moved through London with growing confidence. Friends describe Daisy as a large, vital, and energetic woman, involved in everything, with a huge sense of humor. A friend from her Baghdad school days tells of Daisy shopping at Harrods. Her sons had by then made the family name famous, and as she filled in her name the assistant asked, "Oh, are you related to the Saatchi brothers?" "No," she said firmly. "They are related to me."

Nathan is described by family friends as "a lovely man, very cultured and dignified, proficient in languages, still going into his office daily" (he is over eighty). In the early days of their education, the Saatchis found the children of other Iraqi emigrants at the same private nursery school, but the atmosphere was very English. There is a picture of the three elder Saatchi brothers at a birthday party in 1951, the year of the mass emigration from Iraq, among other children who had left: Jonathan Bekhor, now a leading stockbroker in the City of London, the Shamoons, and others. Interestingly, of the fourteen children in the picture all are Iraqi Jewish, an indication of how close a community they were at this time.

"None of us was really subjected to Bahgdadian influences," says one Iraqi Jew of roughly the same age as the Saatchi brothers. "We all arrived at around the same time, but like Charles and Maurice my earliest recollections are of England. We assimilated very rapidly."

In the mid-1950s, however, financial crisis overtook the Saatchi family. Pakistan and India were producing cheaper textiles than any mill in Britain, and Nathan, for all his shrewdness and hard work, faced ruin. David remembers sitting on the stairs when one day his father came home and emptied his pockets. A few coins fell out. "This is all the money I have in the world," he said. Yet the financial crisis was short-lived. Within months, Nathan was back on his feet with a new business, using his old contacts in the Middle East to open up new trades and new lines of exports.

Soon the Saatchis had moved on into the North London state school system. David was not an academic success. His father desperately wanted his eldest son to go to college, but he had no interest in doing so. He went through the stage of having ferocious fights with his father, then joined the air force for his national service, compulsory at that time. Like many young men, David loved it for the first year or so and from that time on became progressively more independent of his father. Over the next three years he studied accounting, which he hated, but it provided him with the opportunity he needed. One of his clients owned a small pharmacy, which he wanted to sell—and David reckoned he was valuing it too cheaply. He suggested to his father that they buy it, and Nathan, impressed with his son's enterprise, lent him the money. He duly purchased the business, selling it two years later for a considerable profit and repaying his father. He was left with a small fortune by the standards of the day. Nathan was upset when, freed from accounting, David then chose to go to Israel to live on a kibbutz instead of joining the family business.

In fact, David did not settle in Israel but spent the next four or five years traveling around the world, living in Paris for six months, then going to Egypt and elsewhere. In between, he bought himself an apartment in London and began writing "this bad play." At last, at the age of twenty-seven, he went to work for his father, but he didn't like the world of business. In 1967 a family drama occurred when David set off to join the Israeli army in the Six Day War. By the time he got to Israel, the war was over. It was, however, the excuse he needed to get out of his father's business without another row. He drifted on from Israel to America, went back to Britain for a while, and finally emigrated to the United States for good, where he still lives in New York, a prosperous commodity broker who plans eventually to become a sculptor.

Charles, although clearly bright, was also not an academic success. Half a century earlier the Sassoons had sent Siegfried to Eton and Cambridge; Charles went to the more modest Christ's College, Finchley, a nineteenth-century boys' state school of no great distinction. Nor did he leave much of a mark, although he is remembered with a certain affection. "I taught him all I knew about French, and he still seemed to learn absolutely nothing," his French teacher, Ron Oliver, recalled. "He just couldn't grasp languages. But if Charlie wasn't outstanding, he was the sort of boy every mother wanted to cuddle because he was angelic-looking. He was certainly not academic but, like a lot of other Jewish boys, he was a real go-getter." A school photograph taken in 1956 shows Charlie as a well-built thirteen-year-old, his face round and serious beneath a mass of black curly hair, already one of the tallest boys in the school.

Charles was no more distinguished in math. His teacher remembers him as "the boy who was always struggling, always getting detention for bad conduct. He took no interest in school activities, clubs, or sport. He was the sort of boy who made you wonder what would ever become of him." Today Charles's problem would be more quickly diagnosed—he has all the symptoms of someone with a specific learning problem commonly known as dyslexia. His impatience, short-term memory, short attention span, and frustration at not being able to do things he knows are well within his abilities are the classic signs of it. But in those days, particularly in the state schools, dyslexia was not even recognized, and Charles, like so many others with the same problem, was simply put at the back of the class, destined to achieve nothing in the academic world. Both teachers and fellow pupils remember his driving energy and impatience, a kind of pent-up force that set him aside from the others and that was clearly going to be channeled into something—but what?

2
THE JOURNEY UPWARD

From numerous quarters one gathers the impression of Charles as the kind of person who was probably born already set on his own track. Growing up, nothing seemed to deflect him from what he wanted. David recalls that in the middle of their bad financial patch Charles wanted two comfortable chairs and Nathan refused to buy them, so Charles designed and made one; it was rough, clearly amateur, but David was astonished when he saw it. It had been put together with much thought and an extraordinary eye for balance. "There was really a lot of activity within that chair design," says David. Charles was a continual worry to Nathan, who had major fights with him over his clothes—he was very clearly into jeans—his hair, which he wore long before it was widely fashionable, his rock music, and his indomitable will. Nathan was no weak character himself, so confrontations with his willful teenage son were inevitable. Nathan and Daisy found Charles's inability to achieve at school as incomprehensible as the teachers did—and as Charles himself did. Family and friends were left with no doubt that Charles was "the problem child."

For all that, it was a loving and happy household. Nathan and Daisy allowed the boys considerable areas of freedom; they could invite girls home, as long as they were out by breakfast time; and they could have parties downstairs, as long as it didn't affect the whole household.

Charles left school at seventeen, having done little or no work in his last months there. After that, friends recall, came a period of wild partying when Charles would lead a group around London, leather-jacketed and often on motorbikes, staying out late, and generally leading the life of the wilder teenagers of what were then the early days of the so-called swinging London era. Charles would always make a beeline for the prettiest girl in the room, one friend recalls, even if she was the host's girlfriend: evenings often ended up in a fight. Soon he was in the United States, where he seems to have spent about a year, earning enough money to buy a car and see most of the country.

All the while he was an avid TV watcher, absorbing both the culture and the advertisements. What Nathan and Daisy, brought up without television in a strict, work-oriented religious community, thought of this is not recorded, but Charles remained attached both to them and to his

15

home. He would continue to live with them long after he was a million-aire, leaving only when he got married, at the age of twenty-nine. Charles developed another enthusiasm, which he passed on to Maurice. "They were real car freaks," says a friend. "They used to go motor racing all over England every week; Silverstone, Aintree, Brand's Hatch, anywhere there was motor racing."

Charles did more than watch: he raced. When he was twenty and Maurice seventeen, they persuaded their mother to swap her ordinary Mini for a Mini Cooper S, a souped-up version of the transverse-engined Mini that was very much in fashion for rallying and racing in the 1960s. It was not the most useful of cars for shopping and became even less so after Charles and Maurice had transformed it into a racing Mini, stripping out the seats and fitting it with a straight open exhaust. Their mother seems not to have minded.

Charles raced it, but Maurice went along as his faithful supporter and mechanic. Several times Charles crashed but never seriously.

Maurice, in contrast to his elder brother, was quieter, shyer, and academically far brighter. He went to a different school—Tollington Grammar, where he was consistently an honor student. In 1964, to Nathan and Daisy's great joy, he won a place at the London School of Economics (LSE), which was the academic institution probably more in tune with the times than any other. In common with other universities, it was rapidly expanding. That autumn, as Maurice began his academic life, the institution was bursting at the seams with its huge intake of new undergraduates and a growing population of postgraduates from all over the world, particularly the United States.

In the autumn of 1964 an election was looming, and the *Beaver*, the LSE's weekly magazine, in common with many student publications, welcomed the British Labour party's promise of a "scientific revolution and new technological frontiers," led by the man it hoped would be the next prime minister, Harold Wilson. The parliamentary Labour party that duly ended thirteen years of Tory rule on October 10 included sixteen LSE graduates, and among the articulate students of the day there was a distinct bias to the left.

During Maurice's three years there enthusiasm for the Labour govern-ment, the Beatles, Mary Quant (who first made the miniskirt fashion-able), and "swinging London" was at its height. The college was to become, in the words of one LSE professor, "the eye of the storm which was about to burst over universities." In an LSE student demonstration against Rhodesia, twelve students were arrested outside Rhodesia House. LSE students marched on Downing Street, and in the course of the winter of 1965–66, Maurice's second year, there were student union rows between left-wing and right-wing factions over a resolution to send delegates to a "council for peace" in Vietnam. For those there at the time, caught up in the regular demonstrations against apartheid in South Africa or the war in Vietnam or in favor of the Campaign for Nuclear Disarmament, it was strong stuff.

Yet Maurice recalls being remarkably untouched by it. He was not uninterested in politics, but it was far from a passion with him. He watched, according to one of his professors, "with a skeptical eye" the political turmoil at the LSE and the student demonstrations. Professor Percy Cohen, a tall, patrician intellectual who has remained Maurice's main link with LSE, was his sociology lecturer at the time. He says that the young Saatchi was "no gullible consumer of political ideologies." He remembers Maurice as an outstanding student but a person who did not draw attention to himself. Cohen got the impression that Maurice did not *want* to be noticed. In tutorials he spoke rarely, but when he did he was always worth hearing.

His professors noticed many of the same characteristics that his colleagues would later remark on. Cohen remembers Maurice's habit of listening and observing and not committing himself too quickly: "You could never imagine him panicking." Yet Cohen would miss something else: Maurice was absorbing his tutor's style and methods, as he would absorb the best of other people's teachings throughout his life. Cohen had a persuasive way of developing an argument, carefully pulling in the detailed analyses and facts he needed to support each point. He never made a statement or generalization without instantly giving examples. Maurice found this style of exposition extraordinarily effective and would later use it time and time again in presentations and arguments.

Curiously, it was sociology rather than economics or politics that Maurice seemed to enjoy most, and in his final year he won the sociology prize. Cohen ascribes Maurice's interest in the subject to his Iraqi origins: sociology, with its study of class structures, hierarchies, institutions, and the entire complex structure of society, is an ideal way of understanding and coming to terms with a host society.

Cohen was sufficiently impressed with Maurice's academic abilities and capacity for self-discipline to attempt to persuade him to become a full-time academic—even twenty years later he gives the impression that he would have counted it a personal triumph had Maurice become a professor of sociology rather than an advertising magnate. Maurice, however, insisted that he wanted to go into business and was impervious to the prevailing distrust, even contempt, in academic circles (particularly LSE) for business and capitalism in general. When he finished his final exams, Maurice gave his tutor his telephone number and asked Cohen to let him know his results. When Cohen rang the Saatchi home with the news that he had got a first (the highest grade), it was another member of the family who answered, and the response, Cohen recalls, was of great pleasure; he had the impression of great family solidarity.

Meanwhile, Charles had found a job. Through his late teens he was unable to stick to anything, disliking every occupation he tried. He even had a spell in advertising, joining a small agency in 1960 as a lowly office boy—and hated that too. "It was a very bad agency and he thought what they were doing was garbage," said a colleague from his early days. Possibly an impatient young Charles just couldn't get along with small-ness and inefficiency—or his menial position. *Fortune*, in a profile on the Saatchis in 1986, said that "Charles got an old-fashioned start in adver-tising by going to work at eighteen as an agency office boy and rising quickly to star copywriter," but this, like so many of the stories about his early days, is another myth. The same magazine two years before had reported that the Saatchis were "sons of a modestly prosperous North London textile manufacturer whose Sephardic Jewish forebears arrived in England generations ago."

Charles did not rise from that job—he quit or was fired; no one now (including Charles) quite remembers which. Nor does it matter, because at that stage he was not looking to advertising as his chosen profession, and his career was never a smooth progression from agency office boy to star copywriter. He was out of a job more than he was in one, and several years passed before he eventually got a job that interested him. For a time, probably at his father's insistence, he tried going back to college to study design, but that too was a failure. Even when he had no job, friends always remember his interest in clothes—an interest Maurice shared—and Charles always seemed to have a tailor in a back street who would make him West End–standard suits at a fraction of the cost and in a design usually several years ahead of the current fashion. He may have been out of work, but he was never short of money.

Charles was twenty-two before he got his first proper job in the advertising world, two years before Maurice's graduation. In 1965 the creative director of Benton & Bowles, a large American-owned agency based in Knightsbridge, took him on as a junior copywriter. John Hegarty, then a twenty-one-year-old art director, was working at his desk one morning when the company director poked his head into his tiny office. He had hired a new copywriter, he told Hegarty, adding, "I'd like him to work with you, so see what you can do with him."

At Benton & Bowles Charles found something he could do well. Hegarty, young as he was, was already being singled out as a talented art director. "In those days good art directors were hard to find," says Hegarty, "but good copywriters were even harder. This was Charlie's first job in copywriting, but he was obviously very good."

The man who hired him was Jack Stanley, and he knew he was taking a risk. "He had never done any work as a copywriter. He didn't talk a lot, but what he did say made sense. What most impressed me about him was his sense of purpose." Stanley soon felt vindicated.

It is often difficult to evaluate the assessments of early contemporaries of Charles Saatchi. People tend to exaggerate their own role in his career or to suggest that his reputation was overblown. Twenty years later, however, when Stanley was interviewed for *Campaign* in 1968, long before Charles Saatchi's reputation had moved outside the advertising world, he gave his view: "Charles is a really good copywriter. He has a lot of heart about people, which is important if you are not going to treat consumers as a lot of faceless buyers. He has a great color and a sense of salesmanship."

It was not long before Charles was the senior figure on the two-person team, but Hegarty greatly enjoyed working with him, remembering the flow of ideas and energy that came from him. "He was terrific, and we had a great time." But they were both inexperienced youngsters in an agency not renowned for its interest in imaginative ideas. "While he was working with me, he was considered a junior and we would only get half-baked briefs," says Hegarty. "We'd just be tossed things to see what madness we'd come up with."

Not many of the Saatchi-Hegarty ideas even got to the client, let alone into finished ads. Hegarty remembers the atmosphere as stultifying and claustrophobic for the new generation joining the business in the mid-1960s. "Agencies were dominated by . . . management [people] who were basically account handlers of some kind and were not sympathetic to our outrageous creative ideas and thought they would rock the business, upset the clients." He and others like him were among the first generation in Britain who had chosen advertising as a career while still at art school or college and found their elders and superiors were often former journalists, army officers, marketing people, or others who had drifted into the industry as a second choice. "Only we weren't just passing through," Hegarty says. "We weren't on our way to the first novel or working on some canvases in a garret in Chelsea. We actually wanted to be in advertising."

After just two-and-a-half months at Benton & Bowles, Charles met the man who would prove to be one of the key influences on his life. Ross Cramer was five years older and senior art director, and the two met almost by accident one day when Cramer was at his drawing board working on a large poster that featured Biggles and Dan Dare. Cramer barely noticed the tall young man looking over his shoulder until he spoke.

"That's terrific," said Charles Saatchi. "I really like that."

The two began discussing their ideas about advertising, and Cramer responded to Charles's interest and his analysis of the material that was being produced by London agencies at the time. He divided most of it into two categories: it was either "terrific" or "shit," but beneath that simple assessment was a keen analytical mind. Charles frequently stopped by Cramer's desk and soon joined him, with Jack Stanley's active support, as the other half of his team. Stanley recalled that it was his initiative to team them up, "and my hunch paid off. They made a very good team." John Hegarty, abandoned by Charles, did not resent it. "It was good for him," he said, and the two remained friends for years afterward.

It was the beginning of the most important business partnership Charles Saatchi ever had other than that with his brother Maurice. Cramer was a witty, attractive man, always the center of whatever group he was in. He was a perfect foil for Charles. "We just got on terribly well," says Cramer. "He was so enthusiastic about everything."

Cramer was the diplomat of the two, and for the next five years they would work together to produce some of the best ads of the time. That would not happen at Benton & Bowles, however, which even Cramer had come to hate. "It was one of the worst agencies to work for," he says now. The B&B management was taking on bright young people but with no idea what to do with them. In common with many of the other big agencies, they had little interest in creative work yet perceived dimly that their clients required it. Of the many awards the two men were later to accumulate, none was won at B&B.

There was another person at the agency to whom Charles would become even closer. Doris Dibley, a tall, Hitchcock-type blonde, was an American who had read French and English at Smith College, spent a year at the Sorbonne in Paris, and worked as a copywriter for David Ogilvy in New York, then one of the two or three leading figures in the advertising industry. She was seven years older than Charles, but in terms of worldliness and sophistication she was light years away. She knew about food and wine, theater and art; she had traveled, spoke French as well as she spoke English, and moved easily in circles that Charles would never aspire to. Charles's idea of entertainment was an evening at the cinema or, preferably, a game of snooker or poker with his male friends. He had been to Italy a couple of times with his parents and to the United States, but basically he was a gauche, wild-looking, somber young man. She was also, as copy group head, technically Charles's boss. And, to place her even more hopelessly beyond his reach, she was newly married to a racing driver named Hugh Dibley. Charles in her presence was tongue-tied to the point where she barely noticed his existence. He, on the other hand, had fallen in love.

Cramer and Saatchi did not stay at Benton & Bowles for long. Cramer recalls the two of them sitting in their "awful office" one day trying to get on with some work. Very little was getting past the executives, and they were both increasingly frustrated. "Benton & Bowles treated the creative department as if we were rubbish," says Cramer, "while spending huge amounts on the executive floor." In an attempt to placate the two men, a firm of interior decorators had been hired to brighten up their work area. It proved the last straw. "Paint was dropping all over our work," recalls Cramer, who was at the boiling point when an old friend, a photographer named Bob Brooks, walked in.

Brooks had been an award-winning creative advertising person in his day and had always taken a keen interest in Cramer's career. As Cramer and Saatchi moved, he said: "Go to Collett's," meaning Collett Dickenson Pearce, then a new and creative agency. He would set up an interview with Colin Millward, the creative director. Cramer knew all about Millward—"he was the best creative director in London." Within half an hour Brooks rang back to say that he had arranged a meeting.

Cramer did all the talking, showing some of the work the two men had done together, with Charles nodding respectfully in the background. Millward wanted Cramer, all right, but he had no interest in Charles. However, Cramer insisted that they came as a package, and finally Millward commented: "Well, hell, if you want the organ-grinder you've got to take the monkey!" They got the job, and Millward soon came to appreciate the monkey.

Benton & Bowles made a token effort to hold them. "I knew we couldn't keep them," said Jack Stanley in a 1968 interview. "We kept upping their money, but with talent like that some other agency is bound to come along with more." He wished them well, remarking that they were "one of the few teams working together who will stay together for a long time. They are both highly critical of each other and aren't easily satisfied. This is a great virtue in the advertising business."

When they joined Collett Dickenson Pearce, the agency was breaking new ground as probably the most creative of its kind. Founded by John Pearce (ex-Colman Prentis & Varley), it was British-owned, small enough to be hungry, and big enough to have some good accounts. It also attracted some of the brightest talents in the business. Among them was young David Puttnam, who would later achieve fame as the producer of the film *Chariots of Fire*. So too was Alan Parker; like Puttnam, he would make his mark on the world film industry. Ron Collins, an art director who would form his own agency, Wight Collins Rutherford Scott, already had a considerable reputation when the Cramer-Saatchi partnership arrived.

Even among this creative group, however, Charles stood out, not only for the originality of his copywriting and his often outrageous ideas but also for his impatience with his clients and his bosses alike. One copywriter remembers a side of Saatchi's character that soon began to emerge: "Charlie was the brooding kind of manic copywriter who would literally tell the clients to go screw themselves and storm out of meetings if they didn't buy his work. He had mad long hair and really eccentric suits—and crazy cars."

In fact, the long hair and suits emerged only after Saatchi had been at Collett for some months. Before that he had dressed remarkably soberly. Cramer remembers him as "vaguely Ivy League" with conservative suits and ties. Cramer introduced Charles to the man who made his suits, a celebrity tailor called Major, who also made suits for Terry Donovan, one of the most successful photographers of the day. Charles was so impressed that he had Major run off half a dozen three-piece suits, with wide lapels and padded shoulders, the trend at the time. He and Cramer even sported watch chains. But, in contrast to the suits, Charles let his wiry black hair grow out uncut and untamed. "He looked like a golliwog," says Cramer, "just like the one on the label of Robertson's jams."

No one seemed to mind, least of all Colin Millward, an art person whom Charles later atypically recalled as an "advertising genius." That did not stop them from having their differences. Ron Collins, five years older than Charles, remembers walking into Millward's office as Charles was steaming out, still shouting obscenities at the startled Millward. The creative director, says Collins, had not liked one of Charles's ads. "If he didn't like what I did," said Collins, "I would go away and redo it, as would anyone else. But if he criticized Charles's work, Charles told him to stuff it and walked out."

Nonetheless, Charles's reputation as one of the best copywriters in the advertising industry dates from his time at CDP. "He erupted there," says Cramer, "really took off." In that first year, 1967, the two won an industry award for their work for the London store Selfridge's, with ads such as: "A warning to the under-12s. Be on your guard when your parents volunteer a trip to Selfridge's toy department. It could be a bribe to get you inside our barber shop." Or: "The most valuable things shoplifters get off with in Selfridge's are the girls on the cosmetic counter." Trite stuff now, perhaps, but effective in its day. Certainly it caught the eye of the industry.

The next year they made their mark more forcibly, working on the Ford account. Ford was no ordinary account; it was not only large and prestigious but also much sought-after. It had been won by the small creative agency CDP against the big Mather agency (later Ogilvy & Mather) and was its first multinational account. The fact that Charles and Cramer were put on it says a great deal about their reputation at the time.

Rick Martindale, then the head of marketing at Ford, remembers the CDP pitch well. Mather produced a straitlaced, low-key, technical series of ads. John Pearce, the head of CDP, and another senior executive, Geoffrey Pattie, later a minister in the Thatcher government, displayed a much more imaginative approach. Even the highly conservative chairman of Ford, William Batty, and his managing director, Terence Beckett, were impressed.

Batty was a martinet, famous for his dislike of suede shoes, long hair, or any hint of incorrect attire or address. Martindale describes how Batty would stand at the top of the escalator as the Ford executives appeared for work at 8:15 in the morning and send people home if they were wearing the wrong shoes. "Underneath he was really a very nice fellow," says Martindale. "But he put on this attitude and everyone was in fear and trembling of him." At some stage he was going to have to meet the Cramer-Saatchi team, which was now turning out some first-class ads. They were mostly what were called "long copy ads," with lengthy captions by Charles and not much illustration:

> Parking is a lot of fun, especially afterwards
> when you want to get the car out again,
> and you find you've been left four inches in front
> and five inches behind to play with,
> and it's hot, and the sun has turned the car
> into a Turkish bath, and you're working the
> wheel one way, and then the other
> and you're perspiring and turning the wheel,
> and cursing and turning the wheel,
> and crunch there goes a taillight, then finally
> you're out, and feeling just marvelous,
> when a little old lady in a big Zodiac
> tries getting into your space, and she's
> spinning the steering wheel with one finger,
> and for Pete's sake, she glides in in one go
> and you wish you were dead.

The Ford Zodiac was a disaster and the company realized it, but the ads helped to make it a respectable seller. There were other ads for better cars; and there were others that won awards, such as one showing a new Cortina overtaking an older, slower model: "They appear the same—but disappear differently." The Ford people were greatly impressed with these ads, as was the industry. Charles Saatchi was being noted as a rising star.

Martindale finally organized an evening when Charles Saatchi and Ross Cramer could go down to Essex and meet the senior Ford team, including Batty. Martindale's boss, John Pearce, with his respectable air and his little pince-nez glasses, and Geoffrey Pattie arrived first at the Ford country club chosen for the occasion. "Everything was going smoothly, and they were all talking about the cars and things, when I saw Charles arrive," says Martindale. "And he had this Afro hairstyle, really freaky, way-out hair; it stood about six inches off his skull all the way around." Martindale made the introductions, and Batty controlled himself long enough to greet Charles courteously. "But I could see Bill's face freeze," says Martindale. "And I could see he was really wondering what to do. He was going through this schizophrenic thing in his own mind, because *Time* had written this thing about the swinging sixties and we were all supposed to be on a great modern upbeat, and here it was in front of him, and maybe he should be joining it rather than fighting it."

Batty took his head of marketing aside. "How did *he* get here?" he asked, nodding in Charles's direction.

Martindale was ready for that one. "In his Ferrari, I believe," he replied.

"And that absolutely broke him up," says Martindale. "He thought, 'Oh, well, that does it, I know it's me that's wrong. I'm the one that looks strange.' And he almost took his British army tie off and threw it away. And the evening was a great success."

It was while working on the Ford account that, for the first—but far from the last—time in his career, Charles Saatchi found himself in the center of a controversy. The rules of the Institute of Practitioners in Advertising (IPA) forbade "knocking copy," ads that attacked competing products. (The rules have since been changed.) For Ford the Cramer-Saatchi team produced an ad that displayed the merits of its top model, the Ford Executive, against the much more expensive Jaguar, Rover, and Mercedes, with the copy line: "The Ford Executive compares quite favorably with these grand cars." It created a considerable fuss, which only added to the effectiveness of the ad, and persuaded Cramer and Saatchi of the merits of knocking copy, which they would use often over the next few years. "What is a knocking ad?" asked Cramer in an interview at the time. "How can you push one product without saying something bad about its competitors? If knocking ads work, then we use them." Less controversial were other Ford ads such as, "With some 2 litre cars you pay for the name. Ford only charges you for the car." Even twenty years later those Ford ads look and read well and compare favorably to many of today's. Alan Parker had a hand in a number of them, as did Robin Wight, later of Wight Collins Rutherford Scott.

By now Cramer and Saatchi were acquiring significant reputations. Charles was also one of the most highly paid men in the agency. Ron Collins, although older and more senior, recalls how Saatchi would go in to see Pearce or Millward, insist that he was worth more money, and "usually get it, basically just by asking. And he was always asking." He and Cramer had gone to Collett for £3,500 a year each, a reasonable although not spectacular salary for the day. Charles got this up to £9,000 a year when Cramer went to the United States to look at some of the ads being done there, particularly by Doyle Dane Bernbach. Charles let it be known—wrongly—that Cramer was doing the rounds of the big agencies with a selection of their work and that the two would probably soon be going to Doyle Dane. Cramer returned to find that he had been given a big raise.

About that time Charles drove a Lincoln Continental convertible, an ostentatious car in any part of the world but particularly in London, where there were few imported American cars. He was living at home in his parents' house, which allowed him to lavish most of his income on his cars. A Jaguar 3.8S cost £1,741; a Mercedes 200 cost £1,895; so on his salary he could afford what he wanted. Friends also remember a Ferrari, but there were so many cars that no one, not even Maurice, was able to keep track.

Interviews around this time describe Charles as "dark and broody" and are sprinkled with comments such as "Cramer does most of the talking, while Saatchi merely interjects with affable indifference." Close as Charles was to Cramer, it was a work-oriented relationship. The two seldom saw each other in the evenings or on weekends. Cramer was married with young children, while Charles was a bachelor with lots of casual girlfriends but no one steady, at least that Cramer ever remembered. He had the impression that Charles had a close group of friends whom he saw in the evenings, usually to play cards or go to the cinema.

Unknown even to Cramer, Charles was still pursuing Doris Dibley—and was making some progress. Shortly after he left for Collett, he returned to Benton & Bowles for an office Christmas party. Doris's marriage was already in trouble, and Charles may have heard about it. At any rate, he nerved himself to approach her. Doris had not seen the new-style Charles and stared, astonished, at him. "Your hair is quite amazing," she said. He offered her a lift home, and she gratefully accepted. When they arrived at her apartment, he said, "I'd like to see you." Doris was cautious. She was in the process of separating from her husband and didn't want to complicate the issue in any way by dating another man. But she didn't explain any of that to Charles, just simply told him, "Look, this is not really a good time for me. Really, I'm very flattered but I would rather not."

Charles wrote his number on a piece of paper and handed it to her. "If you change your mind, please ring me." Some months later she did. By now she was fully separated and living alone and decided that Charles "would make a very nice reentry into the world of single living." She had been loyal to her husband and knew few single men—except Charles, who had gained in both confidence and maturity in the last two years. Soon they were dating regularly, and Charles moved into her apartment, where he stayed until they married six years later, in 1973.

In many ways the manner in which Charles wooed and won Doris is symptomatic of how he does business. In his private life as well as in advertising he set himself a target that to others might have seemed wholly unreachable—and usually got there. Doris found herself highly flattered by his absolute determination to win her. But she found other aspects of Charles to like too. "We had a similar sense of humor; Charles has this wonderful sense of irony, which I valued very highly. I never doubted that whatever he did would be special."

There was something else that may help explain how Charles thinks and works and may contribute to the student's trying to identify what fired up this wild, unruly young man to achieve the heights he would attain. "I do feel that there is a difference in the American and the British mentality," says Doris, "Americans tend to believe that given enough willpower and brains and money and time any problem can be overcome. But in Europe there is a certain sense of fatigue, a willingness to compromise which can come out of sophistication or wisdom or just the fact that the Europeans have been at politics and civilization longer than Americans have. And Charles had that raw American idea that anything is possible. Another reason we fell in love was because he was an Englishman who loved America and I was an American who loved Europe."

Charles, of course, was not an Englishman or even European—he was an Iraqi Jew, an immigrant, still living with parents haunted by the upheaval of their old lives. He now lived as an Englishman, perhaps, but that was not his culture. Until his early twenties he had never been good at anything—not at school, not at sports, not at work, and the self-imposed pressure to succeed, to be the best, the biggest, to set impossible targets and then achieve them, must date from his early life. He was only too aware of his own inadequacies and lack of social graces—he never joined discussions at any intellectual level because he had no confidence in his ability to argue a case. He never read books and seldom read newspapers. He did read magazines and collected comics, but that and the cinema were about as high as his cultural tastes at this stage went.

"I think he looked upon me as the older, sophisticated woman who could teach him a lot," says Doris. She opened up new worlds to him, took him to Paris and to art shows, kindled his interest (which would become consuming) in modern art, taught him about classical music, and introduced him to a new lifestyle.

The relationship, however, developed only gradually. In the meantime Charles did not neglect his old friends. He went to Cramer's house a number of times and became fond of his children. Cramer recalls an incident when his wife called him to say that one of the children had been hurt in an accident at home and was being taken to hospital. Charles, he recalled, was "as worried as I was" and insisted on driving him in his Ferrari, burning up through the London traffic, to the hospital. All was well, but Charles worried for days about the child.

At work now he was happier than he had ever been, hugely enjoying the atmosphere and the people at Collett. He and David Puttnam became particular friends, going to Majorca on holiday together. To Puttnam, as with a small group of close friends throughout his life, he was open, relaxed, and frequently very funny. Charles even overcame his natural shyness enough to have a party at his parents' house. Cramer, Puttnam, Alan Parker, and others from the office went up to Hampstead to the large house almost opposite the gates of the Kenwood home, one of the most expensive addresses in London.

An enormous table awaited them, set out with a variety of foods, all carefully prepared in advance, presumably by Charles's mother. "The table was so large that Puttnam and I and a few others pushed all the food down [to] one end," says Cramer. Charles himself was ill at ease, and Cramer had the impression that he had never poured a drink before. "Someone asked for a gin and tonic, and Charles just filled up the glass with gin." No one can recall Charles drinking anything at the time, and even later he would at most sip a glass of wine. The room was filled with family photographs, some showing the Saatchi grandparents in their traditional Iraqi clothes, and the food had a definite Middle Eastern taste to it.

And yet Charles didn't stay at Collett. The man responsible for his next move was John Hegarty, his old friend from Benton & Bowles. Hegarty had been fired from Benton for being, he says now, "a pain in the arse" and had ended up in a small agency called John Collings & Partners. It was not a particularly impressive agency, although it had one or two talented people, notably Richard Cope, who at that stage was trying to set up a division with good creative people. Cope asked Hegarty who were the best.

"The two that I know best and that I've got the highest regard for are Ross Cramer and Charles Saatchi," said Hegarty. "Why don't we talk to them?"

They did, and Cramer and Charles decided to make the move. It was a disaster for all concerned. Some said that the pair could never get on with the boss of Collings, Andrew Blair, but Hegarty gives another reason: "It all went foul because nobody there could understand how it operated . . . understand what Ross and Charlie wanted to do and what I wanted to do with it." Charles himself later referred to it in an interview with *Campaign* in 1968: "It was a badly aborted attempt. Basically, I think we had no real desire to fight for minute clients. There's too much talk and intellectual chat in agencies."

The alliance lasted six months before Cramer and Saatchi decided that they had had enough. They had also had enough of working for other people. Neither of them liked the agency scene, although for different reasons: Charles because he was psychologically unsuited to working for anyone else, Cramer because he didn't much like the system under which agencies worked.

They had a new idea: they would form a consultancy that would offer to do creative work on a freelance basis to anyone who wanted to hire it. Both Cramer and Saatchi had considerable confidence in their own ability to produce creative advertising, of which there was a considerable shortage in the industry at the time. They would put together a small team, find an office, and set up on their own.

3
SWINGING GOODGE STREET

W hen Charles Saatchi and Ross Cramer set off on their own, they could not know that they were launching themselves at the beginning of what was one of the most interesting and stimulating times of British postwar history, particularly in the advertising industry. The satirical revue *Beyond the Fringe*, starring the talented quartet of Dudley Moore, Peter Cook, Jonathan Miller, and Alan Bennett, had just opened in London, where its form of humor became a cult among the young. It was soon joined by "That Was the Week That Was," a television satire that lampooned the old order and brought David Frost to fame. Another show, "Monty Python's Flying Circus," epitomized a new style of irreverent humor that would influence the ads made in Britain a decade later when its style of wit began to impress the straighter ads of the New York agencies.

Much of it would not last, but for a decade at least it was exhilarating. Britain seemed in these years to be the most "swinging" of all countries. In the music world the Beatles, the Who, and the Rolling Stones led the way, and even the fashion scene, so long dominated by the chic and expensive Parisian designers, switched to London. Mary Quant and Ossie Clark became international names, and Carnaby Street, just off Oxford Circus, became one of the best-known fashion spots in all Europe. The King's Road and Portobello Road were also international meccas. It was an extraordinary time for fashion photographers born in London's East End: Brian Duffy, Terence Donovan, and David Bailey. There was a new sense of liberation, a break with formal styles that Charles Saatchi and his contemporaries could relish.

The late 1960s would see the first man on the moon, the first heart transplants, performed by Dr. Christiaan Barnard, the legalization of homosexual acts between consenting adults, the Concorde, and Mao's Cultural Revolution. They would also witness the student explosions of 1968, battles on the streets of Paris that almost brought down the government of Charles de Gaulle, bloody confrontations at the Chicago Democratic Convention, the Soviet invasion of Czechoslovakia, a massive anti-Vietnam rally outside the American embassy in Grosvenor Square that destroyed the myth that such political demonstrations could not happen in London, and university occupations everywhere. At the London School of Economics, the *Beaver* exhorted the class of '68 to tear down the walls and expressed its disappointment when the students did not want revolution as much as it did.

It was a culture change that Charles Saatchi could swim in with great enjoyment. His father, like many fathers then, found it hard to cope with the changes and the attacks on so many of the old shibboleths: patriotism, religion, monarchy. But Charles, with his love of new fashions and ideas, his instinctive desire to see change, and his dislike for the status quo, was in the forefront of it—not in the actual physical revolution that was taking place but in the cultural and emotional one. So were his friends and partners. Maurice watched it, as he would many trends, with a more detached and academic eye, responding cerebrally rather than emotionally; but in his own way he was no less a part of it than Charles. And the lessons he would take from the era would prove deeper and longer lasting for him than for most of his generation.

From the outside the building on the corner of Goodge Street, just north of Oxford Street, was unprepossessing. On the ground floor was a restaurant called the Golden Egg, one of those American-style chains of eating houses that appeared around Britain in the 1960s, offering a menu that was halfway between fast-food and proper restaurant fare. Around the corner, Tottenham Court Road was fast developing into London's center for cut-price electrical goods, sold in "pile 'em high and sell 'em cheap" fashion. To the west were expensive restaurants such as L'Etoile and the White Elephant, haunts for some of the advertising executives from the big agencies that had settled in the area. To the east was the City, Britain's financial district, which would later prove crucial for the Saatchis.

The time was 1967, and, wholly by coincidence, some of the most talented people in the media world gravitated to the offices on Goodge Street, which were entered by a door to the side of the Golden Egg. David Puttnam, intent on getting into the film world, left advertising to set up a photographic agency. At the age of twenty-six he was already the leading photographer's rep in Britain, taking 25 percent of the earnings of some of the leading photographers in the country, including David Bailey, David Montgomery, Sid Roberson, and Mel Sokolsky, none of them grossing less than £35,000 a year, which meant that Puttnam was already earning well into six figures. Alan Parker, who had originally taken over at Collett Dickenson Pearce as the golden boy after Charles Saatchi departed, would soon join Puttnam to try his luck in the film industry.

On the top floor was a design agency called Klein Peters, which was composed of Lou Klein, a highly talented American, and Michael Peters, who was to become one of the leading retail designers in the 1970s and 1980s. There was also a young advertising man named Martin Boase, who through the 1970s and 1980s was to become one of the leading rivals of Saatchi & Saatchi with the agency he founded, Boase Massimi Pollitt.

Last but by no means least were Ross Cramer, now age twenty-nine, and Charles Saatchi, age twenty-four, who moved into their first offices in that Goodge Street building.

Puttnam, Parker, Cramer, and Saatchi revolved in the same orbit. They were all young, energetic, and creative, with bags of self-confidence and plans for changing a world that they felt, despite the image of swinging London, was still decades behind what was happening in New York and elsewhere.

That year the best of British creative activity in the film, television, design, and advertising worlds was taken to New York for a major exhibition called "It's Great! Britain." Another bright young designer of the 1960s, Rodney Fitch, was asked to design the presentation. "I met all the top advertising, design, and commercial film people," Fitch recalls. "And that's where I made my first contact with Puttnam and Cramer and Saatchi."

Puttnam was sufficiently impressed by Fitch's work to hire him to design his office. Puttnam wanted something special. Fitch gave it to him. "I did him a really nice office," he recalls. "All done in green baize, like a billiard table." As Cramer and Saatchi were just moving in, Fitch did both offices at the same time, organizing a joint reception area for the two operations. For Cramer and Saatchi he used white Formica, a material that Charles would use in all his offices thereafter, but which was new to the advertising world at the time.

The space Fitch had to work in was not large: basically, two rooms, the larger and brighter one approached by a small stairway where the two principals would have their office, the smaller space occupied by the four or five people they would collect around them. Yet, despite its limited space, everyone who worked there remembers it as the ideal spot for what they wanted to do. Charles would later say that it was only when Saatchi & Saatchi had become the biggest agency in the world and he moved to Lower Regent Street that he had an office as good as he had had on Goodge Street. "Until then copywriters and art directors had worked on different floors," says Fitch. "They were brought together by account directors and conferences and things like that. But the Saatchi people were introducing new work, and they were concerned with the words as much as the visuals. So I created these large white desks where the art directors and copywriters worked together."

Charles was by now a prosperous young man-about-town. He had graduated to a dark blue Rolls-Royce Corniche, and there was also an Aston Martin around this time; he wore the latest suits and had his hair groomed in the best salons. The golliwog style was gone, and his hair was fashionably long, a mass of curls sitting tightly on his head, his sideburns level with his ears. He had moved in with Doris but had no actual place of his own, still keeping his room at his parents' house in Hampstead. He still spent evenings with friends, playing cards or chess or simply going out on the town.

He was already something of a legend in the advertising industry, not just for his ads but for something else: his ability to generate personal publicity. Charles had learned from his earliest contact with the industry that publicity could provide him with a shortcut to success. No one either before or since in the advertising business—and not in many others either—has worked on his publicity as assiduously as Charles Saatchi. Most of it appeared in the advertising press, particularly the weekly magazine *World Press News*, forerunner of *Campaign*, but occasionally it would spill over into other media: for instance, Charles appeared in the *London Evening Standard* as the young man earning the most money in the late 1960s. Colleagues early on noticed that somehow it always seemed to be *his* ads about which the trade press wrote, *his* controversies that caught the headlines. Curiously shy of direct contact, Charles conducted his one-man press campaign by telephone, establishing a discipline and routine whereby he learned the times when the trade magazines *Campaign* and *Ad Weekly* were going to press and would call the editor with his stories. They were not always about himself or even his friends—far from it. He picked all the ad-industry gossip he could—stories about accounts changing hands or executives moving or being fired—shaped it into news items, and phoned them into the magazines. In return he expected some favorable mention of his own activities—and got it.

He cultivated fame in another way too: through recognition for the quality of his creative advertisements. Edward Booth-Clibborn, chairman of the Designers & Art Directors Association (D&AD), set up in 1962 to encourage high standards in visual communication, remembers Charles as one of the young advertising people most active in trying to get his work accepted by the jury that selected the year's most outstanding advertising work and published it in an annual, awarding prizes for the best. In 1967 the Selfridge's ad was included; the following year, the Ford. Appearing in the annual got Charles more attention than anything else in the quarters that mattered to him: the industry, marketing people, and clients. Anyone looking for a new advertising agency—and in those days there were rules against poaching clients—would look at the annual and see the name Charles Saatchi.

There was more to it than that, however. Charles has always been equally fascinated by the creative process and its commercial application. He had discovered in himself a talent for copywriting that he was not even aware he had before he started—although he always had the view that he would be good for *something*. This talent could just as easily have been channeled into, say, screen writing if his circumstances had taken

him in that direction—as they nearly did. Writing advertisements does
not rate highly among the creative gifts even today, and in the 1960s
Charles would have been treated contemptuously for suggesting that it
was an art form. Yet he regarded it as such, approaching it with the same
passion he would later apply to his art collection. Booth-Clibborn has no
doubt about Saatchi's talent. "He was very exceptional," he says. "This
was very much the breakthrough period of creative work in this country.
Up to that time we were copying American slang, and now for the first
time we started to use our own language in advertising. And these
people, particularly Alan Parker and Charles Saatchi, started using
colloquial English that gave a special identity to their work.

"Charles Saatchi was very conscious of doing work that got visibility,
particularly through the D&AD awards, but he and some of the others at
the time really believed in D&AD and what we stood for. They were still
an isolated group in the industry, but they believed in improving creative
standards; that was the important thing." Booth-Clibborn used to make
regular trips to the United States, study the latest advertisements, and
come back to give lectures about them. Charles would be there in the
audience.

The consultancy, which they agreed to call Cramer-Saatchi, was an
idea more common in countries such as Japan, where it is customary for
large firms to employ outside consultants. Cramer and Saatchi dealt
directly with agencies, who subcontracted their creative work to them,
then passed it off as their own. In theory there was to be no contact with
clients—but it did not turn out that way. Those who know Charles
believe that he was at this stage—it would not necessarily be true later—
more interested in enjoying creative free rein than in making money. "He
must have known that people really don't pay you for having ideas," says
John Hegarty. "You make money *making* ideas, not having them."
Cramer was the business end of the partnership, Charles, for a while at
least, content to handle the creative side.

John Hegarty soon joined them at the consultancy. So did an even
younger man straight from Watford Art College. A diffident Jeremy
Sinclair turned up for an interview, showed Cramer and Charles some of
his work, and was told, "Come back—but don't stop taking the dole yet."
When he did return, he was offered a job and started work at £10 a week
as junior copywriter.

The idea was that they would work in pairs, each pair consisting of a
copywriter and an art director: Cramer and Saatchi would continue the
partnership they had already carried across three agencies in less than
three years; Hegarty, an art director, initially hired Mike Coughlan as his
copywriter, but when Coughlan left after a year, Hegarty teamed up with
another young copywriter who also came from Collett, Chris Martin;
and Sinclair, who could never have dreamed that he would one day

become the head of the biggest agency in the world, worked with Bill Atherton, another youngster straight out of the London College of Printing—which had also produced Hegarty and Martin. There was a secretary called Gail—and that was the full team.

The consultancy allowed Charles to try his hand at something he had always wanted to do, something that fascinates him to this day: to get into the film business. Sharing an office with David Puttnam and Alan Parker, both clearly talented, was the ideal opportunity, and within a few months Charles was embroiled in his first venture. Creative consultants could do more than write creative ads—they could write film scripts as well.

"You know, deep down Charlie always felt he got David Puttnam into films," said one of the team at the time. Charles himself would not agree—it was Puttnam who nearly sucked him into films. They had a go at it, creating three story lines that Puttnam then proposed to develop and sell. "One of the stories was an idea that Puttnam had, a story about a little girl who'd run off at the age of eleven with her boyfriend to get married. It was originally called *Melody*, but it was changed to *SWALK*—'Sealed with a Loving Kiss.' Ross and Charlie developed the script and wrote the scenario, and then Alan Parker wrote it as a film script."

The film was made but sank without a trace. "Terrible film—but rumored to have done well in Japan!" says one of the team. However, in trying to launch it Puttnam went to New York, where he made connections he later used to get his own career started. Today, when Charles looks back on these early efforts, he cringes. There was, for example, a satire on *The Carpetbaggers*, for which Charles and Cramer roughed out a story, which was equally as bad as the original. Hegarty is kinder about the scripts than are Charles or Cramer. "They were good. Charlie is a very good writer, not just of ads."

For a time some of the others thought the consultancy would veer away from advertising as Charles became more and more interested in the film business. Possibly, if one of the scripts he worked on had become successful, he might have taken the road to Hollywood with Puttnam, and Saatchi & Saatchi would never have existed. Charles himself would not contradict that view. It is a thought that still intrigues him, and he still follows every movie made by Puttnam, talking to him daily about the films he is working on, listening with fascination to the gossip and problems of Hollywood, half wishing he were there.

But the work poured in for the consultancy, and Puttnam and Parker went their own way to make films such as *Midnight Express*, *Bugsy Malone*, *Birdy*, and many others. Charles, whether he seriously considered a change of direction or not—he was still only in his mid-twenties—

was driven by events and his own success into taking an even bigger step into the advertising world.

Some fifteen of the top twenty agencies in London had hired the services of the consultancy. The money was rolling in and its reputation growing. Then, slowly but significantly, Cramer-Saatchi broke its own rule about not taking on clients directly. The account the team broke it for was the Health Education Council. Like the Conservative party account a decade later, it was not worth a great deal of money, but it made the Saatchi reputation.

The account came in through Ross Cramer. His child went to the same school as the child of a woman who worked for the council. The HEC, working on a small government budget, was responsible for putting out brochures and posters warning people of the dangers of not cleaning their teeth or not washing their hands. As they waited for their respective children, they talked about advertising, and the woman said that her boss, Hilda Robins, might be interested in more professional ads. She would mention it.

Charles Saatchi could have no idea how important this little account would be for him. It was around this time that the Royal College of Surgeons produced the most comprehensive report yet showing the clear links between cigarette smoking and cancer. It was a report that echoed around the world, knocked millions off tobacco shares, and put pressure on the Labour government to curb tobacco sales, even though duties on cigarette sales constituted a key element of treasury revenue. The task of persuading the public to cut back fell to the Health Education Council— and passed on to Cramer-Saatchi. Charles took to it with enthusiasm.

It was one of his most productive periods. The most memorable ad was one of a hand holding a glass saucer into which a liquid stream of tar was being poured. The caption read: "No wonder smokers cough." Below that was the line: "The tar and discharge that collects in the lungs of the average smoker." Another ad featured a stained hand being scrubbed by a nailbrush under the heading: "You can't scrub your lungs clean."

Many of the antismoking ads were good enough for the D&AD jury to select them for its annual. They ran right through 1970, creating a media stir and attracting even more publicity for Charles. Again, he was adept at cultivating it. The whole consultancy worked on the ads at various times, but Charles was centrally involved, writing many of them himself and overseeing the others as any good creative director would. "There were spreads in the *Evening Standard*, full pages in all the nationals— they were everywhere," says Chris Martin. "It was at a time when a full page in the *Daily Express* was probably the pinnacle of advertising media, rather than sixty seconds on *News at Ten*, which is the top now. And we won all sorts of awards."

Charles had already made a stir in the trade press. The antismoking ads got him into the national papers as well. The *Sun*, then just a few years into its relaunch by Rupert Murdoch, devoted a whole page to him and Cramer, with a five-column picture of the two working on new ads in front of a huge "You can't scrub your lungs clean" poster. "Once a week Charles Saatchi plays poker with a few friends," it began. "But in the last month or so he's been less interested in the game than in the fact that it's getting easier to see the cards. The cigarette haze that used to hang over the table is thinning noticeably." Everyone seemed to be giving up smoking, said the *Sun*, because of the "remarkably successful" Saatchi campaign. Charles, in one of the few direct quotes he ever gave to a national paper, is reported to have said of his ads: "Of course they're shocking. But the truth is shocking. What we did was dig out as many facts as possible about what smoking can do to you, and to present them baldly, ruthlessly, clinically."

The *Sun* writer was taken with Charles's assertion that these same facts had so impressed him that he had cut down from thirty cigarettes a day to only two. Several of his team had given up smoking completely. (Charles, alas, has slipped back since—he probably smokes thirty a day again.)

The fuss over the antismoking advertisements, however, was only a foretaste of the publicity to come. That spring he put his team onto the ad that would start him on the road toward becoming a household name. Later, more myths would grow around it than about any other ad. The true story is both simpler and more complex than the myths.

Jeremy Sinclair's first idea that morning in the spring of 1970 was also his best. Instead of a young pregnant woman appealing for help, why not use a pregnant man? A twenty-two-year-old copywriter, Sinclair was working on an unpromising and difficult advertising brief: to promote contraception among the young, basically by producing the kind of posters that line the walls of dentists' and doctors' waiting rooms. It was the tail end of the permissive age that had swept through Britain in the 1960s, but it was also well before AIDS made contraceptives an openly discussed subject. He had to make an impact without being too explicit.

The idea of a pregnant young man inspired the line that would go with it. Hesitantly, Sinclair wrote it out: "Would you be more careful if it was *you* that got pregnant?"

He was pleased with it. It fit the brief given to Cramer-Saatchi by the Health Education Council on which the whole office had been slaving for days. Sinclair imagined the rough shape of a young man with a bulging, pregnant stomach—and then decided that was going too far. He kept the copy line but rejected the image because it was "just a bit sick." For the rest of the day he and Bill Atherton, the art director working with him on the account, thought about other visuals to fit the copy line. Soon they

knew they would have to show their work to Charles, and Sinclair, a
diffident, slight young man, feared—as did the others who worked in
their tiny office—his wrath and scorn. It was Sinclair who coined the
phrase "an ad a day keeps the sack away" to describe the frenetic, driving
atmosphere that Charles had created around him, but the others revised
it to "two ads a day keep the sack away."

Finally, Sinclair and Atherton climbed the few steps that led from the
office they shared with four others into the spacious, bright room
occupied by Charles and Ross Cramer. The roughs they were about to
show did not include the pregnant man—Sinclair had held that out,
although he was only too aware that Charles wanted something very
different for this ad. His antismoking campaign, with its blunt warnings
about bronchitis, heart ailments, and emphysema, had caused hundreds
to write in protest to the Health Education Council. There were profiles
of Charles in the national press as "the man who's put the breeze up half
the nation," whose ads "made previous campaigns look like Mary
Poppins," going for "the punch in the guts—the body blow that stops
you in your tracks." This time, Sinclair knew, he wanted to go even
further.

Charles in 1970 looked even younger than his twenty-seven years; a
dark, slim man just six feet tall, he now had a mop of black curly
hair above his lean, saturnine face. His mood could swing in seconds
from fury when he didn't like something to a great and infectious joy
when he did. The tinge of fear with which Sinclair now approached him
was leavened with a compensating affection, which Charles also inspired.

This was to be one of Charles's more enthusiastic days. He liked the
thought that Sinclair was pursuing. "That's a good line," he said. "I like
that line."

He went through the visuals they had prepared, rejecting them one by
one. "Keep the line, that's good," he concluded, "but let's get another
visual."

"I had this idea for a pregnant man." Sinclair had not even prepared a
rough sketch, but it didn't need much description. Charles picked it up
instantly. "That's great," he said. "Let's see a visual."

An hour later Sinclair and Atherton were back with a rough of a man
with a bulging stomach. "That's it," said Charles. Then more loudly,
"That's it!!"

He burst out of the inner office to show it to John Hegarty, who had
been busily working away on the same brief. Hegarty had only got as far
as lines such as "Who taught your daughter the facts of life?" and a
picture of a gym-outfitted schoolgirl. He needed just one look at Sinclair's sketch.

"I almost died," he says. "It was the best thing I had ever seen. Its
simplicity and audacity were electrifying." Quietly he tore up his own

efforts and went home that evening "depressed and in awe."

Within weeks the pregnant man was the most talked-about advertisement in Britain. Its wit and directness attracted notice everywhere, and the unexpected reversal of the sexes magnified its impact. The health minister, Richard Crossman, raised an eyebrow when he first saw the ad but allowed it to pass. Others thought that even in permissive Britain no government agency should go this far. The national press took up the argument, and soon the pregnant man had become the subject of a nationwide debate. The Health Education Council, a mundane government agency that had already been pushed into the headlines because of Charles Saatchi's antismoking campaign, now found itself either lauded for its adventurousness or reviled for its lack of discretion. Then *Time* magazine discovered the ad, and the pregnant man went international, presented to the world as one of the best examples of the daringly creative things that were happening in the British advertising world. It would go on to win a series of awards and enter all the textbooks of creative advertisements since the War as a classic of its kind.

As Charles was building his business and his reputation, Maurice was making his way in life too. He had his first-class honors degree in sociology and his gold medal and now went looking for a job. With his personality and his ability to marshall complex thoughts and present them coherently, Maurice could probably have found a job anywhere he wanted. The mid-1960s was a time in Britain when the big companies toured the universities in search of bright young managers, and there were far more jobs on offer than there were graduates to go around. Even an average graduate could end up with half a dozen offers—and Maurice was well above average.

Perhaps influenced by his brother's affinity for the trade press, he chose Haymarket Publications, a small but rapidly growing group that owned several publications of great interest to Charles. Haymarket at the time was controlled by Michael Heseltine, one of the brightest of the younger generation of Conservative members of Parliament (destined to become secretary of state for defense in the Thatcher government), and his partner, Lindsay Masters. They had bought most of their publications from the near-bankrupt British Printing Corporation. One of these was *World Press News*, which Maurice remembers as exceptionally dull—it had been around for years, reporting happenings on Fleet Street and in the world of advertising. It contained no scoops or interesting gossip and was going nowhere.

Maurice arrived for an interview shortly after Heseltine and Masters had relaunched it under the editorship of Michael Jackson, who quickly commissioned a feature on the Cramer-Saatchi partnership. It was Masters who interviewed Maurice, and he still remembers the occasion

well. After the usual questions, he was impressed enough with the young
Saatchi to offer him a job.

"Right, when can you start?" They discussed that for a few minutes
before Maurice blinked and said: "We haven't talked about salary yet." It
was Masters's turn to blink. Throughout most of British industry the
standard starting salary for graduates was around £1,000 a year. That
was what he was offering, he explained.

"Ah," said Maurice. "I couldn't possibly afford to come for that." Why
not, asked Masters.

"You see, I've got this frightfully expensive car and I couldn't run it on
that." Masters blinked again. Then he asked him how much he *would*
come for. "It would have to be at least two thousand a year," said
Maurice firmly. Meekly, Masters agreed. It is a story that he tells, years
later, to emphasize the impact from the very first day that the young
Maurice had on him.

Maurice worked as a junior assistant to both Masters and Heseltine
but mostly to Masters. *Campaign* was already a success when he arrived,
but there were new magazines to work on. Haymarket, tiny when
Maurice arrived, expanded rapidly, making Heseltine, with a shareholding worth over £25 million, one of the richest British Members of
Parliament. *Campaign* was an editorial success from the start, featuring
news of the advertising industry on the front page, with well-written
features and columns inside. It was also classic territory for Charles
Saatchi to place his stories in, and for the next seventeen years it was his
main outlet for items of news and gossip he tirelessly gathered, in turn
receiving a steady supply of favorable stories about his own business.

Dozens of young graduates have been through the hands of Masters
and Heseltine before and since Maurice Saatchi. He would stay with
them for only three years and was effectively gone from their lives by the
time he was twenty-four. But both recall him clearly.

"I remember this bright-as-a-button guy, really contributing," says
Heseltine. "He wasn't just taking orders or carrying out instructions; he
was in the dialogue. His ideas you listened to, and his perception and
analysis were valuable. I can certainly remember feeling we had an ace
here."

It was with Masters that Maurice worked most closely, and both
Masters and his wife, Marisa, became genuinely fond of him. With
Masters he was deeply involved in the launch of other magazines,
including *Accountancy Age*, mostly in the selling of advertising space—
and he learned and absorbed the systems used. "Maurice learned a lot
about how to sell here," says Masters. "He was one of those people who
instinctively seemed to know it. Some people learn by staggering around
and falling over all the time, and then pick themselves up. Maurice
doesn't fall over very much. He seemed to be born with it."

Haymarket, unlike most other publishers, had a system of client cards in tin boxes, and Maurice, along with others, had to use them to make a certain number of calls every day to potential advertisers. Today it would all be computerized, but by the standards of the day this was an advanced and streamlined method. It was hard and sometimes humiliating work but invaluable experience that Maurice would later use when he joined his brother. Haymarket in those years had a considerable impetus that, Maurice later felt, could have turned it into a Rupert Murdoch–sized company if Heseltine had not in 1970 become a senior cabinet minister in the new Conservative government of Ted Heath. Maurice watched Heseltine at work looking for new magazines to take over.

"What we did," explains Heseltine, "was we wrote a standard letter to the chairman of every publishing house offering to buy them. We sent out hundreds of letters, and if we bought two magazine groups in a year that was fine. In fact you only need one a year to make it worthwhile." Heseltine cites the example of a phone call that came in from a man in Canada as a result of one his letters. "We're just about to sell to Thomson, and I've got your letter. He's a bit big, and I don't want to sell to him. Are you really interested?" Heseltine leaped into action, worked through the night, and ended up buying a medical publishing company that has made considerable profits for Haymarket since. For Maurice it was an eye-opener, and he absorbed the systems and style like a sponge. Just as he had learned about presentation and how to marshall arguments from Professor Cohen at LSE, now he learned from Heseltine and Masters.

Like his brother, Maurice still kept a base at home. He was far less well paid—£3,000 a year when he left—but he had enough to indulge his passion for cars. Much to the astonishment of everyone at Haymarket, the tall, owlish Maurice traveled to work in his 1966 Corvette, an American sports car almost unavailable in Britain. He also sported smart suits, although they were subtly more conservative than Charles's.

Maurice was no ordinary twenty-four-year-old. It was clear to Masters in particular—and he knew him best—that he was headed straight for the top of whatever he wanted to do. Already his considerable charm, cloaked with his slightly diffident and shy manner, was at work in the organization. He worked hard and thoughtfully, concentrating his energies and intelligence on a course he had carefully worked out in advance. And he had that flash of original thought that already set him apart from others of his age and that would prove so crucial for his future and his brother's.

In early 1970 Charles began to itch for his own agency. He found it irritating that his creative work should appear as the work of agencies who hired his consultancy services. He now had the kernel of a team and something of a track record, and the success of the antismoking ads made him confident that he could attract new clients. He had seen enough of the agency world to despise most of it. Other than the work produced by his old house Collett Dickenson Pearce and one or two others, he felt nothing creative was happening in the British ad world.

At home on the weekends Maurice, observing the ad scene from the outside as a customer and through his connection with *Campaign*, encouraged his brother. And, in turn, Charles was impressed by Maurice's ability to analyze the business, to pick out the weaknesses and the strengths, and by his disciplined hard work.

Exactly when Charles decided to make Maurice part of his new venture neither of them now remembers precisely, but by early 1970 Maurice was preparing to join him. Ross Cramer, to Charles's surprise, proved less enthusiastic. "Look, I'm growing away from all this," he told Charles. "I think I want to go off and direct. I'm getting more involved with films and with this script writing we've been doing. I've decided that's where my love is." He would, he said, direct commercials for a living, maybe move into feature films if it went well. (He never did—but has made a successful career in the commercial ad world.)

"Charlie pleaded with him not to," says Hegarty. "But Ross said, 'No, I won't like what's going to happen; it'll be boring,' and he decided to leave. And Charlie got his brother in to start the agency."

The idea originally had been to call the agency Saatchi, Cramer, & Saatchi. Now that Cramer would not be there, it would have to be called something else.

4
"A BLOODY GOOD NAME"

The first announcement had a limited audience. In the middle of
May 1970 Charles Saatchi emerged from the office he shared with
Ross Cramer. He paused on the top step, looking down at the
room below, and called for attention. He had some news to announce that
affected them all. The days of the consultancy were coming to an end, he
said. They were no longer going to work for other agencies that passed
off the best creative work coming out of Cramer-Saatchi as their own.
They were now going to work for themselves in their own new agency,
with a new type of thinking and approach to the business. The two years
of running the consultancy, which had been a novel idea when it started,
had proved not only that they could do it but also that there was a need
for a hard-selling creative agency. They would need some more people,
and he had some ideas on that. And they would have to move—he was
already looking for new offices, he added.

It was a short speech, one of the few that Charles Saatchi has ever
given. He had some bad news as well as good. Cramer wanted to leave.
He had been in the agency world before and didn't want to enter it again.
Working with David Puttnam and Alan Parker had given him a taste for
the film world. He was going off on his own to make commercials, maybe
other kinds of films.

That caused some dismay. Cramer, although only in his early thirties,
was a veteran compared to the others. He was also a calming, stable
influence on a young group of copywriters and art directors, none of
them older than twenty-six. All of them liked as well as respected him; he
was the only one of them capable of standing up to Charles, the only one
who could talk him out of some of his wilder and more extravagant ideas.
Cramer would be a loss.

Charles Saatchi, however, already had ideas on who would step into
his shoes, he said. Cramer would be replaced—and here there was a
moment of held breath on the part of the audience—"by my brother
Maurice." The others looked at each other blankly. They knew the
younger Saatchi worked for Haymarket and had never worked in an
agency. How could he replace Cramer? Charles nonetheless seemed to
have little doubt. Maurice had other virtues. However, with Cramer
going the name would have to be changed. Cramer-Saatchi, he said,
would become Saatchi & Saatchi. "It's a bloody good name for a new

advertising agency," he went on. "Saatchi & Saatchi—it's so bizarre no one will ever forget it in a hurry."

"I remember him making a joke of the name," says Chris Martin, then a junior art director at the consultancy. "He said they had to have a name that people would remember, so he had got his brother in to make sure they had the right name, almost as if that was the only reason he was joining."

Martin had never even met Maurice at the time but raised no objection; he was twenty-three, doing well, and he was attached to a man he regarded as one of the most creative in the British advertising industry. If Charles Saatchi wanted to start his own agency, Martin was happy to follow. John Hegarty, who although only in his mid-twenties at the time had known Charles Saatchi longer than any of the others, did voice a protest. Unlike Martin, he had met Maurice but only a couple of times. "I thought he was a terrific chap, a really nice guy," says Hegarty. "But I didn't see what he could contribute to us."

Hegarty took Saatchi aside. "Charlie, are you serious?" he began. "He's only twenty-four. Are you sure you're right? It's bad enough that we're just creative people and there's no senior management, but you know . . . what's your brother going to add to that? Are you sure this is correct?"

Charles Saatchi liked and respected Hegarty and was eager that he join him in the new venture. With Cramer going, Hegarty could reasonably expect to be made a partner. Charles realized that not everyone was going to welcome his brother immediately. "Well, it might not be [correct]," he said finally, "but I tell you something, John, whatever happens I know I can trust Maurice. And he won't put a knife in anybody's back. That's worth a dozen of another type of business person that might screw up for us."

Hegarty did not press the point, nor did he take it as a reflection on his own loyalty. He too was enthusiastic for the new venture, and if Charlie believed his brother would add to its chances of success he would accept that. A third member of the team, Jeremy Sinclair, raised no objections. As he would do for the next seventeen years—and is still doing—Sinclair remained loyal and supportive of Charles Saatchi.

"The Saatchis timed their arrival perfectly—or, rather, their parents did," wrote Jeremy Bullmore, chairman of J. Walter Thompson in London, in the *Guardian*. "Before the Saatchi phenomenon, those of us in the surprisingly small industry (only 15,000 people in the whole of this country) were accustomed to obscurity. No agency was a household name, very few people knew what agencies did, the City of London had never met us and didn't want to, and the feeling was mutual. More importantly, we'd all been brought up to believe that the function of agencies was to make brands and clients famous and profitable while remaining decently anonymous ourselves."

Although Bullmore would be one of the early Saatchi supporters, this last, slightly carping note would be echoed for many years by the older generation of advertising people. It would be a long time before agencies realized, as Charles Saatchi did from the beginning, the value of publicity for the agency itself.

Bullmore, however, makes another point that also only slowly became apparent. In the early 1970s, he says, the conventional wisdom in the thinking classes, both in Britain and the United States, was "still mostly conditioned by the title of *The Hidden Persuaders* (few had actually read it), Priestley's *Admass*, and Galbraith's *The Affluent Society*. Few observed at the time that this sector of British business was faster, more responsive, more competitive, and more efficient than any other."

The Saatchis believed this was true only for a small sector of the ad business. Charles was unimpressed with the organizational or creative capacity of most of the big agencies, and Maurice had seen enough to know that the advertising industry could learn a lot from the methods practiced by Michael Heseltine and Lindsay Masters at Haymarket. The structure of the business was disorganized and ripe for the type of semifinancial acquisitive operation the Saatchis would run. Even with the multinational agencies so dominant, concentration in the industry was remarkably low: there were over 600 agencies, none with more than 5 percent of billings. The stock market despised the industry, dismissing it as one largely run for the benefit of the partners in the agencies, with low-quality earnings likely to disappear as clients changed agencies or creative talent left for fresher pastures (wrongly, as we shall see later). It was an industry remarkably vulnerable to a person as determined as Charles Saatchi but even more so to someone as bright and organized as his younger brother.

The name "Saatchi & Saatchi" had not come about as readily as Charles made it sound that day on Goodge Street. Originally, the plan was simply to change the Cramer-Saatchi consultancy into an agency with the same name. Then Charles, impressed by the obvious business acumen of his younger brother Maurice and aware that creative advertising people were not necessarily good at the commercial end of the operation, decided to bring him in. When Ross Cramer refused to join him, Charles had to think again. At the home of their parents the two Saatchis had long discussions, often involving their parents and brothers. Saatchi was such a strange name for the ordinary clients. What would it mean to them? On the other hand, the agency had acquired such a reputation among those who knew about advertising that clients were approaching them directly. They should not lightly abandon the name Cramer-Saatchi.

They discussed all sorts of other possibilities. In the end they agreed that Saatchi & Saatchi was a "bizarre" name, and since they couldn't change it they would have to capitalize on it. "The name Saatchi is something we can't bury," insisted Charles. "We're stuck with it, so let's make it an asset."

Those discussions took place well before Charles made his speech to the staff. Now that the name was decided, preparations for the agency began in earnest. Hegarty, Martin, and Sinclair all willingly agreed to become part of the new venture, which meant that from the beginning it would have a nucleus of talented, creative people with their own reputations. Cramer quietly disappeared from their professional lives, and the tall, boyish-looking, bespectacled figure of Maurice began to be seen bustling in and out, carrying bulging briefcases and files. The offices on Goodge Street were comfortable and airy and had suited them all well but were clearly not right for the new venture. The new office would have to contain more people, be easily accessible to clients who could not be expected to climb the four flights up to the old offices, and have a boardroom and projection room for making pitches to clients. Most important of all, Charles was looking for premises that could be cleverly disguised to make it seem as if his little firm owned the whole building rather than the single floor that he knew was all he could afford. Despite these constraints, by midsummer a suitable office had been found.

Golden Square is an oasis in the throbbing, multicultural world of London's Soho district, surrounded by a mixture of seedy streets full of striptease clubs, theaters showing pornographic films, and shops selling sex videos and pornographic magazines. Nearby is London's Chinatown, offering an array of restaurants that serve up some of the best Chinese food in the world. To the south, just a couple of blocks away, is Piccadilly Circus. The square itself is leafy and surprisingly secluded, the headquarters of some of Britain's largest textile companies and television groups, its respectable Victorian frontages concealing the offices of firms of lawyers, consultants, the better class of wine and spirit merchants, a tailor's shop making tweed suits and dresses for the gentry, and the odd textile gallery. Hundreds of studios and film processors used by the film and television industries are only minutes away. There were better addresses in Adland, but this was fine.

Charles liked the look of 6 Golden Square the first time Maurice and the agent showed it to him. It was one of the most elegant buildings in the square, with carved stone pillars and a high fanlight over the doorway, conveying a feeling that the residents of this office were respectable, solid, and had been around for a long time. The Saatchis took the ground floor and a basement below it, the whole area smaller than the Goodge Street premises but with the potential, with a little creative design, of appearing much larger. The design of it was again entrusted to Rodney Fitch, who was by now making a reputation for his work with Terence Conran; Conran in turn was making a major impact among the younger and trendier middle class with his Habitat shops, specializing in stripped pine furniture and stainless-steel and glass-topped kitchen furniture.

Fitch soon started on Golden Square, working to Charles's and Maurice's detailed instructions. The main area on the bright ground floor would basically be open plan, with everything designed to give the impression that there was more of it hidden away somewhere that the client couldn't see. "It was very clever," says John Hegarty. "It looked really smart, sort of elegant. You went in, and as always with agencies you want the feeling of energy, of people doing things, and it was designed to give you that." Some of the best ads were blown up and hung on the walls, an unusual feature then in agencies but now standard in Adland reception areas. Fitch installed partitions about five feet high so that it was possible when sitting down to have some privacy, but anyone standing could still see what was going on across the room. The reception area had a higher partition that was difficult to see over, but the waiting client could hear that things were going on inside. The room had a high ceiling and windows fitted with modern blinds. The basic working area was divided by four large white-topped tables that served as desks, with aisles running between them. At the back were three partitioned-off offices, still part of the main room, where clients could be interviewed or phone calls made. In the farthest corner was a spiral staircase leading down to the basement, which had a projection room and a long table for conferences and meetings.

The final touch was typical of Charles. He had a brass plate made similar to others around the square that announced firms of solicitors or accountants. Picked out in subdued black lettering were the words: "Saatchi & Saatchi." It was all that would signal to the outside world what went on within.

The office, however, was a minor matter compared to the need to bring in some clients. At that point the Cramer-Saatchi consultancy had only one prestige client that Charles could safely rely on, the Health Education Council. In those final months before the launch, Charles Saatchi exploited the reputation he had built on the health ads for all he was worth.

In fairness, he had something to boast about. The Health Education Council account had initially involved designing brochures and posters, work that Charles left mostly to the young Jeremy Sinclair, to Hegarty, and to Mike Coughlan, who could produce adventurous ads from the most unpromising material. But the others acknowledged that it was often Charles's input that turned their ideas into startlingly good ads. This was true of the pregnant-man ad and was equally true of the "fly in your food" poster, which in its day got considerable notice. It was one of the first ads Cramer-Saatchi produced for the HEC, and Charles wanted something bold. The idea was to show in the most graphic way the dangers of allowing flies anywhere near food. Charles found some text in an old medical book describing how flies vomit on food to soften it up, then "stamp the vomit in until it's a liquid, usually stamping in a few germs for good measure. Then when it's good and runny they suck it all back again, probably dropping some excrement at the same time."

Coughlan added the finishing touch. He wrote at the bottom: "And then, when they've finished eating, it's your turn." The poster got a "special mention" in the D&AD awards in 1970, listing Cramer-Saatchi as the agency, Hegarty as the art director and designer, and Charles Saatchi and Mike Coughlan as the copywriters.

More celebrated, of course, was the "pregnant man" ad, which to this day is often credited to Charles Saatchi. It was one of the key factors behind his reputation when the Saatchi & Saatchi agency opened. "Years later, when we were first buying an agency in New York, the only thing they knew about us was the pregnant-man ad," says a Saatchi employee. The ad was just coming off the drawing board as Charles Saatchi, still running the consultancy on Goodge Street, was finalizing his plans for the agency, and he seized upon it as a heaven-sent opportunity for publicity for the new business. It has become the best-known ad they ever produced, and there is more myth about it than any other. In 1987 the Harvard Business School did a case study on Saatchi & Saatchi and noted that "the agency's first breakthrough came in 1975 when it produced the famous 'pregnant man' advertisement. This established Saatchi & Saatchi's reputation as the UK's 'creative' agency."

In fact, as we have seen, the pregnant-man ad had been written five years earlier. Charles's involvement in it, although important, was by no means as central as legend later had it. What was all Charles, however, was the clever exploitation of the publicity. No one mentioned Cramer-Saatchi—in those days, the client got the credit or brickbats for its advertising and the agencies stayed in the background. But the industry knew—or thought it knew—who had written the ad, and Charles made sure prospective clients knew too. He never attempted to deny Sinclair credit for the ad or to claim it as his own. But he did make sure that it was associated with the name Saatchi. The story ran in the press for months, right through the last days at Goodge Street and the first months in the new office at Golden Square. It continued to crop up afterward in the most unexpected ways.

Unknown even to Charles Saatchi, the model used as the pregnant man was not a professional model at all but a twenty-one-year-old traffic manager for a rival agency, BBDO. It had been a freelance effort on the part of the BBDO creative team, which earned some extra money on the side by working at night for other agencies—without telling their bosses. No professional model could be found for the role, so in desperation they persuaded their young colleague, Dennis Passingham, to stuff a cushion up his sweater. Overnight, Passingham became one of the best-known faces in Britain—but his name was kept secret. Then he fell off his moped and was rushed to the hospital. The BBDO team, which had spent a year worrying that their role would be discovered, now decided to have some fun and leaked the story. The pregnant man gave interviews from his hospital bed, and the BBC ran bulletins on his "confinement." Charles was quoted as saying rather huffily that he did not even know the model's name until then. But the story ran for another week, providing yet more free publicity. The *Sun* newspaper carried perhaps the most memorable headline: "MAN WITH A HUMP GOES DOWN WITH A BUMP."

The Health Education Council was only one client; the brothers desperately needed more. Charles had a friend, Danny Levine, at his old agency, Collett Dickenson Pearce. A junior copywriter, Levine admired the work coming out of the Cramer-Saatchi consultancy. Levine's father was the marketing director of the Citrus Marketing Board of Israel, which sold its oranges and lemons around the world under the name Jaffa and had decided on a big push in Britain designed to take advantage of the growing boycott of South African oranges.

Levine suggested to his father that he try this bright new agency: it was creative and hungry, and with everything at risk it would put its best work into the account, which none of the big agencies would. The Saatchis were asked to pitch and spent days preparing. They got the account but never got to run what they reckoned was their best advertisement: Jeremy Sinclair and Bill Atherton produced a campaign with a biblical feel, along the lines of "And the Lord saith: let there be oranges. . . . " It ended with the line "Jaffa: the Chosen Fruit," but it was turned away by the authorities because it was "anti-Jewish." The authority was unmoved by pleas that "We're Jews and we like it—and the Israelis like it too."

Now they had two clients, but the brothers wanted at least three significant accounts before they opened: otherwise the financial gamble they were taking was going to be even riskier. Another prospect soon appeared. Granada TV was not one of the big accounts by the standards of the multinational agencies, but that summer it was looking for a new agency and a new campaign for its television rental division. The man running it was Brian Wolfson, now chairman of the company that owns Wembley Stadium (home to the English soccer team), then a young executive carving a reputation for himself in the tough world of television rental. Maurice heard about him from his contacts at *Campaign* and rang him. Could Saatchi make a pitch? Wolfson, surprised by the approach, agreed. Again the team worked hard on the presentation material, but as the day approached, Charles began to worry about another problem: they had no suitable premises to make their presentation to the client.

They had no projection facilities on Goodge Street, because they had always been able to use those of the client agencies. Golden Square was not finished yet. What to do?

By a coincidence, one of the last jobs done at the Cramer-Saatchi consultancy was some creative work for a tiny agency called Bowman Harris. The work was intended for an Australian client, and as soon as it was finished, the entire Bowman Harris team, only three or four strong, was to fly to Australia with it. As it happened, Bowman Harris had smart offices that included projection facilities just off Berkeley Square. "Suddenly Charlie thought, this is it," says Chris Martin. "Knowing they were all in Australia, he rang up the receptionist and said, 'I'm just phoning to make certain that everything's all right for the presentation to Granada TV next week.' 'I don't know anything about that,' said the girl. 'Oh, didn't Arnold Bowman tell you? I'd agreed with him that we could borrow your conference room to make the presentation to a client, because of course everyone's away.' Naturally, she said 'fine,' and Charlie went on: 'Will there be a slide projector? And could someone bring in tea and biscuits?' So this wonderful bit of opportunism takes place where the client is directed to these very smart offices, and they actually put a Saatchi & Saatchi sign over the door, and Charlie meets them outside, and then John Hegarty and Maurice make the presentation. And they came back having got the client! It was wonderful."

As important as the clients were, getting the right people to work in the new agency was even more important. Charles decided to do away with account executives, the salespeople most agencies place between the creative team and the client. They were, he insisted, an unnecessary and damaging layer that got in the way of direct discourse between client and creative team. Everyone would have to join in to do that work. (Much of it would fall to Maurice.) However, he needed other specialist skills, and his intention was to fill the team with the same type of person he had working at Goodge Street: young, creative, and aggressive. The secret of much that was to follow was Charles's skill at getting such people to work for him. Later, most of the seven whom he hired as the initial team at the agency went on to found their own agencies or reach the top in another profession. They are now almost invariably wealthy people, established proprietors themselves although still only in their early forties.

Not everyone he wanted joined, however, and the list of those who didn't is almost as interesting as the list of those who did. For instance, Maurice had the idea of hiring a food retailer, which would, he suggested, give them an edge in getting some of the big food and consumer accounts. (The idea was not entirely new—a number of other agencies already employed ex–supermarket people, with mixed results.) He spent weeks trying to woo a young supermarket manager named Ian McLaurin. Still only in his twenties, McLaurin was already head of the northern division of Tesco, then the most aggressive food retailer in the country. McLaurin was tempted but in the end was persuaded by the Tesco management that he had a good career there. He did—today he is chairman.

Maurice had other imaginative ideas. Even before the agency began, he proposed offering clients another service: management consultancy, arguing that it went together with advertising. With his analytical mind, he could see trends perhaps more clearly than his brother, and to him it was obvious that one of the faults of the advertising industry was that it had an image of being "very polite and superficial, even a bit silly. People in it think about it as a hobby," he argued. Consulting, on the other hand, employed a different type of person, a more professional and intellectual type who he felt could make a contribution at a business level. It says something for the relationship between Charles and his twenty-three-year-old brother at this stage that Charles not only listened to him but told him to go ahead.

In between pitching for clients, Maurice approached Peter Foy, a young consultant at McKinsey's, then probably the leading consultants in the world. Maurice deployed all his persuasive charm, but Foy in the end decided to stay with McKinsey's—and is now senior partner.

There was another failure that would later have considerable—and beneficial—significance for the agency. A key role in the new firm would be what is called the "media executive," who buys space and time from the newspapers and TV stations. That summer Charles was propounding to anyone who would listen his theories about how much better a service advertising companies could give their clients by buying media time cheaply and charging their clients a proper fee instead of using the system then (and still) in existence.

Recognized agencies were allowed a 15 percent discount on the price of advertising space; they in turn charged the client the full price, in effect making their profit from the discount. This system was an anomaly that dated back to the time when advertising agencies worked for the newspapers and magazines actually selling space rather than buying it. Although the agencies' role had reversed from seller to buyer well before the Second World War, the system had continued, basically because the advertising industry, which ran itself almost as a cartel, found it comfortable and clients didn't object.

To make his fee plan work—and there were many who told him it was unworkable no matter what happened—Charles needed a good media buyer. The person with the reputation was Paul Green, then regarded as the best media buyer in the business. Green was tempted by the thought of the new agency and by Charles's idea of what could be achieved in the media-buying field through some really aggressive and imaginative bargaining, in particular with the TV companies. However, Green was even more taken by working for himself. Several media people had left to start their own media brokering businesses, and that route appealed to Green. Just weeks before the agency was to launch he backed out. Today the operation he set up, Media Buying Services, is a highly successful one.

Green's withdrawal came as a bombshell to the Saatchis. "Paul Green came to a meeting, he met the people from Jaffa whom we were pitching for at the time, and then at the eleventh hour, really almost the twelfth hour, he pulled out," says John Hegarty. It was so last-minute that Charles Saatchi that very day had dictated a letter to be sent to the media authorities with whom every new agency has to be registered, listing Green as a director of the new agency. "Charlie suddenly said to Gail [his secretary], 'Don't send that letter,' " recalls Chris Martin. "Gail said, 'I've mailed it.' Charlie said, 'Where?' 'Well,' she said, 'it was either in the box in Goodge Street or the one in Tottenham Court Road, or did I post it on my way?' She couldn't remember. There were about six letter boxes she might have used. So Charlie went berserk, and he handed three or four people fivers and said, 'Go and stand by the box until the chap comes and bribe the postman to get the letter back.' And Maurice, Charlie, Gail, and Hegarty all went off. And they got the letter back. And Paul Green was heard of no more. And enter Tim Bell."

When the Saatchis asked who was the best media specialist after Green, Bell was mentioned. A phone call from Maurice brought him to the office within hours; Bell needed little persuading to join—he was already a fan. "Charlie Saatchi was my god," he says today. "I thought he was a genius—I still do. As far as I was concerned, he was the man who had written the pregnant-man ad, the best ad I had ever seen. Only later did I discover that was untrue. At the time I saw him as the new Bill Bernbach. The advertising world in those days was terribly boring and stultifying. Charles to me represented excitement and creativity."

"Lady luck really smiled on Charlie and Maurice when Paul pulled out and they got Tim in," says Hegarty. "Like a lot of things in life, you're dealt what you think is a blow but what in fact is a great piece of luck. Paul Green was an outstanding media man, but in personality terms he didn't balance Maurice and Charlie. The great thing that Tim had was that balance, and without him they never would have built the agency to the size they did."

Bell at the time was twenty-eight, a year older than Charles. Six feet tall, slim, and good-looking, Bell was already heading rapidly up the ladder at Geers Gross, one of the newer and brighter agencies in the industry—and one of the few that Charles Saatchi respected. He also possessed a charm that over the years would become legendary well beyond the bounds of the advertising industry—a profile of him would talk about his being the sort of person "even the dogs cross the street to be kicked by." To the others he was as near a replacement as they could get for the popular Ross Cramer.

"Physically they were very alike; they had that kind of fairish hair," says Hegarty. "And Tim, personality-wise, was very similar to Ross. They were both amiable, and neither ever showed if they were down. They were always in the center of what was happening, very good at remembering the little things that kept people happy, and great at rallying the troops."

5

"TIME FOR A NEW KIND OF ADVERTISING"

B y the end of the summer of 1970, the Saatchi brothers had persuaded most of the talent they wanted to join them. Ron Collins, twenty-nine, was regarded by the others as one of the leading art directors of the day—as he later proved when he went on to found the agency Wight Collins Rutherford Scott. Alan Tilby came from Collett, where he too had a considerable reputation. With Hegarty, Sinclair, Atherton, and Martin, it was a young team, entirely creative except for Maurice and Bell. But how exceptional was it? Each individual member would almost certainly have risen high in whatever agency he chose to join—as indeed most of them did when they later left Saatchi. But there were dozens of other equally talented men and women in the London advertising world at the time; the industry was offering high salaries; it was recruiting young people directly from art schools and universities; and there were many like Hegarty and Sinclair who had chosen advertising as their career. As the manufacturing industry continued its decline and the City of London financial-service sector was in the doldrums, advertising offered an attractive and glamorous career.

So what singled out the nine-person team that Saatchi & Saatchi put together that summer? Several factors emerge. A major part of the answer, certainly in these initial stages, has to lie in the character, energy, and drive of Charles Saatchi himself and in the way he could motivate and bring out the best in others. Hegarty still talks about the special atmosphere Charles could create, a climate touching on fear, but fear in a positive sense. "Creativity is, I believe, an expression of insecurity," says Hegarty, "a desire to win approval. It is in a climate of self-doubt that the creative spark is forced and cajoled into fire." Charles had a way, Hegarty says, of "daring your ability to create a piece of work of even greater artistry."

But the role of Maurice should not be underestimated. Over the years the relationship between the brothers would change. In my research for this book, I initially formed the view, based on interviews with the early Saatchi team, that Charles had most of the ideas, that the broad strategy and concepts were his, and that Maurice, for the first four or five years at least, was essentially a bright and obviously able assistant who carried them out. Only when one analyzes the key decisions made at this early stage and even more important ones made later does one realize that it was never quite like that.

The huge ambition, the overpowering desire to be bigger, richer, more famous—just to be *more* than anyone else—mostly came from Charles. But Maurice was equally ambitious in his own way. The business plans and systems that set Saatchi & Saatchi apart from the run-of-the-mill agency within months were all Maurice's—Charles did not even try to understand them. The takeover plans already being hatched were his too. So were many of the wider concepts, such as the management-consultancy service. It is probably true that in these early days Charles was the X factor, but without Maurice he would never even have thought about public companies, altering the City attitude to the advertising industry, spreading the network worldwide, or so much else that made Saatchi & Saatchi what it is today. Without Charles, Maurice would still probably have built a big business, whatever he had gone into. Lindsay Masters says that he would still have raised money for Maurice, whatever he wanted to do—and at one stage Masters even believed Maurice had plans to create his own publishing business. Over the years people would come to find it impossible to imagine one brother without the other, so well did they work together. But it was never, even in these very early days, the dominant-Charles/little-brother-Maurice relationship that even those who worked closely with them believed it to be.

At this early point, this was not yet apparent, even to Hegarty or Sinclair. None of them had any real idea what they were venturing into—just that they were bright young people starting their own new business with some good ideas, something of a bumpy but creative reputation, a trio of clients, and not much else. Sinclair was undoubtedly a highly talented copywriter, probably one of the most talented of his age; Tim Bell would soon emerge as an exceptional advertising executive whom any agency boss would have loved to have on staff. But advertising history is full of examples of bright young people setting off on their own to form what in a single generation became worldwide agencies. Without Maurice there was nothing especially new or dramatically different about Saatchi & Saatchi. They may have *said* that they were different, that they were going to break the mold, build an entirely new form of advertising agency; but then they would, wouldn't they? What new company does not? But it would have been terribly difficult at this point to spot the chemistry that would make this small agency, above all the other little businesses beginning around that time, grow to such monumental proportions and become so embedded in the corporate folklore of the 1980s. Eighteen years later, Charles could put his finger on what the catalyst was: his younger brother. But he had no way of knowing it then.

Both Charles and Maurice have also displayed a remarkable ability to choose good people suitable to the particular stage of the organization.

They would be right for one stage of the company's development, do their job, and leave—or lag behind the advance of the brothers. Of the team now assembled only Jeremy Sinclair would live with the brothers' pace for the next seventeen years. All the others, including Bell, would drop away or assert their independence. For each new stage of the company, people with different specialties and areas of expertise would be required, and the Saatchis did not hesitate to go out and hire them.

Charles was always contemptuous of his own industry, voicing again and again that summer his view that most advertising was just a waste of money; the clients might as well dig a hole and bury the money for all the good it did them. He would point to full-page ads in the papers that he reckoned no one, "literally no one," would read. His team was going to be genuinely creative, he kept insisting, and would produce the best ads ever seen in Britain. The very fact that his consultancy had done so well showed how big were the problems inside the big agencies. They had no creative ideas of their own and had to turn to him to help them. Look what he had done for the Health Education Council. Look at his anti-smoking campaign, which had been so effective that it had made even *him* cut down.

There were many who found Charles arrogant and overbearing, full of hubris and not very likable. The realities of running his own agency and dealing with clients would soon bring him down a peg, they prophesied. Anyway, his ideas were unworkable, they warned. He was planning to break with a whole series of industry traditions, but others had tried that too and retreated again. No account executives? Well, Geers Gross managed to get away with none, but having to deal with clients as well as produce imaginative advertising imposed an intolerable burden on the creative staff. Bigger discounts from the media and pass the rebate back to the client? That was just a gimmick, fiddling with figures. The clients wouldn't understand, anyway, and couldn't be bothered to try. (The brothers had already discovered that with Granada Television Rentals.) Cold calling clients? That would just annoy them and wouldn't produce a single extra client, or at least not a good one. The big accounts were not going to move because some twenty-four-year-old rang up and said, "Hey, we're a new agency with some creative ideas, and we'd like to have your account, please."

Charles either didn't mind the criticisms or ignored them. What he did care about was being noticed, and he was achieving that. No new agency had received such publicity in the trade press before a launch. That summer he made sure that *Campaign* in particular received a steady supply of stories, whipping his staff to greater efforts. "He used to go around every Monday before press day on *Campaign*," says Chris Martin, "and he'd say, 'Give me a story for *Campaign*. Get out there and get in the pubs—any tidbit you heard this week, give it to me and it will be passed on. If you don't know one, make it up!' And every single week he'd ring *Campaign* with a story. Not necessarily about Saatchi's. They made the front page week after week. It was incredibly time-consuming to do it, but that's what Charlie used to do."

That summer was a busy one for both brothers, as they prepared pitches at the Goodge Street office, hounded Rodney Fitch about the new premises in Golden Square, and worked out their business plan. Hegarty, Sinclair, and Martin were used to Charles's pressure and didn't worry too much as long as his irritation wasn't directed at them. During the years they had known him they had seen him work himself into a fury, the invective and obscenities pouring forth in a great stream on top of the unfortunate recipient. They already talked ruefully about being "beaten up" by Charles, not physically but verbally. They had seen him rip up bits of artwork that had taken days to prepare when he didn't like them, hurling the pieces around the office, shouting that it was "fucking crap." He was uncompromising about the product that came out of his agency. Several times someone had shown artwork to clients who liked it, only to have Charles throw it out because *he* didn't: "Fuck the client, what does *he* know about it?" But if Charles was unhappy with an ad, he took infinite pains to get it right.

"He could argue all night about a point," says one of the team. "He would continually say: 'I don't understand what you're trying to do. Tell me what it is you're trying to say.' He has an incredibly clear mind that gets right to the heart of it." Sinclair, like the others, soon learned to keep the conversation with Charles to a "basic level. He has no interest in philosophizing or intellectualizing about advertisements, replying impatiently to any such attempt, 'Yeah, yeah, you keep your philosophy—just tell me what you're trying to say.' "

Getting the money together was Maurice's job, and he took to it with flair. The brothers had to find most or all of the £25,000 capital themselves; they would take a few of the others in as partners, but their intention from the beginning was to keep control. Charles had for several years been a big earner, legendary even before he moved into his own consultancy for the high salary he could command. He lived at home, but even so had saved little. His earnings in 1970 were £25,000, a huge salary for a twenty-six-year-old in the Britain of the time; but he drove a Rolls-Royce Corniche, dressed well, and generally lived the good life. Maurice's £3,000 a year at Haymarket, good for a twenty-three-year-old, did not allow him to save any capital, particularly with his Stingray. The brothers would not ask their father for capital but would raise it outside.

It is an indication of Maurice's relationship with his then-boss Lindsay Masters that he chose him as the person to ask for capital—and a manifestation of Masters's affection for Maurice that he should respond. When Maurice told Masters he was leaving to join his brother, the

Haymarket boss first tried to dissuade him, then, seeing that was hope-less, decided to help him with advice, contacts, and office space until he was ready to go. "I liked him very much," Masters recalls. "He had done a wonderful job for us and one felt very warmly disposed towards him." For some time after he had offered his resignation, Maurice remained at Haymarket, and Masters would occasionally discover him working on budgets and plans for the agency. "I didn't mind—it was fine," says Masters.

When Maurice came to see Masters to ask him for £25,000, Masters told him he had a problem. Because Haymarket owned *Campaign*, he was concerned about the propriety of investing in a company about which the magazine would be writing. He would, he decided, bring in other investors for Saatchi & Saatchi. Masters, of course, was a wealthy man and had some even wealthier friends.

It is perhaps typical of the Saatchi & Saatchi story that these investors were not faceless people. Mary Quant in 1970 was at the height of her fame—or notoriety—having just come up with a new idea she called "Makeup to Make Love In," a range of cosmetics that a woman "could kiss and cuddle in all night without looking smudged." She had married one of her original partners, Alexander Plunket-Greene, and it was to them and another partner, Archie McNair, that Masters went that summer. Maurice Saatchi, he explained, was a very bright young man who worked for him and needed £25,000 to start a new business with his brother. Would they help him? "Would *you* invest?" he was asked. Masters explained that he would indeed, but he had a problem with conflict of interest and preferred not to. Mary Quant and her husband agreed—but only if Masters invested too, a condition that irritated him. Reluctantly, he accepted and took a share of the investment. "The thing was done by all of us as a sort of well-inclined and friendly gesture and not really as an attempt to get massively rich," says Masters. His partner Michael Heseltine was much keener to invest, but it was just too late for him—the Heath government was now in power, and Heseltine was one of its bright young ministers. There are strict rules governing the invest-ments of government ministers, so Heseltine ruled himself out as an investor.

There is a revealing little tale that attaches to Masters's particular investment. Much of the talk between him and Maurice took place at Masters's home, and his Italian-born wife, Marisa, admits she developed other designs on the younger Saatchi. Her eldest daughter was about Maurice's age, and she thought he might be an ideal match. On several evenings she brought her daughter into the room where the discussions were being held; but as the evening wore on and Maurice developed his plans and arguments for the agency, the young woman fell asleep. Romance never blossomed.

Mrs. Masters herself listened to Maurice's plans with considerable interest. She had worked in London as a translator and kept her savings in a beautiful Victorian box she had found in an auction room. It was, she explains, "my little nest egg," which all good Italian women put by without telling their husbands. In this instance, the Victorian box had been safely deposited in Coutt's Bank in the Strand; in it she had £6,000. She would invest it, she decided, in Maurice's new business.

Her husband wouldn't hear of it. He had gone to Quant and Plunket-Greene because of his worry over his conflict of interest, and his wife could not invest for the same reason. Recalling the same events, Marisa becomes quite emotional: "I wanted to give my money to Maurice because I loved him as a human being, and I trusted him so much. I really loved him. I begged Lindsay. I said I would invest in my Italian name. It is the first time in my life I want to use my money, the first time in my life I know that I can trust someone completely. But he wouldn't let me. I said I will give my money to Mary, and she can invest in her name, and I won't even have any documents. But Lindsay is such an honorable man. I begged, I cried. But no, he wouldn't."

Just in case he weakened, Marisa took Lindsay's driver to Coutt's Bank and got her Victorian box out. She hid it in a cavity under her bath and waited. The discussion between Masters, Maurice, and Mary Quant went on for weeks. Lindsay, she says, always used to complain after the meetings because he would have a stomachache. "Maurice was quite stingy in those days, so they always had dreadful dried-up sandwiches."

Lindsay still refused her the chance to invest, partly for ethical reasons but also because he didn't believe that a new company was the right place for her nest egg. Some months later she and her husband went to a reception. When they got home, they found that a back window had been forced. The burglar had found her box, smashed it open with her own tools, and taken her nest egg. "I cried for three months with anger and shame," Marisa says. She never knew until years later that Lindsay had invested after all.

The brothers now had the capital they needed, found entirely by Maurice, another example of how crucial he was at this point. Maurice had also completed a detailed five-year plan, which he hoped would position them for a public stock offering. With that in mind, he drew up a projection of what the profits needed to be to hit that target. The company would have to make £25,000 in the second year, then £50,000, then £125,000, and £250,000 in the fifth year. It was the plan he showed to Masters and to Mary Quant. Now he showed it to the manager at Coutt's Bank, who was even more impressed. "He said it's the best new company plan he's ever seen," Maurice later told Charles.

Everything was going as planned. By another stroke of luck the economy was picking up under the new Heath government. Neither brother had much interest in politics at the time, Charles in particular dismissing all politicians as useless. The economy was still in poor underlying shape, but the advertising industry dealt with foreign and British companies alike; it didn't matter who made the goods, just so long as someone had the money to buy them.

Many years later there would be a great deal of speculation about what was in the Saatchis' minds at this point. Were they setting out to become the biggest ad agency in Britain, the biggest in the world? Were they set on revolutionizing advertising, taking not just London but Madison Avenue by storm, making themselves into household names while building a business-services conglomerate that would be the biggest of its kind in the world? Years later, the study of Saatchi & Saatchi by the Harvard Business School stated that "their initial strategy was to shake up the staid British advertising world and to produce the most creative advertising in the country." In 1970 when they started that would have seemed a considerable ambition, but by the standards of what they have achieved, it now looks modest.

"They always seemed to believe the total market was theirs," says Chris Martin. "And not just advertising." That is supported by the attempts to bring in a supermarket executive and a management consultant from the first day. Jeremy Sinclair recalls the ambitions for the new agency as being threefold: "We were going to be big, we were going to be good, and we were going to be profitable. Everyone was keenly aware of those three things." But no one else remembers thinking that—or indeed anyone saying it. It is yet another rationalization after the fact. The truth is that there really was no grand design, no well-developed plan that encompassed even a tenth of what occurred. Mary Quant and Lindsay Masters thought they were backing a couple of bright young men who with a bit of luck might do a little more than survive in the advertising world. There was nothing in the business plan, presented to them by Maurice with all the carefully rehearsed skills of pitching to a client, that indicated that theirs was going to be anything more than a medium-sized agency. Even those involved did not seriously believe that what they were doing was fundamentally different from what other agencies did.

What they did grasp was that Charles and Maurice were abnormally ambitious, imaginative, and energetic. Yet even this is exaggerated with hindsight. "With gargantuan ambition burning behind his owlish spectacles, [Maurice] went into the advertising business with his brother in 1970," wrote *Fortune* magazine in a profile of the Saatchis in 1984. No one who knew them then would recognize that picture; but it was not hard to see that they were going places. Working around them was a group of bright young people who had picked up the fever, and it was infectious. All the newcomers knew from their own experience how vulnerable the rest of the advertising world was. It should not be impossible, they reasoned, given a fair chance, to carve out a niche and make a decent living—and enjoy it at the same time.

Robert Heller, the editor of *Management Today* and someone who knew the Saatchis better than most, attributed to them rather grander ambitions. Writing in 1987, he said: "They arrived at a time when rising American domination had been accompanied by a pervasive blandness and repetition in the actual creative work of advertising. It gave British agencies, mostly new, the chance to become the Greeks to the Romans of Madison Avenue. A rolling tide of brilliant British advertising reset the standard and the style. The Saatchis shared in the flood. The difference was that their ambitions were Roman in scope. They wanted an empire."

Heller seemed to have forgotten that the Romans took over from the Greeks, not the other way around. But even then there is simply no evidence that the Saatchis really wanted anything more than to be moderately rich, well respected, and innovative. They may have dreamed dreams, but not even in their wildest imaginings could they have foreseen the $500 million takeover of Ted Bates and their becoming the world's number one agency just sixteen years later.

Today, the brothers themselves have difficulty recalling what their motives were, and even if they could remember, could we rely on their recollections? What they can remember is that they had no thoughts about "globalization" and only dimly perceived moves beyond the advertising industry, and even then only as an extra service to get more advertising business. An international agency seemed a long way away, and their ambitions on that score, says Maurice, only began to develop a couple of years into the agency. "We were just hoping that it wouldn't fail," says Maurice. That is almost certainly a rationalization at the opposite pole from Heller's or *Fortune*'s. The Saatchis had greater ambitions than Maurice cares to remember.

"I never recall thinking, 'Wow, this is going to be enormously successful,' " says Chris Martin. Yet he was aware of an extra dimension even before the agency started. "Charlie loved playing poker with his mates; that was his great thing in those days. And his mates were all the guys from North London that he'd gone to school with, grown up with. I know that he was very strongly influenced by the fact that most of these guys had gone off into the City or property or whatever and they were making big, big money. I can remember him saying one day that the motivation for Saatchi & Saatchi was the fact that he'd gone to school with a lot of Jewish boys who were now all millionaires, all really going for it. Although he had a fast car and a big salary, he wasn't accumulating the sort of wealth that they were putting together. So I think Charlie said, 'OK, I've come into this business; I think my pride tells me that I can't admit that was a mistake and then go off to the City and do anything else. I'm going to bloody make some money.' "

Maybe that was a factor too. But if it was, it was not an important one, because this was not Charles's preserve at all but Maurice's. He instinctively understood the financial side of the advertising industry in a way that Charles never would. He would learn to pull the right levers that made the City of London react; he would in time become skilled in handling bankers, brokers, and financial editors; people would like him in a way they would never like Charles, and Maurice in turn would move through the financial and advertising communities in London and New York making many more friends than enemies.

The brothers are both, when they want to be, attractive, clever, and witty men; the essential difference is that Charles never had the patience or desire to cultivate new friends or even to keep up more than a handful of old ones. Maurice still let very few people get close to him but assiduously courted a wide circle of acquaintances and contacts. Born with a natural charm, he polished and perfected it, using it on colleagues and potential clients alike. As the agency grew into a company and then into a multinational, this quality was crucial. Maurice was born to cope comfortably with a big organization, big business, and big money.

Charles too would grow with the business, and his imagination, energy, and ambition looked over horizons; but his best day was now, when the agency was young and the product was essentially his—with some input from the clever creative people such as Sinclair, Hegarty, and Collins, whom he had gathered around him. As the business grew, so Charles would retreat more and more until he became almost invisible in the group, a hidden but still powerful presence. And curiously, the more reclusive he became, the more his reputation grew, until he began to assume almost mythical proportions inside his own company. Many believe he planned all that deliberately and coldly; others argue that Charles is a natural recluse, and he simply turned his natural shyness into a virtue.

A number of the Saatchis' friends and distant relatives were emerging around this time as leading City figures, and all the talk was of share prices and takeovers. This was the era of City figures like Jim Slater, James Hanson, and Jimmy Goldsmith, a time when young people were making fortunes by taking over staid old companies with nothing more than high-priced paper and stripping the assets. Charles Saatchi lived in that world as much as he did in the advertising one, but it was Maurice who saw that the route to really big money lay in the City, and the best way to get there quickly was by takeover.

In the United States advertising agencies were going public at a rate of almost one a month, and although almost all of them were now having trouble, the principle was appealing. In London a stock-market listing quotation was still relatively novel for an advertising agency, and the two ad agencies that had followed that route were held in low esteem by the investment community, with consequent low ratings. One of them was

Dorland Advertising, which was taken over by John Bentley, a young whiz kid who bought it in 1971 for the real-estate assets it owned. Bentley sold it three months later, minus its properties. (Dorland eventually became part of the Saatchi empire and today, under the Saatchi banner, is the second largest advertising agency in London—after Saatchi & Saatchi.) The Bentley move frightened the only other quoted company, S. H. Benson, which immediately sought shelter under the corporate umbrella of Ogilvy & Mather, an American agency founded by a Scot, David Ogilvy.

In 1970, however, both were still listed, and despite their modest ratings, Maurice had fixed his eyes along that route. Even from the earliest days he talked about takeover plans. At the time it all seemed absurdly ambitious.

That summer Maurice came to know Vanni Treves, a solicitor who represented the Quant consortium. Treves is now senior partner of McFarlane and in 1987 joined the Saatchi & Saatchi board. The solicitor carefully worked out a share structure and articles of association for a public stock offer. Maurice carefully incorporated them all into his five-year plan. That summer he made frequent visits to the City to show the plan around. At home the brothers also showed it to family and friends, seeking their reactions. They were never too concerned about raising the money—that was the easy part. On the other hand, they were very concerned about keeping the equity tight, ensuring that backers such as Quant and Masters received only a nominal amount of shares while still getting a good return on their money.

The brothers divided the shares on the basis that each of them had 40 percent. Another 15 percent was owned by the Mary Quant consortium; 5 percent of the shares was spread between Ron Collins, Tim Bell, and John Hegarty, with Collins and Bell getting the biggest slice. The details were gone over again and again by Maurice and Treves, with Charles continually asking for progress reports, for changes, for the inclusion of often unworkable clauses that would ensure that the brothers always kept control, pushing always to the limit and beyond.

Most new businesses would feel that they had now done enough to ensure that they had a reasonable chance of success. The publicity in *Campaign* almost every week that summer created an air of expectation in the industry. Three good clients were aboard, guaranteeing that most of the bills would be paid even if there was no new business. The team was in place. The offices were developing nicely, with Fitch now laying the floor covering: wide diagonal strips of linoleum in two shades of beige. The £25,000 had been raised and bank facilities arranged. The "pregnant man" story was still making the rounds, adding to the reputation of Charles Saatchi as the creative genius of the advertising world.

Charles still wanted more. There had to be yet another gesture, something that would make an impact beyond Adland, something that would establish the agency from the beginning as something genuinely different, set it apart from other advertising companies, and catch the imagination of the world beyond. Early in September 1970 he hit on it.

The result appeared on the morning of Sunday, September 13, the day before the agency was to open. It was a full-page advertisement on page 7 of the *Sunday Times* with the headline: "Why I think it's time for a new kind of advertising." It cost the Saatchis £6,000, nearly a quarter of their capital. Later, Maurice Saatchi would say, "That ad put us on the map," but that is a high claim for it. The general readership of the *Sunday Times*, which then (as now) had a circulation of about 1.4 million, almost certainly ignored the ad. It was of no interest to them, nor was it aimed at them. What it was designed to do—and what it achieved—was to surprise the industry, get itself talked about, and gain for the new agency a reputation for boldness and imagination. In all of that it succeeded. "I can remember reading that ad," says Bill Muirhead, who joined Saatchi six months later, "and how it sent a cold shiver down my spine. I was an ambitious young account man, and here was this ad telling me I was about to become a waste of space. The account man was redundant."

No one had ever done anything quite like it before. "That caught people's breath. It was the forerunner of their becoming a household name, a prelude to their leading advertising out of a closed-shop industry," says Chris Martin. He remembered the lesson well. Years later, when he set up his own agency, Martin did almost exactly the same thing with a full-page advertisement announcing, "Now the famous brothers represent the 'mega' agency!"

The *Sunday Times* ad, although costly, thus proved another clever bit of self-promotion. For it to work effectively, the brothers decided that the piece had to be attributed to a named writer. The person chosen was Robert Heller, whose *Management Today* was another Haymarket publication. Heller wrote a management column in the *Observer* every week and had also written a series of management books. The brothers gave him a rough draft of what they wanted to say, and Heller pulled it into shape. "It was about the easiest assignment I ever had," he says.

For those who knew Charles and had listened to him and his brother that summer, this ad was familiar stuff. Its starting point was that most advertising is a waste of money. The central philosophy of Charles's simple approach to advertising was set out in the third paragraph: "Expenditure of shareholders' money is only justified if it ultimately produces a quantifiable and adequate return in the same terms—money. In advertising language, this means that a campaign only succeeds if it ultimately helps create new sales for a client, and does so efficiently and economically."

Heller quoted a recent survey in *Management Today* that showed that most advertising did not even set out with this objective but was aimed at improving a company's image or improving brand awareness. "Images and brand awareness are meaningless if they fail to achieve greater turnover: the test is the cash in the till," Heller wrote.

He then went on to set out some of the points that Charles insisted on stressing to single out the new agency from the rest. There was an attack on the role of the account executive, "the middle-man between the advertiser and the people who are paid to create the ads." Others in the industry were trying to come to terms with this; and then a new agency, Kingsley Manton & Palmer (KMP), had a new open-plan office where creative people and account executives all worked together; Lonsdale Crowther had split itself into self-contained units, each with its own creative and account-service staff. Saatchi & Saatchi would go further: it would totally abolish the account executive and replace the position with a "co-ordinator who is not briefed by the client, does not brief the creative people, does not pass judgment on ads, and does not present ads to the clients, but works with the creators as a day-to-day administrator."

This was an exaggeration. There weren't any "co-ordinators" among the staff—unless one counted Maurice. The copywriters and art directors were in effect being asked to take on the role of servicing the client, something people such as Jeremy Sinclair felt singularly unfit for—and rightly so. Within weeks of the new agency's opening, Charles Saatchi was already busily hiring account executives, and six months later he had six doing almost exactly the job his ad condemned so roundly.

The ad went on to quote the "hard-selling creative" record of the Cramer-Saatchi consultancy, making the point that it had thrived because it could take a fresh approach to tired old advertising problems. Just as Bill Bernbach "came back to Avis with the unwelcome news that the only thing which he could find to say about Avis was that it was Number Two: the rest is advertising (and selling) history," Saatchi & Saatchi intended to extend that "freshness" from consultancy into agency.

Then came the bit that made the advertising industry sit up and take note. Saatchi & Saatchi would not take the traditional 15 percent commission on billings. Its charges, the ad said, would average 22 percent, which would be paid by the client. What traditionally happened was that if an agency placed an ad costing, say, £10,000, it demanded and got a 15 percent discount, so it paid £8,500 for the ad. But the agency charged the client £10,000, taking its profits on the difference. The agency therefore had a vested interest in the newspaper or TV company charging the highest possible amount for its space or time. (The actual costs of making the ad were already charged directly to the client.) The quid pro quo that Saatchi was now offering for its 22 percent fee was "a promise of the cheapest possible buying of space and time." This would have been the role of Paul Green but would now be up to Tim Bell to achieve. "Our ploy was that it was going to buy media cheaper than anyone else," says John Hegarty. "We were saying we'll make your media money go further. Charlie was going to balk the 15 percent commission fee and charge 22 percent but guaranteed he would save you money on your media—which meant that you were in fact paying less than 15 percent. In practice that's not how it worked out. It was really a brilliant kind of juggling with figures." Like so many other ideas offered in the ad, this proposal was soon abandoned. Saatchi & Saatchi from the beginning was certainly aggressive at media buying, and that has remained one of its hallmarks, but its methods of charging never caught on, and the system it said was "dying" has remained remarkably intact.

The ad finished by making "the unlikely boast" that the salesmanship line would cut Saatchi & Saatchi off from half its potential clients. As others remarked, that still left a few to go for.

Heller delivered his copy, but as it got closer to publication, he suddenly had second thoughts. He consulted Lindsay Masters and others at Haymarket and decided that by putting his name on the ad he was endorsing the new agency, something that an independent editor probably should not do. That left the brothers with a problem: whose name would go on it? They chose Jeremy Sinclair.

The brothers later claimed the intention had always been to put Sinclair's name on it, but that is an example—there will be many others cited—of what their critics call their "ability to rewrite history." Sinclair was bemused when he was told the ad was to be signed by him. He had very little to do with the advertisement, which was now to be seen by nearly four million *Sunday Times* readers. It is symptomatic of so much to come that neither of the Saatchis would put his own name on the ad, although theirs was the name on the agency and they were largely the authors. Although Charles was keenly aware of the need for publicity, he also had an almost paranoid dislike for personal promotion. As far as the outside world was concerned, the author of the ad was an unknown copywriter named Jeremy Sinclair. The advertising industry, on the other hand, knew full well who was really behind it.

The brothers were too excited to wait for the *Sunday Times* to be delivered. On Saturday evening, as the presses of the paper began to roll on what was—and is—the biggest print run in the Western world, Charles, Maurice, and John Hegarty went to the Gray's Inn Road print works to watch. "We went right down into the pressroom," says John Hegarty. "And I can remember thinking: 'Bloody hell, that's us.' When we launched we really did launch."

6
GOLDEN DAYS IN SOHO

The Saatchi brothers launched their little agency only dimly aware of the secular changes going on around them. Even historians seldom recognize change until long after it has occurred, and there was little of the historian in either Saatchi. What they could see was an industry growing quickly—total expenditure on advertising in Britain had tripled in the 1950s and doubled again in the 1960s. That growth was visible even from the worm's-eye view, and Charles and Maurice both had a natural instinct for taking a higher perspective.

"The joke at the time in the advertising industry was, what do you want to do, fall off a log or make money? Answer: make money—it's easier," says a senior Saatchi executive. Charles was keenly aware that the industry was only on the threshold of still bigger change and, even more important, greater opportunity. For Britain was taking to color TV in a big way, and the agencies that exploited the new medium best were going to dominate. In retrospect that seems obvious, but even by the late 1960s there were agencies in London that were having trouble adapting to commercial television, let alone to color TV. The people running the agencies had grown up in an age of print, and although they had seen the importance of commercial TV to their industry (as John Kenneth Galbraith put it, TV "allows of persuasion with no minimum standard of literacy or intelligence"), they would never be comfortable with it. But a generation that had been brought up on television, that had learned as children to love the advertisements and sing along with the jingles, was now coming to power. Charles has always been a compulsive TV watcher, a devotee of the soaps and the serials, and from his earliest memories a fan of catchy commercials. Those who worked with him remember him combing through the TV listings in the daily papers, muttering: "What's on the box tonight?" Although he had until this point done most of his work in print, his day had arrived.

The 1970s promised to be a boom time for consumerism, which would be spearheaded by advertising on TV. Color TV was still in its infancy in Britain a decade after it was widespread in the United States, and only 10 percent of British homes had color sets, but they were the fastest-selling items in appliance stores. In June the Conservatives had come back to power with renewed promises of returning the country to economic health and expanding consumer spending. In this new era and with a new

medium, the old-fashioned agencies would be at a disadvantage compared to the younger ones, which were offering the type of creative work
that touched a chord even in the most traditional clients. At least, that is
how the newer agencies perceived it, and up to a point they were right.

Charles Saatchi and his friends had already detected a movement away
from what they saw as the staid, multinational houses toward a new kind
of advertising. A hunger among clients for more creative thinking had
become apparent in the three years of the Cramer-Saatchi consultancy.
Britain in the 1960s had changed, and the Saatchis told each other that it
was high time for advertising to reflect this change. What they failed to
perceive was that the larger agencies were changing too, and that no
business, however it might appear to the outsider—and Charles Saatchi
was never an "insider" in the sense of being privy to the strategic
thinking going on in the bigger agencies—is static. Their picture of the
industry, which was never wholly accurate, was of a business that was
"soft" in the sense of being poorly managed, poorly capitalized, and
vulnerable, both creatively and financially, to newcomers willing to work
hard who were unencumbered by the baggage of traditional advertising
values. The Saatchis would never have agreed with the view of Jeremy
Bullmore of J. Walter Thompson that in 1970 the industry was more
responsive, competitive, and efficient than any other.

If Bullmore is correct, then the Saatchis' achievement has been all the
greater, for over the next decade they were to slice through their industry,
not only challenging the might of JWT, which then stood on top of the
advertising world, but actually topping it. Bullmore's view, however, is
not supported by others of the Saatchi generation, who even in the better-
run agencies felt stifled. John Hegarty might have been joking when he
said that at Benton & Bowles, where he and Charles first worked, "a
period at the end of a headline was considered a breakthrough," but
there was an element of truth in that too. There was a joke in the early
1960s that all JWT's print-media advertisements had a headline, a
squared halftone illustration, a few lines of copy, and a pack shot in the
bottom right-hand corner.

But if that is an unfair jibe—in fact, JWT was competitive and
efficient—it proved remarkably easy for Charles Saatchi to establish his
new agency with a reputation as "creative." It should not be forgotten
that Charles had already been at least partly influenced by his experience
at Collett Dickenson Pearce working with Cramer. Nor should the input
of some of the older hands he came across, such as John Salmon and
Colin Millward, be underestimated, although Charles himself was never
free with his gratitude. There were a number of bright young people with
similar creative experience and ambition as Charles working in the same
direction at the same time. Unlike the older generation, they were unapol-
ogetic about their profession, rising for the first time above the social
stigma that had attached itself to advertising.

John Kenneth Galbraith's *The Affluent Society*, which was on the bestseller list in 1958, was followed by two further books that reinforced the point that advertising was the method used by large companies to "manipulate" the consumer into desiring goods and services primarily because it suited the objectives of the large organizations. In the late 1960s Galbraith was still a powerful liberal voice. The new generation, however, was more influenced by Bill Bernbach and David Ogilvy than by Vance Packard or Galbraith, and Charles Saatchi, who seldom read books, was also blessed with a total lack of introspection.

The point is that 1970 heralded a new era in other areas besides advertising. Powerful consumer, social, and economic trends were moving into new phases too. In the early days the sheer novelty of TV ads meant that they had a major impact on viewers and produced dramatic effects on sales. By 1970 the novelty had worn off, and clients and public alike were looking for a new kind of advertising. By the 1960s, advertising in the United States had already changed, taking a much more imaginative approach than had been seen in earlier decades, but these new ideas had largely missed Britain, where many companies were still debating not which advertising house to go to but whether they should advertise at all. The 1950s and 1960s had been decades of bumpy but considerable growth in consumer spending in Britain, which would slow in the 1970s. The nature and habits of Britain's work force had changed sharply in the postwar years, with many more women going out to work, resulting in a demand for convenience foods and one-stop shopping.

During the 1960s Britain had replaced the corner shop with the supermarket, which was more responsive to brand success and showed a marked preference for products that were promoted on TV. The significance of that was not lost on the Saatchis, which is why they had tried to persuade Ian McLaurin to leave Tesco and join them.

In 1970 another trend had also reached its zenith, again without anyone noticing or recording it. The age of the great multinationals was changing, to be replaced by what the Saatchis would later adopt as their own doctrine: globalization, a word then seldom heard outside the study halls of a certain Harvard professor, Theodore Levitt, who would later become very important to the brothers. In 1970 the multinational corporations such as IBM, Ford, Shell, Bayer, and the Swedish group SKF were generally regarded in Europe as sinister organizations to be feared and loathed. Their annual sales, it was pointed out, were as large as the gross national products of many countries, their growth rate much faster. They could—and did—transfer vast quantities of money between currencies, precipitating financial crises. They could, in theory at least, transfer production from a factory in one country to an identical one in another in the event of either a strike or a better deal—an ability that made them greatly hated by the unions.

Most of the multinationals were American, and dislike of them became inextricably mixed up with anti-Americanism, less prevalent in Britain than in other European countries but nonetheless a growing factor. In 1967 Jean-Jacques Servan-Schreiber had published his classic attack on American business, *The American Challenge*, and it had aroused as much interest in Britain as everywhere else. The following year there was an attempt at a British equivalent, *The American Takeover of Britain*, written by two *Daily Express* journalists, James McMillan and Bernard Harris. This book listed all the American brand names marketed in Britain and raised the question: "How far does Britain's economic dependence on the United States compromise her ability to remain politically independent?" In retrospect many of the fears and forecasts raised in *The American Challenge* and by subsequent books and articles were absurd, but then critics of Galbraith would say the same of him, particularly when market and supply economics came to dominate the politics of both Britain and the United States in the 1980s. The rise of the big American advertising agencies spearheaded the spread of the multi-nationals.

The news broke where Charles Saatchi wanted it to—and exactly according to plan: the new agency, Saatchi & Saatchi, would open for business on the morning of Monday, September 14, 1970. The *Sunday Times* ad was set for Sunday, September 13, so the previous Friday *Campaign* carried a front page lead story under the headline: "Saatchi starts agency with £1 million." It dominated that week's issue, with pictures of the brothers—Charles, his hair now a respectable length, wearing a light-colored suit and striped tie, and Maurice, his hair longer, more soberly attired in a dark suit. The story announced that Charles, "the copywriting partner of the highly reputed Cramer-Saatchi creative consultancy," was setting up on his own. He would have five accounts, with billings worth £1 million, it said. Maurice was not mentioned until the fourth paragraph, where he was said to be responsible for new business and "marketing the agency."

The story contained a number of fallacies that would become parts of the myth surrounding the agency's beginnings. For instance, even the most generous of accounting could not add up the billings to anything approaching £1 million; those who worked for the Saatchis suggest that they were worth no more than £250,000 and that "Charlie was anticipating events—as he always did." It was a trait that has characterized him ever since: announce that you have made such and such a figure, then go out and make it.

Then there was the financial backing: no mention of Quant, Plunket-Greene, or Lindsay Masters. Instead, the article explained, "The agency is being backed by a City financial group plus a considerable investment from the elder brother." It would have been slightly embarrassing for

Campaign, even if it had been aware of it, to reveal that its own proprietor, Lindsay Masters, was a shareholder, although Masters had invested only reluctantly and with the best of motives. His involvement, brief as it was to be, remained secret for years. There was, of course, no City group, unless one counted Quant and Plunket-Green as "City"— they did meet in Vanni Treves's office in the City for regular reviews of their investment. Nor had the "elder brother" put his hand in his pocket.

Inside, *Campaign* carried a full-page feature on the agency; the two brothers were interviewed and, in contrast with their later legendary reticence, were positively loquacious. According to the article, "Both are excitable, sound very much alike, use the same expressions (most advertising is either 'terrific' or 'shit'). If one stops talking, the other instantly takes up the script. Each is caught up in the infectious enthusiasm of the other."

Charles made much of the concentration on creativity, stressing the importance of two newcomers to the agency: Ron Collins from Doyle Dane Bernbach and Alan Tilby from Collett Dickenson Pearce (where Collins had also worked when Charles was there). "The creative function is the main one, and one of only two services an agency should provide: the other is media buying," said Charles. "They are the two services necessary to fulfill the agency's one function—to sell the clients' goods. We don't understand any other service." Charles also made the point, which he had been expounding all summer, that there would be no account executives, insisting that the creative advertising people would work directly with the client.

"All our creative people have to act as if they were salesmen," said Charles. "They have to imagine themselves in the client's position all the time. They have to see themselves with a warehouse full of the product which has to be sold. Most agencies have replaced the basic function of selling with myths and mystiques about marketing and research. But agencies and clients have become too sophisticated, whereas advertising is not a sophisticated business at all. It is a simple business."

It is worth examining this comment, not least because it is one of the longest on record from Charles. There is a certain amount of hypocrisy in it, since Charles always hated having any contact with a client and would become progressively more distant from such contact as time went on. Charles might have intended that his creative staff should talk to the client rather than go through the traditional account executive, but he had no intention of doing so himself. *Campaign* allowed itself a skeptical note here: "It will be interesting to see whether this is as meaningful in practice as the Saatchi brothers fervently believe." As events would prove, it wasn't.

There is another point of interest about the interview. By 1970 most London agencies were, as Charles said, offering detailed research and measurements of results. In 1964 J. Walter Thompson had set up "creative workshops" to try to substantiate how advertising worked and from this had evolved a complicated system, which it called its "T-plan," which talked about advertising being a "stimulus" that produced a "response." Other agencies had their own variations, attempts to provide a technical discipline to what had been until then a far from scientific industry.

Charles wanted none of that. Research? If he needed it, he would buy it. Advertising was about selling more of the clients' products or services. Good creative work and good buying of media space—that was what it was all about. "They will say we don't offer the services. We will say, 'We don't understand what other services there are.' But whatever we say, they will never understand."

It is easy enough to spot the holes in Charles's comments to *Campaign* that day. He had never run an agency and was about to learn some important lessons. Today, Saatchi & Saatchi offers its clients every service it can think of, from advertising to management consultancy, legal research, packaging, direct selling, and public relations. Yet there is a fair amount of consistency here too. To Charles, advertising was, and remains, essentially a simple business. His own special genius was his ability to distill a complex argument into a single-minded message. It was what he trained himself to do in his best creative moments and in fact was probably the only way he could work. Charles could not sit and absorb vast quantities of research, as Maurice could, and he made a virtue out of his own disability: keep it simple, put across the message, don't let the research obscure what you're trying to say. He has retained an extraordinary ability to see through the jargon and the complexity that inevitably creep into any industry and made it one of the strengths behind Saatchi & Saatchi, not just as an advertising agency but as a full-fledged public limited company. Charles felt then, and still to some extent feels, that research and other modern methods can get in the way of the purpose of advertising, which is, after all, to sell. This attitude worked for him as a copywriter, and he made sure it worked for him as a businessman.

Even at this embryonic stage, Charles that week did not neglect a wider dissemination of his message. It wasn't just the British trade press that recorded his launch: *Advertising Age*, the U.S. weekly trade paper, did too. There was a little piece reporting that Saatchi & Saatchi "is the first agency to throw aside completely the 15 percent commission system. With his brother, Charles Saatchi has evolved a method of payment which costs clients an average of 22 percent. He remarked, 'That makes us just about the most expensive agency in the business.' " It may not have been a great scoop for *Advertising Age*, but this would be the first of many stories on the Saatchis the periodical would carry over the years— and gave forewarning of Charles's ability to generate publicity even 3,000 miles from where he had his business.

Saatchi & Saatchi had been going a week when John Hegarty met Doris Dibley at a business reception. Hegarty, slim, fair-haired, and one of Charles Saatchi's best art directors, was somewhat in awe of her. The tall, long-legged American copywriter was more and more to be seen in Charles's company, and Hegarty was aware that they were more than friends.

"How is it, John?" asked Doris. "Doris, it smells great," said Hegarty. "You just feel it's going to do something. It just isn't like anything else. The way the office is laid out, the way the whole thing looks, the way it feels like a new idea in advertising—I just have a feeling something great is going to happen."

That did not mean it was comfortable at Golden Square. From the beginning there was an air of tension that was not always positive but that most of the Saatchi team would later recall as Saatchi & Saatchi's "golden era," named after both the period and the Soho address. Ron Collins, several years older than anyone else, found it hard to adjust and never settled into the pace demanded by Charles. Others, however, thrived on it. Tim Bell, although brought in as the media-space buyer, soon moved to center stage, more because of his personality than anything else. Within a matter of months he had assumed as if by right the position of number two to Charles and Maurice—not that it meant much. There was no question who was running the place.

From early morning to late evening Charles strode the floor of his little empire. He had assigned himself and Maurice two of the little offices at the back of the big open-plan floor where all the others sat, but he was seldom there. "Charles's office was where he happened to be—which was sometimes in the middle of my desk, sitting up there cross-legged, with everybody sitting around, shouting suggestions at him," says Hegarty.

Although Charles was as volatile as ever, there was a new aspect to him that Hegarty, who had known him longer than anyone except his brother, now noticed. "From the day Charles decided he was going to start the agency, he changed totally," Hegarty says. "From being this lunatic creative guy who screamed and shouted and stormed out of meetings, he became a businessman. He cut his hair short, he wore sober suits, he bought club ties that he had no right to wear, went to Turnbull & Asser and got shirts made. It was incredible."

Charles emphasized again and again to the others the importance of giving the impression that the agency was bigger, busier, and more established than it was. The offices were designed around that principle. Maurice added a little touch too. He had Bill Atherton design their "Saatchi & Saatchi" letterhead in a very sober type. "Make us look like a bank," he told him.

In these early days, Charles handled clients himself—and did so with skill and courtesy. No one in the agency had any doubt of how charming and convivial he could be when he chose; but all had seen him change abruptly into a raging, contemptuous figure, as liable to wheel on a client, however large, as he was on one of his own staff. For several months, however, even while he stormed around the office shouting for more effort, more business, and better ideas, with clients he was remarkably restrained. "It was like somebody threw a switch," says Hegarty. "He was terribly concerned to get the right image and the right publicity. When clients walked in, they thought, 'Gosh, I've got to see these mad creative people and they'll probably be wearing psychedelic shirts' and instead they met Charlie, and he looked like a bank manager—a very elegant one."

While Charles was dominating the creative output, preparing pitches and even presenting to clients, Maurice was drumming up new business. He had learned a great deal at Haymarket and had soaked up the cheeky but effective methods he had observed work so well for Michael Heseltine. The principal one was that the more phone calls you made, the more business you brought in—something unheard of in the advertising industry, where agencies traditionally relied on clients' word of mouth, and reputation. Maurice enthused about this method to Charles, who saw the possibilities for the new agency. Haymarket, under Heseltine and Masters, was probably the most advanced publishing house of its day in terms of organized selling of advertising space. The Saatchis would employ exactly the same technique, even using the same files of names and telephone numbers, to solicit new accounts. Haymarket required its advertising salespeople to make twenty-five calls a day, the optimum number Haymarket reckoned anyone could reasonably handle. From the first day, Maurice was in one of the small offices at the back working through a Rolodex file of company names—making twenty-five calls a day.

Years afterward, Maurice can still recite his little introduction by heart: "Hello, my name is Maurice Saatchi, and we're a new advertising agency. Although you're probably very happy with your present advertising agency, I think it would be worthwhile your coming to talk to us and see a presentation we have prepared for you."

Even to the younger members of the team this method of getting business came as a shock. None had ever seen it before—or even heard of its being done. It broke all the rules of the industry, which expressly forbade poaching clients. The Saatchis, however, never much cared for convention, and soon Tim Bell was joining in the phone calls. Charles himself, in a quiet moment, would also grab a Rolodex and begin calling, invariably giving someone else's name—Bell's or Ron Collins's or Jeremy Sinclair's or a wholly imaginary one. No one ever remembers him making a call under his own name.

And it worked. "They got streams of people in," says Hegarty. "It was phenomenal." Translating that success into actual billings was another matter, and the brothers knew it would take time. They were laying the groundwork, sowing the seeds. "You get someone in, and three months later they remember you and they come back. Six months later they're reviewing their account, and maybe they come and see you again," Maurice explained to the others, just as Michael Heseltine had explained it to him.

Many marketing directors were affronted by a "My name is Maurice Saatchi" phone call, but no one in Golden Square minded making such calls. Bell and Maurice made a game of relating the best reason yet for being turned down, and the others would roar with laughter when they staggered out of the back office to relate the latest refusals. In those early weeks the others quickly learned to appreciate and respect the younger Saatchi for his discipline, his devotion—and also his humor.

"Maurice was great," says Hegarty. "He'd come out saying, 'Another one just slammed the phone down,' and he'd be dying of laughter. And Charles would join in and then say, 'Back in, Maurice—another twenty-four calls today.' And he'd go back and get the old digit going."

If the marketing manager at the other end of the phone responded, Maurice would invite him to Golden Square for what the Saatchis called a "house presentation." Marketing directors were used to this, and there was enough talk around about this new agency for them to be sufficiently curious to go. There they got a surprise. The normal system was that an agency in a house presentation would tell the client all about the agency— and nothing about his views on the client. Maurice, however, did his homework assiduously and when the client appeared would give him an analysis of the position as he saw it. "It became something of a joke in the agency, because people would say, 'Good god, you must have seen our latest research,' " says a Saatchi employee. It was a simple yet effective bit of marketing; Maurice knew his way around the company card index and press-cuttings files, and an hour's research was often enough for him to identify a company's basic problems or opportunities.

Maurice himself recalls this particular period with mixed feelings. It was tough but also exciting. He and his brother were building their own business and their own fortune. They brought in David Perring to look after the financial details (he is still there); but Maurice, between chasing new business, preparing presentations, and filling in wherever there was a gap, was also the man who had to report to the shareholder's group, represented by Lindsay Masters, Mary Quant, and Alexander Plunket-Greene. It meant that every few months he made the journey to the office of Vanni Treves to explain how the company was doing. Treves remembers the youthful Maurice, tall and gangly, with a curious mixture of diffidence and confidence, presenting the latest set of accounts at these meetings. Years later the minutes make interesting reading: "Maurice Saatchi reported that he was concerned about the rent bill of £1,100 a month." But if Maurice was concerned, Treves reckons he was the only one who was. The shareholders were more than happy with their investment and with the quality of the reporting. From these meetings Treves developed a lifelong relationship with the Saatchis and a considerable respect for Maurice in particular. (Treves is now a main board director of Saatchi & Saatchi.)

From the first day everyone was busy. The main account was still the Health Education Council, with an aggressive new antismoking campaign. The "pregnant man" ad had raised expectations high, and Charles was conscious of how much depended on getting the new campaign right. It was not a simple campaign: it was what is known in the jargon as "attitude-change" advertising, one of the first times advertising had been done in Britain in this way. The first commercial from the new agency— for television—showed lemmings leaping off a cliff, intercut with London commuters walking across Waterloo Bridge, smoking cigarettes. The voice-over said: "There's a strange Arctic rodent called the lemming which every year throws itself off a cliff. It's as though it wanted to die. Every year in Britain thousands of men and women smoke cigarettes. It's as though they want to die."

This campaign, the work of Jeremy Sinclair, proved as controversial as some of Charles's earlier efforts—which is what he wanted. "It was the making of Saatchi's," says Tim Bell, "because the controversy got them talked about in the national press—something which happened more and more as the years went on until the agency itself became a household word." There was another series of ads featuring a quizmaster saying that if you smoked forty cigarettes a day you could win a case of chronic bronchitis and an ad, written by Jeremy Sinclair, with the line, "I gave up smoking by eating prunes," followed by three columns of text with helpful suggestions on how to give it up, including eating prunes, chewing gum, and even hypnosis. "Every ad got talked about," says Bell.

There was an element of hypocrisy to all this. Several of the Saatchi team, including Bell, were chainsmokers, and Charles, although he had announced he was giving up cigarettes, was still an occasional smoker. Ron Collins recalls a TV crew coming around to film Charles about the antismoking campaign. Charles was hesitant and nervous, and it took him several takes to make his righteous condemnation of smoking. Exhausted by the experience, he waited for the camera crews to pack up, then said, "Shit, someone give me a fag [cigarette], I'm dying for a smoke." In those early days, Charles could—and did—make a public virtue of being antismoking even while the room he worked in was heavy with cigarette smoke.

It was fashionable for some agencies to boast that they had no cigarette accounts. In New York Bill Bernbach maintained that boast for thirty-three years, but his agency, Doyle Dane Bernbach, took on Philip Morris eleven weeks after his death in 1982. Similarly, Ogilvy & Mather had a policy of no cigarette accounts for many years. It would be 1983 before Saatchi & Saatchi, after parting company with the Health Education Council, took on its first cigarette client, Silk Cut, for which it then produced some award-winning ads featuring a pair of scissors slicing across a bed of silk. And right to this day the conflict between running antismoking campaigns and at the same time acting for cigarette companies remains. In April 1988 Saatchi & Saatchi hit the headlines again when RJR-Nabisco, the American food and tobacco company that later that year became the subject of the biggest-ever takeover bid, removed $84 million of its advertising because a Saatchi agency produced a commercial for Northwest Airlines showing passengers applauding a ban on smoking. The fact that Saatchi did not handle any of Nabisco's tobacco products made no difference to RJR-Nabisco.

Ron Collins and Alan Tilby were regarded as the "heavyweights" on the creative side: they had been hired to add depth and strength to the reputation of the team, which otherwise consisted of mostly unknown youngsters. Collins and Tilby were assigned the Jaffa account—the Citrus Marketing Board of Israel. The two men soon discovered that they did not get on, although they shared one of the four large, square, white-topped tables in the room. Collins had won a number of awards at Collett and at Doyle Dane Bernbach. His work on a Martell brandy campaign with French scenes including an outdoor wedding reception had gained him a considerable reputation. Painstaking and thorough, he liked to research and think about a campaign for some weeks. He resented the fact that in most agencies the art director was regarded as the junior creative person to the copywriter and wanted to change that at Saatchi's. Tilby, a short, square man considerably less polished than the style-conscious Collins, irritated him by sitting with his feet on the desk, endlessly snipping bits out of newspapers and magazines. Like Collins, Tilby liked to work deliberately and also found it difficult to respond to the speed and urgency that Charles demanded from him.

The other two teams, Jeremy Sinclair and Bill Atherton working at one table and John Hegarty and Chris Martin at a third, were familiar with the Charles Saatchi work pattern, the pressure to produce rapidly and well—the "two ads a day keeps the sack away" syndrome—the continual drive and impatience, the sometimes savage dismissal of material that had taken weeks to produce, and the uncanny way Charles had of seeing through to the heart of a campaign. Collins and Tilby, the only two newcomers to the creative team, were not sympathetic to the Saatchi style. The others regarded them as "prima donna-ish." Charles Martin says that neither of them was "very impressed by the Saatchi thing," which is borne out by interviews with both men. The concept of the Jaffa ads was to persuade the British public to eat more Israeli-produced citrus, particularly the humble grapefruit. Collins and Tilby produced the line, "And all you ever did was sprinkle sugar on it," with the suggestion that grapefruit could be used in a variety of ways. For a person with Collins's gifts it was dull stuff to work on, but he tried hard; and when Charles contemptuously dismissed his work, he stalked out of the office for a couple of days. When he came back, he discovered that Charles had given the go-ahead to his campaign, which later won an award.

This was nothing in comparison to a row that blew up when Tim Bell, by now working as an account person, altered one of Collins's layouts. In one of those incidents that has passed into trade mythology, Collins stormed into Charles Saatchi's office and threatened to resign. In the outer office there was a hush as the voices inside grew more heated. Three people, including Collins himself, relate the climax, when Charles suddenly shouted: "Who the hell do you think you are, Ron—Michael-fucking-angelo?"

Collins, however, often glimpsed another side of Charles. One of the new clients was a London store called Escalade, which was a small account. Collins remembers going to see the client to work on the latest press ad, which would feature some new French-made jeans that it would sell at £5.25—expensive for jeans in those days. He came back complaining that he didn't see how he could get much out of that. Charles immediately grabbed his pad and pencil and said: "Well, let's see. French jeans, are they? What's 'French jeans' in French?"

Collins had some schoolboy French and produced "Les Jeans Français." Charles wrote it down.

"Now, what else can we say about them?" Tentatively, Collins proffered the information that they were for both men and women.

"Right," said Charles. "What's that in French?" At Collins's dictation he wrote down "pour un homme et une femme," then added "Escalade."

"What price are they? Right." Between them they added the final line, "Un belle bargain à £5.25."

It had taken about ten minutes. Charles threw the pencil down and said, "Right, get a nice picture of a couple wearing the jeans and get it off."

Like many things that Charles did, it attracted notice—and won an award. "People came up to me and said, 'That was a sweet ad,' " says Collins.

Despite such moments Collins did not have the temperament to enjoy the frenetic existence of the early days of Saatchi & Saatchi. Hegarty, although exhausted by it, remembers events differently: "Charlie stimulated great tension to create better work. It was always constructive tension, if that makes sense. In the creative process, if you had a violent disagreement, it wouldn't be because he thought the work was too daring. He would say, 'I don't think it's creative enough. I don't think you're going far enough on it.' You might feel creatively exhausted, because you've put everything into it, and he's just saying to you, 'I think you can go further.' "

This is a familiar message about Charles and central to answering the question, "What is special about him?" There is no doubt he had—and has—exceptional creative talent, but there were others who were talented too who have not achieved anything like his success. What was evident from these early days is the extra dimension to Charles, what one person calls "the spark," which displayed itself as a ferocious drive to go one step further than anyone else. One of his lifelong friends, a man as successful in his own business as Charles is in his, says: "Charles is a visionary. He's got tremendous balls, more courage than anyone I've ever met. He tells you about an idea, and you think he's just joking because it's so unbelievable. And then he has the guts to go ahead and do it." What of the other side? "Everybody fights with Charles," says the same friend. "There are times when he can be unbearable and do the more terrible things, but you always forgive him, because he's Charles. At the end of the day you just have to say, this guy is different, the normal rules don't apply." These characteristics would become more apparent in the corporate leaps Charles would take once he got into the takeover game.

The person driven the hardest was Maurice, regarded by Charles in these early days almost as an extension of himself. The others soon realized that it was no accident that the name on the door was that of the two brothers; they had a relationship that only brothers can have, particularly brothers brought up in a tight family environment. Their fights would become legendary, and every Saatchi employee has a "Charles beats up Maurice" story. Most articles on the Saatchis describe incidents of Charles hitting Maurice with a chair, and all those who were there describe such occasions, with variations. Several remember hearing Charles shouting at Maurice, "We never came out of the same womb" (another incident deep in the Saatchi mythology), and Tim Bell was once just in time to see a chair hurtling across the office with Maurice ducking—too late.

"The level of violence between them was sometimes awful," says one Saatchi director. "They were two Jewish brothers, and no one else was allowed to interfere. They had forgotten all about it minutes later—or at least Charles had. Tim always thought of himself as the third brother and could never understand why they would not accept him. He was the only one who tried to get between the two brothers when they were fighting, but all that would happen is that they would wheel on *him*. Tim once got hit with a chair when he got in the way. The brothers would always round on the interloper. So few people were trying to do so much, and there was great tension, but people understood it, and we could all live with it."

Others recall having to explain to visitors what the row was all about. "Don't worry," they would say, "it's only the proprietors having a fight."

"The clients loved it," says one director. "It was the type of creative tension they couldn't get in their own lives. They would come down from the Midlands or wherever and they would walk into the type of madness that wouldn't be tolerated in their own world, and they thought it was great."

Charles was by no means the only one who shouted; the others picked up their tone from him, and sometimes there would be major slanging matches going on around the office. Maurice, unable to bear the tension any more, would go for a walk. So would Bell. This gave rise to a new competition: the "How far did you get?" battle. Maurice got halfway down Piccadilly one day, probably half a mile from the office; Bell got farther. Charles would be waiting for them when they got back, probably having already forgotten the row.

All of them soon learned that Charles's bouts of anger could give way within minutes to a mood of great friendliness and charm. Ron Collins says that there really were three brothers in the firm: Charles, Maurice, and Charles: "Charles was two people: one, the nicest, most charming, and wittiest man you could meet; the other a terror."

Maurice never took mortal offense. Bell suffered much more, as much at the rejection of him as "the third brother" as at the insults thrown. "But everyone always came back," says Bell. "You can't win an argument with Charles. He shouts at you, his invective is often amazing, and he never admits he's wrong."

Even those who didn't much care for Charles Saatchi still found the atmosphere in that little office in Golden Square exhilarating. "You had to learn to take criticism," says Alan Tilby, now the creative director at Boase Massimi Pollitt. "You held things up for the others to look at and people would say 'shit!' It was a great way of working, really, because it knocked all the rubbish out of you. You had to accept the fact that you were in a highly competitive environment." Tilby found it quite a change from Collett's: "In Collett's we'd learned to live in a kind of spoiled environment, when you could go away and reshoot things. Or send the account man back down if he failed to sell the work. It was an elitist organization, and Ron Collins was used to that mode of existence, and I got quite used to it. Saatchi's was different—it was cheapskate, it made you work hard."

Cheapskate or not, Tilby was impressed by Charles Saatchi's refusal to compromise, at least at the beginning. On one occasion Escalade refused to sign off one of the ads Saatchi & Saatchi had prepared, and Tilby and Collins came back to the agency to explain. "Look, we've been down to see them, and they won't accept it," Tilby told Charles. Saatchi exploded. "Tell him if he doesn't accept it, he can roll it up and stick it up his arse!" Tilby and Collins trooped back to Escalade to tell this to the client, albeit in a slightly censored version. "That's strong talk," said the Escalade executive, but he accepted it.

Hegarty, who was a Charles Saatchi admirer, felt that compromise had begun to creep in within the first year. Only a matter of weeks after getting the account, everyone realized that Saatchi should not be working for Granada TV Rentals. The TV-rental business, which was for many years an industry unique to Britain, was booming on the back of the growth of color television, and Granada, immediately after it had given its account to Saatchi, had taken over the much bigger Robinson Rentals. It could rent out every set it could lay its hands on. Robinson was a much more conservative company and had never done national advertising before—not surprising, since it wanted customers in each locale to go to the shop nearest them. The Robinson team didn't see much point in a national campaign and had no interest in the creative ideas coming out of Saatchi. On the other hand, Charles was loath to abandon any account, however unpromising. Relations became strained as the Granada marketing people turned down anything other than the most staid of ads, but Charles managed to remain civil to the client. Back in the office, John Hegarty remembers him saying angrily: "Right, if they want shit, I'll give them shit. I'll give them the best shit they've ever had. If that's what they want, that's what they'll get."

By now the agency was getting bigger and the staff was growing. Bell was doing some of the presentations, and as he and Maurice proved far better at them than anyone could have hoped, Charles began to do fewer and fewer. He would still undertake them if forced, however, and the others recall when the marketing director of the German car manufacturer Audi insisted that Charles himself make the presentation before he would consider the agency. Charles was furious but went along, dropping little anti-German jokes into his presentation, giving mock Nazi salutes, and generally making himself as offensive as he could. Audi was a major client and a prestigious one, but Charles seemed not to care. The Saatchis were offered the account but in the event didn't accept it—on the same day that it came through, they were also offered the British Leyland corporate account. They took BL.

Another Saatchi worker remembers a pitch to Hygena, one of the leading British kitchen manufacturers. Considerable preparation had been done, and Charles joined the others to make the presentation. "He could feel that it wasn't going down particularly well," says one of the team, "so he stopped. It was just a wonderful piece of theater, because he had a huge pile of ads to show, and he put the ads down and walked around the table. And I thought, 'he's going to do something barmy here, something's going to happen.' Everybody just stopped and watched him. He picked up a pack of cigarettes—he never smoked enough to have his own—took one out, and lit it. This seemed like hours, the tension was terrible, and he walked back. Then he began again, and I could see the client immediately began to pay attention. Charles finished, then walked out of the room, ignoring the client, and he hid until the rest of us came out to see if we had got the account." This time they hadn't.

Even as the agency took on more staff, there was one glaring gap— there were no women. Doris particularly commented on this as one of the areas she and Charles quarreled over. In many ways Charles was the modern, trendy, switched-on young man of his day. But in other ways he had not shed his own background; his parents' marriage had after all been an arranged one, and Charles's views on women were often, Doris found, very old-fashioned. This proved to be something of a disadvantage in pitching for a major cosmetic client when Charles suddenly realized that he was not going to get the account unless a woman handled it. Doris by now had quit the industry, largely because she had found herself effec- tively unemployable as a copywriter due to Charles's growing impor- tance. It was now common knowledge that she and Charles were living together, and rival agencies were not keen on having her in on their secrets. Charles drafted her as part of the team pitching to the cosmetic client. They got the client, who returned a few weeks later to discuss the campaign. Where was Doris? Charles had forgotten that she had to be there. "Oh, she's sick today," the client was told hastily. Later Charles said that she had gone to Collett Dickenson Pearce and eventually that she had quit the industry. "These guys kept asking about Doris, and Charlie kept making up new stories," says a Saatchi & Saatchi employee.

To Doris pitching to clients was fun, and she would have enjoyed keeping up the facade. She often joined in the gatherings in the evenings when the staff was still small enough to fit around one table, and she became fond of Hegarty and the others. At the time, she remembers, Charles would leave for the office at 7:30 A.M. and return home at seven or eight at night—long hours by the standards of the advertising industry in London then—and would invariably work through lunch. But he did try to keep weekends free, which increasingly they both devoted to their art collection.

Soon Tim Bell was being used everywhere in the agency and could no longer cope with the media side on his own. It was he who hired his own number two, Roy Warman, a tall, thin media specialist, from Geers Gross. Warman took to the Saatchi atmosphere from the first; he is now joint head of the agency. The others could hear him on the phone in his odd slack moments: "My name is Roy Warman, that's W-A-R-M-A-N, from Saatchi & Saatchi, that's S-A-A-T-C-H-I, and again. And we are a new advertising agency with ideas we think can help you, and I won- der . . ." In most cases the reply was "no," sometimes said vehemently, but Warman joined in the Bell-Maurice game of topping the others with the latest reason for rejection, laughing along with the rest.

When Warman joined in January 1971 the agency was four months old. Another hire who was to go high up the Saatchi & Saatchi ladder joined early in 1972. Bill Muirhead was a tall, blond, twenty-four-year-old Australian whose interview is instructive of the way the agency operated at this time. Muirhead was to be interviewed as the first full-time account executive, helping out Maurice and Bell, whose duties had spilled over into that area. On the appointed day Muirhead turned up at Golden Square and was immediately taken with the atmosphere. It was in SoHo, which is bohemian, but this was respectably bohemian. The brass sign on the door would have done a dentist or lawyer proud; Muirhead knew nothing of the company's history, and it struck him as an establishment that had been there for some time. Inside, there were large blown-up ads—common enough in agencies today but then unusual in London. The reception area was screened off from the main room, but a tall person could see across the whole room, although he could not see the other people inside if they were sitting behind other screens. It was impossible to know that there were just four large tables, three small cubicles at the back, and a conference room in the basement. To Muirhead the offices looked solid and large, and he was under the impression that Saatchi & Saatchi occupied the whole building.

The effect of the office on Muirhead, mirrored by others, is worth noting. Charles and Maurice had spent some time with Rodney Fitch, and all who worked in Golden Square remember the offices and the atmosphere as perfect for the image they wanted to create: young, creative, dynamic, thoughtful.

David Ogilvy had long preached that the physical appearance of an advertising company's offices was important: "If they are decorated in bad taste, we are yahoos. If they look old-fashioned, we are fuddy-duddies. If they are too prestigious, we are stuffed shirts. If they are untidy, we look inefficient." Ogilvy's text was almost a bible to aspiring advertising people, but Charles Saatchi arrived at what he wanted intuitively rather than through any conscious learning process. At Golden Square he set a tone for the agency that it has never quite lost, even in much more institutionalized circumstances.

While Muirhead was sitting in the reception area, a head peered over the partition and examined him intently. Before he had a chance to speak, it was withdrawn, and a few minutes later Muirhead was ushered down a spiral staircase and into an oval room with no windows; it had aluminum chairs, rush-mat carpeting, and a long black table—very modern and clean. There he was interviewed by Maurice Saatchi, whom he remembers as "charming and intelligent." Tim Bell "hovered," passing occasional notes to Maurice. Everyone seemed young and energetic, and there was a discernible buzz. On the way out Muirhead passed the same head that had watched him over the partition, now complete with body and sitting at one of the desks. Charles Saatchi did not spare him another glance; he must have been satisfied with what he had seen the first time. Bill Muirhead may never have heard of Charles Saatchi at that stage, but Charles had made inquiries and had heard of Muirhead.

Muirhead was soon working on his first account: the *Daily Mail*, which arrived at Saatchi & Saatchi at more or less the same time he did. The young recruit was made the *Daily Mail* account executive and a few weeks later went down to Fleet Street for a meeting with the client. An hour later he was back in the office again, searching frantically for the *Daily Mail* ad; the man who had taken the client's brief, Mike Johnson, had forgotten to pass it on. John Hegarty, the copywriter involved, eventually produced an ad, and Muirhead went back down to the *Mail* to do his presentation with material he had never seen before. He was now very late for his meeting, so he took a cab—something unheard of in those days for junior Saatchi employees, who were required to travel by bus or subway. In the cab, he looked at the ad for the first time—and found to his horror that he could not understand it. Going up in the elevator he prepared his opening gambit. He would say: "This is an extraordinarily difficult brief, and we've been struggling with it, and I don't think we've really cracked it. This is as far as we've got."

A few minutes later he made this little speech to the marketing director of the *Daily Mail*, produced the ad, and waited for the flak to hit him. "It's brilliant," said the marketing executive. "Marvelous! I love it." It was a bemused and shamefaced Muirhead who arrived back at Golden Square to relate this event. He still didn't understand the ad, but he had made a sale and he decided that there was a new technique here that he could develop, if only he could work it out. At that moment Charles Saatchi appeared. He picked up the ad.

"What is this shit?" he shouted. John Hegarty was at the next desk, watching with some trepidation. Muirhead explained that it was the ad the *Daily Mail* was using the next day to promote itself. "It's crap," said Charles. The ad was stapled to a strong cardboard backing, but even so he ripped it apart, using all his strength, and hurled it onto the floor. "But the client loves it," Muirhead managed.

"You'll just have to ring him and tell him you're going to do something better." Muirhead rang the *Mail*. "You know that ad you loved? We've done something better now."

Charles sat down opposite, calmly asked, "What's the theme?" and worked on it. Muirhead went back with the new ad and was received with even greater enthusiasm. "It was the most amazing thing I'd ever experienced in my whole life," Muirhead told a friend later. Another Saatchi employee who witnessed the incident says: "Bill loved Charles for that, because the most wonderful thing about him is that he has instant judgment, which confirmed Bill's initial thought. People look at a painting and they say 'great' but they don't really mean it, because they don't really understand it. Charles said, 'I don't understand this—it's crap,' and was prepared to say to the client that something he liked was rubbish."

Everybody who worked at Saatchi & Saatchi has heard the story of how Charles posed as an office cleaner. As with the chair-throwing story, it crops up again and again in the profiles and the feature articles on the company. As with most other anecdotes, it has at least some truth in it, although over the years the truth has tended to become embroidered.

The incident happened in 1972 when the agency was bulging out of Golden Square, just before their move to larger premises. One of the big clients the agency was after was Singer, the sewing-machine group, which in the early 1970s was a considerable advertiser. It had taken some hard work, but eventually Singer had been persuaded to come in for a pitch. Immediately Maurice and his team went to work, doing considerable research, and Charles sat in on a full-scale rehearsal the night before. The office had to look busy and full, and he was determined that when the Singer team arrived just after lunch, there should be plenty of people around. Everyone, he instructed, must ring their friends and contacts and get them to come in around that time. They must all be on the phone, or pretending to talk to clients. The story is told that when he was still not happy with the general air of busy-ness the next day, he sent people out into the street, offering passersby £5 to come in and look busy. "We got cleaners, truck drivers, and shop assistants in and said, 'Pretend you're talking on the phone,' " says one Saatchi executive. Tim Bell also confirms the incident, and the brothers themselves chuckle when they are reminded of it.

At any rate, the Singer team arrived at three in the afternoon to find an office buzzing with activity. They were taken down to the conference room in the basement, and Bell and Maurice began their pitch. It was to be a marathon eight-and-a-half-hour effort, going on until 11:30 that evening, the longest pitch anyone could remember. Charles had been very much caught up in the preparation for it, but by now he seldom saw clients (and soon would not see them at all, no matter how important they were). Every so often he would enter the little projection room behind the main conference room and peer in through the thick glass. He could not hear, but his own team inside could see his head, with its distinctive mop of curly black hair. Finally, he got bored hanging around, went home, changed into jeans and jacket, and came back. He had just entered the main room when he heard the others coming up the spiral staircase. Unable to get out without being seen and heard, he had a sudden fear that one of his own team would not be able to resist stopping beside him and introducing him, which at that moment was the last thing in the world he wanted. Quick as a flash he grabbed a cloth and began dusting down the partitions. All four of his own team, including Maurice, Bell, and Roy Warman, recognized him and began to giggle, while Charles, his head bent, furiously went on polishing. It was too much for Maurice to resist. Very deliberately, while showing the clients out, he paused beside Charles. "When you've finished that, could you make sure you clean my office?" he said. A glower promised trouble for Maurice, but he ignored it, enjoying for these few minutes a fleeting ascendancy. "God knows what hell Charles gave him later for that!" says one of the Saatchi team who was there that night.

Chris Martin has another anecdote—"the Golden Square chairs." Before moving to SoHo, Charles had sent his secretary, Gail, out to Habitat to buy cheap, light, modern chairs. "They were fold-up chairs, with canvas backs, the sort you print 'director' across the back of," says Martin. They were not sturdy enough for the punishment they received in their new home, and one by one they broke and were piled up at the back of the conference-room basement. "When you've got someone the size of Charlie bringing them down on his brother's head, they don't last long," says Martin. "So after a few months there was this pile of matchwood and canvas that had been these chairs. And then one day Charlie saw them, and I heard him say, 'Gail, take those bloody chairs back to Habitat and get our money back on them. They're no good.' And off she went."

All this time the agency was expanding. Maurice's relentless twenty-five calls a day were bringing in clients, some better than others. Saatchi & Saatchi was also being tested. Great Universal Stores (GUS), one of the canniest companies in Britain, asked them to pitch for an account, with a view to giving them more business if they did well with it. It was a run-down jean manufacturer that the company had acquired as part of a larger takeover. There was a denim surplus, and the jeans factory was losing money; but the Saatchis were continually asking GUS for accounts, and here was an opportunity to discover their mettle. "There was an attitude to us that said: 'OK, you're arrogant sods who reckon you're better than anyone else. Well, see what you can do with this one,'" says a Saatchi executive.

Saatchi & Saatchi responded to the challenge. Designer jeans were just coming in, and the Saatchi team reckoned that this was a promising area to explore. Why not turn out more fashionable, higher-priced jeans and market them hard? Roy Warman was given the job of making the presentation for the account, and he traveled up to Speke, near Liverpool. He had made a token protest to Charles before departing, saying, "I don't fancy doing this; it will be a completely hostile crowd." Charles, to his surprise, was conciliatory: "Look at it this way: if they hate it, you'll never see them again. If they love it, we'll get the account. All you can do is your best. Go for it."

Another Saatchi employee remembers similar encouragement from Charles. "It's typical of him. It's his 'Don't look down' syndrome. Let people make their mistakes. Kill them for dumbness, but not for trying."

Warman got the account, then a few months later, just as the sales began to lift off, GUS sold the company—as it had always intended to do. "GUS very cleverly thought that if they gave us the account and built up the image for a very small amount of money, they could flog it for five times what they paid for it," say Hegarty. However, GUS became—and still is—a client.

There were other tough accounts, some of which Saatchi & Saatchi could do nothing with, some of which grew into much larger ones. "The big corporations would say, 'Well, these guys might be mad, they might be bright, or they might be daft—let's give them this nitty-gritty problem we've always had and see what they can do with it,' " says Hegarty. "That way you had to prove yourself with them."

It was hard work, but Charles worked on spreading the word through the constant feed of stories to *Campaign* and the rest of the trade press. There was another factor that was increasingly helping them win accounts: Tim Bell, now the main presenter. Even so, it was still Charles who set the style for presentations, paying considerable attention to the way they were done. "Charles insisted we had to counter this thing that people just thought we were a mad group of creatives," says Hegarty. Presentations were full of charts and plans, and Charles also insisted that the presenters show a chart of the structure of the company and talk about organization. He insisted on introducing more and more titles into his small group. "I was deputy creative director," says Hegarty, "and someone else was creative director, and he was account management supervisor. And right down to the guy in the studio, Melvynne Redford. Someone spelled his name M-E-L-V-I-N and we were doing a rehearsal and somebody said, 'That's not how Melvynne spells his name.' And Charles said: 'Don't be daft, that sound likes a lunatic; I want it spelled like this.' And from then on that's how it was."

All this time Maurice was filing monthly trading statements, a profit-and-loss account, and a balance sheet with Vanni Treves. Treves in turn reported back to the directors of Mary Quant Ltd. These reports contain fascinating snapshots of the state of the business in these early days. On May 3, 1972, for instance, when Saatchi & Saatchi had been going eight months, Maurice Saatchi wrote to Archie McNair, Quant's partner, to say that the Saatchis were now "working very hard to get the first really big client, which they all regard as the breakthrough" (this would be Singer). Treves in this letter already conveys something of the impression that the younger Saatchi brother had made on him: "If one believes

Maurice (and there is no reason for not doing so), the company's reputation is spreading quickly and the quality of its work and ideas is thought by many people as second to none." The Saatchis, Treves went on, were proposing to spend money on advertising "to maintain this momentum of nascent goodwill." Their only misgiving, he added, was "the prospect of spending in one shot such a large proportion of the presently available profit balance (£13,480)."

Treves was convinced by now that the Saatchis were going to achieve their breakthrough, and he told McNair that they "deserved it." He also reminded Maurice around this time that the interest on the money from Mary Quant had not been received, but Treves seemed satisfied with Maurice's response that the original invoice from Mary Quant "was wrong and a corrected one took a long time to arrive." Treves was not uncritical of the way the Saatchis carried on business. "Saatchi & Saatchi keep all their creditors waiting for not less than one month as a matter of policy," he noted. "I personally do not think it is a very good one, but it is for the board to decide," the "board," of course, being Quant, Plunket-Greene, and Archie McNair.

At the end of the first year Maurice had good news to report to the board and to Treves. The agency was on target. It had made a profit of nearly £20,000 and now had enough clients to make it viable. It was expanding and taking on extra premises around SoHo Square. It was being talked about more and more, and its reputation for creative advertising was established. The first hurdle—survival—had been jumped. Now it was time for bigger things.

7

THE THIRD BROTHER

By the end of the first year Charles Saatchi discovered that he had two unsuspected assets. The first was Maurice, who had taken to the advertising industry as if he had been born to it. He was not greatly involved in the creative side, although he often shyly offered suggestions on lines; but it was his other attributes that now came to the fore.

At first he had been seen as a gofer for Charles, a young, inexperienced, but keen brother who would faithfully run errands, do research, make his twenty-five calls a day, and pick up the many pieces that Charles left in his wake. As we have seen, that view of Maurice was never right and in any case did not last long. Within weeks he had earned the respect of the others by grasping the more complex tactical and strategic points of running a business. He was the only university graduate among them, although several of the others had been through art college, and they soon learned to respect his analytical skills even if they worried about his inexperience. He also proved to be an excellent new business getter and presenter; although quiet-spoken and even younger-looking than his twenty-five years, he had a curiously persuasive power that in later years he would employ to considerable effect. He was also a natural organizer, making the simple machinery of the office function in between the myriad other tasks Charles set for him. During the early months he had been very much under Charles's shadow, but as time went on he emerged more and more as a partner—albeit a junior one. How much of this Charles knew or suspected before he invited Maurice to join him in the agency is impossible to know, but he has an instinctive feel for the strengths and weaknesses in people, and he was never a believer in nepotism for nepotism's sake.

The second asset was as much good fortune as good judgment. Tim Bell had been a late choice for the job of media director, and nobody, not even Charles, could have guessed how important he would prove to be. Unlike most of the others, Bell had a middle-class background and had not set off for the world of advertising as his first choice for a career. He was born in 1941 and brought up in London. His mother was Australian; her second husband, Tim's stepfather, was an alderman and mayor of Marylebone. Tim went to a North London grammar school and in his late teens set his heart on becoming a jazz musician—he played a variety of instruments, including the trumpet, piano, and vibes, though none of them well enough to make a living. When he was nineteen, he says, "my mother decided she did not want me hanging around at home," and he was sent off to the Stella Fisher Employment Agency in Fleet Street.

It was a time of full employment in Britain, and for a bright, personable young man finding a suitable job was no problem. Bell came back with a choice of three interviews: one in publishing, one in insurance, and the other with ABC Television. Bell chose the last. "It was my generation who could, almost unconsciously, see the power of television and, by inference, the power of advertising in it," says Bell. However, when he presented himself at ABC, advertising was the last thing on his mind: "I saw myself as a star in the making—an actor or a producer." Instead he was assigned to shift bits of cardboard around on the big board in the advertising department, his first introduction to the industry.

Two years later he moved to the agency Colman, Prentis & Varley (which, among other accounts, did some work for the Conservative party) as a junior media buyer. His next move was to Hobson Bates (taken over by the American agency Ted Bates, which would later become part of Saatchi & Saatchi) as media group head, then to Geers Gross as media director. It was at Geers Gross that Bell, now twenty-eight, got a call from the Saatchis.

From all accounts, during this time Bell was arrogant and flashy but very popular. At the new agency, he rapidly established himself as the person around whom most of the others gathered. John Hegarty took to him instantly, regarding him as the replacement they all needed for Ross Cramer, still much missed.

Media buying—negotiating the best deals for TV time and newspaper space—was intended to be one of the key jobs in the new agency when it was launched, but Bell outgrew the position within three months. He gloried in the pressure, happy to camp in the office overnight or sleep under a desk when they worked—as they often did—through the night on preparations for a pitch to a potential client or on a new campaign. He established a routine of being one of the first in and the last out, a routine he would maintain most of the time he was at Saatchi.

It was at presenting that Bell excelled. Charles could be awkward, impatient, and often rude to clients, unless he put himself out—and increasingly he wasn't interested in making the effort; Maurice was much better, although he did not yet have the self-confidence to put himself out front. Bell, by contrast, turned on potential clients a charm that would later often be remarked on. Charles and Maurice soon put it to good use.

"Tim was the best presenter I've ever worked with," says one of the Saatchi team. He remembers Bell presenting a pitch he had written. At the end the client turned to the younger Saatchi, who had sat silently watching.

"Maurice, you have a brilliant presenter here," he said in front of Bell. "I know," said Maurice simply.

"Tim, I knew, had not seen the work before, so he was looking at it new," says the Saatchi writer. "I mean, we'd got a lot of strategy, a lot of logic, objectives, and preparation that go into a presentation for a major piece of business, and he hadn't seen any of it. And he's pitching it, and he's doing it for the first time, and I'm thinking to myself: 'How can this man do it? This is an act of sheer brilliance.' "

There is an element of hyperbole here, as pitching to a client, whatever the circumstances, is not technically a difficult business. What the Saatchi team could often see was that Bell was better at it than they were, and he seemed to do it without apparent effort. He seldom needed to prepare, although he usually did some preparation. The harder the task, the more he relished it; yet the others noticed something more complex about Bell too. Despite his considerable self-confidence he seemed to depend on the brothers. "I sometimes used to think that his brilliant presentations were more to please Maurice than they were to please the client," says one of the early Saatchi & Saatchi workers.

"Tim completely revered Charles," says another. "In the later years Charles became very, very important to him, but in the early days of the company it was both Maurice and Charles." Most of those who knew Bell well say there was something incomplete about him, as if he could not function without the brothers, Charles in particular. "The agency in those early days had something special—and I think what it had was Charles. Until 1978 he was the catalyst, the center, all the energy," says one senior Saatchi & Saatchi executive. "On the other hand, Tim's a coward in that he likes things to be nice and for people to get on. He hadn't the guts needed for starting a business of his own."

"You got the impression that Charles didn't mind if the whole business went down the drain—he was prepared to take that sort of risk," says the Saatchi executive. "He was a real entrepreneur. Tim never had that."

Bell was prominent in developing one of the agency's major accounts, British Leyland. In 1970 Keith Hopkins, the head of public relations for British Leyland—which still had over 40 percent of the British car market—first met the Saatchi brothers. Leyland's advertising manager, David Welch, had heard about them and suggested to Hopkins that they were people he ought to know. Welch (who now works for Saatchi), Hopkins, and the brothers met at a restaurant in Shepherd's Market. There was, Hopkins believes, no question of Saatchi & Saatchi doing any advertising for him at this stage, but soon afterward the Saatchis managed to get a foot in the BL door with a tiny corporate advertising account, reporting to the office of the chairman, Lord Stokes, in Berkeley Square.

From that followed a bigger but still small account, Triumph, one of the smaller selling lines of the BL empire at the time. Hopkins was not involved in giving Saatchi & Saatchi that account, but Welch was. Martin and Hegarty prepared the creative work, and Charles himself decided to make the presentation in the basement at Golden Square. It was another of those days when the office had to be especially filled with passersby. "Charlie went out and got people in off the street," says Chris Martin. "He just went up to them and said, 'Come on, here's a quid, come and make this place look lively.' "

Welch appeared with a number of senior Triumph executives, and the party was ushered down the spiral staircase, with Charles, immaculately clad in blue pinstripes, at his most engaging. When they emerged a couple of hours later, he was the perfectly mannered host—but they had an unpleasant surprise. It was now around 6:30 and the office was nearly empty, except for the man Charles probably least wanted to meet at that moment. Joe Andrews ran his own photographic studio and frequently dropped into the Saatchi office where he was one of the outside contractors. His appearance was extraordinary. Chris Martin describes him: "He had long streaked hair down to the waist, like a gypsy, with a great bald pate in the middle, huge piratical earrings, makeup, jeans that showed more grizzly leg than was covered, leather jacket, huge cowboy boots with jangly spurs, all topped off with a Stetson hat. And he was deaf—he had a huge hearing aid."

He was also loud, cheerful, and very Cockney. He was in the reception area collecting some work when he saw Charles's head appear over the partition, and he greeted him in his usual effusive manner. "Cor blimey, Charlie, still at it are we, me old cock?" he shouted. According to Martin, he then grabbed Saatchi round the neck and gave him a huge kiss on the cheek, leaving lipstick—although the others do not remember it going that far.

Says Martin: "Charlie says under his breath, 'Joe, lovely to see you, but I've got some clients here.' And Joe says, 'Sorry, Charlie, me old mate, have I cocked it up for yer?' And these Leyland people fell about. It was so funny, I'm sure that's what won the business." Both Hegarty and Martin remember Charles carrying the whole thing off remarkably well, formally introducing the Triumph executives to Andrews and retaining his good humor and his manners. It would be one of the last presentations he would do.

It was to be another year before Keith Hopkins entered the picture again. BL's problems, severe enough at the end of the 1960s, became catastrophic in the early 1970s, when its share of the mass car market plummeted. Its hopes for recovery were pinned on a key new model, the Austin 1800-2200, later rechristened the Princess, into which BL had poured its best design skills and engineers. Before the launch of the Princess, Stokes reshuffled his management, putting Hopkins into the all-important role of head of the mass car division, Austin-Morris. If the

Princess failed, Austin-Morris would never recover, so the launch of the car was going to be a major event.

Hopkins invited the company's existing agencies to make a pitch for the launch account. Benton & Bowles, D'Arcy Masius & Williams, Dorland, and Murray Parry all duly traveled up to Longbridge, near Coventry, to try to get the account. At the last moment Hopkins included Saatchi & Saatchi in the "beauty contest" on the grounds that they were creating a stir in the advertising world and seemed to be doing a good job for Triumph, and he thought it might be worth seeing what they could do for him.

The pitch took place in a conference room in the huge Longbridge complex, then one of the biggest factories in Britain. When Hopkins entered, he was taken aback by the size of the Saatchi & Saatchi contingent: "There seemed to be the world and his wife there, whereas my team was three or four." Hopkins noticed one vaguely familiar face in the Saatchi crowd, "a rather pubescent young man with large glasses who hardly said anything"—Maurice. Otherwise Hopkins knew nobody and wasn't sure what to expect.

At that point Hopkins had never heard of Tim Bell, who rose and began the introductions. Then Bell launched into his presentation on how to sell the new car to a reluctant public. "He was absolutely spellbinding," says Hopkins. "By the end of it I knew I wanted this guy on my side. None of the others featured, except to pass him a couple of bits of copy or a drawing. It was the best presentation I've seen, either before or since. And of course I decided to award them the account and subsequently gave them a lot more business. It was Tim that did that, Tim and Tim only."

In the end the Princess was never a great success, but that was because of early design and production faults rather than the advertising. Saatchi & Saatchi produced not just advertising but a marketing strategy as well, which Leyland adopted for its whole range of cars. "We had a thing called Superdeal, which was the most successful extended campaign of all time," says Hopkins. "We had an awful lot of cars to sell, and we did in fact accomplish some phenomenal sales results. Superdeal was fundamentally dreamed up, at least the sharp end of it, between Tim and myself. We worked very closely indeed. Then we had a very big television campaign, which was drafting the Leyland cars' identity onto all our diverse brand names."

The decision to turn down Audi and go with British Leyland had been justified. But unfortunately for Hopkins and the British car industry, almost every car of his Superdeal was sold at a loss, and through the 1970s and 1980s what remained of the company was kept going only by large injections of government cash. As an important and prestige account for Saatchi & Saatchi, it dribbled away. No amount of advertising could sell models that were seen as out-of-date, unreliable, and technically inferior to the flood of Japanese and European cars that soon came to dominate the British market. Today different Saatchi agencies handle Renault, Nissan, Saab, American Motors, Mercedes, Toyota, and Chevrolet around the world.

Behind all the shouting, no one ever doubted that Charles Saatchi had an inner coolness, a clear-thinking business brain, that would not easily let the business go down the drain. He would take risks, but they would be calculated ones. The scale of his ambition at this early stage was steadily rising and was being matched by that of Maurice. Perhaps their ambition is always destined to stay several stages ahead of what is achievable.

Charles's impatience to get up there among the big players was even greater after that first year than it had been before the Saatchis started. He said again and again that Saatchi & Saatchi would be the biggest agency, first in Britain, then in the world, at a time when such expectations seemed absurd, and his listeners turned away in confusion and embarrassment. But he was always a shrewd, hard businessman, unwilling to surrender an inch if he didn't want to.

There are many examples of his tough business stance in these early days, either in holding expenses down or in bargaining with contractors. Hegarty cites an episode when some artwork for the Jaffa oranges campaign didn't turn up on time and Charles refused to pay for it. "They [the Citrus Marketing Board of Israel] brought their lawyers in to discuss it, and they just didn't realize who they were dealing with—they thought they could sit down and have a reasonable argument," says Hegarty. "Basically he told them to fuck off. He wasn't going to pay their bill, and if they wanted to sue him, go ahead. 'You didn't deliver and I'm not paying. You should have told us you couldn't deliver.' And there might have been a gray area where somebody said, 'Look, it's going to be tight, but we'll do our best for you.' But not with Charlie."

Bell could watch with a certain degree of humor when Charles suffered the odd humiliation. There was, for instance, the incident of Rodney Fitch's bill. Fitch claimed that he was still owed money for his work on Golden Square, and Charles either wouldn't or couldn't pay. The sum involved was small—about £1,800. "It was my first introduction to the world of finance," says Fitch. "Until then I was just—perhaps I still am—a designer." Charles refused to talk to him, and Tim Bell kept putting him off and off. "Eventually my lawyer suggested that we put something called a garnishee order on them, which duly was served. And the solids hit the fan!"

Bell remembers the incident very well: "Charles didn't know what a garnishee order was and threw it in the wastepaper basket. He didn't tell anyone about it until the men from the sheriff of London's office arrived."

A garnishee order is not something to ignore. It froze the Saatchi bank accounts and meant they could not pay either staff or suppliers until they had paid Fitch. Bell learned this when he rang his father, a lawyer who explained how serious it was. "Charles was furious and went around shouting about it for days," Bell says. Fitch, on the other hand, learned a valuable lesson. "It's the most marvelous scheme, and I've used it several times since. We got paid very promptly. There was a great deal of bitterness from Charles about that, yet what I found amusing was that when they moved to Lower Regent Street they asked me to help out."

Bell relates this story (he actually told it years later in an afterdinner speech at the London Hilton with Fitch on the dais beside him) to emphasize how naive everyone at Saatchi & Saatchi was in business matters in those early days. They were learning fast, but Charles and Maurice had a natural instinct for the business; Bell didn't. He watched with a hint of awe the hardheaded way Charles and Maurice tackled suppliers and creditors and with genuine respect their approach to new accounts and to expansion through acquisitions.

By nature Bell is gentler and softer than the brothers and was willing to trade a great deal for a happy atmosphere and a pleasant working life. He hated their fights and always felt obliged to intervene when the brothers shouted at each other, unable to understand that fighting was second nature to them and meant as little to them as a shouting match between a husband and wife. "Tim used to say, 'They only hired me as the referee' as he went in to try to part the brothers and stop them tearing each other apart," says Chris Martin. "And he'd come out with the broken chairs. But Tim was very important to the whole agency—he was a complete adman. As it grew, he was the catalyst."

Others don't agree with the "complete" adman bit. A senior Saatchi employee notes one major gap in Bell's armory. "Tim couldn't judge an ad to save himself," he says. "He could neither judge them nor write them. His clients would get the impression that he wrote them, art-directed them, and did all the work. Not that he would have said that, but he would give that impression. His judgment was sometimes dangerously out, and if you did the opposite to what he said, you'd probably be right. But once you told him the work was great, then he'd go out and sell it superbly."

What Bell wanted more than anything else was to turn the duo of Charles and Maurice into a triarchy, not just in working terms but in personal terms too. Given his contribution and the tiny size of the agency this did not seem an unreasonable request, but the brothers would not even consider it. The more he tried, the more hurt he became; as the years rolled by, that sense of humiliation and hurt would grow. To this day, Bell has never understood why he was shut out. The reasons are complex and probably go back to the brothers' close family solidarity—they were very conscious of their Iraqi Jewish background, and Charles in particular always found it hard to share his private interests and passions with anyone who was not family. Bell, try as he might, would never be family. Martin noticed something that others have remarked on: the more junior you were, the less you got shouted at by Charles; and the higher up you went, the more you were subject to his wrath. Maurice got the brunt of it, but now Bell too was feeling the lash. "He used to beat you up in the morning," Bell says, "not speak to you in the afternoon, then ring at ten in the evening to make peace—but not to apologize. He never, ever, did that."

For Bell, the "beating up" was purely verbal, but he found it exhausting just keeping up with Charles. "He plays mind games with people all the time. It's innate in his character. He's always totally in control of things, and he thinks with the speed of light, seeing your sentences finish before you do, often just playing with you for the intellectual hell of it." However well Bell did, Charles always wanted more from him.

At the end of the second year Bell and Maurice decided the company was doing well enough to buy Charles a car. He had owned most models, so it had to be something special—a Rolls-Royce. "He had been so bloody-minded, and we thought it might make him behave better towards us," says Bell. "But it never made any difference."

As it happened, the thought of a Rolls-Royce had already occurred to Charles. The others can remember him frequently throwing the rhetorical question at David Perring, the company secretary, every time the subject of money came up: "Can I buy a Rolls-Royce yet, David?" And Perring always said no—until one day he said, "Yes—a secondhand one."

Chris Martin recalls Charles bursting in the door saying, "Let's all go for a drive." Outside on the pavement was a Rolls-Royce, on test from Jack Barclay's of Berkeley Square, the main Rolls-Royce dealer for the West End. It was not a successful trip. According to Martin, they stopped at a set of traffic lights in Shaftesbury Avenue, and another Rolls pulled up beside them, driven by the photographer Terence Donovan, an East Ender who had already established himself as one of the leading— and highest paid—photographers of the 1960s. Charles recognized Donovan and began winding down the window to greet him. According to Martin, he never got the window all the way down. "Terry's got one of the new ones, with electric windows, and he just goes *bzzzzz* and leans over and says: 'What's up, Charlie, can't you afford one of the newer ones?' Then he went *bzzzz* again, put the window up—and drove off. Charlie drove straight back to Berkeley Square, parked outside Jack Barclay's, and told them he didn't want it."

Finally Maurice and Tim Bell ordered Charles a Corniche—and Bell got a Porsche, which he wrecked within two days, impatiently reversing into a ramp in an underground car park. But the company was doing increasingly well, able now to pay larger salaries and reward those who the Saatchis thought were doing well. Bill Muirhead came in one morning to find an envelope on the corner of his desk. Inside was a check for double his monthly salary—a present from the brothers. On another occasion his wife told him that a swimming-pool firm had been in to measure the garden. Charles had asked what Muirhead might like, and someone said he was an Australian and all Australians swim. Muirhead was hugely embarrassed by Charles's gesture—there was no room for a swimming pool beside his little semidetached house in Kent.

Bell by now was the most favored employee, but he was still an employee—he had a small stake in the agency, but it was still the brothers' agency, with their name on the door. Yet it never seriously occurred to him, as it was now occurring to Ron Collins, Alan Tilby, and even John Hegarty and Chris Martin, to look elsewhere, start their own agencies, seek their own fortunes. The Saatchi & Saatchi agency was clearly going places, and Bell was going with it.

Toward the end of their second year, the Saatchis decided to buy out the original investors, Lindsay Masters, Mary Quant, and her husband, Alexander Plunket-Greene. The brothers had been clever enough to structure the company in such a way that most of the outside money was in the form of a debenture, with no rights to shares. The Masters, Quant, and Plunket-Greene holding, held through Cannon Holdings, was 15 percent, and the Saatchis wanted it back before the agency became too valuable. They would soon be a public corporation, and 15 percent would be worth a great deal of money. It had been nice to have the backing of Quant and her husband, but they had never been asked to do anything other than invest; now perhaps they could be persuaded to sell—if there was enough incentive.

Maurice began a careful but firm negotiation through Vanni Treves. Quant and Plunket-Greene were not eager to sell; Lindsay Masters was in even less of a hurry. "Look, you're showing a good profit on your investment, and we'd like to buy back the shares," said Maurice. Quant and her husband succumbed; Masters hung on a bit longer—"he had to persuade me a bit harder"—but eventually Masters agreed to sell too. (His wife, Marisa, later told Maurice that such was her faith in him that she would *never* have sold, which would have cost the Saatchis a great deal of money in the long run.) None of the parties involved can recall exactly how much money was involved, but most agree on a figure in the region of £100,000. The investors had quadrupled their money and went away reasonably satisfied, while the Saatchis had consolidated their position.

Later, of course, Masters, Quant, and Plunket-Greene would all look back and try to calculate how much they would have made had they kept their holdings. It would have been well into the millions. Michael

Heseltine too muses on this. Masters had offered to take him in as a partner when he first invested—as they were partners in most things. Heseltine had refused then because he had just become a junior minister in the new Health government; later he decided he had been far too scrupulous: "Having read the rules of ministerial behavior perhaps more cautiously than I should, and wishing to remain 100 percent within the spirit of them, I thought it would not be right to have been involved. That was rubbish. Having read them again now, when I have had time years later, in a detached way, it would have been absolutely right and proper for me to have been involved in such an investment. Nobody could have said that I was influencing it, or that it was a high proportion of the shares, or anything of that sort. I wasn't going to play a managerial role. It was the sort of investment ministers are fully entitled to make."

He had, Heseltine believes, "misunderstood in the anxiety of a new ministerial life the restraints that are imposed on ministers." He said no to Masters and took no shares in the Saatchi business—a misunderstanding very beneficial to the Saatchis.

"What is of real interest," says Heseltine, "is that Maurice very rapidly wanted to buy out this significant shareholding; and although I was never involved in the negotiations—as I had no money in it—I heard about them, the offers and the counteroffers, the blandishments and the persuasion used by the Saatchis to buy out the original investors.

"The interesting question that historians can pose—and no one can answer—is: if I'd had shares in it, would they have actually succeeded in buying us out? If I'd been with Lindsay and there had been two of us, instead of Lindsay on his own, we might have reinforced each other. Whether Maurice would have got away with it—I've often laughed about that."

The question of the other shareholdings turned out to be less tricky. Ron Collins remembers being summoned to Charles's office where he was abruptly told that he "had a problem."

"You've got more shares than Tim Bell," Charles told Collins.

"Yes, Charles, but that was the agreement on which you hired me."

"You're not understanding me. You have a problem. Now I want to know what you're going to do about it."

Only gradually did it dawn on Collins that he was being asked to transfer some of his shares to Bell. Shaken by this realization, Collins refused. Charles, says Collins, presented it as *his* problem, although as far as he was concerned it had nothing to do with him. Bell was clearly the senior in the hierarchy, although Collins was older and more experienced, and when he had been hired *he* had been the senior.

He decided to go. When he told Charles this, he brought up the question of the shares. Collins—and the others—had even less idea about financial matters than Charles, and he had never seen these legendary shares that Maurice seemed to keep locked away somewhere. When he was hired, he had been given a lengthy contract that looked impressive. "He was always arguing about points in his contract," says Hegarty. "He consequently never signed it." Charles had originally told him that he would have "share options" in Saatchi & Saatchi, which Collins understood even less than the shares themselves.

The legend among old Saatchi hands is that when Collins asked about his shares Charles told him they were still only share options.

"Well, how about my options?"

"Oh—we've decided not to take them up," Charles is reported to have said casually.

Collins himself does not deny this outrageous version, although he says that, "financially naive as I was," he was never quite that silly; but he still left Saatchi & Saatchi without his shares and without any compensation. Bell later received over £3 million for his smaller holding. Collins did see a lawyer, who told him the contract, signed or unsigned, was barely worth the paper it was written on. He could still have sued Saatchi but decided it was not worth the hassle. Collins has since made his fortune through his partnership in Wight Collins Rutherford Scott and lives in a comfortable house in Essex, from where he acts as a consultant.

Collins was not alone in drifting away from the Saatchi brothers. Alan Tilby lasted just over a year; he had been brought in to do TV ads, and Saatchi & Saatchi in those early days did not have much TV work. Tilby had fallen out with Charles when Alan Parker's first feature film was screened, and Parker, a close friend, invited him to the preview in the middle of the afternoon. Charles was less than enthusiastic when Tilby requested the afternoon off to attend the screening: "Right, you can go. But you're going to have to make up the time after work." A furious Tilby stomped out. He, like Collins, could never tune into the atmosphere at Saatchi & Saatchi and was discouraged both by his own prospects and those of the agency.

"To be honest, I couldn't see it going anywhere," Tilby says from behind his huge desk in Boase Massimi Pollitt, laughing uproariously at his own shortsightedness.

The Saatchis didn't mourn long for either Collins or Tilby, but when John Hegarty and Chris Martin announced that they were going, that was a different matter. Hegarty had worked for Charles for more than five years when in 1973 he decided to move on, and the brothers were genuinely fond of him. "I suppose I left because I thought, quite rightly, that it was called Saatchi & Saatchi. Charlie was going to run it, it was his agency, and he'd run it his way, and there wouldn't be the opportunity for me to do the things I wanted," says Hegarty. "I resigned, and Charlie didn't speak to me for two years. It was about family, and I was leaving the family."

Hegarty was called an "associate director," but he was wise enough to know he would never be considered a partner. Like Collins, he went off to found his own agency, Bartle Bogle Hegarty, where he too has grown wealthy. "Charlie was terribly upset when he left," adds Chris Martin. "He was actually shaking—the most upset I've ever seen him. Not for me, but for Hegarty, who had played a big part in his career. He saw that John was also very talented, which he has gone on to prove, but it was more than that. I think Charlie had this Jewish family feeling that you kept everyone together, and you were loyal to them and they were loyal to you, and now we were going."

There was a time when Jeremy Sinclair, the longest-serving and (today) the closest person in the organization to Charles other than his brother, decided he was leaving too. Unlike Hegarty, Bell, and Collins, he had received no shares (or even "options") when the agency started. By now it was becoming known that he was the creator of the pregnant-man ad, and he was approached by a competitive agency before most of the others. Ron Collins recalls that Charles took Sinclair out into the little park in the center of Golden Square and talked to him for hours. They were still there when dark descended. When they came back, Sinclair was aglow. He wasn't going after all. "This agency is going to be the biggest and the best in the world," Collins remembers him saying.

New people were coming all the time—Terry Bannister, later to become joint managing director of the agency, came for a client, Fison's; Ron Leagas, who would later also rise to become managing director of the agency, joined. There were now just a few of the original nine left, with Roy Warman and Bill Muirhead coming through as people with considerable potential.

The departures left Tim Bell even more firmly installed than ever as number two to the brothers. He was taking his role more and more seriously, trying hard to apply to Saatchi & Saatchi some of the disciplines he had learned at other agencies, behaving as he believed a good executive should, although he had limited experience in management. Hegarty, before he left, recalls Bell badgering the Saatchis to hold proper board meetings. "Charlie would never have them. He'd say, 'What for?' And Tim would say, 'Charlie, you've got to do this; we're building a big company.' And Charlie would just refuse, insisting, 'What do I need to go to a board meeting for? We've made all the decisions, haven't we? Just go around and tell them.' You had to kind of respect him, because he just wouldn't have bullshit. And he thought boards were bullshit. As he said, 'Power is doing a great ad. That's power in this business. If you want power, do a great ad.' "

It was around this time that the trade press began to refer to Bell as "the third brother." Bell loved it—in fact he may even have initiated the use of this name, although he now denies doing so. "It was the trade press that started it," he says. "I thought it was a great compliment. But they hated it, to think that this middle-class guy should be attributed to them." The Saatchis probably never spared a thought for Bell's class; like him, they have classless accents, particularly Maurice. (The brothers have uncannily similar voices, and on the phone, or if one closes one's eyes, it is almost impossible to tell them apart.) But it would be another ten years before Bell discovered he never could be the third brother, not even an adopted one. He began to mock himself by describing himself as "the ampersand in Saatchi & Saatchi" rather than the third brother.

Others would have their views on Bell's contribution at a later stage. Would Charles and Maurice have built such a big agency without him? Hegarty, who had no contact with Bell after he left in 1973, that year gave his own view: "I do genuinely believe that Tim was the third Saatchi," he says. "Much as Charlie may disagree, I think he'd agree on his [Bell's] contribution. Charlie was terrific at bringing out the best in whomever he worked with, and he used Tim's abilities to the full, and Tim's abilities in turn helped him build an even better agency. Just as Maurice was a marvelous counterbalance to Charles, so Tim was a marvelous counterbalance to the two of them. And they all worked as a marvelous trio."

By the end of 1973 the shape and structure of the agency were altering rapidly. Saatchi & Saatchi now had offices all over Golden Square to house the overflow. Maurice and Bell were making the agency run more and more as a business, and Charles was already pulling back, seeing much less of the new staff who came in than he had of the old. He no longer saw clients, even when they insisted that they would take their business elsewhere unless Charles dealt with them personally. The company was growing as much from acquisition as from new business. It was time to move to new and bigger premises. The Golden Square days were over, and with them went the "creative hot shop" atmosphere in which the agency was founded. Saatchi & Saatchi was now a business; this would bring problems as well as rewards.

8
REVERSE TAKEOVER

At the end of its second year of operation, Saatchi & Saatchi showed a profit of £90,000, after paying expenses, salaries, and taxes—not at all a bad result for a new business and certainly enough to cover the cost of Charles's new Rolls-Royce. The third year, 1973, was also a good one, although profits rose only by £10,000 to £100,000. Then came 1974, and the whole advertising industry dived into its worst recession in years. The recession did not affect just advertising—the period from November 1973 to the spring of 1975 was one of the gloomiest in postwar Britain. The Saatchis were about to hit financial troubles for the first time in their corporate lives.

The Yom Kippur War and the immediate threefold increase in oil prices caught Britain at a bad moment. Long before the first oil crisis, Britain's economy had been running into serious problems. The Conservative government of Edward Heath had overreacted to a rise in unemployment in the 1971–72 winter by slashing taxes and freeing public expenditure from restraint; and by rescuing first Upper Clyde Shipbuilders and then Rolls-Royce the government had, in the words of economist Sam Brittan, handed an invitation card "to every lame duck to call on the Department of Trade and Industry." The result was that from mid-1972 onward the economy began to run faster and faster and by mid-1973 was growing at 6 percent—a desperate overheating that was already causing the rate of inflation to rise. There was a huge overload in the construction industry; Hoover rationed its washing machines to retailers; industry reported shortages of reinforced concrete, steel, and timber; electrical motors were in such short supply that there was a twelve-month delay on deliveries. In the job market, vacancies were at a record low and, despite a government incomes policy, wages were starting to rise rapidly. Economists warned of the serious consequences of letting the money supply expand at 20 percent, and in the summer of 1973 there was another sterling crisis, which the government countered by pushing the Bank of England's minimum lending rate up from 7½ percent to 11½ percent.

The summer of 1973 was still a boom time for advertising, however, and the Saatchis, as caught up in the euphoria as everyone else, spent lavishly on a move to new offices in Lower Regent Street, on new cars, and on taking on further staff. To the man on the street it was a time of plenty—there was more spending on everything, particularly by the government. House prices boomed to the point where a new phenomenon entered the scene: "gazumping," when a buyer persuaded the seller, for an extra consideration, to sell to him, breaking a contract the seller had already made with someone else. Commercial property was enjoying its biggest-ever boom, with prices well past the point where the rents could meet the interest payments. And a raft of new and largely unregulated finance companies and fringe banks were pumping out loans to anyone who would take them, offering the extra incentives of TV sets and free holidays.

The boom had to end, and it did—abruptly. Panic in the Heath government set in early in November 1973 when the effects of war in the Middle East became apparent. The price of oil, which had fluctuated between $2 and $3 a barrel through most of the 1960s, had risen to $3 in the middle of 1973 and now rose straight to $12. The OPEC cartel organized effectively for the first time and cleverly cut its supply so as to have the maximum impact on price. Britain, still without its own North Sea oil, was hit by rationing as well as price increases. And by something worse still: in November the National Union of Mineworkers, which had already won a national strike two years before, began a strike against working overtime. In December Heath declared a state of national emergency, and Britain entered a three-day workweek, with the lights going out even in offices in the City. Heath reluctantly called a general election at the end of February on the issue of who was running the country: the government or the unions? He narrowly lost, then lost a second time, more convincingly, in another election in October.

The new government, headed by Harold Wilson, was perhaps the most left-wing that Britain has ever seen, at least in its first eighteen months of office when, in the words of economist Sam Brittan, it gave the impression that "irrespective of wage claims or restrictive practices, union leaders would be saved by government cash if they priced their members out of jobs." The Labour government of 1964–1970 had left behind social and libertarian reforms that were sensible and would last, and its economic aims were growth without inflation.

By contrast the new Labour government's economic policies had two major aims: redistribution of wealth and the furtherance of trade-union objectives. There was a sustained attack on wealth, with the introduction of a poorly prepared capital transfer tax; increasingly industry and the financial community felt the effects of the antagonism flowing from Whitehall. Much of it was more imagined than real, but the rhetoric left the clear impression that profits and private wealth were under genuine attack. Industrialists and the City were demoralized. The new government continued the Heath policy of bailing out lame ducks, notably British Leyland and the British end of Chrysler; and in its attempt to expand its way out of inflationary recession the new government borrowed huge amounts from overseas creditors.

The result of all this was the biggest financial crisis and stock-market crash Britain has seen in this century—far worse than the 1929 crisis. The economy plunged into recession, and it would be more than a dozen years before industrial production recovered to its pre-1973 level. Share prices fell by over 70 percent in nominal terms, nearly 90 percent in inflation-adjusted terms—the equivalent of the Wall Street crash of 1929–1933.

It was against this background that the Conservative party, early in 1975, rejected Heath and elected its first female leader, Margaret Thatcher, who gathered around her a group of advisers that was increasingly influenced by the monetarist doctrines of the Chicago school of economists led by Professor Milton Friedman and propounded in Britain by Ralph Harris and Arthur Seldon at the Institute of Economic Affairs. This influence was to have profound importance for the Saatchis in the years ahead.

In 1975, however, the brothers did not spare much thought for Thatcher and monetarism; they had their own problems. Saatchi & Saatchi, like so many businesses in Britain, was in trouble.

The brothers had actually coped well with the early months of the recession and ended 1974 with billings of £10.8 million, profits of £190,000, and a nineteenth-place ranking in ad-industry billings. However, the whole of Adland faced a tougher and tougher time as the year wore on. In inflation-adjusted terms total expenditure on advertising in Britain had grown from £554 million in 1970, when the brothers started their business, to £716 million in 1973—an increase of 30 percent. In nominal terms it had grown from £554 million to £874 million—nearly 60 percent. No one in the industry could have known that it would be nearly ten years before advertising expenditure in real terms again matched that 1973 figure. Or that, for three years in a row, it would fall steeply, reaching its low point in 1976.

If Charles and Maurice Saatchi had known the future, they would certainly not have hired Rodney Fitch again to design the new office in Regent Street. The brothers had taken advantage of the property crash to purchase a lease on the building, and it was typical of Charles that he would ignore the battle of the garnishee order at Golden Square and ask Fitch to design his third office. Fitch's instructions were the same as they had been when he designed the office at Golden Square: "Make us look bigger than we are." The offices had once been occupied by Cunard in the days when it ran the *Queen Mary* and *Queen Elizabeth* liners across the Atlantic, and the shipping company had left behind a handsome reception area with considerable quantities of marble, while the proportions of the building were far more generous than those of the tiny Soho premises. For its part Saatchi & Saatchi now had a great many more people to go inside—it was becoming a respectable-sized agency.

That Christmas, however, Maurice suddenly became aware of the scale of some of Saatchi & Saatchi's mistakes. The particular cause for worry was a company called George J. Smith, which Saatchi had bought for £90,000 only to discover its liabilities were far greater than they appeared on the balance sheet. The Saatchis also discovered that the money owed to the company was not so great as the figure shown. They had, in short, bought a company that was virtually insolvent.

The implications of this were just coming through when someone—the various suspects have denied to me their personal involvement—decided to play a practical joke. December was normally Christmas-bonus time, but in 1974, given the troubles ahead, the brothers decided to cut back. Tim Bell, now installed as managing director, sent a memo to all the staff. There would be no bonus this year, he said, but to show the company's appreciation of their efforts everyone would be receiving "a small gift."

A few days later came another memo, this time under the name of the office manager, Tony Hewitson. This stated that further to Tim Bell's memo he was now writing to say that instead of the Christmas bonus, everyone could have a choice of gifts: shares in the company or a turkey. "Please get your order in quick," the memo went on, "because we're running out of turkeys."

Even some of the more senior executives believed in the authenticity of this memo. Bill Muirhead put it aside, making a mental note to ask his wife if she had bought their Christmas dinner yet, while several secretaries asked Maurice where they could get hold of the turkeys. No one asked about the shares. Maurice was not at all amused. Hewitson, completely innocent, was summoned, and under Maurice's withering attack he became so flustered that he admitted authorship. He was close to being dismissed—a very rare event at Saatchi & Saatchi—before the truth of his noninvolvement dawned.

It was Christmas Eve when the full impact of the business downturn finally hit the brothers. On December 21, three days earlier, they had lost their biggest account: the Singer sewing-machine group, won so strenuously two years before, pulled out. Singer accounted for nearly half the agency's billings, and Maurice and the accountants calculated the impact of that on profits for the coming year. The figures arrived on Christmas Eve: the agency was heading for a major loss in 1975.

They could see no hope of relief from the British business world that year. The financial crash was nearing its worst, and there was much talk that the London stock market would cease to exist altogether by the spring. Young people with whom the Saatchis had grown up and who had made fortunes in the City in the 1967–73 period were falling even more rapidly than they had risen, their paper wealth melting away to be replaced by impossible borrowings. Maurice went home that Christmas

Eve feeling that the world was coming to an end.

The strength of the Saatchi brothers is that they have a facility for thriving in adversity. They don't actually seek it, in the way some entrepreneurs do, but they are not afraid of it; and once they have a problem they have an exceptional ability to solve it. "The brothers don't actually see obstacles," says Anthony Simonds-Gooding, who got to know them a decade later. "They simply go straight ahead and then look back and say, 'Oh, that was an obstacle?' " It is entirely consistent with their later history that they should see in their current troubles lessons to be learned—and opportunities to expand.

They tackled their problems in the best way they knew—by going even more aggressively for new clients, by getting more out of the business they had, and by cutting costs. January 1975, with the bankruptcy of Burmah Oil, marked the bottom of the worst bear market on the London stock exchange in a century, and from that point on the recovery began.

By the end of September 1975 and the end of their financial year, the Saatchis not only were solvent but also showed excellent profits. During the year, far from going bust, they had raised profits from £190,000 to £400,000, a 113 percent increase. They would weather this crisis, but it was a clear lesson that expansion could lead them astray.

The brothers had begun trying to take over other agencies in 1973, their third year of operations, applying much the same technique used in their search for new business. Besides his twenty-five calls a day Maurice was also responsible for writing a series of letters to other agencies. He worked out the wording very carefully, aiming to avoid giving offense—which was difficult enough, considering the effrontery of this tiny agency proposing to buy older and often larger businesses—but at the same time indicating a genuine interest. The concept was to approach as many firms as possible. Although the failure rate would be high, there was a good chance of finding someone who just at that point was suddenly deciding to sell or who would keep his letter and come back a year later when it was time to find a buyer.

Maurice's letters were polite but to the point. "I am sure this will be the last thing on your minds, but I wondered if you felt it would make sense to dispose of your company," they began. These letters went out in large batches and even went to the giants of the day, causing much ribald laughter in the industry. The story is told of how Jack Wynne-Williams, the august head of Masius Wynne-Williams, received just such a letter. His agency was J. Walter Thompson's only serious competitor for the top position among British advertising agencies. (Now, after a series of mergers, it is American-owned and known as D'Arcy Masius Benton & Bowles.) He is said to have written back to say that he had looked in the petty cash to see if he had enough to buy Saatchi & Saatchi. Maurice does not remember the incident. There is another story, probably true, of how at a meeting of advertising heads one agency chief pulled out a letter from Maurice and boasted of the takeover approach he had received that day. Three other agency heads pulled out identical letters.

Saatchi & Saatchi held talks with a number of agencies. There was an approach to Boase Massimi Pollitt, old friends from the days with Ross Cramer at Goodge Street, and with Murray Parry. Charles also leaked a story to *Campaign* that he was about to buy an agency in the United States—big talk indeed for such a tiny business. There was another *Campaign* story about the creation of a subsidiary in Paris called Saatchi Damour, which never happened. Intentional or not—and it probably was—the advertising world got the message that Saatchi & Saatchi was developing into a bustling international agency.

There was another set of talks that also came to nothing at the time but would later lead to perhaps the most important deal the brothers would ever make. S. T. Garland Advertising Service was started in 1928 by a former *Daily Mail* ad sales rep, Sidney Garland, and in 1960 was one of those old British agencies that the big American multinationals looked for to give them a place in London. In this case, it was Compton Advertising of New York, which bought 49 percent of S. T. Garland Advertising Service with an option on another 2 percent, thus giving it effective control of a new company that was called Compton U.K. Partners and that owned 100 percent of the agency Garland-Compton. But by the early 1970s a group of its managers began to chafe at the American control, and they worked out a plan for taking the company public, diluting the Americans' holding but giving them a substantial profit. Ken Gill was the Garland executive behind this plan, and it was he who talked the Americans into accepting it. The method of going public, however, was not his but that of one of the sharpest City entrepreneurs of the day: Pat Matthews, who ran the First National Finance Corporation, one of the new fringe banks and finance companies. (It was to go spectacularly bust a few years later, to be bailed out by the Bank of England.)

Matthews employed a roomful of young people who eagerly examined every public company, looking for hidden value or a way of making a quick profit. One of the companies they had come across was the Birmingham Crematorium company, which was exactly what its name suggested: a burial company based in Birmingham, except that most of its assets, with the grisly exception of a bone-crushing machine, had now gone. Birmingham Crematorium was what is called a "shell" company, one without assets or earnings that for historical reasons retains its listing on the stock exchange. Before the rules changed, "shells" provided a convenient shortcut for a company seeking to avoid the lengthy process of getting a stock market listing in its own right, with all the requirements and regulations it would have to meet.

The popular game among entrepreneurs such as Matthews was to buy a company, strip the assets, then inject another company into the "shell" that was left. In this instance, Compton U.K. Partners was reversed into Birmingham Crematorium, which issued new shares to acquire Compton U.K. Partners and then changed its own name back to Compton. By this little device it had transformed itself from a private company into a public one with its shares quoted on the stock market. Gill, who now became chairman, found himself for the space of a day owning the bone-crushing machine. He hastily sold it without ever seeing it.

Matthews emerged as a shareholder, appointed one of his people to the board, and began looking for other acquisitions for Gill to make. Gill was happy to let him do so: he had seen at an early stage the advantage of size to an advertising agency and also realized that many agencies had no idea of their worth. He himself was on the takeover trail and put out feelers to a variety of smaller agencies, several of which were absorbed into Compton. It was during this period that the Matthews people invited him into the City to meet two young people also keen on mergers who might be of interest to him.

It was in a banking parlor on Fenchurch Street in the City that Ken Gill first met the Saatchi brothers. They questioned him closely: how had he gone public, what differences had it made to the agency, what accounts did he have, how did he like working for Procter & Gamble? Compton had a number of clients the Saatchis would have given a great deal for: Procter & Gamble, the biggest advertiser in the world with its legendarily well-organized marketing setup and its huge list of brands, was their dream. Compton also worked for Rowntree, United Biscuits, and a variety of other blue-chip clients. Gill in turn was interested in the Saatchis, but not in an acquisition sense—not then. The brothers talked brightly about the way they saw the industry developing and about international networks—the word "global" had still not crossed their lips. Gill and the Saatchi brothers parted and didn't see each other for another three years.

The Saatchis did make a couple of acquisitions in 1973. There was a small company called Brogan Developers, which was used to house Charles's growing art collection, and they paid £130,000 for a Manchester agency, E. G. Dawes. This allowed the brothers to expand their Manchester office, which they had started in 1973 to service Great Clowes Warehouse, owned by GUS.

The bad times of 1974 offered them more opportunity. The acquisition of Notley Advertising, now an almost forgotten incident, was actually both highly successful and significant. It cost practically nothing and almost doubled Saatchi's size; the Notley people were absorbed into the Saatchi agency (some of them are still there), boosting both business and staff numbers substantially. The appearance of so many new faces at once was a culture shock to the old hands like Jeremy Sinclair and also meant that even with the additional premises around Golden Square Saatchi & Saatchi had to move. It was that acquisition that finally pushed it down to Lower Regent Street.

Then came the acquisition of George J. Smith, which was based in Manchester, with a division in London. Charles is said to have blamed the disaster on Maurice, and more than one Saatchi employee dates the chair-throwing incident to this event.

Nonetheless, the brothers had learned enough to know what to do—and what not to do—in the future takeovers. By the autumn of 1975 they were contemplating one takeover that, with a single bound, would make Saatchi & Saatchi a major agency. No other takeover they would ever do would have the same thrill or the same impact.

The Saatchi & Saatchi takeover of Compton, the eleventh biggest agency in Britain at the time, with some strong clients and billings of £17.44 million, started in a bizarre way. The brothers were not even thinking about a takeover when Maurice rang Ron Rimmer, managing director of Garland-Compton, which was the operating subsidiary. Maurice was looking for a business manager and wondered if Rimmer would be interested. Intrigued, Rimmer told Ken Gill about it, who in turn recounted his own meeting with the brothers several years before. "Go there and see what they say," he advised Rimmer. "Let's find out what we can."

Unknown to Maurice, Gill was looking hard for a way of expanding his agency. He felt it had got into a rut and lacked "bite," and to reinvigorate it he wanted to inject some of the bright, young advertising talent emerging on the London scene in the 1970s. He had held lengthy talks with Ronnie Kirkwood, who had started his own agency, Kirkwood Company, in 1970, the same time as the Saatchis. Gill had talked to John Pearce at Collett Dickenson Pearce, to Martin Boase at Boase Massimi Pollitt, and to others, often coming across the footprints of the Saatchis, who were following the same route. Were they now after him? For some reason he had been left off the round-robin letter that Maurice had sent out to the other agencies and had felt offended. But the position had now changed.

Rimmer reported back that what the Saatchis wanted was to hire Gill—as an administrator. It was puzzling: surely Tim Bell was Saatchi & Saatchi's managing director? Why did they want an administrator? Even more intrigued, Gill decided to pursue the possibilities. His operation was full of good administrators. What he did not have were bright, young, creative people to inject a spark into his somewhat staid and respectable agency. From what he remembered of them, the Saatchis seemed ideal for the purpose.

It was now Gill who approached the Saatchis, and within days they were in serious negotiations. These lasted for months, with both sides carefully thinking through the implications of the move and arguing intensely over the structure of a new group, should they be able to agree on terms.

It was to be a complex deal, particularly for Gill, who had to persuade his major clients, his staff, and his shareholders to go along with the merger. Of these groups the most difficult would be the shareholders (although the staff was not easy either). Compton of New York, the biggest shareholder, still owned 49 percent, and the deal needed its approval. Gill placed a call to the New York office of Milton Gossett, the fifty-year-old president of Compton and an old friend.

Gill outlined the problem that faced him. The London end was a good, solid day-to-day agency, he explained, but he could not see anyone among the younger people who could provide the new burst of energy needed; he had no obvious successor, and that worried him. Profits that year had fallen, and the agency was only eleventh in the 1974 billings table. But he had met two young men who were producing some of the best advertising he had ever seen; they were financially bright as well as creative. He was thinking of taking over their business, getting them to set the direction of the agency. He would like Gossett to meet them.

Gossett, like Gill, was to play a major role in the business lives of the brothers. Compton in New York, the agency where later that year he would be promoted to chief executive officer, was a reflection of its client list: Ivy League, conventional, conservative. Gossett himself, though, was not Ivy League at all and, unlike most people in the agency, not a university graduate. What college education he did have was in engineering, which was of little practical use in his career as a copywriter or as an ad agency president. He had joined Compton in 1949, originally "pushing a cart around the halls delivering mail and learning that media was not a Greek goddess." He is still there today.

At Gill's invitation, Gossett went to London to meet the two young men the London chairman had in mind. Before meeting the brothers, he was introduced to Tim Bell and immediately fell under his spell. Bell, although not on the main Saatchi & Saatchi board, was managing director and, if the deal with Compton went through, was to be in charge of the joint agency. Bell showed him some of the best Saatchi advertisements, and Gossett recalls being bowled over. "I fell in love when I saw the advertising the Saatchis were doing," he told a friend later. And so Gill arranged for him and for Compton's chairman, Stu Mitchell, to meet the brothers.

The meeting did not go off well. It took place in Gill's flat on Down Street, just off Piccadilly. Mitchell was far more conventional than Gossett, and he needed some convincing. He was not about to get it. The first impression made by the Saatchis was not what Gill had planned.

"These two young, dark-haired, and very emotional young men walked in like wild creatures," says one of the Compton party, "and we were the enemy. We represented convention. Stu Mitchell said about three words, and they stalked out of the room." No one remembers what the three words were: " 'rule of order' or something like that," quips a Compton representative.

It was a major setback for Gill, who had his heart set on the deal. Mitchell went back to New York and announced that he was against any such thing. But Gossett, under Gill's persuasion, didn't agree: "All I see is superb creative work, a couple of guys who are very volatile, and a fellow, Tim Bell, who is marvelous. As far as I'm concerned they're great—why shouldn't we do it?" Gill brought the brothers back to his apartment for more meetings, and the talks got back on track.

The more the Saatchis considered Garland-Compton, the more they liked the idea of getting hold of it, merging their own agency into it, and running the whole show. It made sense to them for reasons other than size. A number of lessons were coming home to them. The shock of losing Singer still haunted them, but there was a more long-term consideration too. They had, they felt, established Saatchi's reputation as the creative hot shop of the industry, but they had always known that wouldn't be enough. They had almost no clients in the fast-moving packaged-goods area: no soap flakes, packaged foods, or supermarket goods, which were the big accounts.

They also had no reputation for marketing skills, although when they started in 1970 they had identified the fact that such a reputation was essential. And they were just beginning to realize that it was very hard to get a reputation both for creativity and for marketing. The two are in many ways opposed to each other. The perception among clients was that the world was divided into bright creative people, of whom Saatchi & Saatchi was a good example, and bigger, more conservative operations, which were strong on marketing. Garland-Compton was very much in the latter camp, while Saatchi on its own, no matter how fast it grew, could never get there. The thought of putting its own creative skills and Compton's marketing reputation together under the same roof became irresistible.

Later the brothers would be stung by criticisms that the conflict between the creative and the marketing skills meant that the merger was a "marriage made in hell," and forecasts that it would disintegrate annoyed them. "It's a marriage made in heaven," Maurice, who could see the possibilities even more clearly than Charles, told his brother that summer. Reluctant at the beginning, they began to push the negotiations faster.

Compton was not the only shareholder whose view Gill sought. In 1975 James Gulliver was generally seen as one of the brightest and most able managers in Britain. The son of a grocer, he came from the small distillery town of Campbeltown, in Argyllshire, had studied engineering at Glasgow University, then won a Fulbright scholarship to the Georgia Institute of Technology. In his twenties he became the protégé of the Canadian food retailer Garfield Weston, owner of the Fine Fare super-market chain in Britain, as well as Fortnum & Mason. By the age of thirty-three Gulliver was managing director of Fine Fare, and shortly afterward Ken Gill came along to make a pitch to him for his advertising account. After a bumpy first few years the two men became friends and the relationship survived Gulliver's eventual break with Weston. In 1975 Gulliver had set up his own company, called James Gulliver Associates, which among other services offered management and investment advice. He had bought into Compton when it went public and now owned just under 10 percent of Compton's shares. He too would play an important part in the merger.

Gill enlisted Gulliver's help, asking him to advise on the Saatchi business and to suggest how the deal might be structured. Should it be done at all? Gulliver, who had a small office on the third floor of the Compton building in Charlotte Street, was initially far from keen. He was busy at the time with a series of investments, but he assigned to the project one of the bright, young people he had gathered around him, Martin Sorrell.

Sorrell, a short, black-haired, heavily spectacled man, had been born into the North London Jewish community thirty-one years before. His father ran a profitable electrical retail business, and Sorrell, an only son, grew up in comfortable prosperity. As a teenager, he traveled to the United States to see the Kennedy clan campaigning and developed a lifelong interest in marketing and advertising. He received an economics degree at Cambridge, toyed with journalism for a while, then went to Harvard Business School. Back in London he worked for Mark McCormack's sports and personality management firm. Then in 1975, just as the Compton-Saatchi saga was developing, he joined Gulliver.

Within days Gulliver told him: "Look, I have this personal interest in Compton, and Kenneth Gill has asked me to give him advice on whether they should take over this company called Saatchi & Saatchi."

Sorrell did a double take. Saatchi & Saatchi? He knew the name, because he had seen it on the office on Lower Regent Street, but he didn't know it was a London advertising agency. "I thought it was a new Japanese hi-fi firm," he said.

Impatiently Gulliver explained who the Saatchis were and what he wanted done. Gulliver went on to say that he was opposed to the deal, although he hadn't told Gill that, but that Sorrell should take a hard, clinical look at the whole thing.

Meanwhile, the negotiations with the brothers continued. By the end of the summer of 1975 they were close to a deal, under which the Saatchis would sell their business to Compton for shares. They would own 36 percent of the combined equity of the enlarged group, and Compton of New York would be diluted from 49 percent to 26 percent. Gulliver still didn't think much of the proposition, but Sorrell was becoming increasingly interested in the Saatchis and their quick minds and different way of doing things. Gill's commitment never wavered, and Gossett, who had succeeded Mitchell, was prepared to go along with it.

As the deal progressed, Gill decided that it was time to check with Compton's major clients. They, like the big shareholders or the staff, were also in a position to veto the proposed deal. If, for instance, Procter & Gamble told him it would take its business away, there would be no merger. P&G is in fact very punctilious about not interfering in the corporate affairs of its advertising agencies—unless it feels its brands will suffer. But it had to be convinced. The P&G people knew and liked Gill and listened politely as he explained the proposed deal.

"Well, Kenneth, if that's what you want, we won't try to stop you," said a senior P&G executive at last. "But I hope you're right."

"I'm sure I am," said Gill. "You'll get a tremendous service out of this, a real shot in the arm. Good creative stuff—you'll enjoy it."

The P&G executive knew enough about Saatchi's reputation to have his doubts. "Well, we'll see."

"You *will* see," said Gill. "You're really going to like it; I give you my word. And if you don't you'll fire me anyway, so it's in our interests to see that you do." P&G demanded a larger team working on its account, and Gill was happy to oblige.

Rowntree Mackintosh and other big accounts took the same line. "If that's what you want to do, we'll back you," Gill was told. Only one client, Ideal Toys, didn't like it and withdrew its account.

The brothers insisted on one condition and refused to budge on it: the name Saatchi & Saatchi had to be retained. It was a difficult point, because technically Compton was taking over Saatchi, although everyone had long accepted that it was a "reverse" takeover in the sense that Saatchi & Saatchi was going to emerge on top. Gill fought against the name, and Gossett didn't like it either. Gill, however, could see its value and the cleverness of Charles in making a virtue of its strangeness in the first place. So the operating subsidiary company, the merged agency, it was agreed, would be called Saatchi & Saatchi Garland-Compton. For a decade there would actually be no advertising agency called Saatchi & Saatchi, yet so powerful was the image and reputation of the two brothers that even those who worked for the merged agency called it "Saatchi & Saatchi."

There was one point, however, on which Gill would not give way: the brothers would have to move lock, stock, and barrel into *his* offices on

Charlotte Street. They had been specially built for Hobson Bates as the premises for an advertising company, and he did not think much of the Saatchi office on Regent Street (which, ironically, is where Gill has his office today). Charles did not want to go but reluctantly gave in. Only later, after he had moved in, did he become enthusiastic.

By September 1975 the deal was ready for signing. So far there had been no rumors, and by holding the meetings at Gill's apartment, security had been retained. Then, with only a week to go before the announcement of the merger, Gill opened his copy of *Ad Weekly* and suffered one of the worst shocks of his career. Charles Saatchi was quoted as saying how much he admired Garland-Compton's work—not a remark he would normally make. Angrily, Gill rang Charles. "Christ, you've blown it," he said. "This is far too specific—everyone will know what you're up to." A few minutes later Gill had a call from Bob Gross, chairman of Geers Gross. "Congratulations," said Gross. "For what?" Gill tried to sound innocent. Gross laughed and rang off. But he was the only one to see what was behind Charles's remark—and the only one of Gill's peers in other agencies to support what he was doing.

Within hours of the news being announced, Gill was besieged by calls from almost every agency head in London, telling him how much he was going to regret the merger. The Saatchis were not popular, and the thought of one of the oldest and most conservative agencies falling into their hands sent a large ripple of unease (and also of envy) through the industry. In a single step Saatchi had moved from London's thirteenth biggest agency to fifth biggest. The brothers were getting into the big time.

But the shocks for Gill and for Milt Gossett in New York were not over yet. They had insisted that the deal should be presented to the outside world as a merger, giving Garland-Compton its dignity and pride of place as the senior of the two partners but also bringing out the importance of the Saatchi presence. "An agency with a much higher profile than ours had come in and it was to be billed as a wonderful marriage," says one of the old Compton people. "Good creativity on their part and sound marketing on the part of Garland-Compton." The announcement was to be made delicately, so as not to upset the Garland-Compton staff and also to save Compton of New York some face.

That Friday's *Campaign* therefore came as a bombshell. Across the front page was the headline "Saatchi Swallows Up the Compton Group." The actual story was factually correct, but the headline did the damage. The shock wave spread to New York, where Gossett was angrier than anyone had ever seen him. In London, Kenneth Gill was devastated; friends reported that he had tears in his eyes as he tried to explain the deal. It was a sour beginning to what was to prove a successful and harmonious merger.

9

NUMERO UNO

I n Maurice Saatchi's office on the sixth floor of that same Regent Street building from which Saatchi & Saatchi had moved a decade before—and to which it moved back again in 1985—Maurice and Jeremy Sinclair look back on the Compton merger. To them it is perhaps the single most successful deal they ever made, a move that worked better than they could have dared hope, although in 1975, as they moved up to Charlotte Street, just around the corner from that first Cramer-Saatchi office on Goodge Street, they had traveled very hopefully indeed. On the other hand, there was a certain nervousness. When they had moved from Charlotte Square to Regent Street, they knew they were leaving behind forever the days when they all sat in the same room and shouted insults and ribald comments at each other, gave each other absurd nicknames, and joined in the success and failure of every individual ad. In the Compton building the atmosphere would be different.

On Charlotte Street, Garland-Compton employed 180 people. Following its own growth and the Notley takeover, Saatchi & Saatchi employed about 100. Together they would still be less than a third the size of JWT and several of the other big agencies in London—a minnow in world terms. But compared with a total staff of nine just over five years ago, it was a lot.

Maurice and Sinclair say that one of the main reasons they were able to cope was that they had already had a practice run with Notley's. The takeover of this agency is seldom mentioned in the company profiles or seen by outsiders as an event of any importance. The brothers and their close colleagues, particularly Sinclair, see it as crucial, the prototype of a long production line. Maurice had used Notley's to pioneer his own form of takeover—the "earnout," with so much paid as a down payment and the rest, dependent on performance, paid over five or ten years. That would be vitally important for the future. He also discovered, only after he had bought it, that Notley's at one stage had been the biggest agency in Britain but had declined slowly over the years. Before they took control, the brothers thought of it as one of the deadest agencies in the business, but to their surprise they found a number of able and talented people, some interesting ideas which they adopted quickly into their own system, and disciplines and procedures that were sometimes better than their own seat-of-the-pants methods. If Garland-Compton had been the first takeover, says Sinclair, it would have been much harder to adapt. Because of Notley's, the Saatchis and their team had adjusted to the notion that it was easier to embrace other backgrounds than to attempt to impose their own—yet another important lesson.

There is another reason they could look back on the acquisition of Compton with some satisfaction. In 1975 the Saatchis ignored the accepted wisdom that creative shops and business disciplines did not belong in the same camp. They put the two businesses together, not just as subsidiaries owned by the same group, which is how they would later control many of their acquisitions, but as a physical merger of the agencies, making a single larger one. Until that time, as mentioned earlier, the Saatchis had never been able to offer a skilled marketing service. They had set off in 1970 with the intention of growing their own but at that point could not attract the right person. If Ian McLaurin had joined, perhaps it would have been different, though marketing skills probably did not belong in that frenetic atmosphere. The Procter & Gambles, Rowntrees, and other big packaged-goods clients would not necessarily have appreciated Golden Square.

By accident or not, with Garland-Compton the brothers completed a merger that made good strategic sense—and then they made it work. The combined entity could now be positioned in a way that would give it a major competitive advantage over the opposition. Perhaps it was the fear of this that caused the other big agency heads to attempt to dissuade their old friend Ken Gill from having anything to do with the Saatchis; but it is doubtful if many of the others, steeped as they were in the traditions of their industry, could see the sense in the merger. They could see the difficulties, certainly—they told Gill about them, but in the end those difficulties melted away before the Saatchi frontal assault. Once again the Saatchis were either unable to see obstacles or else chose to ignore them. In this case they saw an opportunity for doing what they had always wanted and went straight for it. This was to be the most successful corporate move they would ever make.

Shortly after the announcement of the merger, Milt Gossett sat in the Compton boardroom. He and the other Compton directors were still shocked by that *Campaign* headline. The complaints from the Garland-Compton staff, passed on to their friends in what they regarded as their New York parent, were plaintive and heartfelt. They had gone along with the Saatchi deal on the grounds that they were taking over Saatchi & Saatchi, that Gill was buying an injection of new talent and new energy but that Garland-Compton, as the bigger agency, would still be in the ascendant. Saatchi & Saatchi, after all, was moving into their building, Gill was still going to be chairman, and they were long established with a stock-market quotation and all the big clients. Now they read that it was *they* who were being taken over.

Gill was so shaken that he did not want to attend the board meeting, but Gossett calmed him down and insisted that he come. Gossett was not a little disturbed himself, but he took a pragmatic approach. Like Gill, he had fallen under the Saatchi spell and wanted the merger to work. There was also a good fallback in these situations, which few can pass up: blame the press. He could say that *Campaign* had got the wrong end of the stick, had taken the whole thing out of context, and he could point to the press release that went out, which put the whole matter in proper perspective. Pay no attention to that headline and that story, Gossett told the directors: this was going to be a great marriage and these are great guys. He persuaded the rest of the board to support the deal, but it had been uncomfortable. "That was a tough one," he told Gill afterward.

Did *Campaign* get it wrong? There was no question in the minds of Charles and Maurice nor of Tim Bell of what they were doing: they were taking over Garland-Compton. The actual mechanism and details of how it was done were immaterial. The substance was crystal clear.

However, it would have taken even an experienced journalist some time to work out the substance of the merger. The announcement and public statements were all designed to avoid humiliating the Compton side and to persuade its members that this move was a marriage of equals. For instance, on September 25, 1975, *The Times* reported the deal with the headline: "Merger Forms One of UK's Largest Agencies" and went on to talk about Compton Partners, "a quoted company with more than 70 years of trading," merging with Saatchi & Saatchi, "formed only five years ago but with a remarkable growth record." The article said that Charles Saatchi and Kenneth Gill would be joint chairmen, that the merger would give Saatchi & Saatchi access to a New York office, "a long held ambition," and added that both companies welcomed the merger, Saatchi & Saatchi because it gave it access to the stock exchange as well as a "greatly expanded scope of operation" and Compton because it "injects new and aggressive young management and creative expertise." That was the line taken by most other papers that reported the merger, not because of any interest in Saatchi & Saatchi but because Compton was a quoted company and therefore merited attention.

Campaign, in contrast, cut through the public-relations flimflam and declared that Saatchi & Saatchi had indeed taken over Garland-Compton. The assumption in Adland was that *Campaign* had been briefed by Charles—which almost certainly it had. Everyone had seen that comment from him the week before, and the whole of Adland knew—and resented—his closeness to the trade press. Inside Garland-Compton the *Campaign* piece had damaged Charles's credibility. But outside? It certainly hardened the view that Saatchi & Saatchi was aggressively on the march, that it was taking the initiative rather than the other way around.

This was the first time the brothers had ever received attention from the financial press. From now on it would become a regular event, yet curiously Charles, so keen on being mentioned in the trade press, never transferred his attention to the financial pages, where he could probably have achieved a great deal more. Maurice's business savvy would bring him out from under his elder brother's shadow. By the mid-1970s many British company chiefs had discovered that a good press image worked wonders for their City reputation too—and therefore for their share prices. A high share price meant one had to pay less for acquisitions. There were plenty of public-relations firms around to advise the Saatchis on how to set about cultivating publicity. James Gulliver could have done so if he had been asked, as Gulliver, in many ways not dissimilar to Charles in his speed of thought, his huge ambition, and his drive, had learned to cope well with the financial press. But to this day no more than a couple of financial journalists in London and none in New York have ever met Charles Saatchi. It is not that Charles, like many advertising people, is not good on figures—he can find his way around balance sheets perfectly well. It is that, while he is wholly at home discussing ads and ad campaigns, he is less eloquent in other areas and is self-conscious about it. He is also naturally shy.

Although neither of them recognized it at the time, this was probably a turning point in the relationship between the two brothers. Until now, Charles, with his volatile and forceful personality, had dominated not just the agency but also his younger brother. Maurice had more than earned his place as a partner, but he was still the junior partner, the one who meekly ducked when the chairs were flying; he might have argued with Charles, but it was always Charles who seemed to get his own way. Charles had been totally dominant in the hothouse atmosphere of Golden Square; he had still been the major influence at Regent Street. But now Saatchi & Saatchi was a public company, with outside shareholders, a staff of nearly 300, and aggressive plans for using its stock market listing to advance its position. This new status required new disciplines and new thinking, and Charles would never learn them. For one thing, they didn't interest him—and Charles has probably never in his life done anything that doesn't interest him. And second, he had his younger brother, whom he still probably viewed as an extension of himself, to do it for him.

It is worth pausing here to note the significance of this. Both brothers today firmly believe that their ability to use the stock market in the way it should be used—for providing risk capital to new and growing businesses—was the most important factor in their growth from this point on. Charles in his more reflective moments freely acknowledges his debt to Maurice in this area in particular. If Charles had gone into business with Ross Cramer, Martin Boase, his friend Frank Lowe, or even Tim Bell, he would have created a decent-sized business, perhaps even the biggest in Britain (although that is doubtful), and lived a prosperous life. His qualities were of leadership, creative imagination, and an ability to find and motivate other talented people. But there are others in the advertising world who have similar abilities, maybe not always as pronounced as Charles's talents but good enough to mean that Charles was not dramatically different from his peers. What now emerged was that Saatchi & Saatchi had not only Charles's talents, but the much more important corporate abilities of Maurice as well. Just as Charles would always have made a good living, so too would Maurice almost certainly have created a large company, no matter what field he had gone into. Lindsay Masters and Michael Heseltine recognized that from the beginning—Masters, indeed, would not have minded what business Maurice was starting; he would still have backed him. From now on Charles and Maurice really did work as partners.

Charles probably never had any real intention of becoming joint chairman—he could not bear the thought of having to stand up in front of shareholders and handle a meeting or talk to investment managers, as chairmen of companies are expected to do. All of that side of the business he would leave to his brother. It was not just that Maurice was good with figures; he also had the interest and the ability to apply the same intellectual process he had been so fascinated with when used by Professor Cohen at the London School of Economics to advertising as an industry. Thus Maurice wondered why advertising had such a low City image and stock-market rating. What caused advertising to have such a low profile and was it justified? He did the research to find out; and when he had proved to his own satisfaction that it was not deserved, he set out with his strange mixture of self-effacement and charm to convince others of his findings. It would take him several years, but he eventually succeeded far more than perhaps he had ever hoped. In doing so he opened the way for Saatchi & Saatchi's expansion far beyond what Charles, despite his huge ambition to be number one, could ever have achieved on his own. To change the investment image of Saatchi & Saatchi, Maurice had to change the view of the whole advertising industry. The fact that he succeeded made it possible for many other advertising agencies to follow Saatchi & Saatchi into the public arena over the next ten years. And it would be entirely through the process of using a high stock-market rating to raise capital that the bastions of Madison Avenue would eventually fall to the British.

Jennifer Laing waited nervously for her new boss to appear. Along with everyone else from Garland-Compton, she had gathered to hear an address by people she had never met. The daughter of a plastic surgeon, Laing always called her decision to join Garland-Compton her "first lucky break"; she had rapidly worked her way up from a trainee on the accounts side to account handler for Rowntree when the merger with

Saatchi took place. She was twenty-four at the time but already seen as one of the brightest people on the London advertising scene. Now, along with all the others, she was anxious to find out what lay in store for her. That *Campaign* headline had given everyone the jitters.

A few minutes later she caught her first glimpse of Tim Bell. He appeared suddenly from the back of the room and strode confidently through the waiting Compton staff to the front. He wore a light brown suit and a golden suntan, and his hair was bleached. With him was Charles Saatchi, more soberly attired in a pinstripe suit. Bell, a cigarette in one hand, told the audience that the merger was the most exciting thing that had ever happened in any of their lives; theirs was going to be the greatest and most famous agency in the world; the combination of the two teams would be unstoppable; they would win major new business and huge new accounts. Bell was going to be in charge of putting the two businesses together, and he was looking forward to working with everyone in the room. "He put it all across in this wonderful sexy voice," says Laing. "It was fascinating watching the effect on the audience."

When Bell had finished Charles stood up very quietly and gave the longest speech anyone can ever recall him making. He did it well, insisting that this was a merger, and he was looking forward to working with Kenneth Gill and everyone else. By the end the damage done by the *Campaign* headline had been more than reversed. "It was a landslide," says Laing. "Everyone walked out of the room feeling they really wanted to work with these guys. I remember someone turning to me and saying, 'Well, Jen, you just went into the advertising industry.' "

An early casualty of the merger was Ron Rimmer, the man who had inadvertently brought it about. He had readily accepted Tim Bell as his boss and had shifted sideways to a financial role; but within months he quit and went to McCann Erickson. "It was the methods of working that worried him," says a former colleague. "He didn't understand all this fiery behavior at all."

There was a successor at hand, however. The deal had been completed in September 1975. Four months later, in January 1976, Martin Sorrell suggested to his boss that they offer the services of the James Gulliver Associates consultancy business to the Saatchi brothers. Gulliver Associates had seen something of the Saatchis during the bid negotiations, and Sorrell had got on well with them. Gulliver was agreeable. He had set up office in a London suburb, Welwyn Garden City, and was at the stage of starting a company that within ten years would make a £2.5 billion bid for the Scotch whiskey group Distillers, only to be beaten, through controversial tactics, by Guinness in what became the financial scandal of the decade. Maurice went to lunch with Gulliver, Sorrell, and Alistair Grant, then Gulliver's joint number two (today the chairman of Argyll Foods, owners of Safeway supermarkets and the third biggest food retailer in Britain). Gulliver, particularly in his own lunchroom, was always formal and invariably served the same food, Dover sole. Sorrell watched with some amusement his expression as Maurice, who sported bow ties in those days, took off his jacket. Gulliver simmered but let it pass, but Maurice had not risen in his estimation.

The Gulliver approach came at the right time, because the Saatchis were indeed looking for advice. Maurice was now coming to grips with the problems of running a public company and wanted some ideas on how to use the stock market. He was already hitting the frustrating wall of the financial community's dislike for advertising agencies and for "people businesses" in general, as marked in London as it was on Wall Street. Saatchi & Saatchi could not borrow in the way an industrial company, with concrete assets and a predictable business, could always raise money from a bank. The company's shares sold at around three times earnings, a miserable rating by any standards, less than one-third the average rating for the rest of the stock market. This meant that raising money or making acquisitions by issuing new shares was prohibitively expensive. Maurice was casting around for a way out of this problem and knew that Gulliver was well qualified to help, and Gulliver in turn assigned the project to Sorrell, who began spending a day a week in the Saatchi office; gradually it became more.

The financial setup at Saatchi at this time was far from sophisticated. David Perring had joined as a company secretary when Saatchi & Saatchi started at Golden Square, and he still had that role (as he has to this day). He was competent but was not a qualified accountant. Mike Johnston was the nearest thing the agency had to a finance director, although with the merger Ron Rimmer and Douglas Blaikey had expanded the team to four. However, Rimmer was never a proper finance director in the sense that most companies understand that position, nor was Johnston. They were administrative officers, the men who looked after expenses, chased overdue accounts, paid bills and salaries, and generally made the group work. Both Rimmer and Perring were meticulous, but neither would be much use to Maurice in talking to the City and organizing new takeover bids. Tim Bell, Jeremy Sinclair, and of course the brothers themselves were bright, adaptable, and ambitious enough to expand as the business had grown, but that did not apply to all the people taken on at Golden Square.

The first advice that Gulliver and Sorrell gave to Maurice, therefore, was to hire a finance director. Maurice readily agreed, and a firm of headhunters was appointed. Finance directors of advertising agencies in those days, in London at least, were not high-powered people, and the headhunters went to the traditional trawling grounds: other agencies and Fleet Street papers. "These guys came in to see Maurice mostly in the morning, because if they had come in after lunch it would have been embarrassing," says one former Saatchi worker. Finally, Maurice, who had lost Rimmer at this stage, snapped at the headhunter: "What I want is someone like Martin Sorrell." "Well, have you asked him?" said the headhunter. Maurice did—and Sorrell came aboard.

Ken Gill relished the new atmosphere in the agency. To the other agency heads, who expressed their forebodings whenever he met them, he was uncompromising in his praise. "It's wonderful," he said, and he meant it. The merger was a new lease on life for him and for the agency. Tim Bell was working from early morning to late at night, often right through the weekend, putting the two agencies together—and doing it well. Other than Rimmer there was a limited fallout; the Saatchi staff moved in to take most of the key positions—Bell as managing director of the agency, Jeremy Sinclair as creative director, Roy Warman as media director, and Terry Bannister and Bill Muirhead also moving into senior roles. Above the agency was the holding company, which had Gill as chairman (Charles never did join him as joint chairman, although there was no doubt in anyone's mind who was the real boss of the business), David Perring, Mike Johnston, and of course Maurice.

The brothers found rooms for themselves on the sixth floor and had them redecorated. They were far from grand: Charles's looked out onto the roofs and enclosed courtyard at the back of the building. Across the corridor Maurice's office was no larger, but he made it bright and pleasant with the now traditional Saatchi style; everything, including the desk, was gleaming white. Bell moved his office onto the ground floor; he had not been on their floor on Regent Street either but was only a single flight of stairs away. Now there was a considerable physical separation between him and the two brothers. That, too, may have been significant. By the standards of the day the brothers were running a medium-sized public company and were increasingly thinking in strategic terms, working on more takeover bids and on expanding the network into Europe, the United States, and the rest of the world. Charles still involved himself in the creative side, but his presence was more and more remote. Many of the Garland-Compton people complained that they had never seen him, and some never would, except perhaps fleetingly in the elevator or the foyer.

For those working in the agency in these years Tim Bell was the hub—and the brothers let him run things. Unrecognized by Bell until it was too late, he and the brothers now began to go their separate ways, gently at first but gathering pace as time went on. Once Saatchi & Saatchi had become a public company, the advertising consultancy agency became only a subsidiary. In these early days it was effectively the only subsidiary, all there was to the public company, and Bell in effect was responsible for generating all the profit. If Maurice's plans came to fruition, however, there would be other subsidiaries, other businesses, which would eventually reduce the importance of the Charlotte Street agency. Bell, relishing the role of running the business, did not pause to consider the wider implications of what was happening. It was a time of extraordinary growth, when the agency seemed to be able to get almost any client it pitched. And a new phenomenon emerged: clients would come to Saatchi, asking it to take on their accounts without even a "beauty contest."

Yet it was Ken Gill rather than the Saatchi brothers or Bell who got the new business off to a flying start. For months before the merger and all the way through it Gill had been talking to Schweppes about moving its account to Garland-Compton. Schweppes was one of the biggest and most prestigious accounts in Britain and had become something of a legend in the 1950s and 1960s with its "Schh . . . You know who" campaign. The marketing director of Schweppes, Keith Holloway, was an old friend of Gill's, and Gill had finally persuaded him that it was time to move from Ogilvy & Mather. Holloway had also quietly let it be known that he favored Garland-Compton, although the agency would still have to pitch. Holloway knew nothing about the Saatchi deal, but as luck had it, the Garland team was preparing for the pitch when the merger took place. Jennifer Laing was one of the people involved in preparing for the pitch, but she now had the added contribution from the Saatchi side. She went along with Tim Bell and two others to make their presentation—and they got the account. To the outside world it looked as if the magic name of Saatchi & Saatchi had clinched the deal for Garland-Compton, and Gill quietly let the Saatchi team have the credit. He could see the impetus this would give to the new agency—and he was right. The Schweppes account had a galvanizing effect, both internally and externally. "That really was a turning point for the doubters," says Laing.

The first report and account of the public company Saatchi & Saatchi Compton Ltd. makes interesting reading. The cover was white, with an embossed rising-step formation, signifying rising profits (or at least rising something). Across the top is the name "Saatchi & Saatchi Compton," in the restrained and ultraconservative script that Bill Atherton had chosen back in 1970 to make the fledgling agency look respectable and established. Subsequent accounts replaced the word "Compton" with "Company," but only the sharp-eyed would ever spot the change. Within a year the parent company was called Saatchi & Saatchi Company Ltd; Saatchi & Saatchi Compton was a subsidiary, and Saatchi & Saatchi Garland-Compton was the name of the agency (it is now called Saatchi & Saatchi Advertising). Compton was already being Saatchified, the first of many major acquisitions to get the treatment.

Maurice used the first report and account to tell the world how much faster the agency was growing than any other. He also identified the best campaigns they had run during the year: Leyland Cars' Superdeal; Schweppes; Brutus jeans; the launch of a new soap powder, Fairy Snow, for Procter & Gamble; Kronenbourg lager; and many others. He also made some wider points. The report declared: "The fact is that the advertising industry is a cornerstone of the survival of a free enterprise mixed-economy in Britain." There should be more acquisitions and mergers in the industry "to bring about the much heralded concentration that the industry needs"; advertisers should stop complaining so much about "account clashes and conflicts that are often more apparent than real" (the Saatchis that year had been forced to resign one beer account when they took on another). The final two pages were aimed shrewdly at the City. They pointed out that the Saatchi & Saatchi stock-market rating was a miserable one: its shares sold at 3.9 times earnings, which meant that the whole company was valued at only £1.3 million (and their own stake at 36 percent of that). The record was far better than the average, yet "we are still 'rated' only half as well as the average listed company!"

Even half was an improvement on what the agency's rating had been at the beginning. The Saatchi share price was beginning to rise at this time (it started at the equivalent of 6p and hit a peak of £7 in 1986) but too slowly for Maurice. In the previous year, partly as a result of his continual campaigning, shares in the tiny advertising sector had risen by nearly 60 percent, almost twice as fast as the rest of the market. "There has clearly been a change in investor sentiment towards advertising agencies," wrote the *Sunday Times* in April 1978. This was despite a nasty incident at Charles's old agency Collett Dickenson Pearce, where the Inland Revenue had launched criminal proceedings against the chairman, John Pearce, the managing director, Frank Lowe, and others. The *Sunday Times* picked Saatchi & Saatchi as "standing out from the crowd" in terms of the quality of earnings, track record, and prospects. But there wasn't much of a crowd. Other than Ogilvy, Brunning, and Geers Gross (Collett now disappeared as a listed company), there wasn't an advertising sector—all the big agencies were American subsidiaries.

The brothers had been struck by the difficulty of persuading major clients to change their agencies, regardless of the work produced for them; for instance, Kellogg and Lever Brothers had been JWT clients for forty-one and fifty-two years, respectively, in 1979. Procter & Gamble and Rowntree Mackintosh had been with Compton even longer. Maurice that year calculated that on average, accounts worth only 2½ percent of total advertising switched agencies each year. This fact came as a revelation to him and then to the others when he related it. Here was his key for opening up the financial markets. Quality of earnings, he could argue, was not at all bad in advertising, and contrary to the accepted wisdom, the business did not go down in the elevator every evening. It was actually remarkably stable, far more stable than anyone had realized before. He began making the point that once you were up there with the big accounts, you were there to stay, even if your hottest creative people and best account managers left. Size really did matter in the industry. On the other hand, that 2½ percent was worth £1 million a week—well worth chasing. Saatchi & Saatchi still had less than 5 percent of the total British advertising market, so there was plenty to go for. Maurice, by now employing financial public-relations adviser Brian Basham, renewed his efforts to raise the status of the industry, and soon articles were appearing making many of these points. In that first year of owning Garland-Compton, Saatchi had profits just under £1 million, which the agency could record as an increase of 145 percent, although that included Compton's profits for the first time. The following year Saatchi & Saatchi made £1.2 million, then £1.9 million, and by 1979, the year it became the number one agency in Britain, profits were £2.4 million, and the stock market was beginning to take notice in a big way. By that time the price-earnings ratio had not only caught up with the stock-market average but had actually passed it. By 1980 Saatchi would become a glamour stock, leading the advertising sector, which by then was starting to become larger as other agencies sought to be listed.

Already the brothers were looking for more acquisitions, and Martin Sorrell was deputed by Maurice to find them. Initially Sorrell was appalled by the Saatchi acquisition policy. He had been schooled by James Gulliver, who was, and is, probably the most thorough person in Britain when it comes to planning a bid—Gulliver's detailed examination of Distillers before he made his bid in 1985 is a classic example. Gulliver was working on a number of acquisitions at the time, and his method was to send Sorrell and his own finance director, David Webster, to the offices of County Bank, a subsidiary of National Westminster. There they were required to go through the Exchange Telegraph cards, a widely used company information system that gives the financial history and details of every listed company. By applying the special criteria that Gulliver had worked out, Sorrell and Webster then built a list of fifty possible candidates, studied them in greater detail, and whittled that down again to produce a short list of perhaps five. That list would then be subjected to an even more detailed study before Gulliver would even begin opening up talks or buying shares. Compton had been a target in his sights at one point, which was why he bought the shares. (He had sold them in the market after the bid was announced, still not convinced it was a good deal.)

At Saatchi it was different. "Maurice's approach was very much to have the whole universe," says Sorrell. "Then it was like Weight-Watchers: you'd have a regular weekly meeting, and people were called to account. The list was divided up, and we all had to go to talk to these companies and see whether anybody was interested in selling their business. People were chastised if they didn't contact a large number."

To Sorrell the Saatchi approach was a blunderbuss in contrast to the fine rifle-shot policy of Gulliver. But once he realized that Maurice was working on his own carefully thought-out plan, Sorrell changed his mind. "It's actually a very intelligent system because what it does is register your calling card. What you're saying to people is: I'm interested. Any decent business should not be for sale the day that you ring up; but one day it might be. The best deals that I've ever been involved in all took three, maybe five, years."

Even without acquisitions, Saatchi & Saatchi was expanding rapidly. The advertising accounts continued to pour in: Allied Breweries, new accounts from British Leyland, British Petroleum, Black & Decker, Dunlop, more from Procter & Gamble. The gap with JWT at the top was narrowing. Then in 1979 Saatchi & Saatchi declared billings (the equivalent of turnover in a conventional firm, used as the yardstick for measuring size) of £ 67.8 million and claimed the top position. It was the front-page story in *Campaign* and the rest of the trade press. Charles was uncharacteristically modest when he told *Campaign* that "as the positions of the four leading agencies are so close, it is not especially meaningful which one emerges at the top for any given period." In Charlotte Street, however, there was jubilation. For years Charles had been openly talking about being bigger than anyone else—and had been laughed at. This change in position was therefore very "meaningful": Saatchi & Saatchi was no longer a little hot shop to be despised and jeered at for its precociousness by the rest of the industry. It stood at the top of the castle and from now on would take on a different reputation: it would be the target for everyone else to try to topple. There was still another year or so while other agencies, notably Masius and McCann as well as JWT, disputed that top position, but finally the impetus that Saatchi still enjoyed left no doubt. JWT, after a reign of twenty years at the top, was number four in 1978–79, and since that time Saatchi's position, if one includes all its acquisitions, has looked as unassailable as JWT's once seemed. Saatchi & Saatchi's slogan, "It's good to be big, it's better to be good, but it's best to be both," dates from this time.

At the end of 1979 Saatchi & Saatchi employed 744 people, earning average salaries of £6,041 each. Its turnover was £71 million and its profits £2.4 million; every year from its start it had increased its profits margins so that by 1979 they stood at 3.4 percent, more than twice the industry average. Saatchi & Saatchi was by now a proper business, its stock-market rating rising every year. The "twenty-five calls a day" system of getting new business had long been replaced by a sophisticated computerized one that Maurice had put into place, where companies were approached on a well-organized and rotational basis. Maurice had visited Procter & Gamble and discovered a whole new world of management and organizational techniques that he had copied and absorbed into Saatchi.

Meanwhile, the advertising industry was no longer the same business the brothers had entered in 1970 but had become much more professional, bigger, and better managed. The economic crisis of the mid-1970s had caused all agencies—even Saatchi—to contract or go under. British industry was still trying to rebuild itself after the ravages of those years and was hitting new problems in the shape of a strong pound, pushed up from $1.53 to over $2.40 by the second oil crisis of 1979 (when Britain *did* have its own oil) and by the emergence of tight monetary controls and high interest rates under the new Conservative government. Advertising expenditure in real terms had increased by 17 percent during the 1970s, which did not make for a great growth industry but was actually faster than most businesses grew in Britain during that decade. Within that overall figure, whole new sectors of advertising had emerged: in 1970 detergent and food manufacturers dominated TV advertising; by the end of the decade the retail sector was the largest, and record companies, films, cars, financial services, and travel were the growth areas.

Another factor, which again Maurice's analytical mind fastened on and played some part in encouraging, was the change of attitude advertisers now had toward recession. Traditionally in bad times the first items of expenditure a company cut were research and development—and advertising. Maurice argued that this was the worst decision a company could make—it merely made the downturn worse and damaged the images of the brands. Without strong brand images consumers would simply switch to more aggressively marketed goods or take the own-brand labels from the supermarket shelves. To compete with the advertising being done by the big retailers, such as Sainsbury and Tesco, the manufacturers should not cut back. By 1979 many manufacturers had arrived at the same conclusion—and the Saatchis willingly gave them a further push. "Brand reinforcement," they forecast, was going to be the priority of the 1980s. They were right.

Every year in Saatchi & Saatchi's annual report the Saatchis published their views on the trends in the industry; they were far from the only people doing so, but no one did it as effectively as they did. Maurice delivered the message to the financial journalists, explaining how and why Saatchi & Saatchi believed it had accomplished only a fraction of what it was capable.

There was little retrospection in Charlotte Street. Charles had set a target, achieved it, and moved on. What had happened yesterday was gone, and he didn't even want to talk about it. Maurice was now setting the pace, with Charles urging him on from behind. Tim Bell may have been running the agency, but Maurice was busy too, thinking beyond the British advertising scene to advertising in the rest of the world and laying plans to conquer other industries.

Here is another part of the answer to the question, "What was different about the Saatchis?" It was Maurice who pointed out that advertising, after all, was still a small industry, even if you became the biggest in it. Charles on his own would probably have stayed in it and would not have dared—or been able—to make the jump beyond. But Maurice was not wedded to advertising and already saw it as a strictly limited industry. Charles, with all that pent-up energy, still drove, and Maurice responded to his impatience and his demands for more, always more. More what? More clients, more markets, more share of the market, more profits, more quality, more people—and more acquisitions. "Charles was the goad," says a senior Saatchi & Saatchi director at the time, "the grit in the oyster that produced the pearl." He was distant, but he was there—and everyone knew it, even if they were not aware that a subtle but significant change had taken place, and Maurice was now the brother framing the ambitions and controlling the direction.

The acquisitions continued to flow: Hall Advertising gave the group a major presence in Edinburgh; O'Kennedy Brindley in Dublin took them into Ireland. The latter was an interesting buy, bringing in another fifty people and some good Irish accounts but also beginning, in a modest way, the march to an international network.

The brothers had used N. M. Rothschild, the London merchant bank, to advise on the Compton merger and still went to Rothschild with their ideas of takeovers. Martin Sorrell soon got fed up with this procedure: "We used to go along to these marvelous portals in St. Swithin's Lane in the City, of which our fees wouldn't cover one square foot, and see James Joll [now finance director of Pearson, the group that owns the *Financial Times*], and he used to read us the book of Jonah and the whale. He always thought we had these insane ideas—he was probably right." Jacob Rothschild still talks with regret of how "we let them get away from us"; Saatchi & Saatchi was too small for Jacob himself to get involved. Joll, a former financial journalist, remembers the brothers' impatience to get on and buy things and felt it was his role to urge a degree of caution.

Neither the brothers nor Sorrell were much interested in that type of advice. There were other banks willing to take a more imaginative view. So far the brothers had not used Saatchi & Saatchi's stock-market listing to any advantage, but they were building toward it. That year's annual report informed shareholders: "We are currently exploring opportunities for the company in the U.S. market—though we regard this as a long-term move and our plans are still at an early stage."

By 1979 the Saatchi brothers were beginning to become quite wealthy. In 1976 they paid themselves less than £25,000 each and their dividends came to £64,600—the top rate of tax then was 83 percent. In 1979 their earnings were still less than £45,000 each, and their dividends had doubled to £120,000 (shared between them). Others in the industry were paid larger sums, but the brothers were far more interested in watching their capital value climb through the increase in their share values—they had over 2 million shares between them, now worth over £1 million, and they could borrow money against that. They also had, like every other senior manager in the agency, their company cars and other perquisites.

Both men were now married. Charles lived with Doris for six years before they were finally married in 1973. Maurice by then had been married a year; his engagement in 1972 to Gillian Osband, daughter of Samuel Osband, a wealthy North London property man, had been a lavish occasion, attended by most of the Jewish community with whom they had grown up. The Osbands were near neighbors of the Saatchis in Highgate, and Nathan and Daisy must have been pleased with the match. Maurice was twenty-five at the time and Gillian was twenty-four. They moved to a gracious home in North London, where Maurice kept some of his growing collection of cars, including his great pride: an AC Cobra sports car of 1950s vintage, capable of speeds over 150 mph, which he had lovingly restored and which he drove sparingly on Sunday mornings. A friend visiting them was later surprised to discover that they had no children: the house seemed to be full of toys and children's books, but that is probably explained by the fact that Gillian worked as a children's book publisher—or maybe because Maurice collected toy trains.

Charles's marriage was a different affair. Maurice's wedding had taken place at his father's synagogue, the Spanish and Portuguese, in Lauderdale Road in North London. Charles's was much quieter, at the Kensington Register Office, with only a handful of guests present. Doris had been born Doris Lockhart in Memphis, Tennessee. Her mother was a White Russian, brought out of Russia by Doris's grandfather just before the revolution and raised in some comfort in America until the 1929 stock-market crash. There was just enough money left to pay for a year in business college; the 1930s found Doris's mother working for the Department of Employment in Memphis. Doris's father was a reporter in Memphis who had just graduated from Penn State and who each week went to collect the unemployment figures.

"They were both extraordinarily good-looking people and they made a dashing, romantic young couple around Memphis," says Doris. "My mother had titian red hair and she got written about a lot in the papers because of her escape from the Red hordes in Russia across a frozen river in a cart carrying just a silver teapot her grandmother gave her." Doris learned later that her mother had been spotted by Hollywood talent scouts but had decided that the Hollywood kind of life was not for her. She married instead, and Doris was the eldest of three children—and the only daughter.

Doris's father had moved to Washington during the war to become the head of censorship of magazines and newspapers and after the war moved to New York, where he worked for Jack Howard, founder of United Press International. The Lockhart family lived in Scarsdale, where Doris remembers being brought up in a very cocooned and protected household. "Our cultural life was centered on New York City, and I was taken at an early age to the art museums, ballet, plays, and all the rest." After attending Smith (which she hated) and the Sorbonne (which she loved) she got her first job in Boston working as a secretary in an advertising agency "with promises of becoming a trainee copywriter" that were never kept. So she moved to a smaller agency, did her training, and then drifted to New York.

The agency she wanted most to work for was Ogilvy & Mather. "It's rather interesting that I married Charles Saatchi because David Ogilvy had at that time come out from Britain and taken the Americans by storm with his long copy series and his dignified ads," Doris remarks now. She took the Ogilvy copy test, passed, and got a job at a time when the agency was still small enough that one could meet David Ogilvy himself in the elevator or the corridors. "He was one of those extraordinary people who would ask quite surprising questions out of nowhere. One day in the elevator he asked me what the wonderful perfume I was wearing was. And it *was* an unusual perfume, not your usual Arpège or Chanel."

Ogilvy later chose Doris as one of three copywriters to write the presentation ads for the U.S. Travel Service, an account won at the time when America began waking up to the fact that American tourism should not be one-way—foreigners might want to come and see America too. Doris grew to regard Ogilvy with considerable reverence: "He was a great leader. I think he could have done anything he wanted to do. His people just adored him—I would have followed him anywhere."

There were lessons she could, and did, teach Charles, whose style could not have been more different from Ogilvy's. She and Charles were now living together in Bedford Gardens in Kensington. Charles was twenty-nine; Doris, whose previous marriage had been dissolved, was seven years older.

Although Charles had married outside the Jewish religion, Nathan and Daisy were resigned to it. Doris was welcomed with open arms, particularly by Daisy, who must have despaired of becoming a grandmother. After his years as a bachelor, Charles seemed to be settling down. The older Saatchis were delighted. "I think his mother was so relieved that he'd found a woman she actually liked, and I turned out to have two arms and two legs and a smile on my face, that she would have welcomed anyone at that stage." In any case, marriage outside the Jewish religion, something unthinkable in the old days in Iraq, was happening with growing regularity among the younger generation of British Jews, who were more prosperous, better educated, and more assimilated than their parents.

Marriage did not greatly alter the lifestyle or habits of either brother. Charles did discover, late in life, the sport of tennis, playing with a level of aggression quite at odds with his ability. Opponents tell of Charles's insistence on serving, both first and second serves, at the same reckless speed, sometimes double-faulting four times in a single game. He hated to lose and is today often accused by those he plays with (Frank Lowe, for instance) of invariably choosing a semiprofessional for his partner to make up for his weaknesses. Over the years, however, Charles took tennis more seriously than any other game he ever played and now plays a good game, often dropping by clubs when he is on vacation to have a workout with the coach. He can be tremendous fun on the court—as he can be in the small group of friends he has gathered around him.

Maurice was more domestic and developed an interest in interior decoration and design that would later blossom; he and Gillian were more gregarious than Charles and Doris, often seen at cocktail parties and other gatherings. They also entertained at their own home, particularly on weekends. Among their close friends were Josephine Hart, the Irish girl whom Maurice had met at Haymarket, and her husband, Paul Buckley, another Haymarket director; the two couples were often to be seen dining together. Neither brother had any children yet, a point that often distressed Daisy and Nathan (neither David nor the younger brother, Philip, have any children), so marriage brought no great culture shock for either Charles or Maurice. They had always lived in a comfortable and relaxed home, and they continued to do so.

In the late 1960s Charles developed another interest that in the 1970s, fanned by Doris, who initially at least was keener than he was, turned into a passion: contemporary art. It was the age of Minimalist art, when New York artists such as Sol LeWitt, Don Flavin, Donald Judd, and Carl André, with his neat rows of bricks, were beginning to emerge at the center of a major art movement. Charles began to collect Minimalist art, at first desultorily and then with growing conviction and excitement, buying works for a few thousand dollars, ahead of the big rush of American investors who recognized its investment potential several years later (when prices had soared).

As he grew more prosperous and his collection grew, Charles and Doris moved back to North London, to Langford Place near Regent's Park. They bought an old chapel and then added the ground floor of the house next door, which Charles used as a private gallery for himself and Doris.

The house, far from opulent, was behind a wall, and visitors, coming in through a gate, were greeted by a massive tubular sculpture. Inside the house was a sitting room about twenty-five feet by thirty feet and a high ceiling, the apse of the chapel. The room had built-in sofas, a table full of magazines—Doris was a magazine addict—and a TV; the rest of the room was taken up by one of Carl André's brick arrangements (literally 120 firebricks the color of dirty sugar in a two-tiered rectangle, five bricks wide by twelve bricks deep), which had caused such a sensation when it was exhibited in the Tate Gallery. There was "art" all over the place: a crushed car here, a Warhol there. In the dining room were tiled murals by the young American-born artist Jennifer Bartlett. Most of the floors were old stone, a relic of the chapel. The modern kitchen was equipped with glass-front refrigerators, filled with Dom Perignon, and state-of-the-art appliances that often excited as much interest among visitors as the art did.

There were another four or five rooms, all of them devoted to more paintings and sculpture. Upstairs there was just one bedroom, a bathroom, and a dressing room. One visitor remembers being struck by the bedroom in particular: "It had this enormous double bed with a fur rug on it, which was underneath a great Anselm Kiefer painting—a very dour, strong German painting, which had an almost uncanny echo of this almost-wolf rug on the bed." There was no spare bedroom, no space for visitors to stay. On the stairs were life-sized figures, and in the back was a tiny garden with a swimming pool. It was a house that would have been impossible for a family to live in. "It was like a marvelous theatrical set," says one frequent visitor.

Charles drove to the office every morning, using a Jeep, an E-type Jaguar, or one of the other cars from his sizable stable. Maurice too drove in from his more modern, neo-Gothic house, often using a jeep version of the British Leyland Mini. Neither of the brothers had chauffeurs, although Tim Bell and Kenneth Gill did, and sometimes Maurice would either ride with Bell or Gill to meetings or use their cars if they were available. Alternatively, he would go by taxi. Neither of the brothers, according to those who worked with them, was interested in company cars or other status symbols of the kind that interested more ordinary executives; but then, with their names above the door they didn't need any more symbols of their status.

Their lifestyles had obviously changed since the early 1970s but not to any significant degree. Those who know the brothers well say they are much the same people today as they were eighteen years ago. Maurice in particular worked hard, unwilling even to take vacations. "His idea of a holiday was going to Capri for a five-day break, or if he had a meeting in America, taking a few days off and going to Long Island. But he had to be forced to take a holiday," says a former Saatchi director.

Charles, on the other hand, was keen on his vacations. Each summer he hired a boat in the Mediterranean and went there with Doris and

Michael Green, a close friend and the chairman of a thriving company called Carlton Communications, and Green's wife, Janet. Charles never learned to swim but still loved boats, probably because he became so quickly bored in hotels and in a boat could move on. But his inability to swim never stopped him from tearing around the water in speedboats. Every Christmas he and Doris flew to the Caribbean, stopping off in New York on the way to visit Doris's father (her mother died the same year she and Charles were married) and see the art galleries. Janet Green, daughter of Lord Wolfson of Great Universal Stores, was almost as keen a collector of modern art as Charles, and today the two of them have the best collections in Britain, if not in the world. (The Greens have since separated.)

Charles's style of working had not changed much either. He may have been more remote than he had been when Saatchi & Saatchi started, but he still had around him a similar group of people. His attention span had not lengthened with age, and his executives knew that they had about three minutes on average to tell him what they needed. Kenneth Gill cannot recall Charles being present at a board meeting and remembers him at only one annual meeting, when Gill was due for reelection as a director. Charles had no title, nor had Maurice until he took over as chairman in 1986 after Ken Gill had a heart attack.

"They [Maurice and Charles] never worked in another large company in any senior position, so they never had a ladder to climb," says Nicholas Crean, who was their personal assistant in the late 1970s and early 1980s. "They made their own ladder. They weren't aspiring to be one day on the board of a company, so they didn't think in terms of hierarchy. They could never understand the fuss people used to make about wanting to be directors of Garland-Compton, the advertising agency, or associate directors. Maurice and Charles were just Maurice and Charles. And because they were not particulary aware of hierarchies or position, they didn't have the trappings of what you would call corporate status."

Outside the business Charles maintained his lifestyle much as before: playing snooker with his friends one night a week, playing cards another, usually playing chess with Jeremy Sinclair in his office at lunchtime. His impatience and low threshold of boredom spilled into his private life too. He loved going to see films, but often walked out before the end. If he managed to see a film all the way through, he would bounce into the office the next day and enthusiastically insist that everyone go see the picture. He often went to the theater, but again seldom stayed for the final curtain. He was still a TV buff, insisting that his staff videotape serials such as "Star Trek," his favorite, so he could watch the show at home later. "If we forgot to record 'Star Trek,' it was like turning up at a presentation with the wrong material," says Nick Crean.

Charles made other odd demands on his staff. One night he went to the

Embassy Club on Bond Street, which was very popular in the 1970s with the younger set, of which by that stage Charles was at the upper reaches. The next day he gave Crean the task of getting all the records he had heard the previous night. Crean had to ring the club, get a list, then track the records down, even ordering some flown over from New York.

Being personal assistant to the brothers was an unusual job. Maurice would send Crean to the City to do some detailed research on potential acquisitions, combing through the Exchange Telegraph cards the way Martin Sorrell had done for James Gulliver. "You'd be doing this when Charles would ring up and say: 'Where are my records?' " says Crean.

The personal assistant also had to look after Charles Saatchi's dog, a schnauzer named Lulu who most days was brought into the office. The dog was Charles's rather than Doris's and contrasted oddly with the rest of his lifestyle. Some saw the schnauzer as a child substitute, but Charles, although fond of other people's children, never indicated regret that he had no children of his own. The switchboard operator normally had charge of Lulu during the day, but the personal assistant might be required to take her for walks or even mind her in the evenings.

This, then, was the brothers' lifestyle in the late 1970s; it was, at least on Charles's part, idiosyncratic perhaps, but many of the most successful people in business don't fit the conventions. Saatchi & Saatchi was clearly an unusual company by any standards, with talented young people running it in a way that had had a galvanizing effect on the whole industry. The Saatchis were much talked about in Adland and becoming better known, at least by reputation, in financial circles; but outside those worlds the name meant nothing.

However, in 1978 and 1979 something else was happening to the brothers and to their agency, something that would have a far greater effect on them than anything they had done so far. Among all the accounts they had taken on, one in particular was about to propel them into the public arena in a quite new way.

10
"LABOUR ISN'T WORKING"

The day, in early March 1978, that Saatchi & Saatchi won the Conservative party account neither Maurice nor Charles turned up. Nor did Tim Bell, who was to make his reputation running it. A young account executive was the only member of the Saatchi team who appeared on time at Conservative Central Office for the formal appointment to what was to be the most important account the agency would have.

Gordon Reece, just appointed by Margaret Thatcher as director of communications at Conservative Central Office, waited impatiently. Charles Saatchi, he had recently learned, would not appear—Charles simply never met clients and would not make an exception even for Margaret Thatcher. Reece had yet to lay eyes on him. Maurice, normally punctilious and prompt, was to represent the agency, but at the appointed time of 9:30 A.M. he was not there.

Reece had already cleared Saatchi & Saatchi's appointment with Mrs. Thatcher. The company meant nothing to her, and she had simply told Reece that if the agency was what he wanted, it was fine with her. However, it still had to be cleared formally by the party chairman, the august former Chancellor of the Exchequer, Lord Thorneycroft, who would have to pay the bills and was, strictly speaking, the client.

Reece had promised Thorneycroft that he would bring along for his approval the team that would be working with the party. Tim Bell would be running the account, but he was on vacation in the West Indies. In any case, Bell's name meant little even to Reece, who had simply identified Saatchi & Saatchi as the brightest and most suitable agency for the job.

Now Reece had only one junior account executive to show Thorneycroft. Reece decided he was not going "to bugger about waiting for Maurice Saatchi." He brought the young Saatchi executive in and introduced him to Lord Thorneycroft as "the top man who handles all these matters at Saatchi & Saatchi."

The meeting was something of a formality. Reece had already persuaded Thorneycroft that the party must have a proper advertising agency. Having made that decision, Thorneycroft was quite happy to leave the choice of agency to the professionals. The aristocratic old Etonian, a minister in Harold Macmillan's government, did not concern himself with the world of advertising. He nodded distantly as Reece and the Saatchi & Saatchi representative explained what they wanted to do and at the appropriate moment agreed that the account should indeed go to Saatchi's.

As they emerged from the office, a taxi drew up, and out bounded a flustered Maurice Saatchi, full of apologies, all primed to make his pitch. "Well, we've just finished, you can go home again," snapped Reece. "You've got the account."

For all this apparent casualness, the brothers were fully aware of the importance of working for the Conservatives. Vanni Treves met Ken Gill that day at the Carlton Club, and Gill was ecstatic that the account had been won. Treves could not understand what was so important about the account but was impressed by Gill's enthusiasm. Over lunch Gill explained that this was the first occasion that a British political party had hired an agency to run its advertising on a professional basis, that it was going to attract an enormous amount of publicity, and that it would establish Saatchi & Saatchi at a new level.

Even then both Gill and the Saatchi brothers wholly underestimated the impact that the new account would have on their lives, both private and business. Within six months the name Saatchi & Saatchi would be a household name closely identified with all that Mrs. Thatcher and her new-look Conservative party stood for, a key component in an election campaign that was almost certainly the most important in British politics since 1945.

It all began in February 1978, when Thatcher had summoned Gordon Reece back from California to help her prepare for an election that everyone assumed would take place later that year. Reece was forty-six years old, a professional TV producer who at that point was working for Dr. Armand Hammer in Los Angeles as a vice president of Occidental Oil, advising on publicity. Reece's role in the Saatchi & Saatchi story is a vital one, for without him the brothers would almost certainly never have gained the Tory party account, never have become so well known, and their task in New York a few years later would have been that much more daunting.

On the other hand, there are those, notably Reece, who would claim that without the Saatchis and their advertising campaign the result of the 1979 election might well have been different and so would the course of British political history. No one anticipated that the agency itself would become one of the issues not just of the forthcoming election but also of the two elections that followed in 1983 and 1987.

Reece's links with Margaret Thatcher go back to the 1970 British general election when, on a purely voluntary basis, he was responsible for the technical job of putting together the Conservative political broadcasts. A team of professional advertising people, led by Barry Day of McCann Erickson and Jim Garrett, a close friend of Edward Heath, wrote the broadcasts and produced the artwork, and they were filmed in a little studio in Soho. Reece, who had produced numerous TV programs in the 1960s ranging from "Emergency Ward 10" to series shows with Eamonn Andrews, Dave Allen, and Bruce Forsyth, acted as "a sort of editor, putting the whole thing together."

Thatcher was one of the Tory politicians filmed for the broadcasts, but the footage ended up on the cutting-room floor. By common consent, she was stilted and shrill, unable to project herself. When the Tories, led by Heath, unexpectedly won the June 1970 election, she became minister of education, and Reece, in partnership with the veteran BBC newscaster Cliff Michelmore, formed a videocassette company backed—and later acquired—by EMI. In the four years of the Heath government, Reece got to know her slightly, and then in 1974 Mrs. Thatcher, by now more proficient in public but still far from her eventual level of expertise, played a more prominent role in the two elections that took place that year, both of which the Tories lost. Again, Reece had the job of editing the party's political broadcasts and schooled Thatcher on how to present herself to the camera.

After the second defeat, in October, the move to replace Heath as leader gathered steam, with Sir Keith Joseph as the ostensible challenger from the right wing of the party. Reece, however, made another suggestion: Thatcher herself, the person who had once forecast that Britain would never see a woman prime minister in her lifetime. "I think that I was the first person to mention that she should run for the leadership of the party," said Reece. "She didn't want to do it—she wanted Keith Joseph. And it wasn't until Keith stepped down that she agreed to run."

Reece was given a leave of absence from EMI to help Mrs. Thatcher with her campaign. When she won, she asked him to stay on, and for the next three years he advised her on her public relations and appearance. Later, Reece's role in changing Thatcher's appearance would be greatly exaggerated, and he himself has always been loath to talk about it. But Thatcher aides are in no doubt of his contribution. He had some simple rules for her: it was important "not to wear a lot of fuss" on television. Edges looked good, but scoop necklines were out. The ideal outfit was a tunic dress with a shirt underneath.

Privately, Reece was offended by the image of himself as Mrs. Thatcher's private Norman Hartnell, "mincing around with a strategic powder puff," as one newspaper put it. He had *not* redone her hair—she had done that herself, advised by people far more expert in hairstyles than he was. But he *had* suggested that she have it done and guided her toward the right people to do it. Nor had he softened her voice. What he *had* done was urge her to act naturally, relax more in front of the cameras, follow her own political instincts. He had certainly schooled her in speaking into the microphone, getting her to slow down and talk more deliberately—made her "more effective," which was the whole object of the exercise. "It was really straightforward editing stuff," says one of the people involved. "He corrected her as a director would correct any performer, making her redo things, showing her how to act in front of the camera."

Later the belief that Saatchi & Saatchi had restyled and repackaged Mrs. Thatcher became almost unshakable, and the brothers, although pointing out the real story in private, did little to discourage this mistaken belief. It became part of folklore, to be denied when it was damaging but generally to be enjoyed, particularly after Mrs. Thatcher began winning elections. The truth, of course, is that advising on Thatcher's appearance was never part of Saatchi & Saatchi's job, and the changes had already occurred before it appeared on the scene.

In her years as leader of the opposition Mrs. Thatcher came to rely heavily on Reece, and he in turn was said to regard her with "near veneration." His influence during these years in opposition was considerable. "If there is such a thing as Thatcherism, Reece, because of what he did in 1975–80, is at least partly responsible," wrote one newspaper. His work attracted a considerable amount of flak and even ridicule: Mrs. Thatcher, it was said, was being molded by the media and was no longer entirely herself. However, that criticism did not last long; once she became prime minister, it was replaced by complaints that she was too strong a character, dominating a cabinet of yes-men.

Reece was born in Liverpool in 1930, the son of a car salesman. He went to school at a Roman Catholic establishment, Ratcliffe, where he was known as a devout Catholic, sometimes visiting churches up to four times on a Sunday, largely to hear the Mass sung. "Church services," he would enthuse, "are so wonderful that they ought to charge for them." At other times he would forecast that "religion is the coming thing. People are ready for it."

He graduated from Cambridge with a law degree and went into newspapers, working for the Staffordshire *Evening Sentinel* in Stoke, the *Liverpool Post*, and for a brief period the *Sunday Express*. In the early 1960s he made a critical break into TV. Now in 1978 Thatcher had brought him into Central Office in a key role, and Reece immediately began making changes. One of his first moves, he decided, would be to find an advertising agency to replace the voluntary efforts that had been used before.

Reece was a man of some style. Slight and dapper, always immaculate, with pocket handkerchiefs matching his ties, well-cut suits complete with watch chain, and an ever-present cigar, he was referred to variously as the "image maker" or more often, in what became a well-worn Fleet Street cliché, the "champagne-tippling Svengali." He certainly liked his champagne, preferably one of the better vintages. Lord McAlpine, the

Tory treasurer, still tells the story of how Lady Janet Young, then deputy chairman to Thorneycroft, complained that it was disgusting the way Reece spent so much in expenses on champagne, and it must be stopped.

"Do you have a car, Janet?" McAlpine asked.

"Yes, a small one."

"But you have to buy gas for it. You see, if you have a Gordon Reece, you have to run him on champagne."

Unknown to either Maurice or Charles, Reece had come across Charles's work before. In the late 1960s Reece was making a TV commercial when the client, the *Daily Mail*, decided it wanted a different slant, some new writing. "And they hired a strange person by the name of Saatchi who had his own creative shop. And he was jolly good."

Reece thought no more about Charles's involvement in the *Daily Mail* campaign until a decade later when he began his search for an advertising agency to work for the Conservatives. It had never been done before by any party, but Reece had learned a great deal from his time in the United States and wanted to import some of the techniques used so successfully by presidents Johnson and Nixon. There was—and is—one crucial difference between promoting politicians in Britain and in the United States; in the latter, a party can simply buy time on television or radio (there is no limit in either country on newspaper or poster advertising), but in Britain the political parties are allotted, free of charge, a set number of political broadcasts. Even within these constraints Reece had persuaded Thatcher that a bright, creative agency could make all the difference for her campaign.

Until 1978 the Tories, like Labour, had relied for political broadcasts on the voluntary contributions of supporters in the advertising industry. That by no means meant that the ads were bad. Barry Day and Jim Garrett in 1970 had studied the advertising in the Nixon-Humphrey race of 1967 and made a series of party election broadcasts for Ted Heath in 1970, featuring anchors Geoffrey Johnson-Smith and Chris Chattaway, both Tory MPs and broadcasters. These broadcasts marked a major change in TV promotion of political parties and probably contributed to Heath's unexpected victory. Day had been particularly impressed by one ad in the Johnson campaign, made by Bill Bernbach, which showed a small girl picking the petals off a flower while the soundtrack used the countdown to a nuclear blast—a reference to Barry Goldwater's hardline policy. The techniques of commercial advertising became an accepted part of electoral communications in the United States in the 1960s, and Day in 1970 used some of these techniques in projecting the Tories. It was, says Day, "the first *conscious* effort to use the established techniques of commercial marketing on the British political scene." The Tories did employ an agency, Colman Prentis & Varley, but only for posters and newspaper advertising, which were at that stage not much talked about, while Day and his team wrote the broadcasts that were finally edited by Reece.

The same team had been involved again in the two elections of 1974, but by then no one, including Day, was pleased with the product. Too many people had become involved in the process of making the ads, and the 1974 Tory campaigns were essentially gloomy affairs. Reece wanted a new approach.

"I've always thought a committee approach to running a political campaign is a very bad idea," he says. "One of the reasons is that they're all chiefs and there isn't a single Indian there. And when you end up trying to get rid of someone it's the Battle of Hastings, because he resigns in a huff and you have to explain it to the newspapers and it becomes a major cause célèbre. If you've got an agency, you simply tell the managing director to change a chap because you don't get on with him, and he is changed."

Saatchi & Saatchi, says Reece, virtually picked itself to handle the Thatcher campaign of 1978. Reece had to have an agency that was big enough to have muscle but not so big that it wasn't hungry. "You wanted somebody who said, 'God, we could get really famous if we did this properly.' " He also decided that the agency had to be one "whose talent was on the creative side, not the media-buying side," because unlike in the United States, there was no media buying involved in British politics. Finally, he thought the agency should be British, which ruled out most of the competition.

Reece soon settled on Saatchi & Saatchi. The reputations of Tim Bell, Jeremy Sinclair, and of course Charles now stood very high in the industry. A friend of Reece's, Terry Donovan, the photographer and director of commercials (and the man with the electric-windowed Rolls-Royce that Charles had envied in the Golden Square days), told Reece that he must talk to Charles, so Reece called the agency. "I want to see Charles Saatchi; when will it be convenient?" The reply was instantaneous: "This morning."

When Reece arrived at Charlotte Street there was no sign of Charles, and it would be another six months before Reece saw him; he did see Maurice, who greeted him courteously on the sixth floor. Reece did not know enough about the brothers to understand Charles's reticence, but he was happy enough to meet at least one of the Saatchis. Reece announced to Maurice that he was no longer willing to make do with a few volunteers to run the advertising for the Tory party. He wanted an agency to handle the account, and he had narrowed the list down to two; he didn't name the other candidate.

Reece never did have two agencies in mind. He had toyed with the idea of the Masius Wynne-Williams agency, but it was more renowned for its ability at media buying than its creativity. "I didn't want a beauty parade," Reece says now. "I can't understand why any company in its right mind asks agencies to pitch. The best work goes into the pitch and is therefore wasted. Anyway, as far as I was concerned here was this wonderful agency, and I went down into the engine room to see who was running it. I had heard about this chap Tim Bell, who was so frightfully clever, but he wasn't there." Reece asked to meet all the people who would be working on the account and was introduced to Jeremy Sinclair, Andrew Rutherford, a copywriter, and few others. "I met all these people, but Bell didn't show up. 'Obviously there is some reason he won't be working on this account,' I thought."

"These are the people, are they?" Reece asked. Maurice nodded. Even without Bell and Charles, Reece was impressed. The more he saw, the more he decided here was the place to go. "There was a dynamism about the place. It was the coiled spring, the kettle bubbling. I felt I had to get them appointed."

Charles and Maurice easily saw through Reece's ploy about the second agency. Once they knew what he wanted, they realized there was no other agency that fit the specifications as well as Saatchi and Saatchi. The account was theirs—if they wanted it.

In Barbados that same day Tim Bell had a phone call from Charles. "What do you think?" Charles asked. Bell didn't think much of the account at all. "It's a bad idea," he told Charles. "It will be completely disruptive to the whole agency. I don't think we should do it."

Bell had been a young media buyer at Colman Prentis when *it* had handled just a part of the Tory party account, and he had seen the problems running a campaign caused for the agency at election time. "I knew perfectly well it would fall to me to run the business, because Charles and Maurice didn't handle accounts. I reckoned it would be tremendously disruptive," Bell recalls, "and I didn't think it was worth any money. I was just vaguely negative about the whole thing, but they were extremely enthusiastic, particularly because Gordon Reece was asking them to take on the account without even having to make a pitch."

Maurice's interest in politics at the time was, by his own admission, "above average" but no more, and his immediate reaction to Reece's proposal was a commercial one. Saatchi & Saatchi, he said, was certainly interested in the account but would not act on a voluntary basis. It would run the Tory ad campaign the same way it would run any other account, although obviously it would assign its best people to the campaign and at election time would give the campaign all the commitment needed. But theirs would be a professional relationship—Saatchi & Saatchi would have to be paid. However, Reece recalls Maurice saying, "We would like it very much; and we are all Conservatives."

Bell was by far the most politically involved of the team. "I was a very committed Conservative, but it's not something I ever discussed with the brothers. We never talked politics at all. We were businessmen influenced by the political environment, and it never occurred to us to think about how we could influence the politicians." Now he was being given that opportunity and was less than enthusiastic.

By the time Bell arrived back in London Thorneycroft had confirmed Saatchi's appointment. Sure enough, Charles and Maurice asked Bell to handle the account. Bell was now warming to the prospect, picking up some of the enthusiasm the brothers were generating. "I'd be delighted," he said. Reece was anxious to recover from the first meeting and was insistent that the whole team, particularly Bell, parade before the party chairman as soon as possible, so they all went down to Central Office to start work. They gathered in a meeting room downstairs, and Reece brought Thorneycroft in. It was there that Reece met Tim Bell for the first time. "And of course he was brilliant, absolutely brilliant," he says.

That day there was nothing for Bell to present, but he was already bubbling with ideas. Reece wanted a party political broadcast to go out on TV in April, only a month away, so time was pressing. He also had other ideas, which he bounced off Bell. "We had a major political problem," Reece says. "The Labour government had been unpopular for some time, but we all believed an election would come that autumn. I was sure of it. And my experience of politics was that during the summertime governments do extraordinarily well, particularly if it's warm. People say, 'Things aren't so bad, perhaps we shouldn't have a change, perhaps we should leave things as they are.' Therefore I wanted to have a campaign right in the middle of summer, hit them with everything we'd got in August. But it was now March, and it takes three months at least for an agency to pick up. I wanted to get things moving quickly."

Back in Charlotte Street, Bell and the team set to work. Even as they started, the polls suddenly showed a fall in support for the Conservatives, putting the Callaghan government (which had been elected in 1976) ahead for the first time in two years. Labour, which had appeared dead only months before, was recovering. Living standards were improving. The government had survived cuts in public expenditure and defeats on key parliamentary votes. Conservative morale was sagging.

It was against this background that Saatchi & Saatchi's first broadcast for the Tory party appeared in the spring of 1978. Saatchi had come up with a novel idea for attracting extra interest: they ran a "teaser" in the tabloid press with the message that if one missed television at nine o'clock that night one would regret it for the rest of one's life. The teaser would have been far more effective if the name of the advertiser had been left off, but the law in Britain requires the name to appear; nonetheless, the teaser attracted the interest the Saatchi team was looking for.

The ad itself was Saatchi at its most creative. Scripted largely by Jeremy Sinclair, it depicted everything in Britain going backward. There were shots of people walking backward over Waterloo Bridge; of Stephenson's rocket steaming backward; of the Comet, the world's first jetliner (and British-built), landing in reverse; of climbers inching their way *down* Mount Everest, and so on.

"This country was once the finest nation on earth," intoned the voice-over. "We are famous for our freedom, justice, and fair play. Our inventions brought the world out of the Middle Ages to industrial prosperity.

"Today we are famous for discouraging people from getting to the top. Famous for not rewarding skill, talent, and effort.

"In a word, Britain is going backward."

The final sequence showed Michael Heseltine delivering the line: "Backwards or forwards because we can't go on as we are. Don't just hope for a better life—vote for one."

It was slick, fast-moving, and attention-catching. The short takes of different politicians, often just delivering one line, had never been used before: the public had been accustomed to seeing "talking heads" on its political parties' broadcasts. The viewers found the Saatchi approach to be more fun.

Although there is no evidence that it shifted the Tory ratings, what the ad did do was suddenly raise the profile of Saatchi & Saatchi—and Gordon Reece. The Labour party machine was discomfited by the ad's professionalism, although publicly Labour's reaction was to complain that the Tories were selling soap rather than policies. Behind the scenes, however, there was a wave of disquiet in the Labour camp. On April 4, 1978, Labour's adviser on political advertising, Edward Booth-Clibborn, sent Callaghan a memorandum, setting out his concern at the presence of Charles Saatchi in the opposing camp. "Saatchi & Saatchi are not only London's fastest-growing and most successful agency in financial terms, they are also a force to be reckoned with in the execution of the work they undertake," he concluded. Callaghan does not seem to have been overly impressed at the time, although later he may have changed his mind.

Tim Bell and his team were now hard at work. There was a considerable amount of research to be done, and a team went off to the United States to study the impact of advertising on the Nixon victories of 1968 and 1972 and Carter's victory in 1976. What lessons were there for Thatcher in those campaigns? Inside the agency Bell and his team conducted a series of group discussions designed to identify what Bell calls "the emotional attitudes that emerge when ordinary people discuss politics." There were hours of discussion about finding the right tone for the ads, which had to be "warm, confident, nondivisive—and exciting," and analysis of what all these adjectives actually meant. There was quantitative research and quality research, much talk about "directional signals," "target areas," how to attract women voters, skilled workers, and much else.

Charles Saatchi may not have wanted to meet the client, but that did not mean he was uninvolved. Bell recalls: "He was wonderful to work with; superb ideas were popping out all the time. It was a little bit like the early days of the agency when it was Charles, Maurice, Jeremy, and me doing things. There were lots of other people helping now, but it was like the old team working together on a twenty-four-hour basis. It was wonderful." One day Maurice said to Reece: "Haven't you met Charles?" Maurice took him across the corridor, and at last the two men met. Reece felt he had been signally honored.

In the middle of it all Mrs. Thatcher decided to honor her new agency with a visit. The whole team—with the exception of Charles—gathered in a ground-floor conference room to receive her, while Bell waited outside on the steps. First the security car drew up, then Mrs. Thatcher's car. Bell ushered her out and into the building, where she gazed around at the reception area hung with blow-ups of some of the Saatchi ads.

Mrs. Thatcher had developed a Jimmy Carter–style habit of greeting people with "Good morning, I'm Margaret Thatcher" and a proffered handshake, and she began working her way through the Saatchi reception area. A rep from a newspaper on his way to the media department was flabbergasted to be suddenly confronted by her. Shakily he accepted her hand. She finally arrived in the conference room. "Good morning, I'm Margaret Thatcher," she greeted Jeremy Sinclair. "Good morning, I'm Jeremy Sinclair," was all he could reply. From that moment on Sinclair was a fan—and would write some of his best ads for her.

Later, as the Thatcher party was leaving, Lord Thorneycroft gazed about in wonder at the display of cars parked in the Saatchi basement. The full panoply of the brothers' favorite hobby was on show. Maurice's two Mini-mokes were there, as well as some of the other cars the Saatchis owned. Other Saatchi & Saatchi executives, including Bell, had caught the bug too, and the brothers were generous when it came to rewarding them with flashy cars. In between the Ferraris and the Aston Martins was a Jeep, which Charles had driven in that morning. On the front was a large grid, which the chairman of the Conservative party stared at for a moment. "Who drives that?" he asked. Someone explained that the Jeep belonged to Charles. Thorneycroft grunted. "I didn't know you got many stray cows in Hampstead."

The Saatchi team was now preparing what would be the most controversial ad they would ever make and almost certainly their single most notable contribution toward Mrs. Thatcher's election campaign. Reece was well advanced on his plans for a summer advertising splash, designed to unsettle Labour in the summer recess and to stem, or even reverse, its rise in the polls. The Liberal-Labour pact was falling apart, and an autumn election looked more and more likely. Thorneycroft was against a campaign, insisting that no one would be around in the summer, it would be expensive, and it would serve no useful purpose. Alastair McAlpine, unflappable as ever, promised Reece he would find the money somewhere. Mrs. Thatcher allowed Reece his head.

In June Tim Bell was due to make his first presentation to Mrs. Thatcher, and the Saatchi creative department under Jeremy Sinclair worked feverishly on a series of posters. It was Andy Rutherford, a wizened, bespectacled copywriter, who one Sunday morning wrote the poster that would match the impact made by the "pregnant man" nearly a decade before. Rutherford had been asked to concentrate on the economy and industry, and, noting the increase in unemployment that year, he hit on the line: "Labour isn't working." All the ad needed was a long unemployment line and it would work very neatly, he thought. He roughed it out with some others and brought it in to show Charles Saatchi, Tim Bell, and Jeremy Sinclair. Charles and Sinclair, he thought, would instantly see its subtlety and impact. Instead, their reaction was lukewarm.

"They quite liked it," says Rutherford, "but they preferred other posters I had done and, even worse, posters other people had done." Rutherford's poster was put into a pile of "possibles," with a decision to be made definitely the next day. "I guessed what that meant," says Rutherford. "It would be given the old heave-ho when I wasn't looking." He got into the office early the next morning and slipped into the room where the posters had been sorted. Sure enough, his "Labour isn't working" was in the "out" pile, just as he had suspected. Quickly he moved it into the "in" pile.

Reece was given a preview of the posters, and he stopped at Rutherford's when Bell came to it. The poster now showed a line of workers snaking out from an unemployment office and disappearing into the distance. The title "Labour isn't working" stood out boldly, with underneath, in much smaller type, "Britain's better off with the Tories." This was the ad Reece wanted.

"That's a wonderful ad," he told Bell. "Keep it for the last, put it at the end."

The presentation took place in the opposition leader's room in the House of Commons. Margaret Thatcher was never an easy person to present to, and Bell barely knew her. He took her through the poster ads Saatchi's had prepared, then with a flourish produced "Labour isn't working." Thatcher gazed at it for a long time. "Wonderful!" she said. It would be the poster the Tories would go with in August.

Bell soon found it was not to be as simple as that. "I had the most awful battle getting the Party's approval," he said later. "The objection was that since few people would actually read the copy beneath the title the effect of including the name of the Labour party in the title would be counterproductive. Yet whatever the veracity of this argument the poster will probably go down in history as one of the most effective political posters ever produced."

When the ads appeared, government ministers hit the roof. Denis Healey, the Chancellor of the Exchequer, complained bitterly about the tactics, and in the silly season that summer the press took up the story, giving it front-page news coverage. The story ran in the newspapers every day for a week, with photographs of the poster and attacks on it from Labour. "The extraordinary thing is we didn't run it much," says Reece of the ad. "I think we only spent about £50,000 on it; it probably went up on only twenty sites, but it became the most famous poster in the country. The mileage we got out of it was incredible—so much so that it became a sort of lead for all stories about the campaign and the work of Saatchi & Saatchi."

Healey came out with the revelation that the unemployed workers were not real workers at all but Saatchi employees. This caused a further storm. Saatchi & Saatchi was able to deny it, creating yet further publicity. "It was absolutely untrue," says Bell of Healey's statement. But those in the ad were not genuine unemployed people either. "The truth is that they were Young Conservatives from South Hendon." Not that it mattered anyway: Reece and Saatchi & Saatchi had achieved far more than they ever imagined. "Healey made a great song and dance and it [the ad] got shown on every television broadcast," says Bell. "Then it got shown on discussion programs. It must have had £5 million worth of free publicity."

But did the poster work? Many claimed so, and it may even have been a powerful influence on Callaghan. In early September all the polls showed the Conservatives ahead by between 2 percent and 7 percent. The summer had not brought the swing in support to the government that had occurred in twelve of the previous eighteen years. "The government's failure to advance was attributed in part to the skill of the large-scale Conservative advertising campaign, 'Labour isn't working,' in August mounted by their advertising agents Saatchi & Saatchi," said David Butler and Dennis Cavanagh, two of Britain's leading political academics, in their book on the 1979 election.

When parliament went into recess at the end of July 1978, some members who were not running again were so convinced that an election would come in the autumn that they cleared their filing cabinets and gave farewell parties. Without a majority in parliament, few could see how Callaghan could get through the vote that always follows the Queen's Speech, the first business of parliament when it resumed in the autumn. By the end of the recess, the first week of September, the Saatchi team had its whole campaign worked out.

It was then that the skills of Maurice came into their own. On strategic matters Bell deferred to him. So did Charles. "Maurice is a brilliantly talented man at understanding communications strategies," says Bell.

"He doesn't have great political flair. I would be very good at saying what the politicians thought and how they thought it was going, and he would be very good at ignoring that and saying, 'Fine. Well, they don't know what they're talking about—now let's work out a good communications strategy.' "

The strategy that emerged came under the slogan "Time for a change," which Saatchi & Saatchi actually copied from the former Australian Labour prime minister Gough Whitlam, though it was far from original: the phrase has probably been used in one form or another in elections since Roman days.

Maurice was off and running. From the earliest days of the agency, he and Charles had developed a technique for reducing new accounts to an easy, logical flow, using the simplest of words and as few of them as possible. It was a technique much favored by Michael Heseltine, who had influenced Maurice, and greatly pleased Charles, with his short attention span and unwillingness to read long documents. Maurice produced a document setting out the combined thoughts of the team after hours of discussion and research; the report covered a single sheet of paper. It started with the deceptively simple proposition that "governments lose elections, oppositions don't win them" and that everything therefore had to be aimed at increasing the level of dissatisfaction, or in other words turning the original proposition around to one of "oppositions win elections by ensuring that governments lose."

"Thatcherism" was at that stage ill-defined, and the Saatchi & Saatchi team spent hours trying to work out clearly what the message of Mrs. Thatcher's campaign was to be. That too was carefully defined in Maurice's document: a Conservative vote would be a vote for freedom, choice, opportunity, small government, prosperity. "The notion was that if you asked people what a vote for the Tories means, they would snap out with an answer that in some ways reflects these associations," says Bell. "We weren't talking about incomes policies or tax cuts or industrial-relations legislation or public expenditure. We were talking about the emotional meaning of a Conservative vote."

Maurice explained to Gordon Reece that he didn't really know if he was writing this document on behalf of the Conservatives or because Saatchi & Saatchi thought it was a good philosophy (he didn't really know whose philosophy it was); but it was the best and most simple exposition Saatchi & Saatchi's team could devise of what they believed the Conservatives and Mrs. Thatcher could and did stand for. Maurice remembers Reece reading it and exclaiming, "Well, if you can convince people of that, that's it."

Maurice waited for the document to be shredded and the full anger of the Tory party machine to point out to him that he had woefully misinterpreted "Thatcherism." To his astonishment, nothing of the kind happened. "Somehow the whole thing seemed to be accepted and it sailed through," says one Saatchi executive. Looking back he now sees Maurice's one-page analysis as "a very good exposition of what has now become known as Thatcherism." That exposition became the basis on which the 1978 campaign was prepared.

It was around this time that Gordon Reece suddenly discovered how Lord Alastair McAlpine intended to finance the summer advertising campaign. McAlpine went to see Maurice and asked him how much was owed Saatchi & Saatchi. Maurice replied that the figure was up to about half a million pounds.

"Phew," said McAlpine. "We haven't got that amount. Now, we're entirely in your hands. We can pay you in a year's time. There won't be any interest, of course." Saatchi & Saatchi was a big enough agency to carry the debt—just—but it made a dent in that year's figures.

As the summer wore on, everyone waited on Jim Callaghan. When the furor over the "Labour isn't working" ad was at its height, Callaghan was on his farm in Sussex helping with the harvest—and making up his mind what to do. Should he go for an autumn election or wait for spring? He wouldn't have to call an election until October 1979 if he could muster a majority in parliament. He had promised to tell his cabinet colleagues of his decision when they held their first meeting after the recess on September 6. Although most of the advice he got favored the spring, his own Labour machine was gearing up for an election in late September or early October. At Conservative Central Office and at Charlotte Street there was even greater activity. Saatchi & Saatchi had to have a campaign ready to go the instant Callaghan signaled the election was on—as everyone assumed he would do in the first week of September.

Callaghan later revealed that he made the decision in August to delay the election until the spring of 1979, choosing April 5, the last day of the tax year, as the likeliest date. A few days later, on August 18, he invited himself to tea at Denis Healey's house nearby. "It was a lovely summer's day and we sat in the garden while I told him what I had decided," Callaghan recalls. The rest of the country was left guessing.

When Callaghan addressed the Trade Unions Congress at Brighton on September 5 the press, his own aides, and certainly the Conservatives still expected him to announce an autumn election. Instead he was ambiguous, singing a little tune about leaving the bride waiting at the church and leaving everyone still uncertain. He was playing right into Tory hands. "I made a mistake in allowing the speculation to build up almost to a feverish crescendo without uttering a word to cool it," he said later.

On September 7 Callaghan made a TV broadcast and announced his decision: "I shall not be calling an election at this time." It was a surprise everywhere. In Central Office there was rejoicing: the political strategists there reckoned the Tories would lose in October but would win in the spring. There was, according to Butler and Cavanagh, "some self-congratulation at Central Office among those who had sponsored the Saatchi & Saatchi advertising, which perhaps had checked any adverse tide during August and September." Reece remembers the atmosphere in Central Office as something more: "There was wild cheering that you felt could be heard for miles around."

At Charlotte Street there was no celebration. Jeremy Sinclair, working at his desk preparing another ad for the campaign, kept an eye on the TV in the corner of the room. When Callaghan made his announcement, Sinclair threw his pen down disgustedly, desperately deflated. Bell remembers being "savagely depressed," and it was forty-eight hours before the team could pick itself up and get going again.

As events were to turn out, there is little doubt that Callaghan made a disastrous blunder in not going to the country in the autumn. Within a month of Callaghan's broadcast the polls had swung back to favor Labour, and by November he was 5.5 percentage points ahead. Margaret Thatcher herself has since voiced the view that she would probably have lost that autumn, and there was little confidence in Central Office that the Tories could pull it off. No one, of course, could have forecast the "winter of discontent" that followed, with the unions humiliating the Callaghan government and sweeping aside the incomes policy under which Callaghan tried to hold wage settlements down to a maximum of 5 percent. The dam broke when Ford made an offer in line with the government guidelines; its workers instantly went on strike and after three weeks settled at 15 percent. When Callaghan sought powers to impose sanctions on Ford, the government was defeated by 285 votes to 283, although it won a vote of confidence the next day. Now settlement after settlement broke the 5 percent guidelines. When striking technicians threatened to put the BBC off the air over Christmas, they received a settlement of 15 percent, bringing forth the bitter comment from a Callaghan aide, "We sold our pay policy to have *The Sound of Music* on Christmas Day."

The public sector, taking its lead from the BBC, now erupted. There were walkouts, militant picketing, and violence by oil-tanker drivers, all of them in pursuit of wage claims the economy could not afford. In Liverpool local government workers refused to bury the dead. In London three trade-union members were dismissed for allegedly switching off hospital boilers in the middle of January, and local officials called a strike of the whole hospital. Local government manual workers put in a claim for a 40 percent raise. Violence flared on picket lines all over the country in the worst winter weather for years. Settlements in the private sector rose into double figures, sparking a fresh wave of demand from hospital and other public-sector workers. On January 22, 1979, over a million local government workers staged a day of action, the biggest one-day stoppage since the 1926 general strike.

Callaghan himself made a further fateful error on January 10 at the height of the picketing and strikes when he returned from a world summit in Guadeloupe where he had been much photographed talking to President Carter. Badly briefed and jet-lagged, Callaghan gave an impromptu press conference at the airport, saying, "I don't think that other people in the world would share the view that there is mounting chaos." This statement was instantly misquoted as "Crisis? What crisis?" which Callaghan never actually said but which became an unshakable part of the story (the misquote now turns up in game shows). Mrs. Thatcher immediately came forward with proposed reforms of the trade unions, which Saatchi & Saatchi turned into a party political broadcast for January 17.

As spring approached, it became clear that Callaghan's gamble had misfired badly. It was only a matter of time before he was defeated in parliament, and he would not have the option of calling an election when he wanted, an invaluable tool in the hands of any prime minister. The rate of inflation was beginning to rise again as the wage settlements came through, and Callaghan's own self-confidence had been shaken by the refusal of the unions to cooperate with a Labour government.

In the end, it was the Scottish National Party that forced the issue by putting down its own vote of censure over the question of Scottish devolution. The Tories latched onto it, and on March 28 Callaghan was defeated in the House of Commons by a single vote: 311 to 310. It was the first time since 1924, when the minority government of Ramsay MacDonald was outvoted, that a government had been defeated on an issue of confidence. Under the British constitution, an election had to be called.

The Saatchi campaign, originally designed for an October election, had long been reshaped for a spring poll. Callaghan called a short campaign, which suited the Tories perfectly. The Saatchi election campaign team moved out of Charlotte Street to a separate office at the back, where they had tight security and were well away from other clients and those not involved in the campaign. It was around-the-clock work. The day was a punishing one: all the newspapers would be delivered at the team members' homes, plus a digest of the press, at two in the morning. They also got a video reel of the previous day's television coverage, which the whole team looked at every morning at six o'clock. There would be a meeting at 7:30 and a press conference at nine. They would meet Mrs. Thatcher at about ten before she went off on her day's tour. Then they would have the rest of the day to get on with their work, prepare ads, get the print production done, buy the space in the newspapers, and get the party election broadcasts (PEBs) together. Then they would meet again at six each evening, and there would be another meeting at ten.

This would be by far the easiest of the three campaigns that Saatchi & Saatchi worked on for the Tories. By 1983 it was defending a government that had been in power for four years, and in 1987 for eight years. In 1979 Mrs. Thatcher was the opposition leader, and the worst that could happen was that she could end up in opposition again. There was little talk of majorities, as there was in the later two elections: the main interest was to win, even by a handful of votes.

Those who worked on the first campaign remember it with affection. "It's classically the way an account should be handled," says one of the campaign team. "You have an account person who looks after the account—that was Tim. You have a creative department, led by Charles and Jeremy—and Charles was very involved, much more so than anyone thinks. And you have a wise mind that you go to with everything that you're doing, and that was Maurice. It was a terrific team effort, twenty-four-hours-a-day, seven-days-a-week stuff, with three or four hours' sleep, often in the office."

Reece came in every day and examined what they were doing. "Do you think that will work?" he would question. "OK—then let's do it." Reece and the Saatchi team developed a close working relationship that was never repeated in later elections. "Gordon understands imagery," says one of the Saatchi workers. "What we brought was the concept of imagery, as opposed to words. Politicians live off words, and they don't think about imagery." Bell and Reece continued to use the lessons they had learned from the United States, not just on advertising but on polling and campaign techniques, and on one occasion organized a youth rally, persuading pop stars and show-biz people to come along, the first time that had been done in Britain.

"Gordon was sitting there saying, give me more, more new ideas, let's do new things," says Bell. "And of course you can do that in opposition because you've no history. There was no point in discussing what was done in 1974 because we lost in 1974. And in 1970 there was a different leader, and we were now in a different set of circumstances and could try new things."

Yet in the end, for all the energy, creative work, professionalism, and new ideas, how much did the Saatchi campaign contribute to Mrs. Thatcher's victory on May 3?

Of the five Conservative television broadcasts used in the campaign itself, the first four had been made before Callaghan called the election; there were another three that were never used at all. The final, fifth, broadcast, was videotaped and featured only Margaret Thatcher talking straight into the camera. None approached the originality and effective-ness of the earlier broadcasts, as both Bell and Reece later admitted. "I'm convinced that the television work we did in this build-up was twice as effective as our work in the campaign itself," wrote Bell a year later. The first broadcast of the campaign, a satirical film showing runners on a track, with the British bogged down hopelessly by weights labeled "inflation" and "taxes," went down badly with the party faithful in the country. Reece defended this ad on the grounds that it was aimed at the floating voter, but a number of the staff in Central Office thought it "inappropriate." The second broadcast was not much better: it used the "What Crisis?" theme (ignoring the fact that Callaghan had never said those words), concentrating on the winter of discontent with shots of rubbish in the streets, empty supermarkets, graves undug, hospitals picketed, and so forth. Like the first, it was flippant and was not a success. Although the Labour broadcasts were made on a shoestring, they were proving more effective. "The Labour broadcasts judged the mood of the electorate better," admitted Bell. "They were more serious; they were more to the point; they had more gravitas in them than our work. We recognized what was wrong, and as the campaign continued we changed the tonal quality of the work."

According to Butler and Cavanagh: "The sober style of the Labour broadcasts with their deliberate emphasis on statesmanship and 'authority' contrasted sharply with the rather gimmicky style of the first two Conservative ones, and the audience appreciation figures for the Labour broadcasts (which cost only £50,000) were markedly higher than those for the Conservatives."

The party's private polls on the broadcasts were at times dismaying. The third and fourth ads featured Lord Thorneycroft, on the grounds that he would provide "style"—a theme that Saatchi & Saatchi had been developing in some of the precampaign broadcasts, one of which had been entirely devoted to a speech by Harold Macmillan to the Young Conservatives Annual Conference and which Tim Bell reckoned was one of the best speeches he had ever seen. Everyone was astonished to find that Lord Thorneycroft's broadcast was the highest-rated of the whole campaign.

Yet somehow all five lacked the spark of the earlier efforts. Reece wasn't too worried. "By that time they had won the war. There were some hiccups during the campaign, as there always are, but, yes, the party politicals weren't their best. They were very good indeed by comparison with a lot of others in the past, but they weren't up to the standard that we had come to expect." The Saatchi & Saatchi team members had learned that making party politicals in "peacetime" and making them during actual campaigns can be very different. The electorate, they discovered, takes its elections seriously. This was a lesson Saatchi & Saatchi would not forget.

The posters and newspaper ads were more effective. "Labour isn't working" was revived as "Labour still isn't working," and Saatchi & Saatchi had another poster, "Cheer up! Labour can't hang on forever," that had actually been prepared before the winter of discontent and was ideal for the new circumstances. There was no doubt that the Conservatives won the press and poster war, but they spent much more too: £250,000 on posters to Labour's £112,000.

Election day itself gave Mrs. Thatcher a resounding victory; she gained two million more votes than Labour and enjoyed the largest margin between the two parties recorded since the war—5.2 percent. Afterward there was much analysis to attempt to identify just how much the Saatchi advertising campaign had helped, but by then it no longer mattered. Even those who had worked on the Labour campaign, such as Tim Delaney of Leagas Delaney Advertising, warned that it was "important for Labour party officials to realize that what Saatchi & Saatchi have done for the Tories is not to sell them like soap powder, but rather to produce the cohesion needed, first, to create a professional communications strategy and then, secondly, to make it work." The Labour party took some of those lessons to heart in later elections, particularly in 1987.

It was time for celebration. Mrs. Thatcher held a party at 10 Downing Street for all those who had helped her get there. Maurice Saatchi, Jeremy Sinclair, and Tim Bell went. Charles Saatchi stayed away. He did not intend to be rude. He simply did not go to parties unless they were given by a few very close friends; and he did not meet any client—even if she was the prime minister.

11
BELL: THE PARTING OF THE WAYS

One of Tim Bell's most prized possessions is a letter of thanks from Margaret Thatcher. He also has a photograph on his wall signed, "From Margaret, with love," given to him at the same time. For Bell they are visible symbols of the fact that he, more than anyone else at Saatchi & Saatchi, had been the one behind the advertising campaign that helped put her in Number 10.

The publicity attached to the campaign boosted Bell's already rising career. In the London advertising world and among the clients, Bell was seen as the person running the Saatchi business. Although it carried the names of the brothers, the agency on Charlotte Street was Tim Bell's shop, with Charles and Maurice seldom seen by either clients or staff. With the takeover of Compton in 1975, Bell had moved his office to the ground floor of Charlotte Street, and from there he ran the agency. With the departure of Ron Rimmer, his nearest rival for head of the agency was Ron Leagas, who was promoted to managing director of the agency in 1978, the same year that Bell was made chairman. Leagas, however, lasted only two years in his position. In 1980 he left to found his own agency, and Bell took over as both chairman and managing director.

The distance between the ground floor and the sixth, where the brothers were, became something more than physical during these years. Bell still referred to himself as "the third brother," but now the phrase had a more plaintive sound to it. The Saatchis' eyes were more and more fixed on the United States, on acquisitions, on creating an international network. Saatchi was beginning to play a much more strategic and financial role than that to which the brothers had been accustomed, and it was Martin Sorrell rather than Tim Bell who would join them more and more in their private thinking. Charles still watched over the agency like a hawk, pouncing on any creative work he didn't like, still shredding artwork not up to his standards; but by the early 1980s Saatchi & Saatchi had become a large business, and Bell, although he was reluctant to accept the fact, had not kept pace with the growth and was further and further removed from the strategic thinking.

"Tim was up on the top floor, chatting, most days," recalls Martin Sorrell. "Like most people in the advertising business—probably most people in life—he was very insecure; he needed continual boosting and reassurance, massaging and reinforcement. The sixth floor was a wonderful working environment, with what I used to refer to as 'corridor conversations,' where things got done. But it could be very frustrating if you didn't happen to be in the corridor when the conversation took place." Bell, working as hard as he was at running the agency, could not always be in the corridor, although he did his best. "There always was that difficulty in everyone's mind about the people on the sixth floor who were interested in the growth of Saatchi & Saatchi the public company and the rest of the five floors, which were interested in the agency," says Nick Crean, then personal assistant to the brothers.

Bell had done an excellent job in combining Saatchi & Saatchi's business with that of Compton. He managed to keep most of the old Garland-Compton staff and almost all the business by molding two opposing cultures together. "Tim really put that whole thing together brilliantly," says Sorrell. "He was very charismatic, and because of his personality and because he worked so hard I think he probably would have liked his name over the door."

Bell made all the major presentations, gave the public speeches, and represented the agency at all the prestigious events. It was his name that appeared more and more in the trade press. Under Bell the agency took on more new business in 1978 and 1979 than during any other years in the industry's history, and with the election victory he was suddenly one of the top half-dozen advertising executives in Britain. "He was a brilliant presenter, the best handler of business, and a very good manager," says one of the Saatchi people. "He could sell anything, any message, any idea." Bell could build relationships with clients that few could hope to achieve. Even now from the top of his J. Walter Thompson empire, Sorrell remembers Bell's abilities with a hint of awe. "For somebody who is so extreme—I mean, if you're sitting in a room with him you don't get a word in edgeways—it is truly remarkable the relationships he builds, whether with the prime minister or whoever. He is very loquacious and people find that overpowering. But he's really aggressive, supportive . . . brilliant. I felt there was nobody who was as good as he was."

There were danger signs surrounding his success. Ken Gill was increasingly concerned about the toll Bell's work schedule was taking on his health. In a profile in *The Independent* in 1987, a former Bell colleague was quoted as saying: "Tim's an obsessive. He's not moderate about anything. The joke at Saatchi's was that he rattled. There was a pill to go to sleep, a vitamin pill in the morning, and so on. It's quite a dangerous personality to have."

Bell's lifestyle was certainly more extravagant than that of the brothers. There are stories of a chauffeur waiting to take Bell the 200 yards down the road to the L'Etoile restaurant on Charlotte Street, where he would often dine with a cabinet minister, sitting in his favorite window seat, visible to anyone passing. To one interviewer, speaking of his Ferrari, Bell enthused: "I work very long hours, and I like to drive to and from work in a lovely car being admired." After the collapse of his marriage he and his girlfriend, Virginia Hornbrook, became a regular feature of the gossip columns. He was on a high. A profile in 1982 described him as "the rollicking Saatchi frontman who, at Chequers weekends, shares snifters with Denis [Thatcher] and wisecracks with Maggie."

Bell was capable of extraordinary, sweeping gestures that could win him the affection not just of the person involved but of everyone who knew him. For instance, when Jennifer Laing left to go to Leo Burnett, Bell was greatly disappointed. She had been a star at Saatchi and was clearly headed for the top places in the agency when she left. Two years later when he heard she was moving on again, he invited her to lunch. Why not rejoin Saatchi? he suggested. Laing rejected the notion instantly. But Bell kept on, talking about a new and enhanced role for her, a job of such seniority that no one could think she had crawled back with her tail between her legs. Finally she relented; but she wanted a symbol, something special, which would indicate to the world that Saatchi & Saatchi had come to her rather than the other way around. "What do you want?" he asked. A car, she replied, "a really flashy car." Fine; but what kind?

Jennifer knew nothing about cars. In fact, she had not even driven since she passed her driving test at seventeen.

"A red one!" she said. Bell pulled out a cigarette packet and wrote on it: "Jen wants a flashy red car."

She duly returned to Saatchi & Saatchi, and a few months later, when she was sitting in her office, someone appeared asking for her. He was delivering the new car she had ordered, he said. Laing went down, not knowing what to expect. Parked outside the Saatchi office was her new status symbol: a red Ferrari.

She had to get her brother to drive her home.

Bell treated the Saatchi business as his own in the sense that he gave it everything he had. He was one of the first in and last to leave the Charlotte Street office, driven, he would say, by "enthusiasm, terrific energy, and a belief that life should be exciting." He was intensely loyal to the brothers, insisting even years later that he owed his success to the Saatchis, "who taught me to believe that all things are possible."

To outsiders, he was the power at the agency, and while a ripple of unease may have gone through Charlotte Street when Bell, in a TV interview, said that as far as he was concerned it was "Saatchi, Saatchi & Bell," in reality it seemed only a matter of time before it became fact.

To the few who actually knew how the agency worked, however, the picture was different. From the beginning Charles Saatchi, largely by force of personality, had dominated Bell and still did. Bell was a few years older, yet Charles was almost a father figure to him. They had frequent shouting matches and sometimes savage fights, but Charles invariably won. Bell came to regard these shouting matches as another sign of his status—Charles shouted only at those he liked and respected. Until 1979 theirs was, for all the fights, a close working relationship, with the brothers prepared to let Bell take the glory as their front man.

Yet since 1984 the Saatchi brothers and Bell have not exchanged a single word, civil or otherwise. They will not even sit in the same restaurant, and in 1987 Maurice canceled his attendance at a dinner party given for an old friend's retirement when he heard that Bell would be there.

What happened? "It's a bit like asking somebody to explain what went wrong with a marriage," says Bell.

Everyone has a different analysis, including the Saatchis, who nowadays tend to talk about Bell's personal problems at the time—his marriage broke up, and he was drinking perhaps more than was good for him. Some believe the brothers had come to resent his power and, jealous of his popularity and reputation, decided to cut him off before he became a threat to their control. There were stories of a cocaine problem, which Bell at the time did not deny but today insists were "libels." Others suggest that the Saatchi organization simply outgrew Bell. "He was much more at home in a small company where everybody knew everybody else," says one executive who worked closely with Bell. "The company was just getting too big, and they were having to bring in new management structures, finance people, and all the rest. He was the 'hands-on' man, running the agency on the ground floor at Charlotte Street, and they had already gone up to the sixth floor to think about the future."

The truth is more complex than any of these individual reasons. The brothers today give no hint of ever having resented Bell—quite the opposite. Both brothers insist that they decided early on that they did not want to run the agency indefinitely and wanted to move on to a more strategic role. Bell, on the other hand, loved running the agency—and was good at it. The brothers were delighted to let him get on with it. Bell, they acknowledge, was one of the reasons Saatchi & Saatchi was so successful up to the time they bought Garland-Compton and then for several years afterward.

But there is another point cited by old Saatchi hands: Bell, they say, opposed all the major steps the brothers took. He was against the takeover of Garland-Compton, the Tory account, the move into New York, and the acquisition of U.S. Compton. "None of them were his ideas, and he needed constant reassurance and stroking; the brothers had to tell him how much they needed him and how great he was," says a

Saatchi staff member. The implication is that Bell wanted to remain the center of the Saatchi & Saatchi universe, and the brothers' expansionary moves threatened that role. "Charles and Maurice went to great pains not to diminish him in any way," says a Saatchi worker. "But Tim developed a fear of not being a one-man band—everything had to be his idea, everything had to come from him, and everyone had to go around making him feel good."

Bell worked harder and harder to retain his central role, but as the agency got bigger, it was not possible for one person to do everything he wanted to do. "He simply couldn't be everywhere, but he kept trying," says a Saatchi executive. "Then a wonderful thing happened to him—the Tory account came along."

Bell's initial opposition to the Thatcher election campaign is put down to the fact that Gordon Reece appointed Saatchi & Saatchi rather than Tim Bell. But once Bell started work on the Tory account, it was a new lease on life for him. For a year he rode a wave of euphoria during which he worked harder than ever. Political accounts, however, are not like others; they have huge highs and then go dead for three or four years before the next election approaches. Bell, however, continued on a high— and this brought a new problem. "From then on it wasn't possible to talk to him for more than a few minutes without Mrs. Thatcher or another minister being mentioned," says a Saatchi employee. "It got a bit tedious for us all, and it got tedious for the clients who became fed up with the name dropping."

The early Thatcher years were some of the hardest yet for British industry, as the new administration imposed tighter money controls that drove up interest rates. It would be several years before British industry saw the benefits of the Thatcher revolution; in the meantime, her name was by no means universally welcome. Yet there are stories of Bell turning up to meet a major client and talking on and on about Thatcher until in disgust the client walked out. "The Tory account was the making and breaking of Tim Bell," says a Saatchi worker. "After that, anything other than politics and advising the prime minister became boring for him."

Soon the brothers and others were filling in the executive gaps Bell left, or in the phrase both brothers use to describe this aspect of their management policy, they "built around" him. Bell ostensibly was still the kingpin in the agency. But in reality he was already being edged aside.

In the two years after the 1979 election the relationship between Bell and the brothers bumped unevenly downhill. The situation came to a head with the takeover in March 1982 of the Compton business in New York. Bell had no role in the takeover, did not participate in the negotiations or the planning—and, worse still, suddenly discovered that under the new structure he was reporting not to the brothers, but to Milton

Gossett, who was appointed head of the worldwide agency, now a subsidiary of the main company. "That was my job," Bell later said, "and they gave it to somebody else."

Charles, according to Bell, attempted to reassure him, saying, "Don't worry, he's going to retire in two years." Seven years later Gossett is still there. Ken Gill, in his roles as chairman of the holding company and elder statesman, also tried to calm Bell. Gill was becoming increasingly concerned by what he could see as a widening rift between Bell and the brothers and did what he could to head it off. For months he had been trying to defuse Bell's anger at the refusal of the brothers even to consider putting his name on the agency. "Can you not see that the name Saatchi & Saatchi is a real power in itself? It's a most unusual name. It attracts attention. If you start fiddling with that, you detract from it." The brothers had had to accept "Garland-Compton" as the name of the agency, but they had always intended to phase it out, and Gill was happy for it to drop away. "What does it mean to have your name up there?" he asked Bell. "It doesn't really matter, you know. You're having a great time, and you have to admit it. You're the one who is being credited with the whole thing." But Gill and the other senior Saatchi executives could also see the problem from Bell's viewpoint. "Milt Gossett was bigger than he was in the organization," says one. "And he couldn't stand it."

With the takeover of Compton, the Saatchis offered Bell something else: head of Saatchi & Saatchi Compton Worldwide. On paper it sounded good, but in practice Bell soon discovered that the subsidiary was rather less than the name implied. "Worldwide" in this context excluded the United States, where two-thirds of group profits were now coming from and which was firmly run by Gossett; it also excluded the London agency Bell had run so successfully in the 1970s. "I've ended up with the Third World," he complained. In fact he had Europe, Australia, and the Far East as well, and with Compton had come a substantial worldwide network that the Saatchis were already busily enlarging with yet more acquisitions (Vander Biggelaar in Holland, Iroda in Ireland); but there was no disguising the fact that Bell, in the now much bigger corporation, was some way down the hierarchy.

For the first time since he had joined Saatchi & Saatchi twelve years before, Bell felt he had a real crisis. He had never considered leaving the brothers before, although he had plenty of offers: Bill Bernbach had even offered him $1 million to run his U.K. offshoot—"he put the check in my hand," Bell told a friend in wonderment later.

He was twenty-seven when he joined the brothers and in the meantime had seen his tiny shareholding become worth over £3 million. He had a large company house, a salary of over £150,000 a year, and he had found fame. Saatchi & Saatchi up to that point had seemed capable of giving him everything he wanted. It was a huge effort to quit. But as part of the reshuffle his office had been moved to a different building, which further removed him from the brothers, and steadily his power slipped away.

For a time Bell tried to make the best of the situation. He made two tours of every Saatchi & Saatchi and Compton agency in the world, ending up with a conference in Geneva, which is still a much-talked-about event inside the company. David Frost spoke at the dinner, and Bell made a presentation of the Saatchi worldwide management philosophy and organization, covering a worldwide media operation (now in place) and a worldwide new-business operation (also in place), and he set out for the first time Saatchi's target of being one of the top ten agencies in every major country (also now achieved). "Maurice and Charles were neither present nor involved and left the whole matter to me," says Bell. He traveled to the United States at least once a month through 1982 and 1983, sometimes making the round-trip in a single day. Yet all the time the gulf between him and the brothers grew wider.

It was this that hurt Bell more than anything. In a curious way his relationship with the Saatchis, particularly with Charles, mattered to him more than money, status, or prestige. Both Saatchis, particularly Charles, are driven people, born entrepreneurs, prepared to take huge risks, relishing the gamble and the tension of pitting their wits against bigger opposition. It is perhaps part of their Iraqi Jewish culture, increased by the natural urge of the immigrant to achieve. Bell, on the other hand, had a solid middle-class English background, and with his charm and good looks success came more easily to him. In a sense, although he did not realize it until too late, he had come to rely on the Saatchis to drive and motivate him.

The relationship was gradually withering when another event accelerated the process. Bell was at dinner one evening with John Perry, public-affairs director of British Airways, when Perry suddenly confided, "You're getting the British Airways account."

Bell was appalled. Not only did he know nothing about the account, but he had been responsible for winning the rival British Caledonian account, which Saatchi had made a success of with its "We never forget you have a choice" ads. The agency could not run both—and Bell felt fiercely protective of his client.

"That's fantastic," he managed to say. "I didn't even know we were talking to you." The British Airways deal would be Saatchi's most spectacular coup, an event that Bell knew would make the front pages not just of the trade press but also of the national papers. Saatchi already had a number of big and prestigious accounts, but none with quite the same high profile as British Airways. The airline under Lord King was making major political and financial waves, and King deliberately kept it in the news as he fought a series of key battles, not just with the unions—he had trimmed over 20,000 workers from the payroll—but also with the government over complex issues such as the write-off of public debt and his air-route structure. A new advertising agency would be right at the heart of all that.

Perry explained that Saatchi had indeed made a pitch and had landed the account, one of the most important in the business. Bell remembers bluffing his way through dinner, trying to hide his deep sense of shock. The next morning he faced Charles. Was it true? Charles, according to Bell, flatly denied it; a week later, Saatchi announced it had won the account.

"The trust broke down," Bell later told a friend. "In retrospect they never did trust me in the way I thought they did. I thought they had a certain relationship with me, and then I suddenly realized they never saw it that way. They never looked at it in the way I did."

There was another incident that did not improve his relationship with the brothers, although it does not seem to have hurt him with his beloved Mrs. Thatcher. He was at a birthday party for Kenny Everett, the zany television personality, at Chez Gerrard one evening, and Bell began to expound about the prime minister and her family, telling a series of ribald anecdotes about Mrs. Thatcher and referring to her son Mark as a "twit." What Bell hadn't noticed was that one of the people who had joined his table was a magazine journalist, who had switched on a tape recorder. Bell's remarks appeared more or less verbatim, causing Bell—and the Saatchis—huge embarrassment. Bell apologized to her immediately, and she seems to have forgiven him equally rapidly.

In May 1983 Mrs. Thatcher called another election, four years after her first victory, and once again Saatchi & Saatchi was in the front line. By this time Bell and the brothers were barely on speaking terms. But he would be leading the campaign for them—Mrs. Thatcher expected, even demanded, that. Bell had his own special relationship with Mrs. Thatcher and with Tory Central Office, and neither the brothers nor anyone else, other than perhaps Bell's assistant Michael Dobbs, had any close ties with the party.

Bell once again assembled his team and moved them to a little office in D'Arblay Street in Soho. This second Thatcher election was very different from the first. In 1979 she was an untried and still largely unknown leader, and to some extent the big question had been, would Britain ever elect a woman as prime minister? Now there had been four years of Thatcherism, and it was Mrs. Thatcher's record that was under scrutiny. "Thatcherism" and "Thatcherite" had come to have a meaning, pejorative or reverential depending on your viewpoint, but there was a clear set of ideas and attitudes associated with her on which the 1983 election would be fought. The victory in the Falklands in 1982 had confirmed her image as a strong leader, the Iron Lady, but there were other clear aspects of her image that the public identified, some of them good, others not: her "Victorian values," reducing the size of government, paying one's own way, making Britain great again, and of course "There is no alternative," or "TINA," her oft-repeated refrain to justify many of the harsh measures adopted during her first term as prime minister.

Ranged against her was the charge that Mrs. Thatcher had not been able to deliver on many of her election promises of 1979. Far from cutting government expenditure as a proportion of gross national product, she had actually expanded it from 41 percent to 44 percent, largely because of the economic recession and the growing number of unemployed—and because huge sectors of the economy, such as the health service, education, the armed forces, the police, and the expensive fabric of Britain's tottering welfare state, were outside even her efforts to control, at least in that first term. Income tax had been cut in her first budget, but even so the tax burden had actually risen. State industries, notably British Leyland, British Steel, and the coal industry, were still receiving large handouts. The denationalization program had barely begun, and the Conservatives had taken only a few tottering steps down the road to Mrs. Thatcher's cherished "capital-owning democracy" where everyone would be a shareholder and every family would own its own home. The one significantly visible achievement was a drop in inflation from over 20 percent in the first Thatcher year to 5 percent in 1983, the lowest level in ten years. But the unemployment rate was 13 percent, and if one added that to the inflation rate to get what is called the "misery index," it came to 18 percent—a very high figure and one that was causing governments around the world to be rejected by their electorates.

Yet by the spring of 1983 the early polls showed that there had been a major shift in the perception of the Thatcher government. The British electorate had begun to accept that economic change would be both painful and long but that it was necessary. There was considerable and growing support for denationalization, a belief that the government had to beat inflation before unemployment, that lower inflation and pay raises did create more jobs, as Mrs. Thatcher kept saying, and that government, both local and central, was too large. In other words, "Thatcherism" was gaining ground, and various leaked cabinet documents showed the government still full of radical plans. If taxes and public expenditure had not yet been cut, Mrs. Thatcher still intended to do so, and there was a visible self-confidence among her ministers that communicated itself to the civil servants in Whitehall. Could that self-confidence be translated into a second election victory?

There had been personnel changes in Central Office that were not to Saatchi's advantage. Gordon Reece was allowed back into Britain by Mrs. Thatcher only after she had announced the election date—"she was supersensitive about the whole timing issue, and every time Gordon came back there would be stories about cigar smoke seen at Heathrow airport, and an election in the offing," says Michael Dobbs. Reece's role at Central Office had been split, with Chris Lawson in charge of marketing and Anthony Shrimsley in charge of communications. Reece found himself largely without a role and Bell without a clear line of reporting.

Dobbs was destined to play a significant role not just in the 1983 campaign but in the 1987 one as well. A tall, rounded, freckle-faced man who looked younger than his thirty-four years, he was one of the more academically qualified people at Saatchi's, having taken a degree at Oxford and a Ph.D. at Harvard, after which he became a journalist in Boston for a few years. In the mid-1970s he returned to Britain and worked as a researcher for Mrs. Thatcher when she was leader of the opposition. In that capacity he had come to know Bell well during the 1979 campaign, and after the election victory Bell offered him a job at Saatchi. Dobbs kept his foot in the political arena, working as an adviser to Norman Tebbit, who was then rapidly emerging as one of the stars of the Thatcher government. Now, with the election campaign running, Dobbs was working both for Saatchi, which paid his salary, and for the Conservatives, a Saatchi client.

Although there was never any doubt in Central Office that Saatchi would play the same role in the 1983 campaign that it had in 1979, this time there was a determination to keep the campaign on a tighter rein and to cut back on expenditure. Saatchi was given a budget of £2.4 million, £150,000 of it for that year's local elections. The flippant ads of 1979 were recalled—there should be no more of those, Bell was told firmly. In January 1983, six months before the election, Bell made a presentation to Mrs. Thatcher at Chequers over a weekend, setting out the central theme: "We must capture the mood for change in outlook, while emphasizing the need for continuity in direction." In April the Saatchi team began work on anticipating how Labour might fight the campaign, and Bell worked out a plan for "rubbishing" the Labour record on unemployment, an area in which the team members knew Labour would concentrate its attack.

In the end the campaign went well, but it had its ups and downs. For its first party election broadcast Saatchi prepared a ten-minute program only to discover that the party had bought only five minutes of air time. Saatchi planned to hire a hospital ward in London's East End to film a sequence about the government's caring attitude on health; the hospital had been closed five months before, a victim of Thatcher cuts. The most effective ad concentrated on the 1978–79 "winter of discontent," with pictures of angry picket lines, closed hospitals, closed-down industry, and terrifying front-page headlines and a gloom-laden voice-over intoning: "Do you remember . . . ?"

The Tories started the campaign 16 percentage points ahead of Labour in the polls, so the central point of the strategy was to keep the Tory lead. With just over a week to go there was the traditional "wobble," when one rogue poll showed the gap suddenly narrowing. No other poll confirmed this showing, and right through the election the Tories kept the lead. The headlines tell the story: "17.5% Lead for the Tories" (*Daily Telegraph*, May 12), "Heading for a Landslide" (*Daily Mail*, May 18), "Mrs. T by Mile Say Key Voters" (*Sunday Express*, June 5), and "The Last Word— 16%" (*London Standard* on election day, June 9).

Bell describes some of the press ads used in that campaign as "the greatest political ads that have ever been done in this country." There were two in particular; the first compared the manifestos of the Communist party with those of the Labour party, showing them to be remarkably similar. The headline read: "Like your manifesto, comrade" and was written by Charles Saatchi and Jeremy Sinclair. The other ad listed fifteen propositions along the lines of, "I agree to have the value of my savings reduced immediately in accordance with Labour's wishes to devalue the pound" and invited the reader to agree or disagree by "ticking the box."

Mrs. Thatcher personally canceled what the Saatchi camp regarded as its best work: three pages of ads set to go into the newspapers in the final few days of the campaign, setting out why voters should not vote for either of the other parties and why they must vote Tory. By that stage it took no great foresight to see that, short of a disaster, the Tories were heading for a very big victory indeed. Mrs. Thatcher increased her majority in parliament from a comfortable 43 to a crushing 144.

To the outside world, Saatchi & Saatchi had orchestrated a good election, but all was not well with Tim Bell, and there were times in the campaign when he was far from well. Even so he had still managed to run the campaign better than anyone else in the organization was probably capable of doing. At one stage, Cecil Parkinson, the Conservative party chairman who had succeeded Lord Thorneycroft, took Michael Dobbs aside to warn him about Bell's health. Parkinson, like everyone else involved with him in the campaigns, was fond of Bell and meant it as a friendly gesture. Dobbs passed Parkinson's remarks back to the brothers, who took them as a warning shot from the party chairman.

Charles Saatchi in particular was now getting very worried about Bell. He told Maurice that Tim Bell was a problem that he would deal with, and Maurice should leave it to him. Maurice willingly did, and Charles rang Bell almost daily. At first Charles was very sympathetic, encouraging him to seek treatment for his visibly declining health.

Despite his poor health Bell could still win accounts. During 1983 he led the pitch for Mattel worldwide and got the Mattel account; he also helped get the Gillette Europe account. He helped organize the worldwide British Airways launch with Bill Muirhead. But he was encountering other problems. In the late summer and autumn of 1983, he split up with his girlfriend, Virginia Hornbrook, with whom he had lived for several years. She went back to Australia, and this crisis in Bell's private life coincided with his final realization that the breakdown with Charles was irreparable.

It was December 1983 when Bell and Charles Saatchi had their worst fight yet. Bell finally nerved himself to ask for something he had wanted for years: could he join the holding-company board? Many of his colleagues felt he should have been there long before, he argued, and it was traditional in the advertising industry for the stars to have their names attached to the agencies. But the Saatchis kept their board very tight. Even though Saatchi was a large public company, it had only five directors: the Saatchis; Kenneth Gill, the chairman; Martin Sorrell, the finance director; and the long-serving company secretary, David Perring.

Charles was furious at Bell's suggestion. "You'll never, ever go on the public company board," he told him. No advertising people went on that board, Charles said. "If they did, then every time we make an acquisition we'd have to put the person we bought on the public company board. It's just going to be Maurice and me and the money men."

That conversation marked the turning point for Bell. "It was a very hurtful conversation," he said later. "I just couldn't understand why he said it. I could understand him saying you can't go on now, or not for a couple of years, but to say what he said—'never, ever on the board'—was a terrible thing to do." (Later, after Bell left, others did go on the board, leaving Bell even more resentful.)

"I don't want to work here any more," he told Charles. He hadn't decided what to do, and Charles initially made a strong effort to keep him, although in a very different role.

"Why don't you set up a public-affairs consultancy?" Charles suggested. "You're very good at that. We'll finance you. You can own 45 percent or 50 percent of it, or whatever you like. It will be yours and we'll own a chunk of it, and it'll be really good."

That wasn't what Bell wanted. Later he would explain that he felt "like you've been somebody's wife, and now you're told you can be the maid."

He was still on Mrs. Thatcher's special list, however, and that Christmas he was a guest at Chequers, a privilege given to only a few of Mrs. Thatcher's close confidants and friends. In a quiet moment he told her of his fight with Charles and his decision to leave. She too had worried about the decline in his health and suggested—as Charles had—that he take a break. He stayed at home in January 1984, persuaded Virginia to come back to him, then went on vacation to Kenya in February. He was back at work in March just as one of the biggest threats to Mrs. Thatcher's rule began—a year-long miners' strike. Bell offered his services to the head of the National Coal Board, Ian MacGregor, who later acknowledged his "able assistance" and "great help" in beating the miners. But during this time Bell was a shadow of his old self, depressed and miserable. It was a bad time for him, and he was further and further removed from any power at Saatchi.

Charles Saatchi thought he had found Bell's successor: for a few months Charles held talks with his old friend David Puttnam, who had just given up on his self-appointed task of changing the British film industry. "The two brothers want to free themselves from the day-to-day affairs of the agency and are looking for a leadership figure," Puttnam was quoted as saying. How Puttnam's appointment would have gone down with Mrs. Thatcher is an interesting speculation: Puttnam had been a Labour supporter and had changed to the new middle-of-the-road Social Democrat party. For a while the film professional was enthusiastic about joining Saatchi, talking about his "very definite ideas on advertising" and the ways it must change. Instead, he went to Hollywood for an ill-fated job as head of Columbia Pictures.

In the autumn of 1984 Bell found himself working on Coal Board ads with his old friend Frank Lowe. Saatchi & Saatchi, because of its political connection, did not want the Coal Board account, so it went to Lowe Howard-Spink & Gosschalk, an agency growing even faster than Saatchi & Saatchi (although one-tenth the size). Lowe knew all about the fallout, not just from Bell but from Charles as well. The Saatchis had tried to buy Lowe's new agency six months after he started it but had eventually decided there was no room for Frank Lowe alongside Tim Bell and had abandoned their talks. Now Lowe, without telling Bell, rang Charles to inquire what he planned to do with Tim. Charles by that stage had no plans. Would Saatchi mind if he, Frank Lowe, made Bell an offer? Charles had no objection at all. Late in 1984 Lowe offered Bell what the Saatchis had refused him: equal status, his name on the door, and a position on the board.

It was a bitter ending. Bell had to buy out his house at its 1985 price, many times what it had originally been bought for, buy out his large bonus, and repay a loan of £1 million to the company . He had to sell £3 million worth of shares to do so, and he reckoned later that it had cost him a net £1.5 million to leave. He was angry about it, although Saatchi as a public company could not have done anything else. Bell still ended up with £2.5 million after paying off all his corporate debts. Charles also made him sign a contract under which he was paid a £24,000-a-year retainer to be available to work on the Tory account for Saatchi & Saatchi for one more election and was forbidden from taking the account with him.

There was one final gesture that still rankles with Bell. His departure from Saatchi was a major news event for the trade press, where every little thing that happened at Saatchi had been front-page news for years. For fifteen years Charles Saatchi had been the biggest source of stories for *Campaign*, and now he wanted a favor. *Campaign* obliged—putting the story of Bell's departure on page three.

Bell's natural good humor has since reasserted itself and he no longer seems to hate the Saatchis as much as he did, but he has not got completely over his hurt. "I was just brokenhearted," he said later. "It seemed to me unnecessary. I don't know why they turned on me. I don't know why we came apart. I don't know why I got written out of the future. They've never been able to tell me." For their part the Saatchi brothers felt a sense of guilt that they did not handle Bell's departure better, that they had in effect grown bored with pandering to him. "Tim should have had the guts to go out and start his own agency years before," says a senior Saatchi executive. "He could have been a legendary advertising man. The Tory party account was a golden age for him, and he was so extraordinarily gifted that he could have been an enormous figure today. If he hadn't screwed up in his last years, he could have taken half Saatchi's clients with him."

A measure—perhaps the best objective one—of Bell's changed status in the industry was the number of Saatchi clients who followed him. When Frank Lowe left Collett Dickenson Pearce, nearly half the clients left with him. Bell had been the chairman and chief executive of Saatchi & Saatchi Compton and the man dealing directly with the clients. For a while at least he would find his feet again at Lowe Howard-Spink & Bell, but he took none of the Saatchi clients with him.

One feels that even after everything that has happened Tim Bell would go back instantly if only the Saatchis asked. He is realistic enough to know they never will. "Maybe they never liked me," says Bell. "Maybe that's what it is. Maybe they never, ever liked me."

12
ONWARD TO
MADISON AVENUE

In 1954 Thomas Rosser Reeves, then head of the Ted Bates agency in New York, made what is generally regarded as the first real commercial advertisement for television. It is an advertisement that is instructive both of the Ted Bates style and of the thinking about advertising on Madison Avenue at that time. The sixty-second spot showed hammers animatedly hammering away at agonized skulls; it was an advertisement for Anacin, a headache remedy. The commercial cost the client $8,400 to produce, but Reeves boasted later that it "made more money in seven years than *Gone with the Wind* did for David O. Selznick and MGM in a quarter of a century."

The ad was to make Ted Bates the hottest agency in New York in the mid-1950s. Television had appeared and become the most powerful sales tool ever devised. Reeves, known as "the blacksmith" for the way he hammered home a simple, repetitious message, was the champion of an aggressive form of hard-selling advertising. The way to sell most effectively, Reeves argued, was to find in a product what he called its "unique selling proposition," or USP, which made a claim for the product that was untouched by the competition.

Reeves was one of the giants of Madison Avenue in the 1950s and 1960s, commanding the heights that the Saatchi brothers could only dream of as they set out in the early 1980s in their quest for a major New York agency. Another giant was Scotsman David Ogilvy, today one of the legends of the industry, whose *Confessions of an Advertising Man* had been required reading for young people entering the business when the Saatchis were starting out. Ogilvy's approach was more genteel than Reeves's: Ogilvy once described the perfect advertising executive as combining the tenacity of a bulldog and the charm of a spaniel. He believed in scientific data and research, insisting that "factual advertising outsells flatulent puffery." Ogilvy was fascinated by salesmanship and brought to the industry new marketing disciplines and a belief in the long-term image of each brand he advertised. "Every advertisement is part of the long-term investment in the personality of the brand," he wrote.

The son of a Gaelic-speaking Highlander, Ogilvy lived as a boy in Lewis Carroll's house in Surrey, went to several public schools, was expelled from Oxford, and became a salesman for Aga Cookers in

Scotland. At the age of twenty-four he wrote in *The Theory and Practice of Selling the Aga Cooker*: "It does not cook the cook. It civilizes life in the kitchen." His life story, up to the point when he arrived, age thirty-eight, on Madison Avenue, is an extraordinary one: he worked in the kitchens of the Hotel Majestic in Paris and later went to the United States to work for Dr. George Gallup. It was Gallup who, in 1932 at Young & Rubicam, had begun the new scientific methods of measuring radio audiences and newspaper, and thus advertising, readership.

One of the chapters in *Confessions of an Advertising Man* starts: "Fifteen years ago I was an obscure farmer in Pennsylvania. Today I preside over one of the best advertising agencies in the United States, with billings of over $55 million a year." Now *there* was a precedent for the Saatchis. And there was another: Ogilvy had originally been financed in his Madison Avenue venture by his elder brother Francis, then head of the agency Mather & Crowther. The Saatchis were thus not the first British brothers to tackle successfully the apparently closed and giant world of American advertising (colloquially but incorrectly referred to as "Madison Avenue," in the same way the British press was still referred to as "Fleet Street" long after the last newspaper had moved out).

In a short history of the Ogilvy, Benson, and Mather agencies, written in 1975, Stanley Pigott says: "Francis Ogilvy fulfilled his vision. He had contrived, against all the odds, to start a British-owned advertising agency on the American advertising scene. He knew that his brother's genius would make it succeed." Was there inspiration, or at least encouragement, in the Ogilvy brothers' success for the Saatchi brothers? Despite Doris's high view of David Ogilvy, he was never a really influential figure for either brother. Charles, with his distaste for research, did not much care for his style of advertising. Maurice could appreciate Ogilvy's ability to build and run a business but never saw him as a great thinker about the longer-term trends in advertising. Ironically, few advertising people would come to resent the Saatchis' move into New York more than David Ogilvy.

But Ogilvy in the 1960s and 1970s offered hope for many aspiring young advertising workers. He pointed out how in 1937 Walter Chrysler gave the Plymouth account to Sterling Getchel, then only thirty-one; how in 1940 Ed Little awarded most of his Colgate account to a dark horse named Ted Bates, predecessor of Reeves and founder of the agency. And how General Foods discovered Young & Rubicam when that agency, later the biggest in the world, was only a year old. There was nothing sacred about the pecking order of the Madison Avenue agencies. Ogilvy himself had proved that.

But it was neither Reeves nor Ogilvy who was the inspiration for Charles Saatchi and many other bright young advertising people. That honor went to a third advertising giant of the day. If Reeves was the blacksmith of Madison Avenue, Bill Bernbach was the Picasso, the man who would lead the industry back into what became known as the "creative revolution." Again and again Charles Saatchi, Ross Cramer, Jeremy Sinclair, Ron Collins, and so many other young creative stars of the day refer to Bernbach as the most powerful influence on their formative years. Yet that influence was confined in Charles's case to the creative side; the agency he and his brother built after the first few years owed little or nothing to Bernbach and perhaps more—although they would not welcome the thought—to Ogilvy. Ironically, in view of what was to occur later, the giant to whom they owed nothing whatsoever was Rosser Reeves; his work and his agency lay well outside their orbit.

Born in 1911 in the Bronx, Bernbach was the son of a designer of women's clothes. He moved easily through various public schools before studying English, music, and philosophy at New York University, displaying, in the words of one biographer, "the sort of easy eclecticism that allowed him later to range across a variety of disciplines in his advertising career." Like so many others, he drifted into advertising by accident, joining Grey Advertising, and soon proved to be an inspired copywriter. By the late 1940s, however, Bernbach was increasingly disturbed by the research methods that dominated the business. In 1947 he wrote a memo to his boss that set out some of the themes he would espouse for the rest of his career:

> I'm worried that we're falling into a trap of bigness, that we're going to worship techniques instead of substance. . . . I don't want scientists. I don't want people who do the right things. I want people who do inspiring things. . . . Let us blaze new trails.

In June 1949 Bernbach, then thirty-eight, set out to blaze his own new trail. With Ned Doyle (accounts) and Maxwell Dane (administration and finance) he created Doyle Dane Bernbach, hinting at their departure from the norm by including no comma or ampersand in the name. The agency had thirteen employees and $500,000 in billings, and its first office was on the top floor of 350 Madison Avenue, a floor and a half above the last elevator stop. Bernbach lived most of his life in an unfashionable part of town, traveling by subway, and claimed that he and his two partners probably did less entertaining than any agency in the business. "We're just three guys who live very modestly and don't cater to clients [simply] because we need the money."

In many ways Bill Bernbach was the opposite of Charles Saatchi. Short and stocky, with bland features, mild blue eyes, and graying blond hair, he was also sane, well balanced, and uneccentric to the point of dullness. A former copywriter of Bernbach's, Bob Levenson, described him in a book intended as a tribute to his old boss as "a quick-witted package of ego, ambition, confidence, determination, and energy"— which gave Charles something in common with him. His hobbies included music, literature, and the philosophy of Bertrand Russell, whom he often quoted: "Even in the most purely logical realms, it is insight that first arrives at what is new."

Bernbach's era was about to dawn. By the 1950s the big American advertising agencies had expanded with the great consumer boom, of which they were an integral part—some even said its cause. These big agencies were regarded as fulfilling a vital economic function in the new "affluent society." The deprivation of two decades of depression and war had created a seemingly insatiable demand for consumer products. America in the 1950s had virtually no unemployment, inflation was 1 percent a year, and there was cheap and plentiful energy.

As the nation's great factories mushroomed, the imperative was for consumers to consume—and for the advertisers to persuade them to do so. By the end of the decade the United States had 25 percent of the world market share in manufacturing and, before the days of Japanese penetration, 95 percent of U.S. cars, steel, and consumer electronics were made in its own factories. Madison Avenue became the background for films, plays, and novels: Doris Day and Rock Hudson acted out their innocent romances in agency offices; Gregory Peck starred in *The Man in the Grey Flannel Suit*; Frederic Wakeman's book *The Hucksters* appeared in 1946 and painted the industry as unscrupulous and manipulative; Vance Packard's *The Hidden Persuaders*, which appeared in 1957, exposed the evils of the scientific methods widely used in the industry.

All this time Bill Bernbach had been producing a new and different kind of advertisement, called the soft sell, which began to replace the brain-pounding repetition of the USP. Bernbach rejected the proposition, expounded by many large agencies, that "once the selling proposition has been determined, the job is done." Research, in his view, perpetuated mediocrity and led to dullness: "There are a lot of good technicians in advertising. They know all the rules, and they talk the best game. But there's one little rub. They forget that advertising is persuasion, and persuasion is not a science but an art. Advertising is the art of persuasion." He favored what he called "the intuitive flashes of inspiration that defied scientific investigation." His philosophy was based on the simple principle, as he often remarked, that "human nature hasn't changed in a million years."

Bernbach became high fashion. He made a splash with his first client, Orbach's department store, which he took with him from Grey's and relaunched with ads such as "Liberal Trade-In. Bring in your wife and just a few dollars . . . we will give you a new woman." He produced most of his best ads within a space of a few years. In 1959 he got the

Volkswagen account and "like an earthquake broke new ground in every direction," in the words of one of his fans, the British advertising executive David Abbott, who worked for him.

Volkswagen was already selling 150,000 cars a year in the United States when Bernbach came along, but he considerably boosted that rate with a series of iconoclastic and daring ads that became the talk of the industry. Bernbach capitalized on the obvious defects of the car, which was still closely associated in those days with Hitler's Germany. He poked fun at it with ads such as one that showed a set of snow tracks on a desolate country road—with no car to be seen. The caption announced that here, finally, was a beautiful picture of a VW. Or there was a picture of a VW being pulled by a tow truck, with the caption: "A rare photo." His ads talked about how "Our funny little engine sure can push our funny little car fast." One ad that broke new ground in the 1960s just featured a line, roughly showing the ugly shape of the VW Beetle, with the caption: "How much longer can we hand you this line?" The trade paper *Advertising Age* later designated the VW ads the best campaign of the half-century. In a Britain being swept by the satirical shows "That Was the Week That Was," "Beyond the Fringe," and later, "Monty Python's Flying Circus," it is easy to see how such ads would appeal to creative young people like Charles Saatchi and Ross Cramer.

But Bernbach is probably most famous for his Avis "We try harder" campaigns. In 1962 Avis lost $2 million and brought in a new executive, Robert Townsend, to rescue it. Townsend in his classic book *Up the Organization* describes how he hired Bernbach. Townsend started by inquiring in the industry which were the hottest agencies, then he asked each agency the question, "How do you get $5 million worth of advertising for $1 million?" Bernbach responded to the challenge on one condition: that the ads he would produce after ninety days of consideration must be run. There could be no argument.

After ninety days Bernbach was back. "He said he was sorry but the only honest things they could say were that the company was second largest and that the people were trying harder." His own research department, Bernbach confessed, didn't like these suggestions. He didn't go for them very much himself. Nor did Avis.

Reluctantly Avis ran Bernbach's ads, and the following year Avis's turnover rose by one-third, and it made a profit of $3 million—a turnaround of $5 million—at least partly because of that ad campaign. As Townsend says: "The rest is history."

By the late 1960s some two dozen American agencies had gone public, little suspecting the hard times that lay around the corner. The early 1970s brought recession and a sharp downturn in consumer spending. After twenty-five years of unprecedented growth, the "affluent society" was suddenly no more. Inflation and recession hit consumption hard, and the big manufacturers cut back their spending on advertising. In 1971 many big agencies, including JWT, McCann, Young & Rubicam, Bates, and BBDO, suffered large losses. The troubled agencies found themselves in a vicious downward spiral: the more their problems became known, the more clients withdrew. The more creative agencies in particular lost accounts and were forced to move to a more conservative, marketing-oriented approach. Abruptly, the creative revolution, which had flourished for only a decade, died. A number of agencies that had gone public now bought back their own shares and went private again. Agencies sought marketing experts instead of creative talent.

David Ogilvy welcomed the change: "Today, thank God, we are back in business as salesmen instead of pretentious entertainers. The pendulum is swinging back our way." In fact, advertising was evolving rather than swinging widely, and creative advertising, as Ogilvy himself was the first to admit, was still of prime importance to the industry.

The 1970s also saw a great wave of mergers among American agencies. Edward Ney took over at Young & Rubicam in November 1970 and proceeded, with an ambitious series of mergers, to build a company that surpassed JWT in size in national billings. Its acquisition of Marstellar in 1979 made it the leader in world billings too. Other agencies followed the same trend. Interpublic bought Campbell-Ewald; Ogilvy took Scali McCabe Sloves (the hottest new agency of the 1970s); Wells Rich Greene bought Gardner. Bates absorbed Campbell-Mithun, and the three biggest public-relations firms were bought by JWT, Y&R, and Foote, Cone & Belding.

By the end of the 1970s American advertising was back in boom times again. Soft sell had given way to hard sell, and the growth of corporate business favored rational content in ads. It didn't appeal to the creative staff, and in 1977 *Advertising Age* announced that "The industry is waiting for the next creative giant to shake us all up." In 1980 *Advertising Age* again said that the industry was "on the verge of a new creative revolution."

So it was, but those changes were shaping up 3,000 miles away. The Saatchis were ready for the New World.

The catalyst for the first major move by Saatchi & Saatchi into the United States was the Cincinnati-based Procter & Gamble. For several years the Saatchi & Saatchi Garland-Compton agency had handled such Procter & Gamble products as Ariel and Fairy Snow soap powders, Head & Shoulders shampoo, and Pampers diapers. Kenneth Gill had made P&G a promise five years before and had kept it: Procter & Gamble was going to benefit from the Saatchi-Compton deal. In Britain Saatchi & Saatchi and P&G had gotten along well, and far from withdrawing its account P&G had given the agency new business; the agency was careful to offer this prestigious client what it wanted, and Maurice and Tim Bell took pains to get to know the P&G people and study the company philosophy. P&G responded by giving Saatchi new accounts.

P&G was not only Saatchi & Saatchi's biggest account—it was also the biggest client of Compton Advertising in New York, and this began to raise certain problems for Milt Gossett. As he learned, often thirdhand, of the brothers' advances to other agencies, Gossett started to think about protecting his own position, feeling that the brothers' expansionary plans were sooner or later going to run them into trouble with P&G— trouble that would brush off on Compton in New York. There were rumors all over New York of the Saatchis approaching one agency or another, many of which would have put them in direct breach of P&G's tight rules governing the agencies it used. Gossett heard of only a fraction of the brothers' activities in New York. In the late 1970s and early 1980s there was scarcely an agency in the business that did not get an approach—and often several approaches—from Maurice Saatchi or Martin Sorrell.

The first talks in 1977 were with a food company that had acquired a medium-sized advertising agency it wanted to sell. Sorrell led the negotiations, which were approaching fruition when a better prospect popped up: Daniel & Charles, a medium-sized agency with which Sorrell then negotiated for several months. Those talks too were making progress when one day Bob Gross of Geers Gross, hearing of Saatchi's interest in buying an American agency, rang up. He had a special relationship with the New York agency Cunningham & Walsh, and he knew it was looking for a buyer. Sorrell immediately switched to this bigger and better prize, and again there were detailed and lengthy negotiations, with Maurice and Sorrell spending weeks in New York, keeping in touch with other prospects while pursuing this one.

What caused Gossett and his Compton team their greatest worry, however, was the news that the brothers were in negotiations with Cunningham & Walsh, which as it happened was another big P&G agency. Aghast at the rumors, Gossett rang the Saatchi office in London to voice his worry. Did no one there realize how determined Procter & Gamble was to spread its business around a number of agencies? If Procter & Gamble heard that Saatchi was going to take over another of its agencies, P&G would as likely as not remove *all* its accounts—from Compton in New York as well as from Saatchi & Saatchi Compton in London. It would be a disaster.

Maurice and Sorrell finally abandoned Cunningham & Walsh to chase another, even bigger, agency: Wells Rich Greene, founded by the legendary Mary Wells, one of the most successful women in the history of advertising. Maurice and Sorrell flew to the south of France, where Mary Wells had a villa at Cap Ferrat, to negotiate, but after some months those talks too were aborted.

At any one time Saatchi & Saatchi might have been talking to half a dozen agencies, to most of them tentatively, to a few of them more seriously. They were particularly keen on Doyle Dane Bernbach. Maurice, who was traveling to New York every second or third week, set up a meeting with Bill Bernbach himself. Sorrell made an approach at a different level: at Harvard he had met Neil Austrian, a relative of Bernbach and the financial executive who became president of DDB in the late 1970s. While Maurice talked to Bernbach, Sorrell arranged to meet Austrian. Tim Bell flew over, and they all had dinner. But the deal was never a serious possibility, Bernbach had no intention of selling, and certainly not to a tiny unknown agency from London. By that time Maurice had decided he didn't want to buy DDB in any case, even if he had been able to afford it. Bernbach, like the Saatchis, had a creative reputation, and what they needed in the United States was something different: a company with solid clients and a rock-solid business— something more like Compton in fact. "Bernbach struck me as a rather flaky outfit," Maurice reported back to Charles, who followed by telephone every move his brother made.

It was painstaking and often frustrating work, but both Maurice and Sorrell were well suited to it. Maurice's disciplined approach and Sorrell's exceptional financial grasp made them a formidable pair at the negotiating table. The brothers were intent on getting their move into New York just right, and this first step had to be a good one. The takeover road in America is littered with the bones of many past failures by overseas companies, and the Saatchis were prepared to spend years if necessary to make sure they were not among them. The style, therefore, was to talk to as many people as possible, to keep putting the feelers out, but to be very hardheaded indeed when it came to putting down any cash.

A typical example of the Saatchi brothers' approach is the experience of John O'Toole, former head of Foote, Cone & Belding. In the summer of 1981 O'Toole was invited to have breakfast with Maurice at the Pierre Hotel in New York. He had been led to believe by the third party who had arranged this meeting that Maurice wanted to talk takeover, and as he drove down on a virtually empty New England throughway that morning, O'Toole was thinking about the "glittering acquisition" he was about to make for Foote, Cone & Belding. At the meeting Maurice soon launched into his well-rehearsed patter about his belief in pan-European and even global brands and told O'Toole that Saatchi & Saatchi needed to break out of its London fetters and gain access to a worldwide network. O'Toole nodded enthusiastically, thinking that Saatchi & Saatchi would make a perfect fit with FCB. "I knew what Jimmy Carter meant by lusting with his heart," he wrote later.

He was halfway through his scrambled egg before the penny dropped. Maurice didn't want to sell his business at all—*he wanted to buy FCB*. "I

have never, in the ensuing years, underestimated the dimensions of
Saatchi & Saatchi's vision or determination to realize it," says O'Toole.

Inside Compton the senior managers were as nervous as Gossett when
they heard of the approaches the brothers were making on Madison
Avenue. The Saatchi reputation had grown enormously with the acquisition of the Tory account and the victory of Mrs. Thatcher, and in the
New York agency no one doubted Saatchi & Saatchi's creativity, but they
did wonder sometimes about its sanity.

Gossett himself expressed his own worries to his directors. "They're a
couple of crazy guys who won't stay by the conventions," he said.
"They're brilliant, but they're crazy." His team had worked well with the
Saatchis, and he had come to like both brothers, who often dropped in
on him during their trips through New York. Maurice and his wife,
Gillian, had spent weekends at Gossett's house, and he in turn had stayed
with them. He had met Charles and Doris as well, and they talked about
art—or at least Doris did, Charles as ever unable to bring himself to
venture more than a few monosyllabic replies on the subject. Tim Bell
had come over a number of times, and he and Gossett had made
presentations together, notably one to Coca-Cola. The relationship
between the two agencies was working well in a technical sense, but all
that could be blown away by one ill-advised takeover, which might
benefit Saatchi & Saatchi but could do severe damage to Compton.

Gossett gradually began to put in place his own defense mechanisms.
He talked to P&G and explained his position—just in case he was hit by
a preemptive strike. The ambitions of the Saatchi boys, he explained,
had nothing to do with him and he couldn't curb them. Then he decided
that he had to either increase his shareholding in Saatchi & Saatchi
Compton and wrest back control or find another agency in London.
Compton's shareholding was no longer in the parent but in the subsidiary
Saatchi & Saatchi Compton, and Gossett had few levers. He broached
the subject of increasing his shareholding with Maurice, and the negotiations began. Like O'Toole, however, Gossett misunderstood what Maurice had in mind. Gossett proposed increasing Compton's shareholding
to 40 percent, and the brothers appeared to go along with the suggestion,
gently and patiently drawing Gossett deeper into their net. The negotiations were at times hectic, and the Compton side soon lost count of the
number of times one side or the other stormed out. Finally, however, the
Saatchis seemed to agree: Compton could go up to 40 percent. The
papers were drawn up and everything was prepared for a meeting in Milt
Gossett's office. Both brothers turned up for the signing. Then at the last
moment Charles suddenly said, "No, I don't want to do it," stood up, and
walked out, with Maurice close behind him. This maneuver was almost
certainly completely premeditated. Gossett was being lured in deeper
and deeper.

It was Maurice who reopened negotiations. He rang Gossett one day to make his proposition: "Why don't you buy all of us?" Instead of buying 40 percent, why didn't Compton buy 100 percent of Saatchi & Saatchi? The strategy was now becoming clearer. The brothers had been able to reverse their own agency into Compton in the United Kingdom with startlingly successful results six years before. Why not try such a reversal on a larger scale? That caused Gossett to begin thinking hard. Many of his senior managers were of that postwar generation who were—as he was himself—moving toward retirement.

The agency was coming up to a generation change, just as Garland-Compton had been in London six years before. But were the Saatchis, with their essentially London base, the right people to provide this change? Gossett may have been tempted to go with the Saatchi brothers, but he did not have much support from his own team. "Our relationship with the Saatchis was pretty similar to what it would be if they were Martians or people from the planet Saturn," says a former Compton employee. "We had no idea how to deal with them. But Milt had an immediate and easy relationship with them, and he was incredibly impressed with their creative work. Compton's creative work was pretty poor then, and the Saatchi creative work was everything Compton's was not."

Gossett, however, decided he could not recommend Maurice's proposal. He believed he would never get his management to agree and didn't think all that much of it himself. Even so, they resumed talks, and here Gossett had another eye-opener. Maurice began with one of his beautifully presented expositions on the Saatchi philosophy and his view of the industry. He showed how Saatchi had increased its earnings per share by an average of 30 percent over the past five years and its billings from £13.7 million in 1971 to a forecast £100 million in 1981. He outlined the need for advertising agencies to have international networks—he didn't have to remind anyone of how McCann Erickson had used the Coca-Cola account in Brazil as a lever to grab the U.S. account too.

Compton, like many agencies, had no corporate plan. Gossett himself was a former creative pro and freely admitted he was not very good when it came to figures. The Saatchis seemed to have everything thought out years ahead. Gossett still didn't want to make the deal, but he decided he had better get moving with Compton before it was too late. He had his financial team draw up a plan for expansion, and Compton went on the acquisition trail, buying up Klemtner Advertising and Rumrill-Hoyt.

Then one day Maurice rang him with a suggestion. "Why don't we buy all of *you*?" Gossett laughed uproariously. It was the most outrageous suggestion he had ever heard. "You're crazy," he said. Despite Saatchi's rapid growth, Compton was still twice its size and had a much more established position. Gossett would not even consider the proposal. Yet when he had rung off, he did consider it, and the more he thought of it, the more it made sense to him. The trap had been sprung, and Gossett, although he had not yet realized it, was inside the net. Now the problem would be getting his senior managers to go in with him.

Meanwhile, every week seemed to bring a new rumor that the Saatchis were in talks with someone or other. There was almost no agency they could buy, it seemed to Gossett, that would not raise some conflict or other with P&G in particular—unless it was Compton. There was only one thing to do: he had to have his own agency in London. It was his final effort to wriggle free.

More in desperation than anything else he traveled to London and bought Britain's seventeenth largest agency, KMP, an agency that had been started in 1964 with as big a splash as Saatchi made years later and by 1974 was actually fifth in billings. In the economic crisis of the mid-1970s the company fell apart, lost £210,000 when one of its clients, Brentford Nylon, went bust, and was briefly owned by the Guinness brewing group. Then it went independent again—and now became part of Compton.

Having signed the deal to acquire KMP, Gossett called in on Charlotte Street to see his old friend and Saatchi chairman, Ken Gill. As a matter of courtesy, he told Gill about KMP. Gill, however, had something for Gossett. From his desk he took a letter that offered to buy the whole of Compton Advertising in New York. The Saatchis were drawing the strings of the net tighter and tighter.

Gossett was furious as he began to realize what was happening. "This is obviously a ploy," he said. "You knew I was going to tell you this afternoon we were buying a London agency. But you're not going to change my mind. We're still going to buy it."

Back in New York, Gossett dropped the piece of paper containing the offer into a desk drawer and left it there for six months. He didn't even tell his managers about it. Every so often one of them mentioned that someone had heard that Milt had an important piece of paper and that the word in London was they all should know what was on it. Gossett was still so annoyed that he refused even to get it out again.

Saatchi meanwhile had made a takeover but not in the United States. The Saatchis were still concentrating their efforts on New York and on Compton in particular, but some of the early feelers they had put out in London were coming to fruition. In 1978 there had been lengthy negotiations with Charles's old agency, Collett Dickenson Pearce. The opportunity to purchase Collett arose because the Inland Revenue had disclosed its intention to charge its chairman, John Pearce, and the managing director, Frank Lowe, with tax irregularities. The price was not right, however, and CDP survived. Soon thereafter, Young & Rubicam bought a 40 percent stake in it.

In 1981 there was another opportunity to make an acquisition; this time the Saatchis did not pass it up. When John Bentley had bought Dorland Advertising a decade before, stripped the assets, and then sold it, the buyer—for £850,000—was Eric Garrott, who owned his own small ad agency. He combined the two agencies under the name of Garrott Dorland Crawford. During the 1970s the agency did well, but in 1981 Garrott fell seriously ill, and with no heirs and no obvious successor, he decided to sell. For patriotic reasons he refused to sell to the American agencies, including Compton, who were after him. Saatchi & Saatchi was quickly at hand.

Dorland cost Saatchi over £7 million, but it was not all paid at once. Ever since the disastrous George G. Smith bid in 1974, the brothers had adopted a new method of paying for acquisitions, devised to an extent by James Joll at Rothschild (and later developed and adopted by Martin Sorrell when he went solo). The Saatchi brothers would agree to put down a lump sum, say, a quarter of the agreed price, then insist the rest of the price be "earned out" over a number of years. This meant that if the acquisition turned out to be a dud, they paid only a proportion of the total price; if it did better than forecast they paid more—the "earned out" portion had a performance element attached to it. The idea was to lock in the existing management and keep it at maximum effort for at least the first few years after the takeover. It was a method that was already widely used in the rag trade and other industries in Britain, and Maurice, guided initially by Joll, a former financial journalist, speedily adopted and developed it. This method of payment would later become clearly identified both with Saatchi and with Sorrell and become all too familiar to New York agency chiefs.

In the case of Dorland, the Saatchis decided against merging it with their existing agency—both businesses were too big for that. The Saatchi staff was now about 700 strong; Dorland in its own right had over £50 million in billings, half Saatchi's size. Garrott lived long enough to see the deal through and to declare, "This is a union of strength and a great day for British advertising" before dying on the operating table. The success of the Dorland acquisition meant that Saatchi & Saatchi had no challenger for the number-one spot in Britain. JWT had fought back to match Saatchi's £83 million in billings in 1980 but could not match the combined billings of Saatchi and Dorland.

The Dorland bid was significant for another reason: it was the first time Saatchi had made use of the London stock market to raise money. The idea was that Saatchi would sell £5 million worth of shares in the market, then pass the cash to the Dorland management, an exercise that Saatchi would later use to the limit when buying Bates. It was a tiny issue, yet it is a mark of the attitude that still existed toward advertising companies that there was no confidence that it would succeed. The

Saatchi stockbrokers, Phillips & Drew, one of the biggest brokerage firms in London, were very nervous about the offering and not at all sure it would be taken up. Maurice and Martin Sorrell drove into the City to address the Phillips & Drew sales force before the markets opened.

"They were all white-faced and worried about it," recalls Sorrell. But the offering went well, and Maurice made a note to use it again. It would become the standard Saatchi method of financing takeover bids, a financing weapon unknown and unavailable to the New York agencies.

During this time there was no contact between Gossett and his team in New York and the Saatchi team in London. Compton now had its own London operation, and Gossett insisted he didn't need Saatchi & Saatchi, although Compton still of course retained its 20 percent ownership in the Saatchi agency. Maurice was still making his rounds of the New York agencies, patiently explaining his plans, sometimes received with courteous interest, sometimes getting the door slammed in his face. No one treated him with contempt: the Saatchi creative reputation went before him, and most agency chiefs were intrigued enough to meet him. Everyone in the New York ad business knew about the "pregnant man" and the "Labour isn't working" ads. That, of course, didn't mean he had anything to offer them in New York, but it gave him a hearing in most places, and the persuasive and earnest Maurice could accomplish a lot with that.

It was still a lonely furrow. He usually went alone or with Martin Sorrell, sometimes presenting his case to a packed boardroom, at other times at breakfast or lunch or a late dinner. Charles never went at all. Gossett was still in the net, but Compton had not yet been reeled in, and that exercise still required careful playing and infinite patience. Ken Gill was still keen to revive negotiations with his old friends at Compton and kept the lines open.

After about six months of silence, Gossett rang Maurice. "This is ridiculous," he said. "We have the international networks, we have the accounts, we have a wonderful opportunity to be together, and we can learn a lot from you." The talks were on again. Gossett, however, was still not ready to surrender easily. He put his chief financial officer, Bob Huntingdon, in charge of the negotiations, knowing full well that Huntingdon was opposed to the merger. If Huntingdon could work something out, it had to be a good deal for Compton. He and Maurice began their talks, and the Compton side soon learned to respect the younger Saatchi brother's grasp of financial detail and his ability to deliver instant decisions without deferring to anyone. Gossett asked that Sorrell be kept out of the talks—Gossett had never liked him and was also slightly afraid of the finance director's ability with figures. Charles never appeared but as always was fully in the picture and driving from behind. He never wanted to be bothered with detail. It was to Charles, as always, a matter of "Do it."

Right up to the last moment the brothers played their fish into the net, steering Gossett into giving them the deal they had always wanted. There was to be a crucial meeting in New York where the final details would be thrashed out, and for this Charles accompanied Maurice. In some ways this merger was almost a rerun of the original Compton bid in the United Kingdom. One of the last details to be settled was the name of the merged company. After long negotiation Gossett had accepted, as Gill had back in 1975, that the Saatchi name came first. But how many Saatchis? At a previous meeting Gossett had agreed that the name would be Saatchi Compton. Now Charles, who had said very little, suddenly spoke.

"I hate to do this to you, but we need both Saatchis in the name."

Gossett stared at him a moment, then snapped, "Well, screw that, that's the last straw." It was his turn to storm out. The talks were off again.

This time, however, Gossett's irritation lasted only a matter of weeks. If the agency had just been called "Saatchi," it would never have been so distinctive—he knew that. It was that second "Saatchi" that gave the name its special effect, as Charles had realized years before. Gossett was now virtually landed, his final struggle over: he would settle for the two Saatchis coming first in the name.

The Compton merger was an enormous deal for Saatchi & Saatchi, many times bigger than anything the brothers had touched so far, and even more significant in that it took them into the big time in world advertising, opening the door at last to Madison Avenue and all that lay ahead. Compton was twice Saatchi's size. The brothers would need to find $30 million immediately and another $24.8 million paid over five years, again on their "earn out" formula—which only the City of London could provide. (Wall Street would never have touched it, either then or now, even in the days of junk bonds.) Once again, Maurice and Martin Sorrell paraded into the City early in the morning, this time to arrange a stock issue of some £26 million, a large sum in relation to their existing business. Their ability to raise money on the London stock market was a two-edged sword, however. Each time they did so, they diluted their own shareholding in a way the big American agency heads would have refused.

This was a turning point for the brothers. They now owned 36 percent of the company. The bond issue they were about to make would reduce their holding to 18 percent. They both hated doing it, and it was Sorrell who laid out the options for them the night before: "Are you prepared to own 18 percent of Saatchi & Saatchi plus Compton or 36 percent of Saatchi on its own?" It was Charles, very nervous, who gave Sorrell his answer: "Do it." Gossett, with 10 percent of the Compton business, would become a rich man, and another 100 of the staff also got handsome payouts.

In dollar terms, Saatchi's billings that year were running at about $350 million. Compton's were $650 million. The combined group would have billings of around $1 billion a year. Overnight Saatchi had become the thirteenth biggest agency in the United States, the ninth biggest world-wide, and with the addition of KMP, which it now acquired with Compton, Saatchi & Saatchi was even more impregnable in London. The deal was formally announced on March 15, 1982, and *Campaign*, for the only time in its history, brought out a special issue on the following Monday to mark the occasion. The British invasion of Madison Avenue had begun.

Baghdad (*above*) where once eighty thousand Jews lived and prospered. The Saatchi family left in 1947; within five years almost the entire Jewish population of Iraq had emigrated.

By 1951, the year of the mass emigration of the Jews from Iraq, the Saatchis were already part of an Iraqi-Jewish community forming in London. Maurice, age five, is at the back left, beside his eldest brother David, age fourteen. Charles, age eight, is at the right end of the back row.

The parents: Nathan and Daisy Saatchi (*right*) at their comfortable London home.

Charles (center back) at age thirteen (*below*), at his North London school, Christ's College, October 1956.

The eldest brother: David (*above left*), seven years older than Charles, lives in New York, where he is a successful commodities broker–turned–full-time sculptor.

The youngest brother: Phil (*above right*), the only one of the four brothers born in England. Seven years younger than Maurice, he was a journalist before going into the music world, first as owner of a recording studio, then as a songwriter, singer, and guitarist; he played on tour with Joan Armatrading and released his first album in April 1987.

The original backers: Mary Quant and her husband, Alexander Plunket-Greene (*below*), who put up the bulk of the £25,000 to start Saatchi & Saatchi. Lindsay Masters (*above left*), who gave Maurice his first job at Haymarket Publishing, put up the rest. Michael Heseltine (*above right*), Masters's partner at Haymarket, did not invest—although he wanted to—because he had just become a government minister.

Above: Charles and his partner Ross Cramer in April 1970. Their Cramer-Saatchi consultancy business, the forerunner of the Saatchi & Saatchi agency, worked for the Health Education Council, for whom they produced a highly successful "stop smoking" campaign—and the "pregnant man" poster.

Left: John Hegarty (seated), an art director who was one of Charles's first recruits; Chris Martin (standing) joined soon afterward. Both men are now directors of their own agencies.

Right: Written in 1970, Jeremy Sinclair's "pregnant man" ad created a sensation that is remembered to this day. A reputation for daring and creativity helped the fledgling agency get off to a fast start.

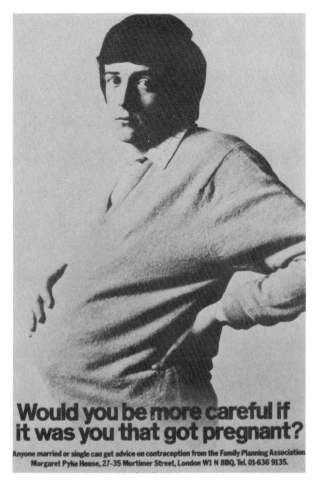

Would you be more careful if it was you that got pregnant?

Anyone married or single can get advice on contraception from the Family Planning Association Margaret Pyke House, 27-35 Mortimer Street, London W1 N 8BQ. Tel. 01-636 9135.

Left: Jeremy Sinclair, who wrote the "pregnant man" ad in 1970—and many others over the next twenty years. Charles Saatchi hired Sinclair as copywriter in 1968, straight from Watford College of Art, and later he became joint deputy chairman of the worldwide group, number three to the brothers.

This "fly in your food" poster (*right*) for Britain's Health Education Council was typical of Saatchi's attention-getting copy. After describing a number of loathesome things that flies do to food, the ad concluded, "and then, when they're finished eating, it's your turn."

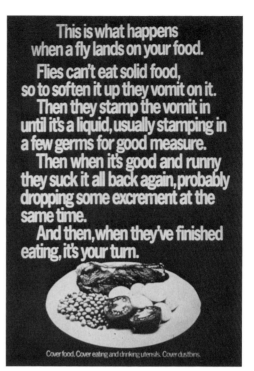

This is what happens when a fly lands on your food.

Flies can't eat solid food, so to soften it up they vomit on it. Then they stamp the vomit in until it's a liquid, usually stamping in a few germs for good measure. Then when it's good and runny they suck it all back again, probably dropping some excrement at the same time. And then, when they've finished eating, it's your turn.

Cover food. Cover eating and drinking utensils. Cover dustbins.

The brothers (*below*), Maurice (*at left*) and Charles, in Maurice's office on Charlotte Street, where they moved in 1976. This is one of the few stock pictures they supply of themselves—they do not like either photographers or reporters.

David Puttnam (*right*) and Alan Parker (*above*) almost tempted Charles into a career as a film script-writer. The three became friends at Collett Dickenson Pearce, where Charles first made his name, and moved to offices in the same building on Goodge Street in the late 1960s. Puttnam and Charles have remained close friends.

Josephine Hart (*left*), the Irish woman who first met Maurice at Haymarket in 1967. She became his second wife in October 1984, and they have a son, the first Saatchi grandson. Josephine is now a major West End theatrical producer in London.

Maurice (*below*), pictured in 1972, became the chairman of Saatchi & Saatchi PLC, the biggest advertising business in the world. Charles has never had any other title than director.

Doris Saatchi (*right*), whom Charles married in 1973. Together they built a collection of contemporary art that is regarded as the best of its kind in the world. It is shown in their own gallery at St. John's Wood. Charles and Doris are now separated.

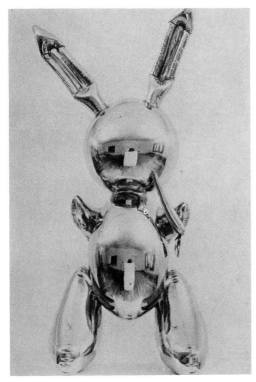

A Saatchi exhibition, "New York Art Now," featured some of the East Village artists in Charles and Doris Saatchi's collection. This stainless-steel rabbit (*left*) is by Jeff Koons, whose work includes porcelain and polychrome pets, toys, and a larger-than-life-size Michael Jackson.

Left: The 1979 election campaign: Margaret Thatcher rehearses with Tim Bell on the roof of the building from which Saatchi ran the campaign. Bell became a fan, and Thatcher in turn insisted that he work on the account in later elections.

Below left: "Champagne-tippling Svengali": (Sir) Gordon Reece is the public relations man who groomed Mrs. Thatcher for power. Wanting an advertising agency that could present her properly to the electorate, he hired Saatchi & Saatchi.

Below right: Lord Thorneycroft, the Conservative Party chairman, was much impressed by Bell—when he finally met him.

Ron Collins (*above*), one of the original Saatchi & Saatchi team. He stayed only a year, left without being paid for his shares, and became a cofounder of Wight Collins Rutherford Scott.

Jennifer Laing (*below*) was tempted back to Saatchi with a red Ferrari.

Bill Muirhead (*top*), an Australian who became Saatchi's first account executive. He is now chairman of the London agency.

Ken Gill (*middle*), chairman of Garland-Compton, played a central role in Saatchi's first major takeover. He became chairman of the enlarged company, until Maurice finally took over in 1985.

James Gulliver (*above*) was asked by Gill to advise on Saatchi's takeover of Garland-Compton. Gulliver thought it was a bad idea—and sold his shareholding.

Tim Bell, here appreciating the initiative of a young man seeking a job in advertising, was once seen as the "third brother." He joked that he was in fact the ampersand in Saatchi & Saatchi. By 1983 he and the brothers were falling out.

Michael Dobbs (*right*) worked in Mrs. Thatcher's private office before the 1979 election, but she didn't offer him a job on Downing Street. He worked as assistant to Tim Bell in 1983 and then became director of communications at Saatchi.

Martin Sorrell learned much from the brothers. He jumped from being finance director of Saatchi & Saatchi to staging a dramatic $560 million bid for J. Walter Thompson, the "university of advertising."

Anthony Simonds-Gooding (*below at left*) was charmed away from Whitbread by Maurice Saatchi, who brought him in as Saatchi & Saatchi's chief executive. This rare photo of Maurice Saatchi was taken when Maurice happened to wander into a photo shoot for Simonds-Gooding shortly before his departure in 1987 to run British Satellite Broadcasting.

Giants of Madison Avenue:
Bill Bernbach (*below*) told Avis that the best he could say about the company was that it was second largest and that its people were trying harder. His ads for Volkswagen and Levy's rye bread were among the best made in America in the 1960s. He was the guru to the new advertising generation, including Charles Saatchi.

David Ogilvy (*bottom*) is regarded as the doyen of advertising. A Scot, he worked as a chef in the Hotel Majestic, Paris, sold Aga cookers in Scotland, and started Ogilvy & Mather in New York in 1949—the same year Bernbach founded Doyle Dane Bernbach.

New York agency chiefs taken over by Saatchi:
Milt Gossett (*top left*), chairman of Compton, initially proposed buying Saatchi & Saatchi, then allowed the brothers to buy Compton in 1982, their leap into the big league.

Carl Spielvogel (*top right*) is a former journalist whose Backer & Spielvogel agency grew even faster than Saatchi & Saatchi before he sold in 1986. He is now the chairman and chief executive officer of Backer Spielvogel Bates Worldwide, created from agencies taken over by the Saatchis in New York, including Ted Bates.

Ed Wax (*bottom left*) is an ex-Compton man who was persuaded by Milt Gossett and Maurice Saatchi to rejoin in 1982. He now runs Saatchi & Saatchi OFS Compton in New York, the biggest agency in the group.

Bob Jacoby (*bottom right*) got $110 million for his shares in Ted Bates—and another $4 million for wrongful dismissal after they fired him. The ensuing battle at Bates, dubbed "MacBates" in the New York trade press when it lost a series of accounts and received a large quantity of bad publicity, gave the brothers the worst time of their corporate careers.

Victor Millar (*right*) was one of two senior worldwide managing partners of Arthur Andersen, then the world's largest management consultancy, when the Saatchis hired him at a reputed $1 million a year to spearhead the drive into consultancy. When Simonds-Gooding left, Millar took over responsibility for communications too.

Martin Sorrell, WWP Group chief executive (*below*), and Kenneth Roman, Ogilvy's chief executive officer, talk about the merger of their two companies in New York in May 1989. Roman at first was totally opposed to Sorrell's proposal but later succumbed to his improved offer and tactical ability. (Reuters/Bettmann Newsphotos)

13
GLOBALIZATION

Maurice Saatchi's reading list is catholic; on his desk at any given time one may find a tidy heap of economic journals, analysts' reports on half a dozen different industries, or the latest Tom Wolfe or Scott Turow novel. The visitor, politely remarking on any of these, will receive an enthusiastic summary, followed by a copy of the book or photocopy of the article delivered to his or her office a few days later. Both brothers like to share their enthusiasms, so if Charles has seen a film or a West End or Broadway show that he likes, everybody *must* go and see it too. If Maurice has found a new novel or writer, then everyone *has* to read the book. This eagerness to share their discoveries is, perhaps, a gesture of bridge-building, of reaching out, the nearest the brothers get to letting the outsider glimpse their inner selves. They don't share their private lives with colleagues or business friends, not because of any overpowering desire for privacy, but simply because they genuinely find it difficult. Charles finds it hard to sustain a conversation of any length with anyone he hasn't known for years and who is therefore unattuned to his shorthand. He and Maurice don't need to say much to each other; they wander in and out of each other's offices all day and talk constantly on the phone or in the car driving to meetings together. Involving others in a book or a film that has caught their interest provides a tiny opening in the curtain the brothers have drawn over the rest of their lives.

There is another factor at work; both brothers, Maurice less so than Charles, have low thresholds of boredom. If something does not interest them, they will not do it. Having done something once, they are not very interested in doing it again. Each successive stage of Saatchi & Saatchi had to have some new element to it that caught the brothers' imaginations and made their agency's climb more than the straightforward progression of a company up the profits ladder.

The Saatchi brothers set out to make money, certainly; but that came remarkably easily and after a few years was not enough. Charles wanted to show that a "hot-shop" agency could grow and become the biggest in the land; several years before that happened both brothers had already mentally discounted that goal and were looking ahead. In the late 1970s they would both get enormous intellectual satisfaction in watching the speed with which the agency pulled in new accounts and in seeing the people they had hired take on and beat the biggest names of the day.

Running the advertising campaign that helped elect Mrs. Thatcher had given them as big a thrill as anything, not so much because of what it meant politically but because it posed a technical challenge to their professional skills and to the organization they had created. Their name and reputation had become closely associated with the new Tories, so winning meant a great deal. And the fame their role in Mrs. Thatcher's election gave them allowed them to do even more, take on things they otherwise could not have attempted.

Buying a big New York agency, never before done by a foreigner, was yet another challenge that engaged their interest, and their imagination could work overtime on seeing the enormous possibilities, then solving the difficulties in accomplishing such a purchase. Each stage of their progress had to have a philosophical justification, often discovered retrospectively, but growth for the Saatchis was never the simple affair it is for many corporate predators. There would be a consistent strand through that philosophy and through their growth, but many times the brothers had little idea where that strand was leading them. That too was part of the thrill, the excitement of making a leap and discovering that the ladder was indeed where they hoped it would be and that they were safely halfway up it already.

It is possible to be highly skeptical about their philosophical utterings, dismissing them as no more than whitewash for a ruthless and single-minded preoccupation with size, power, and self-satisfaction. Indeed, much of what the brothers would claim as their philosophy does not, on first glance at least, justify such a high-blown term.

It is worth looking again at that 1987 Harvard Business School case study of Saatchi & Saatchi, which has a section headed "Philosophy." As the company grew, says the study, so the brothers lowered their profile "to minimize the company's apparent dependence on themselves . . . operating management had been delegated to a number of experienced . . . executives." That appears to be fairly straightforward but on closer examination is what the brothers wanted the world to believe rather than the reality. The Saatchis say that they have consistently, from the earliest days, tried to work themselves out of a job. Thus, within a couple of years, Maurice had turned over to others the whole machine of getting new business, which he started with his Rolodex; Charles stopped writing many of the ads within the first couple of years; and Tim Bell took over first the making of presentations, then the running of the agency. Martin Sorrell took on the financial affairs of the group and also its relationship with the City and the bankers and stockbrokers. Distancing themselves from the day-to-day activities of the agency made the brothers more remote and added to their mystique, and in terms of building a large-scale business it was the sensible thing to do.

But is that really why they did it? It is probably nearer the truth to say that the Saatchis made a management virtue of their own thirst for excitement and the need to keep themselves involved; by the time they merged with Compton in London, they had no interest in running an agency anymore, so they never did it—they gave the responsibility to Tim Bell and probably congratulated themselves on their cleverness in motivating someone so good at it to work so hard for them. Their devolvement of power and delegation of responsibility are good textbook stuff, which the Harvard Business School teaches its pupils; but using these methods of management also happened to be the only way the Saatchis could keep themselves interested in the business.

Typically, having discovered that it both worked and suited them, the Saatchis soon began encouraging their own executives to think in the same way. Maurice, interviewing people for senior roles, would tell them that one of the things he wanted them to do was "work yourself out of a job" as soon as possible, thus freeing the executive for even bigger and better things.

The next paragraph in the Harvard Business School case-study analysis of the Saatchi philosophy is more sweeping: "The twin elements underpinning Saatchi & Saatchi's strategy," it says, "were a belief that being large was important, but being the number one, two or three in the industry was vital; and that markets were defined globally."

The Saatchis undoubtedly always had a belief that "being large was important," as shown by their cheeky offers to the other agencies from their earliest days. They had no interest in being a "creative hot shop" a moment longer than they needed to be; they instinctively yearned after size and prestige, and their instinct was supported by their experiences in the early days when they could not get near the big accounts because their agency was too small. They also wanted to be number one—Charles told everyone that was where Saatchi & Saatchi was headed. But that longing to be number one was because Charles wanted to prove something to the world rather than for any commercial reason. Think of his and Maurice's delight, therefore, when they discovered a philosophical reason for what they instinctively yearned for. Ted Bates, in conjunction with Harvard, undertook a study that produced what it called the "Law of Dominance." Simply stated, it said that unless you are in the top three companies in an industry, you are nowhere, or, as Bates put it: "One, Two, Three, or out." The Saatchis refined this slightly to read: "One is wonderful, two can be terrific, three is threatened, four is fatal."

The Law of Dominance was supported by a number of statistical analyses of the Harvard databases, all of them showing the importance of market share in determining profitability. These analyses seriously questioned whether, in the long run, firms outside the top three could be consistently profitable in any international industry. The study's finding was an argument in favor of "power of scale," which meant that a bigger firm could attract and keep better talent, take bigger risks, invest in research and development, establish a worldwide information system, and benefit from economies of scale.

To Maurice and Charles the Law of Dominance was a revelation, and they seized on it with an enthusiasm they would communicate to the others in the organization. Soon the Law of Dominance had become official Saatchi philosophy, to be spread through the organization and on into the investment world as explanation and justification of where the agency was headed. Here again is another piece of the answer to what made the Saatchis different. Not many organizations have any clear philosophy at all or anything more than the vaguest idea of where they are headed. The Saatchi philosophy may not have been what the Harvard Business School professors thought it to be, but it certainly existed, and it was understood by Saatchi's own senior staff.

The final part of that Harvard sentence was, "and that markets were defined globally." In 1982, when they signed the Compton New York deal, the Saatchis had barely heard the word "global" used in the way the Harvard study used it. They perceived at an early stage the need to be international and had opened offices in Paris, Brussels, Frankfurt, and other major European cities in the mid-1970s, putting the name Saatchi & Saatchi on the door, hiring someone to run these European offices, and waiting for the business to come along. The brothers had not seen Saatchi's expansion into Europe as symptomatic of any great movement in world markets but as a practical solution to the demands of Saatchi's clients, demands the agency was otherwise unable to satisfy. The brothers soon retreated from their European venture, realizing the advertising world did not work that way. No one wanted a Europe-wide agency, particularly as tiny a one as they were offering. An advertising agency had to be worldwide to be of any value to the client. It was one of their more humiliating failures.

Over the next few years the need for a large and well-organized international network was borne in on the brothers again and again. They found that Saatchi & Saatchi would not get on the shortlist for a new client because only the multinational agencies were included. That was bad enough, but there was something more. Saatchi & Saatchi began losing business. Maurice remembers one big client coming to him and saying: "Well, I think you're great, and you're marvelous people, but the decision has been taken back in America that we're going to have a chain. I'm very sorry, it's very unfair, you're the best people, but you'll just have to go." The awareness that business was going to multinational agencies even if they were not as highly regarded as Saatchi & Saatchi was what inspired the talks with O'Toole of Foote, Cone & Belding (who had probably seen the globalization trend before the Saatchis) as well as

Maurice's analysis of the way advertising was developing, which impressed Gossett and others.

With Compton, Saatchi did acquire an international network and was now able to offer a worldwide service. But the brothers, like most people in the industry, had never seriously thought about why an international network was so necessary—they had simply reacted to the pressure from clients to put one in place. They had bought a big New York agency because they had seen, ahead of most of the pack, the direction in which their big clients such as Procter & Gamble were going. They had tried to create their own international network and failed, so they had bought one. Now they were to find an intellectual justification for this move too.

On Maurice Saatchi's regular reading list is the *Harvard Business Review*, an economic and business publication that contains articles mostly by academics, written for and read by America's management elite. Maurice never went to Harvard, but it is one of his few regrets that he did not take off a few years after the London School of Economics to study outside Britain. He compensated by staying in touch with the academic debates going on in management circles, not closely but taking a spasmodic yet intense interest in subjects that fired his imagination. He was continually looking for answers or advice on problems that none of his colleagues in advertising could help with—or understand, for that matter. In mid-1983 an article in the *Review* caught his attention, and as he read it, Maurice became more and more enthralled. The article was called "The Globalization of Markets" and was written by Professor Theodore (Ted) Levitt, a professor of business administration and head of the marketing division of the Harvard Business School. Its subheading read: "Companies must learn to operate as if the world were one large market—ignoring superficial regional and national differences."

Levitt had been making the same point for several years, but as Maurice read it for the first time that day, Levitt's analysis struck him as an exact fit with the circumstances of his own company. Here for the first time was an answer to the "why"—Levitt was explaining precisely what the brothers and most big agency chiefs had found out by trial and error. Levitt's thesis was essentially this: the big multinational companies were finding that their old markets were becoming saturated. New markets, on the other hand, were more and more difficult to find; and if a company had to customize its products to suit the new markets, the extra sales were not worth the trouble. The big multinationals had been so caught up in trying to anticipate what these new markets would want that they had become befuddled and could no longer see the forest for the trees.

Another and wiser group of companies was taking a different approach. This group regarded the whole world as one and the same market; it sold the same advanced, standardized, functional, and reliable product everywhere. Thus, explained Levitt, in Brazil thousands swarmed daily "from preindustrial Bahian darkness into exploding coastal cities" and installed the latest television sets in corrugated huts, or made sacrificial offerings of fruit and fresh-killed chicken to Macumban spirits "next to battered Volkswagens." During Nigeria's civil war, the soldiers listened to transistor radios and drank the very same Coca-Cola that teenagers did in America. "Corporations geared to this new reality benefit from enormous economies of scale in production, distribution, marketing and management," Levitt wrote. "By translating these benefits into reduced world prices, they can decimate competitors that still live in the disabling grip of old assumptions about how the world works."

Levitt insisted that national and regional preferences were gone; last year's models could no longer be sold in the Third World, because no matter how poor they were, the developing countries wanted the latest. And they wanted them at the same prices the multinationals charged in their home markets. According to Levitt, "The globalization of markets is at hand. With that, the multinational commercial world nears its end, and so does the multinational corporation." The multinational and the global company were not the same thing, said Levitt. The former operated in a number of countries and adjusted its policies to each—at a high cost. The global corporation sold the same thing everywhere.

Economists had been making a similar point long before Levitt. Peter Drucker's *Age of Discontinuity*, published in 1969, has a chapter entitled "From International to World Economy," in which Drucker argues that the world was rapidly moving to become one large marketplace for products other than Coca-Cola—the Volkswagen, for instance—and that the wants of affluent consumers were pretty much the same whether they were American, French, or Russian. Levitt took Drucker's argument several stages further, particularly in his assertion about the death of the multinational. The article of Levitt's that Maurice Saatchi read in the *Harvard Business Review* that day ended on a warning note: "The global company will shape the vectors of technology and globalization into its great strategic fecundity. It will systematically push these vectors toward their own convergence, offering everyone simultaneously high-quality, more or less standardized products at optimally low prices, thereby achieving for itself vastly expanded markets and profits. Companies that do not adapt to the new global realities will become victims of those that do."

For Maurice, Levitt's warning was a revelatory message—and one he could use to his advantage. Procter & Gamble, he now realized, had been a global company for years and had long known the lessons Levitt set out. Other Compton clients were also global companies, all of them demanding that their advertising agencies keep pace with their expansion. The world was going in that direction, and Saatchi & Saatchi had been pulled along with it. Now Saatchi must get ahead. Levitt had little to say about the advertising industry in this article (Maurice didn't know it, but Peter Drucker, in his book *Management: Tasks, Responsibilities, Practices*, published in 1973, had hinted at such a trend developing for the advertising business, as had various others), but his theories fit the industry so neatly that they seemed to be tailor-made. Maurice decided to fly up to Harvard and talk to Levitt and to place globalization at the heart of the Saatchi doctrine.

Levitt warmed to the younger Saatchi's enthusiasm, but Maurice was not the only advertising executive to beat a path to his door that year. Another big New York agency, Foote, Cone & Belding, struck first. Its annual report that year featured an article entitled: "Global Markets, Global Advertisers, Global Agencies—The Wave of the Future." The author was the same Ted Levitt whom Maurice now regarded as his private philosopher. The New York agencies were not going to allow the Saatchis to hijack their guru without a fight.

In that Foote, Cone & Belding article Professor Levitt applied his theories along the precise lines that Maurice Saatchi would have wanted. "A powerful new challenge and opportunity faces advertisers and advertising agencies," Levitt wrote, "with results even more profound than the great transformation for which Albert Lasker, the founder of modern advertising, is justifiably credited. Suddenly, commerce throughout the world is getting radically different. Competition has become intensely global."

Advertising, he went on, so far had played a remarkably small role in this movement toward globalization, although the trend had in fact been brought about by communications, the jumbo jet, "digitized and transistorized telecommunications," containerized shipping, and so forth. "What was once known to, and available for, only the affluent and the leisure classes is now becoming known and accessible to impoverished masses everywhere."

Levitt in this article suggested that the advertising industry should do more than respond to the global needs of its clients: advertisers should actually lead the way. "Most important is the necessity for advertising agencies to help their clients to see how the world is changing." He elaborated on the Coca-Cola example, pointing out that Coke was not always a mass-market, transnational, low-cost product, nor did it grow into one by slow self-propulsion: it was created "by imagination in the design of its strategies and the implacability of its executions. The resulting economies of scale and consequent profitability are obvious."

The advertising industry, said Levitt, had to get in step with the new world and turn its multinational clients into global competitors. He ended by quoting from W. B. Yeats's poem "The Second Coming": "Things fall apart; the centre cannot hold," adding that "nothing could be more true regarding the old abnormalities of world commerce. The phrase 'passion-

ate intensity' with which Yeats ends the stanza is appropriate to the way
we must rethink competition in 'The Republic of Technology.' "

What Levitt failed to mention is that Yeats in that poem, forecasting a
world of anarchy, said, "The best lack all conviction, while the worst/Are
full of passionate intensity." Did Levitt intend to imply that the rethink-
ing should now be done by the "worst"? And whom did he mean? One
wonders if the Foote, Cone & Belding directors had ever read Yeats. Or if
they realized that the same poem ends: "And what rough beast, its hour
come round at last,/Slouches towards Bethlehem to be born."

So there were others in the advertising industry alongside, and perhaps
even ahead of, the Saatchis in their thinking about the direction of the
industry in 1983. There were many who were ahead in putting this
thinking into practice. The worldwide Compton network that Saatchi
now owned was not a good one, certainly nowhere near as good as those
of half a dozen of the top New York agencies. The Saatchis knew that,
but it didn't bother them. They could make the Compton network
good—by beefing it up, by making more acquisitions, and by using it
properly for some of the major new accounts. The first real test of the
international network would be the British Airways account.

March 1983: in a small studio in the Saatchi & Saatchi headquarters
on Charlotte Street a small group waits for the lights to go down. One of
that group is a square, heftily built man, now past middle age, whose
jutting jaw and vast, squat hands convey an impression of great forceful-
ness. He sits in the front row, in the center, for this show is in his honor:
Sir John King, appointed by Mrs. Thatcher to take the near-bankrupt
British Airways out of state ownership and into private hands, has put
Saatchi & Saatchi at the center of his marketing strategy. A great deal
hangs on the ads he is about to see.

Beside him sits Maurice Saatchi, his tall, thin figure and his youthful-
ness—he is nearly thirty years younger than King—contrasting with
King's powerful stockiness. Bill Muirhead, Saatchi executive in charge
of the BA account, holds the floor, and the assembled group of BA and
Saatchi executives listens attentively as he makes his presentation.

This is to be no ordinary campaign but will, it is claimed, break new
ground. It is to be one of the few totally worldwide brand-advertising
drives ever attempted and is probably the most coordinated international
marketing push ever mounted by a British company. Television sets in the
United States, Canada, Australia, and Britain will carry the same ad on
the same day. Some twenty-five other countries ranging from Egypt,
Hong Kong, and South Africa to India and Thailand—everywhere that
has a developed commercial-television network and a few passengers who
might fly British Airways—will see it shortly afterward. The commercial
will cost £25 million worldwide in the first year, not an enormous figure

by the standards of Procter & Gamble but a huge outlay for an airline.

Saatchi has latched onto a key statistic: British Airways can boast that it flies more people to more places than any other airline in the world, a function of its inheritance of routes to the old British Empire and its base in London, still probably the most international city in the world. Unlike the United States, there are not many profitable domestic routes around Britain; the big U.S. airlines carry more passengers than BA, but no one carried more *international* passengers—to more places. British Airways flies to seventy destinations around the world, and only Air France comes anywhere near that number. British Airways clocks up 130,728 international aircraft departures a year; Air France is second with 116,700. Saatchi converts this information into the slogan: "The World's Favourite Airline."

There is another statistic Saatchi can make use of: every year British Airways carries more people across the Atlantic than live in Manhattan (1.2 million). The first ad that Muirhead shows reflects this. The ad is a dramatic science-fiction piece of film, designed to illustrate the airline's dominance of the toughest route of all, the North Atlantic. A dog on a nighttime stroll with his master stops, whimpers, and looks up; a housewife in quilted housecoat peers skyward from her doorway; the music builds as a dark shape passes overhead. Then the scene shifts to air-traffic control. "Roger, Manhattan, continue to 2,000 feet," says a controller. As crowds emerge from a Tudor-style village to gaze upward, Manhattan island, its lights blazing, its major buildings recognizable, appears on the flight path for Heathrow airport. A voice-over, shaking the sinister sci-fi mood, suddenly booms: "Every year, British Airways flies more people across the Atlantic than the entire population of Manhattan."

The special effects have been done by the same team that did *Superman*, *2001—A Space Odyssey*, and *Star Wars* and are straight out of the Spielberg genre of the day, with music and effects similar to the feature film *Close Encounters of the Third Kind*. The commercial's director is Richard Loncrane, who has just finished filming *The Missionary*. The group assembled is shown other, less dramatic ads, each of them ending with a film star (Joan Collins, Omar Sharif, Peter O'Toole) checking in at British Airways.

As the lights finally come back on, King leads the chorus of approval. He loves the Manhattan ad. "The dog is great," he says. "It was a great idea to have the dog." King has seen roughs of the ad before and even scripts, but this is the first time he has seen the finished product.

I was one of the small audience in the studio that night, invited by King to see the commercial with him. He was anxious about the impact it would make and, despite his apparent self-confidence, was feeling under pressure. How would the ad go down with the press? With the City? With the traveling public? Maurice Saatchi and several of his team accompanied us to dinner, where King and his chief executive, Colin Marshall, talked about the importance of these ads for British Airways.

King explained that the Manhattan ad, which he had personally approved in the planning stage, was intended for a purpose other than persuading the public to use his airline. "I wanted an ad that would cause the staff to look up," he explained. "That's what the man does who is exercising his dog. I want them all to look up and say, 'My god, did we really do that?' "

King at the time was at a low point in his task of turning BA around and getting it into shape for a stock-market offering. In his first year in charge of British Airways he had shown losses of over £300 million and discovered that on staffing levels BA was the least efficient airline in the world. Its reputation and image were low, and morale in the company was even lower, particularly after he had axed 23,000 employees.

King was one of the few Saatchi clients who had met Charles and had become—and would remain—close to Maurice. He was not the average head of a company but a powerful political figure, a self-made millionaire from humble beginnings who became a Thatcher favorite in the early 1980s and who knew his way around Whitehall and the houses of parliament even better than Tim Bell did. When King took over BA one of the first things he did was precisely what Robert Townsend advises in his famous book *Up the Organization*: "Fire the whole advertising department and your old agency. Then go get the best new agency you can. And concentrate your efforts on making it fun for them to create candid, effective advertising for you."

King had not read Townsend, but his thinking was along the same lines. Foote, Cone & Belding had held the British Airways account for thirty-six years, had coined the highly successful slogans "Fly the flag" and "We take more care of you," and assumed it would hold the account for the same period again. Foote, Cone & Belding's work was good, and BA had been happy with it. But there was another reason for King to make the move. "When I became chairman of the airline, I had the problem of getting people to understand I was there and would actually see it through."

Foote, Cone & Belding executives were used to dealing with marketing people, and King felt he was not getting through to them—or they to him. Two or three times he sent messages asking them to come and see him, but they had never dealt with an airline chairman before and were reluctant to do so now. The chief executive in London, Bill Barry, met King twice, the first time when King told him he was scrapping BA's cheap-fares policy and going for maximum profit per head and on a second occasion when King came along to a presentation at the FCB office. "King told us our TV ads for British Airways were brilliant,"

Barry said later. "But he was unhappy about two of our press ads." As King was leaving, he turned to Barry and remarked, "You have made it very difficult for me to see what other agencies can do, but I cannot promise you that I will not go on looking."

Barry needed to understand King and his task at British Airways to have any comprehension of what was going through his mind at this stage. King wanted a high-profile, morale-boosting campaign that would be talked about outside the industry and lift the visibility of BA and of himself. He was in the political arena, fighting round after round with government ministers and officials as he tried to get them to write off BA's debts, guarantee his routes, and support him in the battles he was having with the unions and the work force. Foote, Cone, he decided, was producing good ads, but he wanted something more.

He unburdened this problem on a friend, a young art-gallery owner, Bernard Jacobson, one day. King at the time knew nothing about the advertising industry, about the relationship between clients and agencies, and never thought about how much of a stir it would make if he took the British Airways account to another agency. Jacobson knew the Saatchis from boyhood days—he and Charles had been school pals, and Charles had supported Jacobson's move into the art world. Jacobson was one of the few people Charles *could* discuss art with.

"Do you know Saatchi & Saatchi?" Jacobson asked. King didn't, although he had heard of the brothers in recent weeks. "They're very good," said Jacobson. Would King like to meet them?

A few weeks later King and Jacobson had dinner with Charles and Maurice at the Mirabelle, one of the best restaurants in London. It is a sign of the importance of the British Airways account (and of Jacobson's friendship with him) that Charles agreed to be present at this meeting; it would, although King did not know it, be the only time they would meet—"I've never seen him since!" The evening went well; King has a wry sense of humor and a keen political sense, and he warmed to these two bright young men, who responded to his warmth. "We talked about the media, we talked about advertising, and of course we talked about my problems," King recalls. "They said they could come up with a program that could do what I wanted, so I made the change." Saatchi had two airline accounts at the time, British Caledonian and KLM, and even with Maurice's highly tuned new business machine and Saatchi's parallel agencies there was no avoiding a conflict of interest. However, it is not often an account as big and prestigious as BA approaches you— and even rarer when the approach is from the chairman personally.

Some weeks later Saatchi & Saatchi made a pitch to BA, the only agency asked to do so other than Foote, Cone. Maurice handled the pitch personally, beginning a rapport with King that would develop into warm friendship over the years. The announcement that British Airways would be moving its account to Saatchi & Saatchi went out in September 1982, making the front pages of most of the national papers. At Foote, Cone & Belding, Bill Barry was furious. Not only was BA a visible and important account, it was also worth over £20 million a year, and losing it would mean firing staff as well as losing prestige. The loss would be a savage blow to his agency, all the worse because it was undeserved. Barry fired off an angry letter to King, complaining that he had been given no explanation for the move. To the press he stormed: "I would dearly love to know the reason. Saatchi & Saatchi have strong political connections, and Sir John was appointed by the prime minister. Here is a political payoff."

King insists he never even spoke to Mrs. Thatcher about making the switch. "I didn't know at that stage that you couldn't change your advertising agent. I thought you could do that the way you changed your newspaper if you wanted to." He would never, he says, even if he had thought of it, have taken the issue up with the prime minister, even though the government still owned the airline and she was his ultimate boss. "It was a purely management matter, and as a matter of principle I would not have taken it up with her."

There is other evidence to suggest the move was not politically inspired. For a start, the only Saatchi person with the ear of the prime minister was Tim Bell, and he, of course, played no part in getting the BA account. Maurice had not seen Mrs. Thatcher for several years, and Charles had still never spoken to her. It is possible she might have encouraged King on her own to switch to Saatchi, but she knew as little about the advertising world as he did.

There were several factors in favor of Saatchi. First of all, its reputation, deserved or not, was higher than that of any other agency in London. Second, it was British. Third, it had the ability to handle the account worldwide. No other British agency had ever been able to deliver such an advertising network. Now Saatchi could—and BA was its first new client gained as a result.

That week's *Campaign* said, "It is no exaggeration to say that the whole world of advertising will be scrutinizing the new British Airways campaign . . . in an attempt to predict the impact it will have on the perception of the airline and, therefore, on its performance in the marketplace."

The British Airways ads, when they appeared in New York, had an immediate impact on Saatchi's reputation. They were the first television ads made on Charlotte Street that Americans had seen. King was even more delighted with the response as the whole press took them up, both in Britain and the United States. He went to New York that week to find that "people were being interviewed on the streets in America and being asked: 'Have you seen that British Airways ad?' and they were saying

'Yes, it's fantastic.' It really caused a stir. It won a series of awards too, and it's in the Museum of Modern Art in America." The Saatchis, King says reflectively five years later, delivered what they had promised: "Our people started looking up again."

There were many critics of the Manhattan ad, too, and of the campaign that followed, which never achieved a standard approaching that first ad. But the Manhattan ad happened to hit the American market just as the more creative shops were producing a new kind of advertising, caused, among other things, by the arrival of video recorders and the remote-control device for the television set. "Suddenly people didn't have to get up any more and cross the room to change from a bad commercial. All they had to do was move their thumb a quarter of an inch," says the head of one of the big New York agencies. "So the time was right for outstanding creative work like the British Airways Manhattan ad—work that totally transfixed the individual and broke every rule of American advertising, like you mention the product in the first ten seconds, repeat it four times, and so on. All that stuff went out the window."

Compton was not the ideal agency to respond to the need for change, and the Saatchis soon began to become nervous about it. Some of the clients were getting unhappy—including Procter & Gamble and Jeep. Compton had never been famed for its creative advertising, but now, to add to its poor reputation on that front, its profit margins were also perilously low by Saatchi—and even industry—standards. Something had to be done. Changes had to be made in Compton's management—a tricky affair given the position of Milt Gossett, whom nobody wanted to lose.

The man the brothers chose to shake up Compton was Ed Wax. A tall, thin, lugubrious man with a bushy moustache, Wax is the son of immigrant working-class parents. He grew up in Lynn, Massachusetts, earned a chemical-engineering degree at Northeastern University in Boston, then went to work for Du Pont. He was twenty-seven when he decided to move into advertising and marketing. However, of the 200 companies to which he applied, only a handful replied, and only Compton offered him a job. He took the position and stayed for fourteen years. Then, in 1977, frustrated by Compton's staid advertising, Wax moved on, this time to a small agency called Richard K. Manoff, which by a curious coincidence was bought by the British agency Geers Gross. By 1981 Wax had moved on again, this time to Wells Rich Greene. It was here that he got a call from his old agency: would he be interested in heading up Compton's European operation? The idea, he was told, was that if he did a good job there, he would be brought back after a couple of years to take over the agency in New York. Compton was a private business, owned largely by the management, and Wax had been offered a chunk of stock. He was just about to accept when on March 17, 1982, he got another call: Saatchi

& Saatchi had bought Compton, thus killing any chance, or so Wax thought, of his accumulating any capital. "The boat's gone, and I was too slow," he told a friend.

Wax was no stranger to the Saatchis. He had been a senior director at Compton when Gossett first brought Maurice over in 1977 and the long round of negotiations that would take over five years to complete had begun. Wax was at Wells Rich Greene when the Saatchis made their abortive bid to take over that agency in 1980. He was impressed with what he had seen and assumed that the Saatchi influence would push Compton into doing more creative work.

Wax rang Maurice and had a long chat; at the end of it, Maurice offered him the same job he had already been considering in Europe. "You have the opportunity to get to know us, to reestablish your reputation with Procter & Gamble," Maurice told him, "and I'm sure at some point Milt would welcome you back to New York to help run the agency." The plan was for Wax to spend three years in London and then head back to New York to take effective charge of Compton.

In the end, things moved faster than planned. The brothers were hearing rumblings from the clients. Wax was known in New York and knew the business there; he also had an outside perspective that would help. Wax took the job with Compton in June and moved in August, looking after Procter & Gamble in Europe. He had seen something of Maurice but had still never met Charles, until he heard Gossett was in town. He called Maurice's office, and found that Gossett had left a message for him: "Meet me in the Dorchester lobby at 2:30." When Wax arrived, he spotted the brothers with Ken Gill and Milt Gossett, just emerging from the grill room.

Maurice performed the introduction. "Charles, you've never met Ed Wax." Charles was less than ecstatic about Wax's presence and demanded, "What's he doing here? I thought he was in Europe."

Gossett took Wax aside to give him his new instructions. "Ed, we're bringing you back to New York." Back in New York, Wax found there was trouble with only a couple of accounts; he managed to save them, but he was careful not to be seen as "the Saatchi boy here to Saatchi-ize the agency." He liked the Saatchi style, but not *that* much. There were far more clients happy with Compton than there were unhappy ones, and as much a fan as Wax was of British advertising, he would only adopt some of its better ideas.

Wax, with his experience of both London and New York, likes to compare the two different advertising styles. Asked in December 1986 by the trade magazine *Across the Board* why American advertising was beginning to look more and more British, Wax replied: "Don't forget, not all British advertising is terrific. There is a lot of crap over there too. But their best has been far superior to anything seen in the United States."

But *why*, pressed the interviewer, are the British better?

"They aren't," said Wax. "But they've developed graphics, sound, camerawork, and production values in such a way that they can be funny and still get the message across." On the other hand, he went on, the British had no choice but to be creative: "They *had* to make their commercials better, because in the U.K. they have fewer commercial breaks during programs than we do. They tend to bank large groups of commercials into each break, which means there is a lot of time for viewers to go to the toilet or leave for a beer or sandwich."

Wax took back to New York with him some of the British ideas of getting "wit and charm" into his commercials, and he was determined to make Compton's ads more entertaining. The British Airways ad arrived just at the right time for him, but he began to change the creative output of Compton, he emphasizes, because he could see the changes taking place in U.S. advertising. Charles and Maurice Saatchi had little or nothing to do with his changes.

The changes at Compton were just one of the many decisions for the Saatchis as they pursued the Levitt doctrine with growing enthusiasm. All the energies they had channeled into developing the agency in London back in the early 1970s were now focused on expanding it in New York. Compton was a step, but there had to be more.

Their planning at this time was meticulous and impressive—and as bold as ever. Maurice was still making his rounds, talking to the big agencies, carefully laying the groundwork for another bid. Compton had taken five years of on-and-off negotiation, but accomplishing the merger had been worth the time spent. He went back again and again to the same agencies, refusing to accept that he could not tie up a deal. In June 1983 he landed one: McCaffrey & McCall, a medium-sized New York agency, was bought for $10 million down and another $10 million to be "earned out" against profits over three years. McCaffrey & McCall was all right; but Maurice was after much, much bigger things.

In September 1983 the Saatchis made another of their leaps. They would get their stock listed on Wall Street, becoming only the third British company (after BP and Tricentrol) to do so, and would raise some new cash at the same time with a stock offering. It was only an over-the-counter listing, not a full stock-market quotation, but Saatchi & Saatchi had to go through the rigorous requirements of the Securities & Exchange Commission to achieve even that. In October Maurice took a team to the United States to begin a road show that would take in New York, Chicago, Los Angeles, San Francisco, and Boston. Only a week behind them was John Harvey-Jones, the chairman of ICI, and soon many other British companies would be joining in with the same idea. The British invasion of the United States, which would gather pace and transfer ownership of many of America's most prestigious assets, from Jacuzzi whirlpools to Brooks Brothers menswear, into British ownership, was under way.

Saatchi's meeting with analysts in Chicago was typical. At noon on Thursday, October 27, 1983, the Cadillacs and limousines delivered the last of the investment analysts for their date on the sixty-sixth floor of the 110-story Sears Tower, the highest building in the world. Maurice was flanked by Martin Sorrell and Saatchi & Saatchi's corporate development director, Simon Mellor. A man from the sponsoring bank, Morgan Stanley, one of the leading houses on Wall Street, made a brief introduction: "Ladies and gentlemen, let me introduce Saatchi & Saatchi, by a wide margin the world's most successful advertising agency."

On what criteria he based that judgment he didn't elaborate, but Maurice didn't object to that assessment as he took the stage. He had his presentation finely tuned by now: he and his brother had founded the business in 1970; today they were the eighth largest in the world. They had an impressive client list: American Motors, Avis, British Airways, Black & Decker, Du Pont, and so on. Biggest in Britain, biggest in Europe, tenth largest in the United States, earnings growth averaging 34 percent a year over the past five years—all of Maurice's claims were backed up with the help of charts and graphs. The American audience had heard of Saatchi in connection with the election of Margaret Thatcher, but it did not know any of this information. Maurice then gave them his little lecture on Levitt and globalization, a speech he and Levitt would give as a double act so often that the myth soon developed that the Saatchis were the first to discover Levitt. "This global trend is something that Saatchi has been working on for years. We have a head start and are geared for it," said Maurice.

The new stock issue duly went ahead, and it did a number of things for Saatchi. First, it gave the company money—it now had some £40 million with which to make acquisitions; second, the issue gave it American-listed shares that could be used to reward and tie in senior American executives; and third, the issue gave the agency a much higher profile in the American financial world, a factor that would become increasingly important as it continued takeover activities. The shares were now monitored by the small group of specialist media analysts in the Wall Street houses. A few months later the *Wall Street Journal*'s "Heard on the Street" column began a piece: "Analysts are recommending advertising agency stocks even though the sector has been sluggish of late." The column ended by pointing out that Saatchi & Saatchi was selling at twenty-seven times earnings, "a multiple reminiscent of the days when agencies were glamour stocks." That rate, it went on, reflected Saatchi's status as a "hot" agency; the article quoted one analyst—Mary Vandeventer of Widmann, Blee—as saying that maybe some of the British glamour would rub off on American agency stocks as Saatchi became better known in the United States. "Well, maybe," echoed "Heard" laconically.

Morgan Stanley was prepared to recommend Saatchi shares, as was

PaineWebber, another leading Wall Street brokerage house involved in the issue; a third house, Wertheim, which had no involvement in the issue, was soon recommending the shares because of the "dynamic outlook." Maurice had come a long way from the days back in 1976 when he set out to persuade the investment community that advertising companies should sell at more than five times earnings. He was not to know for some time that the glamour rating was no more than a temporary phenomenon.

As 1984 progressed, the brothers were widening their field beyond advertising. They bought two more companies, Yankelovich, Skeely & White and McBer & Company, both market-research specialists. They bought an agency in Australia, Gough Waterhouse, making Saatchi & Saatchi the first British agency to do so. There were more buys in Dublin and Scotland.

Then, at the end of 1984, came Saatchi's biggest takeover yet: $100 million plus another $25 million of "earn out" for the American-based Hay Group, a leading international firm of management consultants, with ninety-four offices in twenty-seven countries. Hay was more than just another buy—it was a major diversification that would signal a new stage in the history of Saatchi. The brothers had now, for the first time in their careers, stepped right outside the advertising world and its associated business and into a new realm altogether. Management consultancy is a business far bigger and far more sophisticated than advertising. It is dominated by firms such as Arthur Andersen and McKinsey and is as different from advertising as accountancy is from the legal profession. The brothers had always wanted to offer clients a service more central and more respected than advertising. Now they had taken their first significant step toward another Saatchi target: the creation of the services supermarket where a client could get not only advertising but also public relations, direct marketing, management consultancy, and even—perhaps—banking services.

It was becoming an almost unstoppable advance. Many newspaper articles at the time had the same first sentence: "There is no stopping Saatchi & Saatchi." It was an onslaught never before seen in the advertising industry, and even the biggest groups on Madison Avenue began to become nervous. The clients worried about it too, particularly when they heard the rumors of still bigger takeovers, and Milt Gossett and Ed Wax were continually having to deal with questions about conflicts of interest. When they passed these questions on to the brothers, they were ignored. The Saatchis were on a roll and were not going to turn back until they had accomplished the goal of being the biggest advertising business in the world. Each bid took them closer, but as they pointed out, even at this stage less than 1 percent of all the world's advertising passed through their hands.

In 1985 the brothers talked and negotiated incessantly, yet ended the year having bought no more advertising agencies in the United States. They came close but somehow never made the final breakthrough. Their burgeoning consultancy and other businesses, however, were a different matter—in 1985 Saatchi & Saatchi acquired companies outside advertising at a rate of one a month. The series of bids the brothers had made in advertising was now replaced by a bigger string of bids aimed at widening the services they offered: the acquisition of Hay was followed by nine takeover bids, giving the group a major position in everything from direct marketing and corporate design to sales promotion, public relations, and conferences. Most bids were in the United States, but there were three advertising bids outside the United States too: in Hong Kong, Canada, and Britain.

Saatchi & Saatchi was advancing at a monstrous, mind-boggling pace, but the markets loved it. The shares rose, even though Saatchi was now issuing new stock almost monthly. More important, the company was getting so big and so widely spread that the brothers needed senior professional help to manage it. As they had done when they employed Martin Sorrell, the Saatchis went to a headhunter. And that was how Anthony Simonds-Gooding, chief executive of the Whitbread brewery company, came to join them.

On the day in June 1985 when it was announced that Simonds-Gooding was leaving Whitbread, the brewery's shares fell sharply, knocking £45 million off its market value. Simonds-Gooding was forty-seven and had some advertising experience, both directly and indirectly. He had begun with a short spell at Lintas, where he had worked alongside Frank Lowe, one of Charles Saatchi's oldest friends (and now Tim Bell's chairman), who handled the £11 million-a-year Whitbread advertising account. In 1973 Simonds-Gooding joined Whitbread, one of the more conservative breweries, and for the last three years had been its top executive, a job that most managers would have been happy enough to see them through to retirement. Born in Ireland, Simonds-Gooding was a heavily built, English public-schools educated man of considerable wit and charm who took a keen interest in advertising, particularly Whitbread's own.

When the Saatchis approached him about coming to work with them, he had no intention of leaving Whitbread—he had, after all, one of the best jobs in Britain. But he is a restless man who could not envisage the thought of doing the same job year after year. Nonetheless, he would not have moved had Maurice not, as Simonds-Gooding often told him, "come to me with a rose between [his] teeth." The headhunter effected an introduction, and Maurice followed up. Simonds-Gooding would later refer in almost awed tones to the persuasive power of Maurice Saatchi, and that day he saw it at its best. Maurice complimented him on the "wonderful job" he had done at Whitbread, then went on to point out that, having done it, there was not much else to do. On the other hand, Saatchi & Saatchi was reorganizing itself after a blitz of acquisitions. Maurice himself was taking over from Gill as chairman, but "we really need someone like you" to put the whole thing together. "We've made lots of acquisitions, but we've only just started, particularly in the U.S.," Maurice said. "We need a person of your caliber to administer and run the business and get it into some sort of order. So far we haven't done much with all the acquisitions, but there are enormous opportunities." Why didn't Simonds-Gooding join? Wouldn't it be very exciting?

The two had several more talks before Simonds-Gooding made up his mind: he would take the plunge. His official title was chairman and chief executive of Saatchi & Saatchi Communications, which included all the advertising companies worldwide, as well as all public relations, design, direct marketing, and sales promotion. The fledgling management-consultancy side would be in a separate division with its own Simonds-Gooding-type figure, both of them reporting to Maurice.

Simonds-Gooding's first day at his new job is a vivid example of how the Saatchi operation can function. He had been subjected, as he said to a friend, to "all the love and seduction of Maurice" and had been persuaded to abandon his lovely office and his comfortable, cared-for lifestyle at Whitbread. On that first morning at Saatchi, early in September 1986, Simonds-Gooding came down to earth. He was given Tim Bell's old office on Maple Street, behind the Saatchi building, known in the organization as "Bell's last stand." It was a dark and dingy place, in a semibasement, looking out on a small enclosed yard at the back. Simonds-Gooding remembers thinking, "We should all have sort of blue denims and shuffle around at lunchtime in this windswept courtyard. It was awful." There were a desk, two chairs, and a telephone; no files, no system, no secretary even, no one to welcome him or to tell him what to do, no handover, no introduction. But there *was* something else: masses of flowers, roses everywhere, and a card saying: "Welcome Anthony. Over to you. Love, Charles and Maurice."

They had both gone on vacation for two weeks.

Simonds-Gooding was aware that he was treading in tricky waters at Saatchi. The men and women who ran the advertising agencies—Roy Warman, Terry Bannister, Bill Muirhead, Jennifer Laing, and Jack Rubins in London, and Milt Gossett and Ed Wax in New York—now reported to him, not to the brothers. For the first time in the history of the company there was a filter between the advertising personnel and Charles and Maurice, and the old hands in particular were going to resent this unexpected development. Even Jeremy Sinclair, who played chess with Charles every lunchtime and was a powerful figure in the agency, theoretically reported through the new head of communications.

The power in the organization was on the sixth floor at Charlotte

Street. Simonds-Gooding wasn't even in that building, let alone on that floor—which was overcrowded with no room for a new office.

How to start in those circumstances? Simonds-Gooding soon discovered that the Saatchi principle was that you made your own way. First, he got an employment agency to get him a secretary. Then he sent a telex to Milt Gossett saying he was coming over to New York and he would like Gossett to brief him on the situation there. Gossett, clearly resentful of the new executive, telexed back to say he could fit him in for half an hour over lunch the week after next. Simonds-Gooding replied angrily, stating clearly that he was coming for four weeks and that he wanted to see every single manager in the American organization: could Gossett arrange that for him as soon as possible? Gossett got the message.

There was still nothing for Simonds-Gooding to do in his dreary little office. "At least when you join Whitbread you're given a book, *The Green Jackets* by Arthur Bryant, and *Brewers Since 1703*," he remarked later. Here he got nothing but flowers. But on the second day his phone rang. "Hello, Simonds-Gooding," he said with some relief. Back came a thick Australian accent.

"Thank Christ I've got some fucker at last. It's Cliff Cobbett here, ringing from Melbourne. All my creative staff's walked out, and I wonder what authority I've got because the creative director's coming back from holiday and I want to sack him. Is that OK?"

"Well, Cliff, it's very nice to talk to you," began Simonds-Gooding, "but I've only been here two days, and it's a bit difficult . . . "

"Ah—well, I've only been here for two days too," said the Australian.

Finally, Simonds-Gooding gave him some instructions: "Do as you see fit," he said and put the phone down. He later learned that the creative director in Melbourne was duly sacked—and instantly hired by a sister Saatchi company at a higher salary. Simonds-Gooding found this baffling—and bizarre. Where was the clear philosophy about globalization, benefits of scale, and all the rest of it? Obviously, there was a lot of air in the system, a lot of organization to be done. He departed on a tour of the Middle East, visiting all the Saatchi subsidiaries there, then went on to the United States.

In September 1985 when Simonds-Gooding joined them, Saatchi & Saatchi had 4,000 employees. Within a year it would have 14,000, most of them reporting to him. The buying activity so far was merely a prelude to the biggest bids ever seen, bids that would send shock waves through the whole American advertising industry and force a series of megamergers that would change its shape forever. Nineteen-eighty-six was to be the year of the megamerger—and the year Saatchi & Saatchi climbed to first place.

14

L'EMPEREUR JACOBY

As he trawled Madison Avenue for new acquisitions, Maurice Saatchi often came across the footprints of someone else on the same ceaseless hunt: Robert E. Jacoby, chief executive of Ted Bates, had been there before him. Bates had a history as an aggressive acquirer of other agencies, even before Jacoby's time, taking over AC&R Advertising and Diener-Hauser in New York. But in ten years Jacoby made seven acquisitions, including Stern Walters/Earle Ludgin in Chicago and the Minneapolis-based Campbell-Mithun, which brought with it the prestigious General Mills account. Then Jacoby acquired Conill Advertising, Cole & Weber, Sawdon & Bess, McDonald & Little, and the direct-marketing firm Kobs & Brady. The purchase in 1982 of William Esty, with billings of $450 million, was the biggest advertising acquisition of its day at $55 million and finally pushed Bates into the major league of advertisers with billings topping $2 billion. The acquisitions were mostly houses not dissimilar to Bates itself: agencies with mediocre creative reputations but with solid enough account lists. But these purchases achieved their purpose: Jacoby had decided it was cheaper and quicker to *buy* accounts rather than hope to win them against the competition.

Jacoby was a workaholic, putting in eighteen-hour days during the week and twelve- to fourteen-hour days on weekends. He had always worked hard, from the time he started as an account representative, ironically at Compton Advertising, working on the Procter & Gamble account. He had handled Gleem toothpaste, Ivory soap, and Tide detergent, all deadly dull brands with equally dull ads, but Jacoby saw his tenure at Compton as training for better things. He earned $12,000 a year, commuting into New York from Fort Lee, New Jersey, where he lived with his wife, Monica, and four daughters (born within five years of each other). Later, when he was considerably better off, he would tell stories of his hard-up days, of having to scrabble around the house to find enough Coca-Cola bottles to raise the sixty cents needed to pay his bus fare into town to collect his paycheck. Once he joined Bates, however, Jacoby rose rapidly, making his reputation working on the chewing-gum and candy brands of American Chicle, a division of Warner-Lambert. In 1969 he was made president of Bates and in 1973 became the agency's third chief executive officer.

Bates, always more financially oriented than any other agency, had never gone in for the prestigious offices occupied by most of the big names of the industry. In 1972 it moved into 1515 Broadway, between Forty-fourth and Forty-fifth streets, right beside Times Square. Others may have hated this location, but Jacoby relished it: it was cheap—less than half the $40 a square foot paid on Madison Avenue—and from his own extended office on the twenty-seventh floor he had a superb view of the Hudson River.

Maurice Saatchi may have believed that he was among the first to identify the trend toward size in the agency world, but Jacoby had figured it out years before him. From the late 1970s Jacoby was already making speeches predicting that the ad industry would end with four, five, or maybe six big agencies, and Bates had to be one of them or "get middled," because the ones in the middle were going to be squeezed. It was this realization that spurred his takeover efforts and that caused him to ride his staff hard in search of new takeover prospects and new accounts.

But as his empire expanded, so did Jacoby's behavior become more erratic and dictatorial. He traveled more and more, sometimes spending up to six weeks in the Far East, usually accompanied by a pretty young assistant from his office, whom he openly took to dinner engagements and other functions. At a dinner in South Africa he gave his own special version of "what it takes to become a success in business." His reported answer (which he does not deny) was: "What's important to me is money, sex, and revenge. If I don't get the first two, I'll get revenge on the person who kept them from me." This was obviously intended as an after-dinner joke, but it still had enough truth in it to send a shudder through the Bates empire when word got back to Broadway.

From around the world and at home on weekends, Jacoby bombarded his staff with memos, often described as "nasty" by the recipients. In New York his lunches, at Sardi's or in the back room of some dingy restaurant, dragged later and later into the afternoon. Jacoby's drinking habits were openly talked about by his staff members, who at one point became so concerned that they consulted the agency's lawyers. The lawyers pointed out that Jacoby was impregnable. He owned the controlling interest in the company—a gift from his predecessor, Archibald McG. Foster—and if he wanted to he could dismiss the board.

When Jacoby, away on one of his long trips at the time, heard of the threatened revolt, his reaction was to tighten his control still further. He took up the 6,000 voting shares controlled by the corporate treasurer and general counsel so that he owned all 30,000 voting shares in the company. Nobody could touch him. At board meetings he often produced a nickel-plated pistol, which he kept in his safe, and laid it on the boardroom table.

But even from his twenty-seventh-floor security, Jacoby could still see the looming problems in his own company. Bates's skills at "hard-sell" advertising had left the agency with a strong list of packaged-goods clients but few "image" accounts, and through the 1980s Jacoby was determined to change the balance. In 1982 he hired Mike Becker from Young & Rubicam, then spent $5 million to bring in eighty new employees under Becker to beef up the creative department.

Jacoby, now in his late fifties, had seen other trends too. He had been an early adherent to the new doctrine of global markets, and Bates's worldwide network was certainly far superior to Compton's. Client conflicts increasingly blocked the way of further takeovers in the United States, so in 1985 Jacoby focused his attention even more intensely on the rest of the world. He bought a 51 percent stake in Scholz & Friends, based in Hamburg, and announced that he was looking for acquisitions in France, Britain, and Canada, "where we are not at a ranking commensurate with our total."

There may have been other reasons for these bids, however. Winston Fletcher, chairman of Bates's British subsidiary saw an image different from the one presented to the world by Jacoby. In an article in *Campaign* in April 1988, Fletcher said that he had witnessed the organization in New York being "reshuffled with the regularity of a poker deck" by the "Stalinesque" Jacoby. Each reshuffle "promised to be the dawn of a bright new era" that never dawned.

Fletcher's analysis of Bates is an interesting one in view of the Saatchi brothers' thinking at this time. He says that Bates's USP philosophy was so deeply embedded that it could not be shaken out and was hurting the agency around the world. Bates had been left behind by the changes in the industry in the 1970s and 1980s: "A new generation of consumers had arrived, young men and women who had grown up with television. They had learned to decode sophisticated advertising messages . . . they wanted to be entertained and amused while being sold to." Bates continued to "peddle its muscle-bound USP philosophy" and began to lose market share, a fact that had "been obfuscated by some spectacular acquisitions." The agency had always been highly profitable and had, said Fletcher, "built up a piggy bank with which to fund its growth," which it now did through acquisition rather than through winning new clients. But Bates's "continuing commitment to an outdated and constricting advertising philosophy was a prescription for long-term disaster." Fletcher's sentiment echoes what other people inside Bates had also come to realize.

"By the mid-eighties," wrote Fletcher, "you hardly needed a doctorate in management studies to deduce that Bates was in severe danger of becoming an agency with a great past but no future. I have no doubt whatsoever that the key Bates shareholders in New York reached exactly that conclusion."

Ted Bates had believed in spreading the equity of the business among the executives, but now five senior executives, including Jacoby himself, were approaching retirement age. To buy them out would cost at least $150 million, and Jacoby became increasingly convinced that, given what was happening in the industry, a private company could never raise the capital needed to survive and compete. He seriously investigated the possibility of going public, but there was another way that could solve all his problems at once. Fletcher was right in his interpretation. "I'm going to sell this company within two years," Jacoby told a meeting of his senior executives in Hawaii in March 1986, "and I don't give a damn what anybody says about it."

Word that Bates was for sale had reached the ears of the Saatchis long before that, but for a long time they were no more than moderately interested, putting it low on their priority list. Saatchi had taken a floor in the General Motors building in Manhattan, and Andrew Woods, a young merchant banker who had been hired from County Bank, had set up shop there, combing the market for potential acquisitions, evaluating the lists that Maurice continually thrust at him, and holding round after round of talks with potential target companies. From time to time, some of the more outrageous rumors reached Gossett, and Compton executives would find him with his head in his hands, muttering, "Oh God, what are they up to now?" But the brothers had the bit between their teeth and were determined that not even the wrath of Procter & Gamble, which at times could be felt all the way from Cincinnati, was going to stop Saatchi's growth.

The first meeting between Saatchi and Bates to discuss the takeover set the scene for what would prove another eighteen months of on/off discussion, some acrimony, and not a little humor. John A. Hoyne, Jacoby's quiet-spoken, silver-haired international agency chief, opened talks with Simon Mellor, a young, bright Saatchi associate director who had been put in charge of strategic development by the brothers. Hoyne and Mellor met in January 1985 in the Helmsley Palace in New York and sparred around a number of issues, including the potential purchase of William Esty by Saatchi. But neither had any doubt of what really interested Saatchi & Saatchi: the whole of Ted Bates. By March discussions reached the stage where both Hoyne and Mellor thought their bosses should get together, and Maurice flew to New York for his first meeting with Jacoby.

The venue again was the Helmsley Palace, a suitably ornate setting for one of the more bizarre meetings yet for the Saatchis. Jacoby was accompanied by Hoyne and by a financial adviser, Ned Pugh, former chief financial officer of Avon.

Maurice began with one of his immaculately delivered perorations on the shape and direction of the industry, on how Saatchi had developed and how it saw global markets. The three biggest advertisers in the world, Procter & Gamble, Philip Morris/General Foods, and R. J. Reynolds (which had just merged with Nabisco), had all been involved in "mega-mergers" themselves in the past couple of years, as indeed had almost every company in the Fortune 500. Contrary to the accepted view, the big advertisers were not in any strong moral position to preach against mergers or takeovers in the advertising world. They were the ones who were pushing for greater size and international networks in their advertising agencies, but that could not easily be achieved without further concentration in the industry.

In the past five years the proportion of world advertising expenditure that went through the big eight or nine multinational agencies had risen from 14 percent to 20 percent, which still made it a fragmented industry by any other standards. The big clients were increasingly seeing surveys showing them that 60 percent of companies were centralizing their advertising management and that 75 percent would prefer one global agency to handle their advertising. In the future there would be just three or four "megaglobal" agencies, and if you were in that group—and it didn't really matter if you were number one, two, or three—you could look forward to a secure future. Large global companies were never going to go back to working with nonglobal agencies—that period of history was over. The shift to the large agencies was gathering momentum and would carry them forward for the next twenty years; there were twenty years of growth built in just by being in that big league. As for advertising expenditure, in 1986 it was running at $160 billion a year. So the prize was not only very considerable but also very secure.

Saatchi was also anticipating another trend: clients wanted more than just advertising. They wanted services such as direct marketing, sales promotion, corporate design, public relations, and management consultancy. Thus the agency that could offer all the services a big company needed around the world was going to be ahead of the game. Saatchi had the resources and the organization to ensure it was in that position—and very few companies would dominate that business. Saatchi & Saatchi had announced its intention of getting a 10 percent share of the world advertising market—no one at that time even had 5 percent—and 10 percent of the world market in consulting, market research, and public relations.

Jacoby listened in silence, smoking his cigar, his eyebrows rising occasionally at one of Maurice's more ambitious statements, waiting for this carefully prepared and persuasively delivered speech to end. Bates, Maurice went on, had a number of choices. It could say to itself that it would be one of the surviving mega-agencies and go out and make some acquisitions of its own. Bates had, the Saatchis had discovered, already talked to a number of investment banks about the possibility of going public, which would help it make acquisitions. Or it could join with another agency that was, whatever happened, going to be one of the top three. By merging with Saatchi, Bates would make the combined group the biggest in the world, so its position in the sun would be assured. Jacoby listened abstractedly; he knew all this, knew it long before Maurice Saatchi did. He wasn't interested in any of this. There was only one answer he wanted to hear that day.

When Maurice ran out of words, Jacoby removed his cigar from his mouth and spoke, almost for the first time.

"That's very good, Maurice. Now tell me about the dough."

Abruptly Maurice came down to earth. He made an offer: $280 million in cash and roughly the same again spread over five years, depending on how well Bates performed. A few days later Hoyne reported back to Mellor that this offer had been refused. Jacoby was not interested in an earn-out. The Bates chief wanted his money up front—and the price was $500 million. Cash.

This first set of negotiations would last over a year, with the papers whizzing to and fro over the transatlantic fax machines and by special messenger. When the rumors on Madison Avenue identified Bates as a takeover target, most experts put a price of $200 million to $300 million on it. But Bates, with its high levels of profitability, was too tempting for the brothers ever to walk away from entirely, however much Jacoby irritated them. As the year wore on, the Saatchis, unable to land any of the other big companies they were chasing, began to weaken but still hoped to work out a deal that suited them as well as Bates.

Just before Christmas 1985, Maurice rang Jacoby directly with a new offer. He was now pressing hard to tie up a deal by the end of the year and was well advanced on preparations for Saatchi & Saatchi's biggest stock issue ever, which it would need to pay for Bates. One final hard round of negotiations and they would have a deal, he urged. Jacoby was a tougher negotiator than the Compton board or anybody else the brothers had ever encountered. Jacoby still held out.

Early in January 1986 the Saatchis told Hoyne they were now ready to meet Jacoby's terms. They would pay $400 million in cash down, with the rest a year later—$500 million in all. Could the Bates team come to London, bringing the contracts with them? The teams from both agencies met on January 9, 1986, at Claridge's Hotel, with Jacoby and Hoyne on one side and Maurice, Simon Mellor, and Andrew Woods on the other. There was, as usual, no sign of Charles.

Again Maurice began, not with a peroration this time but along the lines of, "Since we talked last we've been thinking a little bit more about the concept and the price and. . . ." Jacoby and Hoyne caught his drift immediately. The deal was not firm after all. Maurice was not going to meet Jacoby's terms but was putting forward yet another proposal. This was not what Jacoby had come to London to hear. The American listened impatiently for a few minutes, then said abruptly: "Excuse me, we need to confer," and left the room, followed by Hoyne. Twenty minutes passed while the Saatchi team nervously waited. When Hoyne finally reappeared, he was alone. He delivered a hotel card on which Jacoby, now ensconced in the bar, had written his terms: "$500 million cash. No contingencies and no problems." The talks, without Jacoby, carried on for another hour before they broke up, with the parties agreeing to meet again the next morning at eleven.

The next morning Maurice offered $450 million cash with the final payment dependent on certain conditions. Andrew Woods led the negotiating, irritating Jacoby, who claimed Woods was being overaggressive. Jacoby accused the Saatchi side of nitpicking, of raising dozens of small points that were not relevant. His price, he repeated, was $500 million— cash. Finally he left the room, followed by Hoyne, and again there was an uncomfortable silence while the Saatchi team waited to see what would happen next. It didn't have long to wait. From the hotel bar Jacoby gave Hoyne his instructions: "Go back and tell them to go fuck themselves."

Hoyne was more oblique. He reentered the suite, looked around, and said: "Could I have Mr. Jacoby's coat?"

Jacoby had gone, furious that the Saatchis had moved their ground. He was playing a very risky game, because by any criteria the Saatchi offer placed a full (many would say overfull) value on the Bates business. Saatchi was not yet as desperate as Jacoby believed it to be, with several prospective bids still running. True, Jacoby had other offers on the table back home, but those were nowhere near the price he had just turned down. He returned to New York to see if he could tie up something better or perhaps even persuade the Saatchis to meet his full price—up front. "It was a marvelous tactic by Jacoby," says a former Saatchi executive. "We didn't know what pressures he had back home or what offers he had, but we had read the rumors about McCann's and others. If he was trying to screw more money out of us, it was a very effective way of doing it." This executive says that with the benefit of hindsight, however. At this time not even Jacoby was thinking as clearly as that.

The story leaked to the American trade press, and Jacoby denied it, but the Saatchis admitted it. In January *Adweek* quoted an unnamed Saatchi executive as saying: "There have been meetings. . . . This isn't something the Saatchis will walk away from—even if they're struggling to make a deal."

In the light of what happened later, there is an interesting paragraph in this *Adweek* story. It quotes a Bates executive as saying, "It could be Jacoby wants more cash than stock from Saatchi's," seen by the reporter as a reference to "the agency's reported $250–300 million price tag." The trade press contains a number of other references to prices within this

range, which is roughly where Saatchi's valuations put Bates at the time
and is probably closer to what Jacoby might have persuaded an American agency to pay. Jacoby, however, was playing a deeper game and still
believed he could get $500 million for Bates, a price even its good profit
record could not justify.

Saatchi entered 1986 with the big prize still elusive. There were plenty
of balls in the air, and sooner or later one would be caught. But which?
With Bates no longer high on its priority list—although not crossed off—
it was time for Saatchi to revive another old favorite takeover target:
Doyle Dane Bernbach. Bill Bernbach's once great agency would definitely not emerge as one of Maurice's Big Three. It was losing clients,
had no proper international network, and was clearly going to be taken
over. The industry hummed with rumors and stories. The *Gallagher
Report*, a confidential newsletter in the advertising and marketing
industries, reported in April 1986 that Barry Loughrane, the head of
Doyle Dane Bernbach, was "beating the bushes" in his attempt to find a
marriage partner for his $1.7 billion (in billings) agency. Loughrane had
approached the chairman of Needham Harper Worldwide, Keith Rein-
hard, in mid-March "with a bid to reinforce Needham thrust."

Anthony Simonds-Gooding, who had joined midway through the
Bates negotiations, was told by Maurice to get into the bidding for Doyle
Dane and see if it might be retrieved before it was too late. Simonds-
Gooding knew he was starting well behind several other bidders but,
urged on by the brothers, made an appointment to see Loughrane
anyway. Saatchi & Saatchi, Simonds-Gooding said, was prepared to
make an offer in cash that he hoped would at least match, and probably
better, what Loughrane had on the table. Loughrane had set up a board
meeting to consider the various offers, and Simonds-Gooding now asked
to come and address the board. He had an offer in his pocket, which he
planned to pull out, hoping that would tempt the directors away from
some of the more nebulous proposals in front of them. The Doyle Dane
directors, however, did not want Saatchi. "Martin Sorrell had made a
run on behalf of the Saatchis several years before, and there had been
some bad feeling over that," said a Doyle Dane director afterward. "So
we were sort of anti. BBDO and Needham were fellow Americans and
closer."

At the end of April BBDO chairman Allen Rosenshine announced the
first of the season's megamergers: BBDO, the sixth largest U.S. agency,
Needham Harper (number sixteen), and Doyle Dane Bernbach (number
twelve) would get together to form an agency with billings of $5 billion—
and at least a dozen potential account conflicts. BBDO itself had the $225
million-a-year Chrysler account, while Doyle Dane had the $120 million
Volkswagen account. BBDO's $100 million Pillsbury business compared
with Doyle Dane's $35 million Nabisco cereal billings. Augie Busch, the

head of the giant brewery Anheuser-Busch, withdrew his $50 million Stroh's brewing account.

However, Rosenshine had achieved at least one objective. His quote that his new group was the biggest "but maybe only for ten minutes" would become one of the sayings of the decade. The pace of mergers on Madison Avenue was now frenetic. The American Association of Advertising Agencies listed eight mergers in 1984, nineteen in 1985, and eleven in the first four months of 1986.

Rosenshine's new holding company, called Omnicon, to some extent copied the concept pioneered by Interpublic, the McCann-Erickson holding company, which under Marion Harper had merged three agency networks under one holding company a decade before. Now there were rumors of more agencies doing the same thing. Everybody, it seemed, was either taking over or being taken over. There were dark hints about the Saatchis, seen, even after the Bates talks broke down, as the most predatory agency of all. "It's hard to say where a company like Saatchi, with such deep pockets, will strike next," *Time* magazine quoted Abott Jones, president of the Chicago-based Foote, Cone & Belding, in its May 12, 1986, issue. It was equally hard to see where any one of a dozen agencies was going to end up, and the Saatchis at that moment had no clearer an idea than did anyone else which they might end up with.

But the Saatchis did at least have some possibilities—and some successes. While pursuing both Bates and Doyle Dane they had kept open other talks, and some of them, caught up by the merger mania, came to fruition. In the early months of 1986 Saatchi made two acquisitions of New York advertising agencies. Neither of them ranked in the megaleague but were still significant additions to the Saatchi & Saatchi empire.

The first, acquired in February 1986, was Dancer Fitzgerald Sample, the thirteenth largest agency in the United States, with $876 million in billings. Dancer Fitzgerald was another Procter & Gamble house, with a reputation for good creative work and a talented staff led by Stu Upson. It had taken some time and effort to persuade P&G chairman John Smale to agree to allow the sale, and Milt Gossett had to be at his most persuasive. Maurice argued that the whole concept behind the acquisition was to create a second international advertising group, merging Dorland in London with Dancer Fitzgerald to form a network parallel to the Saatchi & Saatchi–Compton one. This argument was based on an idea the brothers had been working on for some time, taking as precedent the way the great Marion Harper, creator of the Interpublic group, had found a way around the irritating client-conflict problem.

The Dancer Fitzgerald deal had first been considered in 1984, and at that stage Smale had killed it. Dancer Fitzgerald had around $60 million of P&G business, and if Smale refused to allow too much of his business under the same roof, then even the Saatchis at that point were not prepared to push for a deal. Later the circumstances would be different.

The closing of the Dancer Fitzgerald deal was a major boost for Jack Rubins, the head of Dorland in London, who since 1981 had run his agency inside the Saatchi empire, keeping its operations—and clients— separate. The new DFS Dorland Worldwide was a fancy name for what was only the sixteenth biggest network, a long way from Maurice's "one, two, or three," but this merger was another step along the way and gave Saatchi some more of the world's top advertisers: Nabisco, Toyota, and Wendy's. It cost Saatchi $75 million.

The Dancer Fitzgerald takeover is significant for an additional reason: suddenly the American advertising industry seemed much more vulnerable to British takeovers than it had in the past. True, Compton had been taken over, but for a number of years that had seemed an anomaly, a special situation that had come about because of the relationship Compton had with Saatchi in London. Dancer Fitzgerald, in contrast, was a straight purchase. *Campaign*, in an editorial, said the significance of the Saatchi bid for Dancer Fitzgerald was that "the dominance of American agencies is no longer unchallengeable. The great networks built up before and after the war by the U.S. pioneers are perceptibly running out of steam as competition becomes fiercer and the generation which created them moves gradually aside." Even the great Doyle Dane Bernbach, the editorial reported, was up for sale.

Campaign ended on a ringing note: "Is there a world role for other British agencies in this changing scene? None is likely to succeed on quite the scale that Saatchi has, for no other outfit has spent the time and energy (or, arguably, has the required business flair), in gathering itself for the transatlantic leap; but there is clearly room for more partnerships in which it is not necessarily the Americans who will have the final word."

Campaign had spotted an interesting trend. Martin Sorrell had by this time left the brothers to set up on his own, and he, for one, began to look closely at what was happening in the American advertising world— would there be a chair for him when the music stopped? It was only now, four years after the Saatchis had gone to New York, that other British agencies began to think that perhaps they could do the same, that there was nothing written that said the global agencies had to start in New York or Chicago and then spread to Europe and the Far East. Expansion could occur the other way too.

In April the brothers fostered another crop of stories along the lines of: "There is no stopping the Saatchi brothers" and "The ambitions of the Saatchi brothers know no bounds." They had bought another agency, smaller than Dancer but more important for other reasons: Backer &

Spielvogel was the twenty-third biggest agency in the United States, with revenues of $500 million. Founded only eight years before, it boasted the fastest growth rate in the business, faster even than the Saatchi agency on Charlotte Street. Its addition took Saatchi to within a single bid of being in first place, with billings of $3.4 billion against Young & Rubicam's $3.6 billion. (Rosenshine's Omnicon merger was then still a fortnight away.)

Backer & Spielvogel was run by a man who would later become important to the Saatchis: Carl Spielvogel. Spielvogel was actually one of the original architects of the Interpublic giant when he had been assistant to Marion Harper and was to emerge over the next few years as one of the leading agency chiefs in the industry.

Born in Brooklyn, the son of a raw-fur processor, Spielvogel was once an advertising columnist for the *New York Times*. He had spent twenty years with Interpublic, the parent company of McCann-Erickson, working his way up to vice chairman before striking out on his own with five other McCann executives. His own agency was regarded as something of a creative hot shop, just as Saatchi & Saatchi had been a decade earlier. Backer & Spielvogel had startled Madison Avenue when it pulled in the entire $85 million Miller beer account two months after its inception, and it had forged close links with a small number of major clients that were well pleased with its service—up to a point.

Backer & Spielvogel in the mid-1980s was a victim of exactly the circumstance that Maurice had described to Jacoby. The six partners who had left McCann had boasted of their independence and had no intention of selling until three events occurred: their client NCR decided it wanted to develop internationally, and Spielvogel was forced to put together a patchwork of independent agencies to accommodate it; in London Spielvogel granted the NCR account to Martin Boase of Boase Massimi Pollitt, carefully avoiding Saatchi because of its position in New York. Then another major client, Philip Morris, took over General Foods, and suddenly there were another five agencies in the Philip Morris family, all of them far bigger than little Backer. The biggest blow was the third: the Miller High Life and Lowenbrau accounts went to J. Walter Thompson. "The loss of Miller sobered us," said Spielvogel. "We realized that you need a critical mass of stability to sleep easy at night. For a long time we knew we had to sell. Miller's loss made us realize we should sell sooner rather than later."

Backer & Spielvogel was an attractive agency, with excellent growth and potential—if someone could supply the global network. Saatchi was by no means the only agency Carl Spielvogel talked to—in those months everyone seemed to be talking to everyone else. He had talks with Don Johnston of JWT, with Bill Phillips of Ogilvy, and with others.

When Spielvogel first met the Saatchis, it was about another matter entirely. He is a man deeply involved in pro-bono public works—a trustee of Mount Sinai Medical Center, a member of the Municipal Art Society's board, and chairman of the Committee on the Public Interest, which helped save New York from bankruptcy. He is also head of the business committee of the Metropolitan Museum of Art, and it was in this capacity that he called on Charles Saatchi the great art collector rather than Charles Saatchi the great advertising man. Spielvogel persuaded Charles to join his business committee at the Met, and the contact, once made, continued.

It was Maurice who one day in the spring of 1986 told Spielvogel that the Bates deal was off: he could not come to terms with Jacoby. That news was all over Madison Avenue in any case. So was the word that Backer & Spielvogel was seeking a home. Maurice offered him one. "We'd be prepared to run you independently at all times. You want access to international facilities; we'll provide that. You want access to direct marketing and promotion; we'll provide that too." All the areas where Spielvogel knew his agency was losing out could be filled in by Saatchi & Saatchi.

Compared to many of Saatchi's other negotiations the purchase of Backer & Spielvogel was a relatively straightforward one. Maurice and Carl Spielvogel did most of the negotiating themselves, and Spielvogel, seventeen years older, soon realized that the innocent-looking Maurice was an astute and experienced mediator. Several times the negotiations broke down, but finally the two men had a deal, and Spielvogel went off to tell his clients about it before finally signing. Unlike Jacoby, Spielvogel had agreed to the Saatchi "earn-out formula"; he and his six partners were paid $56 million down, with the rest to be earned over six years.

Saatchi & Saatchi's acquisition of Backer & Spielvogel was announced in April to an industry now seething with rumors and proposed deals. By then, unknown to Spielvogel, the Bates talks were on again.

During that first week in May 1986, impossible, absurd rumors circulated throughout the industry. Ogilvy & Mather was to team up with Interpublic to form a colossus that would outdo everybody; JWT and Young & Rubicam were to merge. Bates was linked with BBDO—or with any of another half-dozen agencies. A few of these rumors had some factual basis, as most companies were talking to at least one other agency. Several, like Bates, were doing the rounds, negotiating the Saatchi bid price higher and higher. Some talks even ended in deals: Foote, Cone & Belding took over Leber Katz of New York, the Omnicon trio got together, and in London Lowe Howard-Spink & Bell (now including Tim Bell) bought the privately owned Allen Brady & Marsh, while Wight Collins Rutherford Scott, which houses a number of former Saatchi workers, joined forces with FCO.

Meanwhile, Robert Jacoby, who must have been worrying that he had pushed the Saatchis over the limit, let it be known that he favored a deal with Interpublic. At Compton, Milton Gossett, staying closely in touch with the big clients, particularly Procter & Gamble in Cincinnati, was relieved to hear it—Gossett kept passing on messages to the brothers that P&G would undoubtedly remove some accounts if the brothers were so foolish as to buy Bates. Bates had Colgate Palmolive, the big rival to P&G, and the Cincinnati company had indicated clearly that it would not stand for sharing an ad agency with its competitor. Gossett had been brought up to believe that no one ever dared buck P&G, and he was highly nervous about the outcome of the Saatchis' plans to take over Bates. "Don't do it," he pleaded. The brothers decided to ignore him—they would make their peace with P&G later. The whole issue of client conflict was up in the air in the merger hothouse, and the Saatchi brothers would either run Bates as an independent agency, in the same way they were offering to run Backer & Spielvogel, or they would merge it with Backer to complete the second global network under their umbrella. They were once again taking a bold jump into the unknown—and loving the thrill of it.

In April John Hoyne again sent the message that Bates was interested in a deal with Saatchi—but still on his original terms. Jacoby wanted his $500 million. The Saatchi merger team under Andrew Woods looked at the figures again. Bates would cost Saatchi more than twice as much as it had spent on all the thirty-seven acquisitions the agency had made in its whole existence. The war chest was empty. To pay for Backer & Spielvogel Saatchi was committed to a stock issue. It was finally decided to raise all the money in one go: a £406 million issue, one of the biggest the London stock market had ever seen, topped only by that of Lord Hanson and Sir Gordon White when they raised over £500 million to pay for SCM Corp., the old Smith-Corona typewriter company. If the Bates bid fell through, Saatchi would use the money for something else. The issue of shares brought the market value of Saatchi above the £1 billion mark for the first time (and the brothers' stake below 10 percent)—where it would stay only briefly. In value terms at least, if not yet in billings, Saatchi was the biggest advertising business the world had ever seen.

The final deal to acquire Bates took less than a week to negotiate. There was in fact little room for negotiation; Jacoby set his price and his terms, and Saatchi agreed to meet them, reluctantly accepting Jacoby's suggestion that the Bates directors could borrow $57 million from the banks—and Saatchi would assume the loan. In London the press releases—and the headlines—announced that Bates had cost Saatchi & Saatchi $450 million. The true figure was over $500 million.

Shrewd as they were in the area of negotiation, the Saatchis had never come up against a Bob Jacoby before, he knew exactly what the Saatchis wanted to do, knew the options open to them, and saw, as the windows of opportunity closed, that they needed Bates—or they risked being shut out of Maurice's "one, two, or three." Bates would make the agency number one and give the brothers the security for the next twenty years that they wanted so badly. They should pay a premium for it. Jacoby himself would receive $70 million from the deal and another $40 million on top for his voting shares in the agency, which everyone had assumed had little or no monetary value—$110 million in all, much more than anyone had made in the entire history of the agency. This amount would make him nearly twice as rich as the brothers. It was also agreed that he would still be in charge of Bates, with a five-year contract paying him $1 million a year—which was also more than the brothers paid themselves.

In the final weeks before the closing of the deal was announced, Jacoby allowed thirty staff members, many of them low-level ones, to buy more than 1,000 shares each in Bates, thus making some of them millionaires. Those not included grumbled furiously, but Jacoby pointed out that he had helped the people who "got to me first."

The deal, when it was finally announced, had been so often rumored that it was not a surprise; but it was still a major story. This was partly because of the size of the merger, partly because of the names involved— Saatchi & Saatchi and Bates were both well known beyond Madison Avenue—but mostly because the deal brought to a head the concern growing throughout the industry at the enormous rush of mergers and takeovers. On the morning the bid was announced (May 12, 1986) the *Wall Street Journal* quoted Jacoby as already making plans for further expansion: "We have a list of 30 possible acquisitions worldwide. But the opportunities aren't good, because it's been picked over to a fare-thee-well. There's nothing of quality." The next day's *New York Post*, which carried a picture of Jacoby, huge cigar in hand, in his twenty-seventh-floor office at 1515 Broadway, reported: "Wall Street analysts, who had been slow to turn their eyes uptown at what was once thought of as a flaky business, are now recommending that institutions invest their funds in the largest agencies."

If that had been true a few months before, it was no longer true now. The rumblings from Cincinnati were reverberating throughout the country—Procter & Gamble had said it would punish Saatchi & Saatchi if it took over Bates. Now P&G could not back down even if it wanted to. Other clients were less than happy too. The Saatchis, it was said, had gone too far. Milt Gossett was said to be in despair.

Jacoby was widely quoted defending the bid on the grounds that agencies without global capacity "can't go it alone," but that message was not appreciated on Wall Street. "This fetish for bigness . . . is beside the point. It's big for big's sake," said Alan Gottesman, an advertising analyst at L. F. Rothschild, Unterberg Towbin. "When was the last time you encountered synergism, except in a crossword puzzle?" Roy Grace, who had just left Doyle Dane Bernbach as executive creative director because of that agency's chase for "this imponderable size, this mindless size without meaning," was critical too. "Advertising is really a personal service," Grace said, "and the bigger it gets, the more impersonal it becomes. It's not like manufacturing sausages."

These criticisms were directed, at least at first, as much at Rosenshine and the merger he had put together under a new holding company, Omnicon, as they were at Saatchi. However, the criticisms directed specifically at Saatchi soon began to reveal a special edge. "Our industry is going through fundamental changes and consolidation," said John Bernbach, president of Doyle Dane Bernbach International, who had observed the Saatchis at work when he was in London, "and the changed environment is due entirely [to the Saatchis]. We are all living in the environment they created."

Allen Rosenshine found himself rocked by the criticism he now encountered: "Pre-Saatchi the reaction to our merger was 'Wow!' Post-Saatchi, we got mired down in the negativism."

Given what was happening in every other American industry at that time, this is a considerable overstatement. Sooner or later merger fever had to arrive on Madison Avenue, and even the Saatchis' most ardent critics, including Ogilvy & Mather (itself the product of a series of mergers and acquisitions), would not remain immune. Did Boone Pickens change the environment of the oil industry? Or Rupert Murdoch and Ted Turner the media industry? Or Carl Icahn the airline industry? Perhaps; but a historian with a wider perspective might argue that these people and the other predators of the day—Jimmy Goldsmith, Lord Hanson, Irwin Jacobs, Ron Perelman—were only the more visible elements in a much longer-term business of restructuring in which the forces for change were irresistible and that the Saatchis were simply the most controversial part of that change.

Put another way, if the Saatchis had never ventured out of Golden Square, would American advertising—and therefore world advertising—be any different than it is today? We have already seen that the Saatchis were not the first to discover Ted Levitt—and even Levitt was not the first to discover globalization. The Saatchi brothers did not invent the forces that were driving the advertising business into bigger and bigger units; they did not create the retreat of the American multinationals or the fall of the dollar that resulted in foreign companies sweeping into the United States and taking over many of the companies that had come to symbolize Americanization to the outside world. As *Time* lamented in November 1987, "Suddenly, the U.S. seems to have become a country for sale, a huge shopping mart in which foreigners are energetically filling up their carts."

The Saatchis were certainly in the forefront of identifying some of these forces and using them for their own special purposes. What they succeeded in doing was *persuading* the world that they had invented globalization. They were not even the first British agency to buy into America: Geers Gross had done so in January 1978, and another British business, Lopex, bought a minority stake in Warwick, Welsh & Miller, a New York agency, a few years later. It is possible to argue too that Ogilvy & Mather was originally a British invasion of Madison Avenue.

But it is the perception that matters—the Saatchis rewrote history, not deliberately perhaps, but simply by allowing people to persuade themselves that that's how it was.

They also did something more—they contributed to a general undermining of the confidence of the New York agencies in their own creative product. "We've grown up in awe of American advertising," said Maurice Saatchi in 1982. "It's been our mother's milk. But now it's generally accepted that British advertising is the best in the world, and we'd like to wave the flag a little." It wasn't generally accepted then—or even later. Television advertising had developed differently in Britain for a variety of reasons: for a start, it developed a decade later, so it could learn from American mistakes; it grew up on better technology than that to which American business had been accustomed; and because British commercial television groups ads together for less frequent interruptions to programs, it was forced to be more entertaining to catch the attention of its audience.

When the Saatchis arrived in New York, they came as the flag carrier for a whole school of "British advertising." And their ideas worked, at least limitedly. Like it or loathe it, Saatchi & Saatchi today has a reputation in New York as a "creative agency." Ask anyone what they like about its ads, and they will remember three: the pregnant man, "Labour isn't working," and the Manhattan landing sequence for British Airways. Saatchi has gone on winning as many prizes as ever for its creative work, and with Charles and Jeremy Sinclair watching over it, it produces some fine work.

But did it have great new creative lessons to teach the Americans? Ed Wax at Compton, an agency scarcely renowned today for its creative ads, would dispute that; Stu Upson at Dancer Fitzgerald would probably resent it; and Carl Spielvogel would definitely reject it. For their part, the Saatchis were clever enough to know their own limitations; even if they had wanted to, they could never have imposed their own creative ideas on the big New York agencies they acquired. It simply wouldn't have worked.

For better or worse, in May 1986 Saatchi & Saatchi had taken over Ted Bates, with Bob Jacoby and all. The brothers had achieved the objective Charles had set years before: their agency was bigger than any other. No one, not JWT or Ogilvy or anyone else in the world, would ever look down on them again—or so they thought at the time. True, the Saatchis had long since ceased to care about that aspect of it and were focusing several stages ahead; but they could still allow themselves a few hours of celebration—before beginning to sort out the problems they had created for themselves. Many of these they had anticipated, but nothing could have prepared them for the difficulties that lay ahead.

15
MacBates

A fter sealing their latest deal, [the Saatchis] sent champagne to Bates executives," reported *Business Week* on May 26, 1986. "If all goes well, that may be the last they hear from Maurice and Charles Saatchi." The magazine was commenting on the Saatchi way of running its subsidiaries, allowing them autonomy and considerable freedom. It quoted Michael Wahl, chairman of the Howard Marlboro sales-promotion company in New York, which had been bought for $414 million in 1985. Wahl said of the Saatchis: "Their style is not to become involved unless there's a problem."

But there *would* be problems at Bates—perhaps the worst the Saatchis had encountered in their business career. Within months the celebrations had changed to anger and bitterness. Within a year Charles Saatchi would be complaining about the "pain" that the deal was putting the brothers through and wondering plaintively whether it would ever end. If everything had gone right for the Saatchis up to that point, the next eighteen months were a time when everything suddenly went wrong.

The first fallout from the Bates deal was the change in the Saatchi share price. For eleven years it had risen rapidly, taking the Saatchi brothers' fortune with it, so that by April 1986, on the eve of the Bates takeover, the value of the brothers' holding, listed in their joint names in the accounts, was £35 million. By the autumn it had fallen by more than £12 million, and a year after that, after the October 19 crash in 1987, had more than halved. Saatchi & Saatchi's aquisition of Bates was by no means the only cause of that fall; but the deal marked the high point for the stock price, touched only fleetingly again, and in many ways the merger with Bates was the height of the Saatchi magic too. As Anthony Simonds-Gooding began the task of producing some order from the mass of companies that had been acquired, he turned to Charles to say: "You know, you're not a real company until you've gone through adversity and then come out the other side. You've had such a gilded life, you don't know what it's like until you've felt pain." Charles glowered but later turned this remark into a joke, firing it back at Simonds-Gooding. Every time there was a new bit of bad news, Charles would come in the next morning and ask: "Have we had enough pain yet? Are we big boys now?"

The task facing the company was immense. Bates was the thirty-eighth successful takeover by the Saatchis since they began, a fast rate even averaged over sixteen years. However, some of those years had seen no bids at all: the first bid the brothers had made came in 1973, when they had been in business three years; there was nothing in 1976 or 1977 after they absorbed Compton-Garland; and even in 1978 and 1979 the only bids made were to Hall's in Edinburgh for £2 million and to O'Kennedy Brindley in Dublin for £250,000. In 1980 the slate was again blank, and 1981 was the year of the Dorland deal, which cost £7.1 million.

From the moment Saatchi & Saatchi took over Compton in the United States, however, the acceleration began: three bids in 1982, two the following year, then seven in 1984, twelve in 1985, and now three to considerable agencies in the first five months of 1986. Add to this the fact that Bates itself was every bit as predatory as Saatchi, that its billings at the time of the merger were almost dollar for dollar equal to those of Saatchi worldwide, and that there was no love lost between the heads of the different agencies, and one has some idea of the problems the brothers now faced. The atmosphere after the rush of megabids became antagonistic both inside the industry and among some of the clients, and that antagonism spread to Wall Street and to the press. Martin Sorrell had been the person most active in keeping open the lines of communication to the Wall Street analysts, but he was gone, and in these months his absence was felt. Greg M. Ostroff, an analyst in the Wall Street house Goldman Sachs, had followed Saatchi for several years and encouraged a lot of his clients to purchase its stock. Now some of the pain spread to him too:

> At six o'clock in the morning I would get up and sleepwalk to the front door, pick up the *New York Times,* and turn straight to the advertising column. Anything nasty that had happened to Saatchi was put in a box. If I saw a box, my heart would start palpitating; I would get to the office, call London, which did all the trading, find out what was going on, write something up, and try to get on with the rest of my work. If there wasn't a box I'd go back to sleep, then come in and have a normal day. The trade press, which had given so much coverage to the Saatchis since they arrived in New York, was really gunning for these guys, and giving them their comeuppance. I mean, the first eight pages of *Adweek* and *Ad Age* each week were filled up for a six-month period with Saatchi stories: who's going to leave, who's worried about getting merged, and what clients are going to storm out. Stuff like that.

Charlie Crane of Prudential-Bache, another major Wall Street house, also watched Saatchi & Saatchi's change of status with concern for his investors. Says Crane:

> The speed with which they [the Saatchis] had grown their business

in the early 1980s did manage to turn a few heads. And the vehe-
mence with which they claimed they were going to be number one in
such a short period of time was one which was met initially with
skepticism. After they got going and really started rolling in these
acquisitions, people started thinking: "Maybe they can do it, let's
buy the stock and drive up the share price in anticipation of their
succeeding; if anybody can do it, they probably can." I suppose
many of the financial decisions are ultimately questionable in hindsight. If indeed investors bought the concept that they would be
number one, and bought into the shares on that basis, what do you
do when they achieve that goal? What's next? What can you do
when you're already at the top of the heap? Create a new heap?
Probably—that's what they are trying to do with the consulting arm.
And what then? A third heap?

The Saatchi brothers had until this point plenty of fans both on Wall
Street and in the City of London. According to Crane:

> One of the things they deserve an awful lot of credit for is
> positioning their company as one worthy of a high rating on their
> stock. They convinced the City that the agency business was one of
> the few true growth industries for U.K. investors. And they per-
> suaded quite a few people over here too, on a different basis. The
> agency business in the States was a fairly mature one, with some
> growth left, but it was no Silicon Valley. In Britain and on the
> Continent it was a growth business, and in the States they could
> grow fast too by acquisitions, then make them perform a little bit
> better—which is what they did, greatly improving the margins of
> Compton, for instance. It was a good line to pitch to the financial
> community, and they pitched it well. They learned first and foremost
> that it wasn't a bad thing to hype your own story, and their connec-
> tions with the trade press are the stuff of legend.

Crane and other Wall Street analysts who came to follow Saatchi after
the Compton deal all made money for their clients on the Saatchi stock's
price rise. "They really did succeed in improving Compton," says Crane.
"Not so much through devastating head-count reductions, although there
were certainly cutbacks. It was through watching where the money
flowed, making sure it flowed at the right pace and through the right
hands. What I saw was not only a change in the financial strength of
what had been a long-standing unsatisfactory agency, but I also saw the
introduction of a new creative spirit there. The quality of the product that
emanated from Compton was higher, more daring, as if the staff had
been released from their financial worries and were prepared to be freer
spirits."

All these effects of the Compton merger had driven up the Saatchi price and given the firm an image no advertising business had ever had. Most big agencies in New York were run by advertising rather than financial people. David Ogilvy could boast that: "I cannot read a balance sheet, work a computer, ski, sail, play golf, or paint. But when it comes to creative advertising, *Advertising Age* says I am the 'creative King.' " The Saatchis *could* read a balance sheet, particularly Maurice, and from the beginning had a clear understanding of the financial aspects of what they were doing. They had used the stock market to finance their growth in a way that no other agency anywhere in the world had even thought of. According to Greg Ostroff: "One of the problems in covering agencies as an analyst is that they're run by agency people. They don't run these businesses as businesses should be run. The Saatchis were unique in that. They had, up to the time of Bates, been going along well, courting the financial community, raising capital, buying businesses, using rigid financial-management techniques on those businesses to get the proper margin out of them, and making these acquisitions pay for themselves. I guess that on Madison Avenue in general, from a purist's point of view, that was not looked on with favor."

It wasn't. David Ogilvy, in a new edition of his *Confessions* published in 1987, showed how he hated these techniques. In a clear reference to the Saatchis, Ogilvy wrote that one of the major problems facing the industry was "the emergence of megalomaniacs whose mind-set is more financial than creative. They are building empires by buying up other agencies, to the consternation of their clients. They have never heard of the South Sea Bubble."

That view could be heard all along Madison Avenue in the summer and autumn of 1986. The Saatchis, it was said, had taken one step too far. They were in trouble, said the gossip. And if it hadn't been for the damage the Saatchis were seen to be doing to the entire American advertising industry, there would have been an unrestrained air of *schadenfreude* in the Madison Avenue gossip. Bob Jacoby was not widely popular, and he had become even less popular when it became known how much money the Saatchis had paid him. For anyone in the advertising industry to get $110 million was regarded as disgraceful; for Jacoby to get it was almost obscene. That was clients' money, it was argued, and if advertising agencies were so hugely profitable, maybe the clients were paying too much.

"There was clearly an attitude of waiting with bated breath for these guys finally to make a mistake," says Ostroff. "Then every dog would have its day."

The weekend of the Bates bid I found Maurice in his office on Charlotte Street looking relaxed and contemplative. I still have my notes of our conversation, and in light of events since, it is interesting to look back on that meeting. The brothers clearly were not anticipating any problems. Maurice had received a phone call at three o'clock the previous morning from Bob Jacoby to tell him that everything had been worked out with the lawyers and the deal was done. He had also received a large cake, sent to "Charles, Maurice, and the boys" from Sir John (later Lord) King as a celebratory gift from one of their favorite clients.

Later that morning Maurice ran through the wider arguments that he had at his fingertips: the need for size, the impact of the big mergers among the major clients, which were driving agencies into still larger units; the fact that Saatchi & Saatchi was well short of its stated target of having 10 percent of the world advertising market and even further away from the target of 10 percent of the other markets the brothers had identified: consultancy, research, and public relations, plus all the ancillary services that revolved around these. But at least Saatchi & Saatchi now had a critical mass that would guarantee its position for some years to come. He expounded on Saatchi's relationship with Procter & Gamble, which had been so important for it, basically because P&G was in the forefront of global development and Saatchi had been able to observe Procter & Gamble's methods and learn from them. Just that week P&G had appointed a Pampers general manager for Europe, running the whole of Europe as a single market. Managements were being aligned across regional boundaries—in every industry.

Maurice was not interested in talking about Bates; that deal was done, and he wanted to go on. One of the key aspects of the Bates merger was that it was the market leader, so that people would no longer laugh when they talked about achieving market leadership in the much bigger and faster-growing markets of consultancy and research. The combined groups would be the world leader in direct marketing too, so that the Bates acquisition accomplished two goals while making the others look more achievable. It would take some time, but it should be in place by the end of the century. It had taken sixteen years to do what the brothers had done and probably would take an equal amount of time to achieve the rest of their ambitions. By that stage he and Charles would be . . . Maurice paused to work out their exact ages then. "A couple of old duffers," I interjected helpfully. Maurice roared with laughter. "Exactly. A couple of old duffers sitting under a palm tree in the Bahamas!" Clearly he did not mean this remark literally, because in the next breath he was talking about motivation, the desire, as strong as ever in both of them, to get the job done, and the excitement of putting it all together. Sheer size, he said, gave them no particular pleasure; what did excite them both was translating their concepts and ideas into practice, combining size with dynamism in a way few companies could achieve—keeping people motivated.

Maurice had read a new book that had inspired him, which showed how many good companies were run along what the author called the "tight/loose principle." It described Saatchi & Saatchi perfectly, he felt—a combination of loose controls in terms of allowing the individual companies their autonomy, but tightness in terms of financial control. This was the system that Simonds-Gooding was installing throughout the enlarged communications part of the Saatchi group, and that was how Saatchi would be run around the world.

Meanwhile on the other side of the Atlantic Bob Jacoby was enjoying the success of his deal. On May 22, 1986, he held a meeting of Bates stockholders and made a presentation, complete with slides. The agency's book value, he showed, was $390 a share (analysts put it at much less than that). Jacoby then showed another slide giving the price that Saatchi had paid: $853.02 a share. There was a spontaneous burst of applause. Jacoby might not be a hero on Madison Avenue, but he had done well for his fellow stockholders.

It was another few weeks before the full implications of the deal began to come through. That same month Bernard Gallagher sent out a gloomy view to clients of his private newsletter, the *Gallagher Report*. The current megamerger movement among ad agencies, said the report, was the "most significant development in advertising in 20 years," but there would be a major fallout over the next three to five years. Many of the deals were highly leveraged (Saatchi's, financed by stock issues, were not) and had been "fueled by deal-makers," timed to cash in on the merger mentality that was sweeping through the industry. The interests of the clients had been forgotten, and there was no indication of improved services or increased efficiencies. The superagency concept, Gallagher added, was only viable if it was conceived with the interests of the client paramount to the financial rewards of the principals involved. He forecast the reversal of the globalization trend and the return of the "boutique" era of the 1960s with the birth of a new group of agencies led by a new generation of Bill Bernbachs and Mary Wells Lawrences (of Wells Rich Greene).

Indeed, as the Saatchis would soon discover, all was far from well. Forrest Mars, head of Mars Inc., soon let it be known that he was personally disturbed by the Bates takeover. The Mars account was worth $100 million a year in billings to Bates; now Forrest Mars himself ordered a review of the entire Mars $200 million-a-year advertising budget. Worse was to follow. Colgate Palmolive withdrew $80 million of business, and the Warner-Lambert Company, Bates's biggest domestic client with annual billings of $68 million, indicated that it was about to move too.

In June Robert Jacoby was elected chairman of the American Association of Advertising Agencies, the industry's trade group. He found his peers in that organization highly critical of his sale to Saatchi, but at first he shrugged off the criticism. "They're just jealous," he said to his wife. But there seemed to be more to it than that. When the Saatchis heard the rumors about Warner-Lambert, a major rival to Procter & Gamble, Jacoby is said to have assured them that the account was on "solid ground." The Warner-Lambert president, Melvin R. Goodes, took a different line. When he learned of the takeover his first question was: "How much does Jacoby make out of it?" When he was told that Jacoby had received over $100 million, he was appalled. "What is Procter & Gamble going to do about this?" was his second question. Others wanted to know the answer to that question too. Goodes didn't wait to find out. In June he sacked Bates as his advertising agency.

Procter & Gamble meanwhile had no intention of letting the deal pass without showing the Saatchi brothers the full weight of its anger. Milt Gossett was the man who had to field most of the anger, as P&G always had been his special account. For him the Bates acquisition was a bitter blow. The brothers, he said, should never have done it. He had visited them several times in London to try to dissuade them and listened as they in turn inveighed against Bob Jacoby, who they said was really taking them to the cleaners. "Bates is everything that you say you don't want," argued Gossett. "You are buying the antithesis of what this company ought to be. We have a reputation of being creative before anything else. Well, Bates is not very creative." The brothers calmly told him they would change all that and he shouldn't worry; but Gossett did, particularly when P&G warned him of what it would do if the brothers insisted on going through with their plan.

Gossett urged Maurice to travel to Cincinnati, see John Smale, the head of P&G, tell him and the person in charge of P&G's huge advertising budget, Robert V. Goldstein, what he intended to do—and fall back on their mercy. The brothers were against that. They loved to have P&G on their books, but they would not kowtow to any client.

There was pride on both sides. Smale had let the world know of his disapproval, and he could scarcely back off now. On June 16, the *Gallagher Report*, in its terse, shorthand style, made another key mention of Saatchi. Smale, it said, had reined in the brothers and told "the boys to call halt to ad-agency acquisition spree (primarily P&G houses) or face client defections. . . . Maurice takes to road to appease clients."

Maurice had indeed taken to the road. Charles, of course, had never been to Cincinnati, but he urged Maurice to make the trip now. He knew how well liked Maurice was within Procter & Gamble, and it was clear to Charles, as it was to Maurice, that only a personal visit could head off serious trouble.

In June Maurice flew to New York and collected Milt Gossett and Anthony Simonds-Gooding, and together they flew on to Cincinnati, one hour and fifty minutes' flying time from New York, for a meeting with Smale and what seemed to be half the senior executives of P&G.

Maurice's charm did not let them down. Simonds-Gooding was continually astonished by the way Maurice could get on with people, but even by previous standards this trip was a revelation to him. In Cincinnati he found Maurice something of a celebrity among the P&G wives: "Someone would always invite us back to their place for dinner, and all the others would come 'round, and there would be half a dozen top P&G men and their wives, all old enough to be Maurice's parents, and the wives sort of treated him like a little son. 'Well, Maurice, what have you been up to? You've been naughty again, we hear, and caused a lot of trouble, and you really shouldn't do this.' They adored Maurice, and he loved it."

Gossett was also a calming influence in Cincinnati, and he had done his best to keep things on an even keel. Nothing, however, could easily cool the anger of Smale and his colleagues. Procter & Gamble prides itself on being the most professional marketing company in the world—almost a university of the subject. It has systems that have been developed, refined, and added to over decades. It was the biggest advertiser in the United States, spending $819 million in 1986, just ahead of Philip Morris with $815 million and a long way ahead of numbers three and four, R. J. Reynolds and General Motors, both around $450 million. Procter & Gamble has developed tight systems for controlling its advertising expenditure, measuring its effectiveness and its ability to create the all-important brand image. Possibly no company in the world works as closely with its advertising agencies as P&G does. Cincinnati executives boast that they are in daily contact with every one of P&G's advertisers, and agency executives are required to visit Cincinnati every so often for what the industry calls "indoctrination" sessions. An agency with a P&G account has to work within very close confines but in return receives big rewards—and loyalty. P&G does not lightly change its agencies—*Marketing Week* magazine worked out that on average P&G's agencies (largely Leo Burnett, Grey, Wells Rich Greene, D'Arcy Masius Benton & Bowles—and of course, Saatchi & Saatchi Compton) had been working for it for thirty-seven years. Procter & Gamble is big and powerful enough to set strict limits on what other clients its chosen agencies should have—and it hated to have those limits broken. Never in its history had the conventions been flouted as flagrantly as the Saatchis had now done.

The meeting the first morning was a stiff one but went better than the Saatchi people expected. Saatchi would not get off completely—P&G would withdraw its $6 million Encaprin account from Dancer Fitzgerald (now renamed DFS Dorland Worldwide)—but that was only a light slap. There was also a severe warning that P&G was not happy and it would watch events, particularly at Bates, with keen interest. Fond as it was of Compton and Saatchi, Procter & Gamble would not hesitate to protect its products.

Maurice continued his tour of the United States, desperately trying to stop further defections. He saw Forrest Mars in McLean, Virginia, just outside Washington, for another uncomfortable meeting. In Minneapolis he had a tough session with Art Schultze, the president of the grocery-products division of General Mills, who was reported to be taking a hard line over $125 million of billings at DFS Dorland Worldwide, plus another $50 million of spending at another Saatchi shop, Campbell-Mithun. Simonds-Gooding seemed to be living on a plane, dashing from one account to another, in between trying to pull together the threads of his vastly expanded operation.

The losses went on. On June 23 Gallagher forecast further trouble: Bates was about to lose some General Foods business. "Reason: Bates 'compromised' cardinal principle of GF agencies (must retain flexibility in coffee ad efforts)," wrote Gallagher. Bates handled Maxim and Mellow Roast coffees, plus Oscar Mayer and Louis Rich meats; but at Compton the Saatchi group handled Folgers and High Point, two P&G brands of coffee.

Week by week the account losses continued to mount, with rumors of more to come. The Bates takeover was not actually consummated until August 6, three months after it was announced, and by then the losses were considerable, most of them at Bates. RJR-Nabisco pulled out $96 million of billings, Michelob another $38 million, Ralston $12 million, and McDonald's $8 million. Backer & Spielvogel lost some clients too, and so did the other Saatchi agencies: ABC dropped McCaffrey & McCall, and Helene Curtis dropped DFS Dorland. By mid-August the account losses came to $359 million, almost all from Bates—and more were on the way. Early in September Gallagher reported that Saatchi was taking a hard line with General Mills chairman Brewster Atwater: "offer to resign $170 million in GM business. Reason: Atwater adamant over elimination of client conflicts." There had been some gains too, however—Bates had won a $48 million Xerox account, and RJR-Nabisco, dropping $96 million of billings from Bates, had given DFS Dorland $32 million. Even so, the net loss that summer was considerable.

By early September the Saatchi stock price was hitting new lows for the year, and the brothers' equanimity had long faded. Much of their anger was directed at Jacoby, who they felt had not done enough to stop the fallout. Saatchi & Saatchi seemed to be caught in a never-ending spiral of account losses, which damaged morale and its reputation, leading to still further losses—and then to firings. All over Madison Avenue agencies, particularly those involved in the megamergers, were laying off people, creating further bitterness.

The scene was set for the most damaging blow yet—something that was probably inevitable from the beginning but that the Saatchis had not foreseen: conflict with Bob Jacoby.

The departure of Jacoby from Ted Bates was actually not of the

Saatchis' making, at least not directly. The brothers and their head of communication, Tony Simonds-Gooding, found themselves propelled into events because of a boardroom battle between Jacoby and two members of his own staff, Larry Light and Donald M. Zuckert. Light, forty-six, was a Montreal-born intellectual who had cultivated in particular Forrest E. Mars, the domineering head of Mars Inc., makers of Kal-Kan pet foods, Uncle Ben's Rice, and seven of the world's bestselling chocolate bars. According to the *New York Times*, "the superdedicated Mars appreciated both Light's strategic repositioning of Snickers candy bars as an adult snack and Light's ability to bring himself to tears in evocative paeans to Milky Ways and the American consumer." The legendarily frugal billionaire was also said to approve Light's unpretentiousness. "Larry wears the same blue suit every day and his buttons are always popping," a Bates executive was quoted as saying. "To Forrest he's a man of the people."

Zuckert was fifty-three, an overweight, heavily built man whom Jacoby had promoted in 1983 to president of Bates New York—number two in the organization. The two men had not got on, with Jacoby accusing Zuckert of not being tough enough and Zuckert complaining that Jacoby was picking on him. Jacoby, he said, would "cut you to ribbons with a very sharp tongue." On another occasion he declared, "Bob believed in personal conflict and fear."

Zuckert and Light were now to feature at the center of a drama that *Advertising Age* called "MacBates" and that capped for the brothers what had already been the worst summer of their careers.

On the night before the Bates deal was signed, Light refused to accept his new employment contract, thus threatening the merger. He demanded promotion to the role occupied by John Hoyne, who had negotiated the Saatchi deal: president of Bates International. Hoyne had served Jacoby well throughout the negotiations, but faced with the collapse of the Saatchi talks once again, the chairman gave in. He suspected that right through 1986 Zuckert and Light, neither of them close to him anymore, were meeting on weekends to discuss how they could advance their careers inside the agency. Jacoby later accused them of plotting to take away accounts, including Mars. Both men denied the accusation.

Simonds-Gooding spent most of that summer, when he wasn't trying to put his finger in the dike, working out how to reorganize his vast communications empire. He controlled 14,000 people in four agencies. Bates could stand on its own as a global network inside the Saatchi stable, with access to all the various special companies Saatchi owned: Siegel & Gale (corporate design), Clancy Shulman and Rowland (public relations), Howard Marlboro (sales promotion), and so on. What of the others: Saatchi & Saatchi Compton, the first agency they owned in the United States; Dancer Fitzgerald Sample, already merged with Dorland but scarcely a global agency; and Backer & Spielvogel? There were all sorts of client conflicts and staffing problems as Simonds-Gooding juggled the various possibilities.

He was naive enough to outline his thoughts to Jacoby, whose analytical mind he had come to admire, in August. "You are obviously the key player in this, and I look to you as an ally," Simonds-Gooding told Jacoby. "I am an Englishman, and I don't know this market. I need your support." Simonds-Gooding had probably said something very similar to Gossett, Stu Upson, and Carl Spielvogel, but he was, as any good manager would be, anxious to take everyone along with him. Jacoby seemed perfectly willing to oblige: "You paid the money; you tell me what you want, and we'll do it. I'll tell you if it's wrong, but if you want it we'll do it." Simonds-Gooding had heard of Jacoby's reputation as something of a tyrant—the trade press liked to caricature him as Napoleon—but invariably found him pleasant and amusing company. In those months before Bates officially became part of Saatchi he had a series of detailed and constructive discussions with Jacoby, each time more impressed with his grasp of the business and his thoughts on how the different agencies could be run. Whatever else might be said of him, the American was a professional to his fingertips.

At Bates some of the others saw a different and much less cooperative Jacoby. "Here was a guy who had the hammer and sold the hammer, and once you sell the hammer you can't swing it anymore," said Don Zuckert. "Someone here said that once Bob sold the agency he couldn't accept the fact that he was a hired hand." Simonds-Gooding, however, reported back to the brothers that Jacoby seemed much maligned and that Napoleon seemed to be on their side after all: "I'm having no problems with him. He's absolutely delightful."

"Well, you know why that is, don't you?" asked Charles. "He's got about $100 million of our money in his wallet. Cash!" He put his head in his hands in horror. "God, I'd kill for $100 million. I'd do anything for $100 million!"

Maurice looked at him keenly. "Would you really, Charles? Would you run down Charlotte Street naked for $100 million?"

"I'd do that for $10 million," snapped Charles.

"I'd do it for a million," replied Maurice. Clearly the brothers had not entirely lost their sense of humor.

On August 7 Jacoby wrote to both Maurice and Simonds-Gooding to say that he wanted to make some management changes. Zuckert, he said, had done a good job for him, but he was now tired out. "Zuckert is a housekeeper and I would have changed his role whether you bought us or not," Jacoby wrote. He proposed to promote a new employee he had hired in 1985: John H. Nichols, a forty-nine-year-old Texan, whom he had brought in from the Chicago agency Leo Burnett and put in charge of new business. He also wanted to promote John Hoyne, who would become Jacoby's number two, which would mean that Larry Light reported to Hoyne rather than Jacoby. This restructuring would, he explained, free Jacoby to help Simonds-Gooding with the great affairs of state with which he was having to deal.

The Saatchi executives were noncommittal—the message went back that Jacoby should obviously run the company the way he thought fit, but everything was about to be reorganized and the new roles might not fit the organization. They suggested he wait until Simonds-Gooding had got an overall structure clear in his mind before doing anything. However, the brothers were keen to show Jacoby how much they appreciated him. "We have not come across anyone quite as dynamic and determined as you have been," wrote Maurice in a letter dated August 19, 1986. "It is a new experience for us and a very pleasant one." This was one of the rashest statements Maurice Saatchi ever made.

Early in September Simonds-Gooding set off for New York on a week's tour to see all four top Saatchi executives: Stu Upson, head of DFS Dorland, Carl Spielvogel of Backer & Spielvogel, Milton Gossett at Saatchi & Saatchi Compton, and Robert Jacoby at Bates. Simonds-Gooding made the same speech to each one: they were his four top people and he trusted them. They had to help him find a way of pulling all the businesses into an organization that would work and benefit the whole company—and benefit each of them individually too. Everyone must gain from the organization. He was, he said, giving each of the four the same information and he wanted them to confer, then he would come back in a week and they would get down to the serious business of thinking where they should go from there.

Jacoby that morning was less responsive than he had been. Simonds-Gooding spent two hours with him going over his rough plans. As he was leaving, Jacoby said: "You know that organizational thing I was talking about—involving Zuckert and Light? I'd like to do that now." Simonds-Gooding hesitated—he didn't know any of the four people involved and couldn't assess the situation.

"I'll ask you two questions," he said. "Will it militate against any of these maneuvers?"

The answer was no.

"Will it cause any disruption?"

"Zuckert will be happier than a pig in shit," said Jacoby. "He has $22 million, and he can go and think how to spend it, and he'll do administration. Nichols is very good. Larry Light is pleased to have a solid finance executive to help with the business. And of course I will then be free to help you with your dream and make it happen."

Simonds-Gooding agreed and set off on his rounds. That evening, Wednesday, September 3, 1986, Jacoby scribbled a note to Zuckert in pencil, gave one further memo to his secretary, and left with his wife for a camping trip in Colorado—out of reach of everyone except his secretary, who kept this fact to herself. "There was a saying in Bates that among Jacoby's interests were booze, money, women, and revenge. And this was revenge. The deal was over and he was going to put one on Light and Zuckert," says a former Bates executive. The next morning when Zuckert and Light appeared, there was consternation. Light discovered that Hoyne was now senior to him, while Bates executives recall hearing an outburst of shouting from Zuckert's office. The memo Jacoby had drafted told Zuckert he had been replaced as New York president by Nichols.

That day Simonds-Gooding was passing by the Bates office on Broadway, still making his rounds. He needed a bathroom and suddenly decided he might as well avail himself of a Saatchi facility. He went up to the executive floor and ran into Zuckert in the men's room. The Bates executive was still angry. "You might want to look at this," he said, waving a bit of paper. "It's going to cost you two or three million dollars."

Simonds-Gooding assumed the paper must be litigation of some sort. "I don't want to talk about it here. Let's go to your office," he suggested to Zuckert. When he opened up the paper, he found that it contained an announcement of the management changes together with photographs of Nichols and Hoyne and Jacoby's penciled note to Zuckert. There was also a copy of Zuckert's reply, telling him of his extreme anger at the way he was being treated after twenty years of working for Jacoby, that his contract had been broken, and that he demanded to be reinstated in full. Zuckert had also sent a note to the staff along the lines of, "You will have been as surprised as I to learn . . ."—which gave the others some hint of his distress at the move.

Zuckert then gave Simonds-Gooding a long and unflattering lecture on Jacoby and the problems in store for Saatchi & Saatchi. "You didn't think properly about this, you didn't do due diligence," he said, pointing his finger accusingly at the Saatchi executive. Saatchi, according to Zuckert, had brought the problems on itself by underestimating Jacoby, whose last-minute granting of Bates stock to executives, often junior ones, "received notoriety that whipped through the halls like crazy." Zuckert also told Simonds-Gooding that Jacoby was drinking excessively. (Jacoby later denied having a drinking problem to the *New York Times*, which quoted him as saying: "I had to drink to be successful in the advertising business. But I don't think you would find anybody who ever saw me drunk and nonfunctional.")

The Englishman was exhausted after flying the Atlantic and attending his round of meetings and sat there completely impassive. Even Zuckert was impressed by his calm, not guessing its real cause. Finally Simonds-

Gooding said he would see Hoyne, who was at that moment the most senior person present in the agency. "Fine," said Zuckert. "You do that. This is all public knowledge now. There's nothing that I've said which is off the record. I'm giving it to you as a board member." Simonds-Gooding then went to Hoyne, who tried to be reassuring. "Don't worry about it. Relax, it will all pass. If you want me to see Larry [Light], I'll see Larry." By the time Simonds-Gooding arrived at Milt Gossett's office for his next appointment, he discovered the news was out. Gossett greeted him with, "Have you heard about Bates? It's all over the street."

That afternoon Greg Ostroff had a phone call from one of his investors at his office in Goldman Sachs: "We hear Bob Jacoby's disappeared." That was dramatic news, of great significance to the Saatchi stock price. Ostroff rang a contact at Bates. Yes, she said, Jacoby was not there.

"Did you fire him, or did he quit?"

"Well, neither," said Ostroff's friend.

"Then where is he?" There was a pause.

"Well—we don't know!"

Jacoby could not be contacted—he was said to be on a farm without a phone. There was much talk of sending a helicopter to find him, but in the evidence later presented at his case for unfair dismissal it turned out he was in daily contact with his secretary. The story of his disappearance began hitting the press, and there were waves of complaint from clients. Without Jacoby, Zuckert and Light were able to rally a large number of Bates staff behind them, and advertising executives know how to apply pressure on their masters: do it through the clients.

A few days later Maurice Saatchi had a call from Forrest Mars. Mars was terse and to the point. Jacoby learned of the call at his arbitration hearing, and according to his version it went thus: "My good friend Larry Light doesn't like what Jacoby's done, and I don't like it when Larry is unhappy. Fix it." Mars hung up the phone. From Cincinnati came angry growls from Saatchi's biggest client, Procter & Gamble. This was getting to be too much. Clients had received a form letter from Jacoby setting out the changes, and they were resentful. "Who are these guys?" asked one client. "I don't know Hoyne or Nichols from a hole in the ground."

On Monday morning Greg Ostroff rang up his friend at Bates again. The rumors over the weekend had made many of his investors in Saatchi & Saatchi very nervous, and Ostroff was looking for information to evaluate the changes. Just what was going on? "Listen, it's Monday morning, and he's not around. You guys are telling me that you didn't fire him and he didn't quit. Well, he's surely pissed off," Ostroff concluded.

On September 10, the Procter & Gamble volcano that had been rumbling in increasing anger at Saatchi all summer finally erupted. P&G

would not let Saatchi off lightly this time. It decided to withdraw $85 million worth of its food business from Saatchi & Saatchi Compton New York. Out went the Crisco Oil and Duncan Hines business from Compton, while DFS Dorland lost Luv's diapers and Bounty paper towels.

P&G typically was prepared to limit the damage. Greg Ostroff that day sent a note to investors saying: "We have spoken to P&G who report that this does not reflect on the quality of the advertising from Saatchi's agencies but that because of their strict no-conflict policy these moves were necessary. Saatchi retains P&G soaps and detergents business and remains Procter's lead agency worldwide." Nonetheless, this was the most savage blow yet, and it convinced the brothers that they had to take drastic action immediately. They could not risk losing the Mars account, which would almost certainly go if Light left. And Light would not stay if Jacoby did.

Simonds-Gooding finally made contact with Jacoby on the evening of September 10 when Jacoby arrived in Lake Tahoe, Nevada, for the American Association of Advertising Agencies western-region convention. The brothers told Simonds-Gooding what they wanted him to do with Bates: merge it as rapidly as possible with one of the other agencies. The instructions were passed on by Charles, who dealt with Simonds-Gooding almost daily. "Perm any combination you want—but do it fast," he told him. Charles originally preferred to put Bates under the Compton umbrella in the hope that doing so would eliminate some of the Procter & Gamble problems, but Simonds-Gooding soon decided who he wanted in charge of Bates: it had to be Carl Spielvogel. In the cabinet of New York advertising executives he was trying to put together, Simonds-Gooding found that Spielvogel was the only one the others "would bend the knee to." Charles, in his gloomier moments, says Simonds-Gooding prompted him to go a stage further and do a "big bang": merge Bates with both Compton and Backer & Spielvogel to create one huge Saatchi & Saatchi business worldwide and build a Saatchi brand name that would be even greater than that of Young & Rubicam or Ogilvy. The merged business would be run by Spielvogel. Such a merger would have been a dramatic—and probably foolhardy—leap, but the brothers say that they saw it only as their "doomsday scenario" to be carried through only if the account losses became cataclysmic. Simonds-Gooding, however, found himself working on just that scenario for several months.

When Simonds-Gooding talked to Jacoby in Lake Tahoe on September 10, he deliberately ignored the chaos at Bates and the bitter battles still raging there. He came straight to his central point. "I want to meet you to discuss the merger of Bates," he said. Even the tough Jacoby had not expected this.

His contract, Jacoby protested, stipulated that he should run an independent Bates for five years. The Saatchi executive was no longer interested in that. Saatchi owned Bates, and it was going to make whatever changes it wanted. Jacoby could not go on running Bates, not with the present turmoil. He would have to stand aside from the agency, work for Simonds-Gooding directly in the public company Saatchi & Saatchi, and help Simonds-Gooding put the agencies together—a job, argued the Saatchi executive, that was very important and that would still give Jacoby credibility and responsibility. The one role he could not go back to was the chairmanship of Bates—that was over. Further, Simonds-Gooding was reversing the decisions about Zuckert and Light. Nichols and Hoyne, Jacoby's two favorites, would be demoted again.

Jacoby would not move easily. He had no interest in the job Simonds-Gooding was offering him. Disdainfully, Jacoby ordered his portrait to be taken down off the wall on the twenty-seventh floor, and he sent Saatchi a check for its value, saying he wanted the painting for his daughter. Then he went off to Washington for another advertising convention, leaving the Bates staff to stare at the empty space on the wall.

That Friday Simonds-Gooding called the Bates board members together—twenty-eight of them, without Jacoby. Simonds-Gooding was abrupt and to the point. Jacoby had been shifted and would continue in a different role in the Saatchi organization but would not be running Bates. Zuckert was taking over as chief executive officer. They must all act to stem the loss of clients and to restore morale. Jacoby, according to the *New York Times* account, got the news later that day when Steven W. Colford, *Advertising Age*'s Washington bureau chief, interrupted him at the AAAA conference with the question, "Did you know you'd been fired?" When Jacoby got back to New York that night on the Eastern shuttle, his driver, meeting him at La Guardia, confirmed that Zuckert was now the chief executive officer of Bates.

Jacoby, of course, had not been fired. He was still being paid $1 million a year and he continued to go into the office; but his power was gone, and he could not take seriously the job that Simonds-Gooding intended for him. He and Zuckert had booked a skiing holiday together over Christmas, but they avoided each other in the corridor. The rumors continued: Jacoby was said to be about to be investigated by the Securities & Exchange Commission (a story which was total fantasy), while stories of the big stock gifts he had made on the eve of the Saatchi bid became more and more racy—and absurd.

On September 22, the knowledgeable *Gallagher Report* stated that Jacoby had given "the thumbs down" on the offer as assistant to Simonds-Gooding. He had been "shown door in biggest executive purge in ad agency history." However, the return of Larry Light had defused the Mars time bomb—that account at least was safe for the present.

In fact, Jacoby remained at Bates until October 21 when he finally quit

and sued Saatchi for breach of contract. He won his case—getting
another $5 million to add to the $110 million he had already made. It was
this money that now, as much as anything else, became the focus of the
industry's wrath. "Everyone knows that Bob Jacoby got enough money to
compete with the Sheik of Araby," said Leonard S. Matthews, president
of the AAAA. (Jacoby had to resign as chairman of the AAAA when he
quit Bates.)

From the head of Young & Rubicam, Ed Ney, came an even more
damaging remark that is still quoted around New York: "I thought this
particular merger was an unfortunate occurrence, because I never saw
anything said about we're doing this to give better service to the clients.
The reason it wasn't said is it couldn't be said. What was said was we're
the biggest. In the consumer service business that's just nonsense."

Zuckert, whose first action as chief executive officer was to fire John
Nichols, hit back, but he was very much on the defensive. "Clearly I wish
this had never happened," Zuckert said. "It would have been a lot easier
to do a Douglas MacArthur and just fade away. Clearly, we must be the
major new business target of every agency in town. On the one hand
they're saying this is bad for the industry and then they're giving all these
stories to the press about how awful megamergers are. I wish Ed Ney
would put us in Y&R's profit-sharing plan. We've given them half of
their new business this year."

From Wall Street came the view that the ruckus had been damaging for
the whole level of investment interest in the advertising sector. "In the
short run, it will contribute to all the old fears that investors have about
ad agencies," said Charlie Crane of Prudential-Bache. "That the assets
do go down the elevators and that this is not all that stable a business."

As the crisis deepened, so the pressure put on Simonds-Gooding by
Charles to find a solution increased. Through September and into
October Simonds-Gooding pressed ahead at full speed with the concept
of the "great merger." He knew the odds were against such a merger, but
he believed—wrongly, according to the brothers—that it was what
Charles and Maurice wanted. It was to be textbook stuff: everything
would be grouped under the Saatchi & Saatchi brand name, including
the consulting group—one huge and unified Saatchi & Saatchi brand
applying to everything around the world. Taken region by region, Saatchi
was not number one everywhere, but if there was just one Saatchi
business, in the same way there was just one Young & Rubicam, the
Saatchi brand would be a clear world leader. "It was a wonderfully manic
concept that appealed to Charles," says a former Saatchi executive.

Only the concept could never work—and it didn't. Simonds-Gooding
was exhausted, and his strategic thinking was flawed. In London the
brothers had taken such a battering that they were not thinking with
their usual coolness. Organizationally, the merger might have been

possible, with the goodwill of the New York agency heads; but the clients simply would not accept it.

At Compton, Gossett and Wax reluctantly went along with the idea, although they didn't like it. "It was just hell for them, this concept," says a former Saatchi executive. But the two men had begun to realize that in the drive toward globalization even Saatchi & Saatchi Compton was not big enough on its own; it needed more of the Saatchi pieces to keep it ahead. Don Zuckert raised no objections, although Bates would in effect disappear, particularly if Spielvogel was running the whole thing. "With Jacoby gone, Bates is like a headless chicken," Simonds-Gooding told the brothers in London.

Once again it was Smale in Cincinnati who put his foot down, killing any faint hope of Simonds-Gooding's "big bang." Gossett and Wax, the two men least enthusiastic about Charles's dream, were sent out to P&G to sell it on the concept. They came back, as one executive said, "with their tails between their legs." Procter & Gamble's executives would have nothing to do with it. Their dislike of Bates as an agency was such that they would not let it near any of their accounts. They also pointed out that by putting three agencies together all over the world, every Saatchi office in America, Australia, Britain, and elsewhere was going to be turned upside down. The people at Procter & Gamble were not prepared to accept the damage that this would have on the handling of their own business. "They said: 'Forget it,'" Gossett reported back. "They said if you're going to put these three agencies together, they're off. The whole account. It's not on."

Simonds-Gooding was back at square one. He had made no progress in merging Bates with any of the other Saatchi agencies, and abruptly the brothers changed tack. They would not merge anything but would leave all the agencies as they were, separate autonomous units running inside the Saatchi & Saatchi holding company. The defections were now slowing, new business was coming in, the stock was recovering in the continuing bull market and actually ended the year more or less where it had started. The brothers would get on with building the other divisions of the Saatchi group and leave what they called "migraine city" alone for a while.

It was Simonds-Gooding who early in 1987 argued that this route would not work either. Over the autumn Saatchi & Saatchi had pulled back in new business more or less what had been lost, although the new accounts did not have quite the same quality. The point, however, was that the growth had ceased: the whole motive behind taking over these agencies was to produce an accelerated growth rate for the company, and after a year of standstill, increases were 20 percent behind where they should have been. In the meantime the executives of Compton had come to see Wax to urge him to consider a merger of the agency and asked him to work out which agencies the firm could merge with.

Simonds-Gooding finally presented the situation to Charles and Maurice. "We have a real problem, and doing nothing will not solve it," he told the brothers. "Nobody understands what we are about. We have Backer & Spielvogel sitting there, a big agency. We have Bates, still a headless chicken with endless client defections post-Jacoby. We have DFS Dorland, which we pretend is a third-world network but it's not. Compton in New York has lost the P&G business and is bleeding. DFS are complaining that they too have lost Procter business and a lot of Cadbury's [candy] because we now have Mars, and none of it has anything to do with [DFS]; they're not winning the pitches they used to."

He proposed going back to New York and working out a complete new structure for all three of the Saatchi & Saatchi–run agencies. He would talk to the clients, to the agency executives, to everyone who could contribute to the debate. Then he would come back with a plan and put it to the full board. Simonds-Gooding had been at the group long enough to know that Saatchi & Saatchi did not have full board meetings in the way other companies did—Charles was constitutionally incapable of sitting through a full meeting, and no one at Saatchi had ever seen him do it. However, this was an issue that Simonds-Gooding thought was so important that it would have to be considered by everyone, and he would need the complete backing of the directors to put the plan into effect.

The brothers were not enthusiastic about the option that Simonds-Gooding now recommended: one of "manageable units." However, they would go along with it. But "speed it up," they urged him. He flew back to New York.

One morning in January 1987 Carl Spielvogel was in his office at 1140 West Street when Simonds-Gooding came through on the phone. Could he come and see him? He had something important to say. Spielvogel was intrigued. He had watched with some concern the Saatchi share price collapse in the summer, the client defections, and the attacks in the press—at one stage Simonds-Gooding, tracked to his hotel, resorted to putting a paper bag over his face to avoid questions from reporters. Spielvogel had been slightly detached from the events of the summer, but nonetheless they had rubbed off on him too. He hated the controversy into which he had unwittingly put himself and what one Saatchi executive called the "noise, noise, noise" of the critics. Charles Peebler of Bozell, Jacobs, Kenyon & Eckhardt labeled the megamerger trend an advertising version of Chernobyl where the fallout could damage the whole industry—a remark directed straight at Saatchi and those who, like Spielvogel, had sold their businesses to it.

When Simonds-Gooding turned up, Spielvogel thought he looked tired and drawn. The days when the English executive could sit in Tim

Bell's old office with nothing to do had long disappeared. Now he had given up the "big bang" plan and was about to propose something else. He sat on Spielvogel's couch and began: "I'd like you to consider something. I'd like you to consider taking over Bates."

Spielvogel was startled; he had never even thought about the possibility. However, when he did, he reckoned it was not at all a bad idea. Backer & Spielvogel had a reputation as a creative agency and Bates did not. It made sense to do it that way around. He became an enthusiastic supporter as Simonds-Gooding outlined the rest of his plan.

Completing the merger would take months of extraordinarily delicate and painful negotiation, during which time the brothers left him alone, but from the spring onward Simonds-Gooding began putting his changes into effect, merging some of the smaller agencies, including McCaffrey & McCall with Rumrill-Hoyt, and organizing a three-way merger of AC&R/DHB & Bess.

It was June 1987 before Simonds-Gooding finally put the first major stage of his plan into effect. Dancer Fitzgerald would be merged with Saatchi & Saatchi Compton to form a new agency called Saatchi & Saatchi Worldwide, with its major North American subsidiary called Saatchi & Saatchi DFS Compton Inc. The new agency's combined annual billings would be $2.3 billion, and it would have ninety-eight offices in fifty-four countries. Dorland was left out of this merger, becoming again a stand-alone London agency, the attempt at creating a third-world network finished. Jack Rubins departed from Dorland in disgust, but one part of the Saatchi & Saatchi empire now had some order to it.

What about Bates? Simonds-Gooding had put into effect his plan for this troubled agency too. On July 15, after months of rumor, maneuvering, denials, and changes of course, the announcement was made: Backer & Spielvogel would merge with Bates. Significantly, Carl Spielvogel would be the chairman of the merged company, and the name of his agency came first in the new title, Backer Spielvogel Bates Worldwide. Billings would be $2.7 billion, and the agency would have 104 offices in 46 countries. Zuckert was to be chief operating officer (he has since left), but there was no doubt in anyone's mind whose agency this was: the fifty-eight-year-old Spielvogel had emerged on top, and his creative reputation, it was hoped, would set a new tone for Bates. "The wind is at our backs," said Spielvogel on the day the merger was announced. "Let's spread our wings and run with it."

The rest of Simonds-Gooding's plan for the empire was complex but equally practical. He had soon learned that within the Saatchi organization, the Charlotte Street agency, although now only a subsidiary of a subsidiary, was still "the holy grail"; it had, he told the brothers, a "bunker mentality," although in effect the philosophy and the driving force for the whole group came from there. If the philosophy were to be injected into other parts of the Saatchi group, he had to bring the Charlotte Street management much more to the fore. Roy Warman and Terry Bannister found themselves elevated to running a new international division, a reward for the way they had successfully replaced Tim Bell, and Bill Muirhead moved up to become chairman of the agency.

There were still other bits to be sorted out. A number of the smaller agencies were lifted out of the larger agencies altogether: Campbell-Mithun, William Esty, AC&R/DHB & Bess, and Stern Walters/Earle Ludgin reported directly to the Saatchi parent organization.

By the autumn of 1987 the agency side of Saatchi & Saatchi was relatively calm, and the new networks were settling down well. It was then that the man who had done so much of the work at Saatchi revealed that he had decided to leave.

Simonds-Gooding had been headhunted as early as May 1987, just as he was putting the finishing touches to the mergers of the Saatchi & Saatchi agencies. "I was absolutely hell-bent on finishing the task," he says. "The adrenaline was really flowing, and I was going to do it or die—literally die—in the attempt." As the pressure eased, he gradually came to realize that what he was doing was not sustainable and that his personal life had fallen by the wayside. His wife had gone with him to New York, but he had seen little of his children, and the pressure had been extraordinary.

Once the organization was in place, his job was essentially done. The agencies would have to—indeed would insist on—running themselves.

He had come both to admire and to like the brothers a great deal, but he realized that they saw his role in a different light. Simonds-Gooding would always be the person they sent in to clean up the mess their big, bold leaps had created. He was now offered an exciting new job—to head British Satellite Broadcasting, a private-sector consortium that planned to put a satellite in orbit over Britain and offer viewers three new TV channels. This was an entirely new business that offered a completely different form of challenge.

The brothers were gracious about letting him go. Perhaps they felt that he had no real future role in their organization either, although Charles awkwardly offered his thanks for the way Simonds-Gooding had sorted out the problems in New York. He stayed with Saatchi & Saatchi through the summer for the announcements of the mergers, then left quietly in October, when there was a lull in the publicity and the controversy that seemed to follow Saatchi & Saatchi.

As for Jacoby, he linked up with his old mates Hoyne and Light again to make two takeover bids. The former Saatchi finance director Martin Sorrell beat them for control of J. Walter Thompson in yet another bold

British move into Madison Avenue, then Hoyne and Jacoby bought a stake in Ogilvy & Mather but sold out again when they discovered the board wanted nothing to do with them. Jacoby ruminated on his defeat for months afterward at his sprawling ranch house in Saddle River, New Jersey, and planned a comeback: "It would be fun to have something that would get me closer to knocking off the Saatchis," he said. "It's easy to do because I can see these guys are amateurs."

The brothers, however, had for the moment put New York to the back of their minds. There were more pressing problems back in London.

16
ENTER JOSEPHINE HART

T he takeover of Ted Bates and of the other agencies in the United States had not gone according to plan—not by a long shot—but by the time the new Saatchi & Saatchi structure was in place, the analysts in the City of London and on Wall Street had grudgingly come to accept, at least for a time, that Saatchi had probably, after all, got it right. For the fiscal year ended September 1986, which included only a few months with Bates, profits rose 73 percent to £70 million. Much of that increase was accounted for by acquisition; but the bottom-line figure, the one the analysts look at most closely, showed that earnings per share were up 21 percent, dividends rose 20 percent, and profit margins, at 15.8 percent among the highest in the industry, were up 18 percent. Saatchi & Saatchi, whatever its problems, was still a financial success.

The following year, 1987, was the year of the big reorganization of the agencies, the year when all those account losses and Charles's "pain" should show in the accounts. Yet profits still rose another 77 percent to £124 million, a figure beyond the dreams of any company in the history of the advertising industry. Again, both earnings per share and dividends per share rose by more than 20 percent. Financially the brothers remained as surefooted as ever, or so the investment community believed.

From the end of 1986 there was a renewed flow of recommendations coming from the stockbrokers and analysts who followed the advertising sector. In December, Emma H. Hill, an analyst at Schroder Wertheim, the New York investment house, sent her suggestions to her clients, saying that Saatchi & Saatchi "remains our primary recommendation." "It had been," she said, "one of the most eventful years [to date] in Saatchi's dynamic history," but its management "had distinguished itself in two regards—first its vision and second its financial discipline." County Securities USA, a New York subsidiary of NatWest Bank, declared Saatchi & Saatchi's stock a strong buy and went on to say that its recommendation was both "quantitatively and conceptually based." The "quantitative" bit, of course, had to do with Saatchi & Saatchi's profit record and prospects—which looked good. "The conceptual part of our recommendation," County Securities continued, "is that Saatchi is becoming the prototype of the communications/business-service company of the future." Saatchi was the only agency stock listed on Paine-

Webber's "attractive" list that December, and there were several others who agreed with PaineWebber's assessment.

Time would prove the analysts wrong, at least for the next couple of years. Saatchi & Saatchi's shares had bounced back but were again underperforming the rest of the bull market and did not rise above their pre-Bates peak; but as 1987 progressed and the shape of the new agencies became clearly identified, the perception of the Bates purchase changed. Yes, it was agreed, Saatchi had paid a high price, and, yes, Jacoby had done well for himself and for Bates's other stockholders. On the other hand, Saatchi was now so well positioned with its two parallel world networks and good people at the top of each one that the acquisition of Bates had probably been worth it.

This was exactly the message the brothers wanted to get across to the financial community, and it is a measure of the hold they still had on it that they succeeded so well. The modern-day investment analyst, in the City of London just as much as on Wall Street, is a notoriously fickle creature. On the way up, investment analysts compete in their fulsomeness, and many a more level-headed entrepreneur than the Saatchis has made the mistake of believing he has discovered the secret to lasting financial success.

Over the next eighteen months, particularly with the October 1987 stock-market crash and the fallout from the insider trading scandals, the Saatchis would find out the truth. Fashions in the investment world change faster than they do on Fifth Avenue. The brothers, although they did not even suspect it, were no longer on the way up. They had reached, as far as their glamour rating was concerned, the high-water mark. It was to be a new experience for them.

Saatchi & Saatchi celebrated its number-one position by moving offices again, leaving the premises on Charlotte Street, which were bursting at the seams and which they had extended into the adjoining buildings. Ever since the takeover of Compton Advertising in New York in 1982, Charlotte Street had essentially been the home of a satellite agency. From that moment Saatchi & Saatchi had become a holding company, and as acquisition followed acquisition, the need for a separate headquarters became more and more apparent.

Anthony Simonds-Gooding, with far greater experience of big companies than either of the Saatchi brothers, had told them that it was absurd to try to run a world-class company from the cramped sixth-floor space available—particularly as there had not even been enough room on the sixth floor for him. Charles had contemptuously rejected his complaint at the time, but Simonds-Gooding's point had hit home.

The takeover of a small advertising agency and public-relations business, Grandfield Rork Collins, brought with it a short-term lease on the same building on Lower Regent Street where Saatchi & Saatchi had moved in 1974. The brothers went down to look at it and in exploring the place discovered a top floor that was used only for storage. Maurice poked a ceiling and discovered a large skylight. There was another one at the other end of the floor. This was the place for them. They had the top (sixth) floor done up, the skylights uncovered, and moved into the brightest and airiest offices they had ever occupied, the brothers as usual opposite each other, separated only by a small lobby. Simonds-Gooding, Ken Gill, Simon Mellor, and the financial staff moved with them.

The new offices provided space to display more of the Saatchi art collection. Charles and Doris had by now opened their own art gallery in St. John's Wood, but as big as it was it could contain less than one-fifth of their rapidly growing collection. In any case, the public company, Saatchi & Saatchi PLC, owned around 20 percent of the art, so it rightfully belonged in its corridors and offices. The artwork was not to everyone's taste, of course, but no one complained to Charles.

A dozen years had passed since the brothers had last occupied that Regent Street building, and there had been changes in their private lives as well as in the company. The brothers themselves had probably changed very little; physically they were both still trim with no suggestion of paunchiness or gray hair, and despite their wealth and fame, neither had lost any of his shyness. Charles might have been the more reclusive of the two, but he was far from a Howard Hughes—he still played snooker, cards, and chess with the same group of friends; he kept in close contact with the people who interested him—he talks most days on the telephone to David Puttnam, for example—and had made a wide number of new acquaintances in the art world. Doris's interest in contemporary art had brought a new dimension to his life, one that had become as important to him as the advertising business. Just as Maurice had come to know the lobby of every major advertising agency in New York, so Charles knew most of the Greenwich Village galleries. Both brothers went at least once a week to see their parents, who were aging gracefully, and Nathan and Daisy remained a constant in both their lives.

Yet there had been changes, more for Maurice than for Charles. Maurice's marriage to Gillian Osband had originally seemed the ideal match; they had known each other since childhood and had grown up together in the same North London Jewish community. Neither brother had ever lacked for girlfriends before marriage, but of all of the girls Charles and Maurice took home, Gillian must have seemed the most suitable to their parents.

Tall, with a mass of red hair and a considerable sense of humor, Gillian had plenty of admirers. Wealthy in her own right, she continued to be independent of Maurice after they were married, working first as a children's book editor and then as a writer. She kept her own name and her identity, and Maurice seems to have encouraged her to do so.

Colleagues remember her at the Bologna Book Fair, the big event of the publishing season, where "she stopped hearts and turned heads with her miniskirts and her fluffy angora sweaters." She created a worthy enough reputation for herself in the children's book world with her own special style of book; "the archetypal Gillian book is full of jokes and activities," says a colleague. "She puts it all together herself, maps out the ideas—hundreds of ideas—and really keys it into children."

Gillian and Maurice moved to a house in a secluded estate called the Vale of Health in Hampstead. Situated on a very private, very expensive bit of real estate, it was a large two-story villa-style house, set behind an eight-foot wall. The grounds were so spacious that they gave the impression of countryside. One friend described the residence as "one of the most beautiful houses I've been in," although it was not to everyone's taste—other Londoners, living in the more gracious parts of Hampstead or Regent's Park, wondered why Maurice chose to live there. There was a garage big enough to house some of Maurice's cars (although most of them were in the basement garage at the company) and room enough in the house for his collection of antique trains and toys. Gillian was a highly social person, with a wide range of friends and contacts, and she loved to entertain—people from the publishing world, from the film industry, from the music industry, and from everywhere else. To the outside world she and Maurice seemed an idyllically happy couple—which they probably were for a time. But Maurice's closest friends had been aware since the early 1980s that all was not well with the marriage.

The brothers have always had the ability to compartmentalize their lives. For instance, Tim Bell, in all the years he worked with Charles Saatchi, had never been to Charles's house, nor had many of his other coworkers. Similarly, Maurice, although friendly and charming to clients and colleagues, still retained a reserve that few penetrated. Unlike Bell, neither brother had the slightest interest in playing the "friend of Margaret Thatcher" card, and they stayed well away from the cocktail-party circuit frequented by the politicians and City workers. Asked at lunch or dinner parties for his view on the state of the country or the government, Maurice would look embarrassed and make an evasive answer—that wasn't his scene at all, he would indicate. The Conservative party was a client and he preferred not to talk about clients, he would say as politely as possible.

Nor did the brothers mix their private lives with their business lives. Neither Doris nor Gillian was to be seen much about the office, although Doris did turn up from time to time to take Charles off to a new exhibition or a West End show. Doris, more than Gillian, was willing to play the director's wife when it was required, taking some trouble over such tasks as buying Christmas presents for the staff. "Maurice would personally go off on Christmas Eve and buy people strange presents—

bars of exotic soap or something like that—and he would wrap them up or put them in an envelope in his office and come out, be slightly embarrassed, and say 'Happy Christmas' and run off again," says Nick Crean. Maurice was far from ungenerous—just awkward. With Charles and Doris, Christmas presents were something of an event. Doris loved wrapping presents herself and also got considerable fun from giving them, so she organized them, and they came, says one former staff member, "unbelievably beautifully wrapped with ribbons all over them, from Tiffany's or somewhere like that." The odder the present, the more fun Charles had in presenting it. "One present they gave me was a silver key to wind up my toothpaste," says Nick Crean. "It was the sort of present that Doris thought was amusing to give. And Charles laughed and said, 'I bet you can't guess what it is.' Which I couldn't. It was another little game to him."

Doris and Gillian Saatchi had little in common. Doris was ten years older, and despite all the years she had lived and worked in London, she remained an American immigrant in a foreign country. Ask her friends what they think about her, and they say, "She's very *American*," as if that were enough to describe her. They seem to mean a person who never merged herself into her adopted country but retained some of the elements the British tend to classify as American—chatty but cool, given to much more obvious analysis of her friends and acquaintances, with fewer inhibitions—and, of course, an American accent. The art collection occupied a large portion of her time; she also wrote freelance articles for a number of publications, including *The World of Interiors, Artscribe, Architectural Review*, and others, and was for a time the London editor of *House and Garden*. One profile describes her as "blonde, figure kept trim by twice-weekly visits to Dreas Reyneke, bodybuilder to the famous. Mousy or glamorous, depending on who is doing the talking. Typical transatlantic laid-back-but-tough-as-hell image. Keen social-izer." That may have been Doris's image when she was a working copywriter or during her early years as Charles's wife, but as Doris Dibley increasingly became Mrs. Charles Saatchi with all that meant in publicity terms, friends saw a much more vulnerable and tenser person. She was certainly trim, very fashion-conscious, and poised; she was never "mousy," even to those who didn't much care for her.

Gillian lived her own life, keeping her distance from the Saatchi office and staff. Neither she nor Doris had any children, and Daisy complained that none of her four sons had yet made her a grandmother.

Both marriages eventually broke up, Maurice's several years before Charles's. Maurice first met Josephine Hart, a tall, attractive Irish woman who was another of Lindsay Masters's success stories, when Maurice joined Haymarket in 1967. She was working one day in the advertising department when some of the other women mentioned the new arrival in the building. Since he was going to be involved with the same magazine, *Campaign*—Maurice in a more junior capacity—and because the women described him as "young, appealing, and attractive," she went down to see him. Maurice was twenty-one but seemed even younger, and Josephine was twenty-five. She reported back to the other women that he was "not my type at all." However, soon they were working side by side and became friends as well as colleagues. Romance between them would not blossom for another ten years.

Josephine came from a very different background than Maurice—or Gillian Osband. She was brought up in a typically close Irish Catholic family; her father owned a garage in Mullingar, an unlovely town on the edge of the great bog that makes up much of the center of Ireland. She went to a Catholic boarding school, which may not have taught her much about life outside the convent walls but gave her an excellent literary education. Her father, like many Irishmen of his generation, loved poetry and recited to his children endlessly; Josephine from her early years knew by heart most of Goldsmith's "Deserted Village" and much else. English, however, was the only subject she learned in that language—her math, Latin, history, and even French were taught in Gaelic, which under the Irish education system gained her five extra percentage points in national examinations.

Josephine's great love, besides English literature, was acting, and she won prizes in competitions all over Ireland, reciting her prepared pieces to judges from the Royal Academy of Dramatic Art and other British drama schools. One woman, awarding Josephine first prize, said, "This girl breaks all the rules—magnificently." She was the eldest of a family of five, but in her last year at school a brother and a sister died in separate incidents, and she returned home to look after her devastated parents.

For four years life effectively stopped for Josephine; she got a job locally and stayed with her family until everyone was well enough to cope again. Then, when she was twenty-two, she went to London, dreaming of a career on the stage. She worked in a bank in the daytime and in the evening went to drama classes at Guildhall. But eventually she decided the stage was not for her, and she got a mundane job with the Thomson Organisation, working in that same Gray's Inn Road building where the Saatchi brothers six years later watched their full-page ad come off the *Sunday Times* presses. It was at Thomson that she learned the simple skill of selling classified advertisements, and she excelled at it. From childhood she had an exceptional memory, and she now discovered that she was a good organizer too. When she finally arrived at *Campaign* in the late 1960s, both Lindsay Masters and Michael Heseltine said she was far better trained—and skilled—than anyone they had ever had selling ads. Both men soon realized they had hired something more than another salesperson.

Masters appointed Josephine assistant classified-ad manager for the new magazine but was aware that she would outgrow this position. "She took charge very quickly," says Masters. "She was clearly better than the man who was her boss and within a few months she had taken over." Haymarket had never before published a weekly magazine that contained actual news, nor had it ever sold classified advertising. Josephine soon showed Haymarket how to sell ads. "She was quite brilliant at it," says Masters, not easily impressed by ad salespeople. "I had a little thing with her that for every page she sold extra she could have an extra salesperson. Finally I had to say, 'that's enough,' because she had so many. She was the best organizer and trainer of salespeople that I've come across." Heseltine echoes Masters's praise: "She was an extraordinarily polished and sophisticated trainer. And I can remember how thrilled we were to have her." The early issues of *Campaign* featured Josephine Hart as classified advertising manager and Maurice Saatchi as business development manager—and often an article or two about Charles Saatchi.

In 1970 Maurice, very much her junior in the office hierarchy, confided to her his plans for setting up an agency with his brother, and she asked him what he would call it. "We're talking about Saatchi & Saatchi," he replied. Josephine, along with everyone else at Haymarket, thought he would do well, whatever he did. She still remembers a discussion around the lunch table just after Maurice left, when one Haymarket director remarked that the younger Saatchi brother "had effortless superiority." She knew Maurice well enough to agree.

Josephine stayed fifteen years with Haymarket, ending up on the board; she married Paul Buckley, a Haymarket director who had also started as a personal assistant to Heseltine. The Buckleys and Maurice and Gillian Saatchi often made up a foursome in the evening and spent weekends together. Josephine by now had a son, but her marriage, like Maurice's, was beginning to go wrong.

Maurice gradually became more and more interested in the Irish girl who laughed at his dry, witty remarks and whose mind seemed to work on a similar level as his. Her passion for the theater had grown with the years, and although his approach to the theater was on a less exalted level, he shared her love of it. She was less successful in her attempts to kindle his interest in poetry, but he accompanied her to poetry readings, another of her passions. Poetry had played little part in Maurice's life, and although he tried, he never acquired anything approaching Josephine's love of it. After some years he could respond to Eliot and to the Irish poets that Josephine thrust upon him, but he is not a person to be found in a corner reading a book of poetry. Not that it mattered to their blossoming relationship. Above all Maurice found Josephine fun—and she found him funny. "I've always found him the funniest man I've ever met," she told friends. "He's just such a funny man all the time—he has such a quick wit."

In 1984 their separate divorces came through, and in October Maurice and Josephine married, a very different event from Maurice's first wedding ceremony. This time the marriage took place in a register office. Maurice, like Charles, was marrying outside the Jewish religion. By now Nathan and Daisy had long been resigned to a world that had changed since they first arrived in Britain; London's once-tight Jewish community was declining in numbers as more and more Jews married outside their faith, and Nathan and Daisy's own circle of friends, initially almost entirely fellow Iraqi Jews, had been absorbed into the cosmopolitan London community. Nonetheless, there can be few greater shocks to a Jewish mama than an Irish Catholic daughter-in-law, and a divorced one at that. Josephine, however, was welcomed into the family, and Daisy and Nathan warmed to her even more when in 1985 she produced another son, Edward—the first Saatchi grandchild. "The grandparents were in heaven," says a friend. "You've never seen anything like it." (Gillian remarried too and now lives on a farm in Wales where she continues to write children's books.)

Maurice now not only had a son but a stepson, Adam, age eight in 1985. He proved an attentive father to both boys. "He's very good with children," says Josephine, "and it's been a surprise to him how much he enjoys it. None of the other boys was terribly interested in children."

Maurice, Josephine, and the children were now living on Bruton Street, in London's West End, in a house that Maurice spent hours redesigning and then overseeing. They lived briefly in Brompton Square, but Maurice was increasingly happy only in a house he could redesign to suit his own taste. His visual sense contrasted totally with Charles's; the elder Saatchi likes clean, starkly bare space around him, and his houses tend not to be very different from his Minimalist art. Visitors get the feeling that even a coat casually draped over a chair would spoil the visual effect; children would destroy it. Maurice's taste produced a much more peaceful, family effect—a delight for children. Adam told his mother that there was a nice surprise around every corner in Maurice's house.

Psychologists would probably draw interesting conclusions from the fact that both brothers married women older than themselves, both of whom had been married before. Both brothers also married women who had been, however briefly, their bosses—Doris had technically been Charles's boss at Benton & Bowles, and Josephine had been Maurice's boss at Haymarket. Both married not only non-Jews but also non-Britons—Charles chose an American and Maurice an Irish woman. There are other odd similarities too. For example, Doris remarks on the lack of interest in the arts she found in the Saatchi household when she first went there. She had been brought up in a house where everyone took an interest in the arts—and so, in a different sense, had Josephine. Charles was drawn to Doris's love of contemporary art, just as Maurice was drawn to (although he never fully understood) Josephine's passion for poetry.

The property that gives Maurice the most pleasure is a house near Staplefield in Sussex called Old Hall, which he bought in the mid-1980s. He and Josephine began going house hunting on weekends and were driving past when they saw it. "That's it," said Maurice without hesitation. Old Hall was a mock-Tudor red brick house, with its own keep, complete with weather vane and narrow arrow-slit windows, ivy-clad castellated walls, and a small amount of land. Maurice bought Old Hall and began a major reconstruction task not only of the house but more particularly of the garden.

Maurice took to gardening with something of the same passion that Charles brought to art; he bought every book he could find on the subject and toured Kent and Sussex studying the great gardens created by past enthusiasts. On summer weekends he would leave work early on Friday, collect Josephine and the children, and drive to Sussex, where he was instantly wandering the gardens and fields, sketching his plans for the property.

He bought the farm next door, and soon the bulldozers arrived, clearing entire fields, which were to be replaced by lakes and waterways. Josephine joked that if he kept on that way, visitors would have to come in by boat. He built a large Kew Gardens–style conservatory, where he keeps semitropical plants. Around the house he designed a more intimate garden, along the lines of Vita Sackville-West's Sissinghurst, with its own separate "rooms" for different colors and seasons. When he decided on a rose garden, Josephine found him earnestly studying a pile of books on roses before he even began work on the project; he knew the Latin name of every rose. One visitor commented that visiting the Saatchis in June was like something out of *A Midsummer Night's Dream.*

He went to work on rehabbing Old Hall with even greater interest than he had devoted to his London houses. Maurice never uses interior decorators but works out the architectural drawings and even chooses the fabrics to be used himself. Josephine briefly resented the fact that Maurice took all the work upon himself—Doris, for instance, was in charge of interior design in Charles's household until they broke up—but Josephine was soon boasting to friends about his "marvelous eye."

Maurice and Josephine bought a house in the south of France too, at Cap Ferrat, which was semiderelict and had not been lived in for years. It suited Maurice perfectly, with its little jetty by the sea, its own small beach, and views over the Mediterranean, full of boats and windsurfers all summer long. The house at Cap Ferrat is also within easy reach of Nice airport and thus accessible on weekends. He and Josephine enjoyed doing it up, building themselves a bedroom on the top floor, with a view over the bay and a large living area on the ground floor. It is not as grand a house as many in the area, but they love it. Maurice even developed an interest in boats; he bought a Riva Aquarama, a twenty-four-foot heavy mahogany speedboat, the Rolls-Royce of its class, and uses it often when he is at Cap Ferrat, motoring around the coast to moor at a little bay and swim and sunbathe. Several times Maurice's inexpert handling of the speedboat gave him and Josephine cause for alarm; he had never had a boat before and it took him a while to grow accustomed to sudden changes of weather while out at sea. These early scares did not deter him, and he soon learned to drive the boat with much of the same confidence with which he drives his cars.

As Doris had sparked Charles's interest in art, so Josephine persuaded Maurice to become a West End angel. He dutifully attended the poetry readings she organized featuring some of the best actors in London, but with his business training Maurice began toying with another idea. Josephine was the only woman on the Haymarket board and was regarded as a considerable success there, but she was given her own magazine, *Engineering Today*, to run—and it failed.

This was the opportunity Maurice had been waiting for. He had listened for years to her talk about the stage and was well aware that the theater was her first love. She enjoyed publishing, and she was good at it, but her heart was elsewhere. He had often told her the belief that he and Charles held to: "If you want something bad enough, you'll get it. But you have to really want it." She refined this credo to "If you have the will *and the vision* to do something, then you'll do it." She had never gotten over the death of her brother and sister, and she told Maurice that she felt she had once had the vision to become an actress—but had lost the will to pursue an acting career. Now it was too late.

But with the closing of *Engineering Today*, Maurice urged Josephine to set up her own theater-management company committed to presenting new writing in the West End. "This is something you have wanted to do for years," Maurice told her. "You've walked away from it for too long. Now do it!" Josephine had coproduced a number of plays, including *State of Affairs* at the Duchess Theatre in 1985, and in 1986 she set up Josephine Hart Productions Ltd. She was starting in the profession late in life, so to make up for her slow start she was determined to produce only new plays "I can be proud of." She was determined to be commercial as well, but that was not her major objective—nor Maurice's.

Within months of starting up, Josephine and her partners were receiving up to twenty plays a week, and she was besieged with requests to be coproducer of a large number of plays. She created rather than picked the plays she wanted to do, buying the rights to a new Oscar Wilde book, for instance, then persuading a playwright to turn it into a play. Curiously, it was Maurice who came up with one of the five plays she was working on in the summer of 1988—a stage version of Iris Murdoch's novel *The Black Prince*.

Josephine had been a Murdoch fan most of her life and immediately picked up the phone and rang her. "I'm absolutely in love with this novel," Josephine said. "Maurice and I have talked about how we could do it." She had lunch with the Dublin-born novelist, who could scarcely have resisted her enthusiasm. Josephine wanted to do *The Black Prince*, she explained, because she saw at the center of it "a marvelous, harsh moral imperative." The book's narrator and hero, Bradley Pearson, an elderly writer with a "block," goes to prison for a crime he never committed. But he could not escape moral responsibility for the final violent catastrophe. "I just want to hear some of those lines on the stage," Josephine told Murdoch. In the spring of 1988 Josephine began to work seriously on staging the novel.

Maurice was supportive of his wife in other ways too. Josephine soon found that one of the most difficult parts of putting on stage plays is getting the right actors together at once. Maurice became deeply involved in the casting, making suggestions and urging her to wait, get it right, only go for the best. She in turn was deeply grateful to him; he had, she said, been responsible for getting her back to something she had always dreamed of, something she had been forced to give up in her teens.

She was impressed with other of Maurice's virtues, notably his extraordinary self-discipline. From his earliest years, Maurice had always been able to organize and marshall his schoolwork effectively. At the London School of Economics Professor Cohen remarked on how prepared Maurice always was, never flustered or caught unprepared, always using his time to maximum effect. Lindsay Masters commented on his control and discipline, and at Saatchi & Saatchi these combined qualities became one of the principal factors enabling the Saatchis to translate big bold strokes into effective action. He extended this self-discipline into his private life too, organizing himself so that he had time and energy for all the things he enjoyed doing. Both brothers firmly believe that they must get maximum satisfaction and pleasure from both work and play, and they organize themselves to bring about that balance.

Josephine was aware that Maurice was intelligent but gradually realized that his self-deprecating air and complete lack of boastfulness hid a keener brain than even close friends were aware of. Someone told her that Maurice had an IQ of 165, but it took Josephine five years of constant questioning to get him to admit it. When he eventually did, she believed him. Long before they were married, he had confided to her his dreams and ambitions, often laughed at in the outside world—but steadily he had turned them into reality.

He and Charles had a "Star Trek" joke—"to boldly go where no man had ever been before"—but behind it was a grim determination to push past barriers and achieve goals not achieved before in their industry. Maurice, at least as much as Charles, was deadly serious about being the biggest and the best, and Josephine watched keenly the relentless way her husband and his brother pushed on past the difficulties. Yet in all the years she knew him, she never once saw the slightest hint of insecurity or hesitation in him or in Charles, whom she knew much less well. From the start both brothers knew where they wanted to go and were utterly determined to get there. As she would say, "They had the vision—and the will."

The Bates and Jacoby affair might have caused the brothers professional anguish, but it never disturbed the pattern of their lives or caused them to take their eye off the other interests of the group. Just as the Tim Bell affair had been handled by Charles, so the post-Bates problems fell to him, and it was to Charles that Simonds-Gooding reported. Charles was very protective of his younger brother when it came to personnel problems, but he also reckoned Maurice's time was far better spent working out his longer-term strategies than dealing with individual difficulties.

Even as the business grew larger, the brothers hated to see anyone go. Time and time again, they had solved a personnel problem by hiring other people to fill in the gaps left by an executive who had turned to drink or drugs (which occasionally happened in the advertising world). Mike Johnston, for instance, had played a significant part in the early days of Saatchi & Saatchi as the financial man, but when the business grew away from him the brothers left Johnston in place and brought in Martin Sorrell above him. Similarly, the Saatchis had built whole teams around Bell when he had his personal problems. When friends came to them for advice on how to deal with a particular management problem, the brothers gave them the same message: "Build around it." Often this was bad management advice, resulting in crossed lines of responsibility and in confusion. But the brothers preferred confusion to a sacking. If a person became disruptive, they would find an office for him somewhere outside the building, and often he would eventually drift away.

Tim Mellors, now creative director at McCormick in London, cites how the Saatchis and Jeremy Sinclair helped pull him back from the depths of drug taking, drink, a broken marriage, bankruptcy, and a mental breakdown. Sinclair hired him, and Mellors quit drinking, won a series of awards, and even worked on some of the Tory ads. "Then I foundered and got into trouble with drink again, and the agency backed me," Mellors says. "I went into a clinic and stopped drinking. Haven't taken any drugs or drink since. I think only in Saatchi's could that happen. They were fantastic to me. Charlie said, 'Go in there and it doesn't matter how long it takes.' " There are other instances of this generous side of the brothers' characters, as unknown to the outside world as some of the less attractive character traits exposed in this book.

There is a tendency to classify successful businesspeople, probably more than people in any other category in our society, as one-dimensional. The myth is that businesspeople get to the top by single-minded drive and ruthlessness, which shut out more human impulses. Typically, successful businesspeople have no interest in the arts even though they are to be seen at Covent Garden, the New York Met, or Glyndebourne; they have loyal but dull company wives, read only balance sheets and financial reports, and live only for their companies, which in turn pay for all the perks they do not appreciate. In practice, it is impossible to find a successful entrepreneur who fits the stereotype. Entrepreneurs are as varied and multidimensional as people in any other category of human being—in fact, probably more so, since they can afford to indulge whims and interests that others cannot. But even by these standards, the Saatchis are very different and do not fit into any preconceived concept either of self-made millionaires or of advertising executives. They could be as ruthless as anyone in their pursuit of a goal; Charles could throw his angry tantrums, and Maurice could dream up schemes to make them still more millions. Yet at the end of the day the brothers were as human as anyone, with all the failings and strengths that word implies.

The events of 1987 would expose all their vulnerability and test their nerve more than the Bates affair had done.

17
ELECTION OF '87

As 1987 opened, the Saatchis were keenly aware of the major challenge that faced them that year. Although her five-year term was not up until June 1988, Mrs. Thatcher under the British constitution had the right to call an election any time she wanted to—and the view of all the pundits (and of her own colleagues) was that she was almost certain to go to the polls either in the spring or in the autumn. The opinion polls suggested that she was heading for her third victory in a row, but there were other factors clouding the horizon for Saatchi & Saatchi. Although the brothers still paid Tim Bell a £24,000-a-year retainer for his services, they had decided they would not use him in the ad campaign for the impending election. It would be the first time Saatchi & Saatchi handled the Conservative party account without Bell's input. By itself this caused Saatchi & Saatchi no special worries. Maurice and Jeremy Sinclair would become more involved in presentations, and they decided that John Sharkey, an account manager who was bright and imaginative but who lacked Bell's personal charm, would handle the Tory account. But with or without Bell there were enough signs already to suggest that the campaign of '87 was going to be a difficult one.

The circumstances leading up to the election were anything but auspicious. In September 1985 the prime minister appointed Norman Tebbit, one of her most loyal supporters over the years and a man indelibly associated with the Thatcher revolution, as Conservative party chairman. She believed that he, above all her other cabinet colleagues, had the best political skills for handling a campaign that she hoped would see her into the history books as the longest-serving prime minister of the century. But she was now forced to accept that she had made a critical mistake: Tebbit was not entirely well. He was still suffering the after-effects of injuries from an IRA bomb planted in the Grand Hotel in Brighton during the Conservative party conference in 1984; the bomb had left his wife, Margaret, permanently paralyzed. Tebbit, it was said by his colleagues, was not the same man but was instead more touchy and short-tempered than before and was unable to work the long hours that he had once relished.

Within a few months of Tebbit's move to Central Office the relationship was under strain. For a start, Tebbit was even less well than he pretended, suffering considerable pain from a wound on his thigh that stubbornly refused to accept skin grafts. He was also deeply upset by the injuries to his wife and the simple practical difficulties her paralysis raised for both of them: twenty-four-hour-a-day nursing, special elevators, and all the other facilities needed for a quadriplegic. There were emotional moments when they appeared in public together, Tebbit pushing the wheelchair while his wife, Margaret, could do no more than smile, unable even to move a hand to wipe away her tears.

There was another factor that led to dissatisfaction with Tebbit's appointment. Tebbit was a superb politician, a man who relished the cut and thrust of parliamentary debate. But he was not a natural administrator—and the job at Central Office was essentially administrative, making a professional organization from what was an amateurish, poorly run machine. Tebbit's friends argue that his lack of administrative skill was greatly exaggerated and his proposals for reforms, like those of previous party chairmen, were continually vetoed: Mrs. Thatcher did not want a powerful chairman with a highly professional machine of his own because it would pose a potential threat to her. "Central Office had delivered two good election results for her and was on the way to delivering a third," says one staffer. "Norman led the recovery in the polls, but she never gave him much credit for it."

The improvement in the polls, however, only came later, and there were some black moments for Thatcher before the Tories could begin to approach the election campaign with any confidence. No prime minister in British history had been elected three times in succession. Mrs. Thatcher was the first woman prime minister; now she was after still another record. At the end of 1985, however, she suddenly found herself in deep trouble over the affair of Westland, the helicopter firm. The dispute divided her cabinet between those who supported a partial bid to take over Westland by the American Sikorski group and those, led by the defense secretary, Michael Heseltine, who favored a European solution as a way out for the near-bankrupt company. The controversy cost Thatcher two cabinet ministers, including Heseltine, and much credibility. As she prepared for a crucial debate on the morning of January 15, 1986, she confided to a close colleague that it was quite possible she would no longer be prime minister by that evening. In the end the opposition leader, Neil Kinnock, fluffed his chance and she survived; but during those crucial weeks Mrs. Thatcher felt that Tebbit was against her, siding with Heseltine, denying her his support when she needed it most.

In fact Tebbit was *not* against her, but he did not side with her, either. He saw his role as the healer and bridge-builder and desperately urged Heseltine to stay in the government, afraid of the damage his departure would do to the party and its reelection hopes. Tebbit thought he had succeeded in convincing the defense secretary to stay, until Heseltine abruptly got to his feet in the middle of a cabinet meeting and walked out, leaving behind a stunned prime minister. The next day, with the government turmoil at its height, Tebbit went into the hospital for another operation on his thigh. For the next month, as Mrs. Thatcher plunged into the worst crisis of her premiership, the man who should have been her closest ally was out of action. Mrs. Thatcher visited him several times and they talked on the phone, but the rift between them was widening.

It was while Tebbit was in the hospital that the position of Saatchi & Saatchi as the Conservative party's advertising agency was suddenly challenged. The government's ratings in the polls had dropped sharply as the Westland affair and Heseltine's resignation took their toll. The Tories were neck-and-neck with Labour up to Christmas, but in January 1986 Labour opened up a five-point lead—38 percent to 33 percent in the *Sunday Times* opinion poll. Some polls even showed the Tories slipping to third place, behind both Labour and the SDP/Liberal Alliance party. The Tories were suddenly in trouble.

Mrs. Thatcher, unwilling to accept the blame for the party's low ratings, looked for someone else to shoulder it. She complained to her colleagues that there was no initiative coming out of Central Office to reverse the trend. Recent Saatchi work, she said, lacked "edge," and she had begun to feel that the agency had grown so big that it no longer cared about reelecting the Tories. In 1979 Saatchi had been a smaller, hungrier agency, her argument ran. Now it was a huge international business and had lost its creative vitality. At Saatchi there was puzzlement when these comments filtered back; the agency had done almost nothing for the Tories in months—it had been a dead period on the campaigning front. But most observers agreed with Thatcher that Central Office was not performing as it should.

The prime minister had never had the same relationship with Saatchi & Saatchi since Tim Bell left, and she continued to find fault with the agency's recent work. During the early part of 1986 she complained that Saatchi ads had become "too gimmicky" and that the advertising done by Labour, which had learned much from earlier Saatchi campaigns, was often better. Again, the Saatchi camp was taken aback: what ads was she talking about? There had only been a couple of party political broadcasts, and they had been in response to Tebbit's request that, with an election still probably two years away, they should do "something adventurous." Saatchi & Saatchi's recent work for the Tories had been an experiment only—surely she was aware of that?

Thatcher was at a low point in her fortunes when in February 1986 she held a meeting of her political advisers. Among them was a man named Geoffrey Tucker, a veteran of many election campaigns, who was working as a consultant to Young & Rubicam in London. That weekend Tucker offered Young & Rubicam's help: a detailed statistical analysis of the government's ratings, its public standing on a series of issues and policies, and some suggestions on how Mrs. Thatcher could effect a recovery. Y&R had developed a sophisticated system for looking at the electorate in a different way, and several cabinet ministers, including Lord Young, had been impressed enough to persuade the prime minister to see it. The approach had originally been offered in 1984 to Central Office by Tucker and Ed Ney, the head of Young & Rubicam Worldwide, who had advised Ronald Reagan in 1980 and 1984; the staff at Central Office had occasionally used Y & R's method, but Tebbit and his staff were unimpressed by it. "It didn't conflict with anything we were doing," said a Central Office representative later. "We just weren't convinced of it." Now it was being offered to the boss herself.

The Y&R method was an adaptation of fairly standard U.S. "psychographic" research on what is called "values and lifestyles"; Y&R called it "Cross-Cultural Consumer Characteristics," or CCCC, and it was based on the premise that consumers (or voters) hold similar attitudes the world over and can be divided worldwide into nine categories. Y&R developed its research in great secrecy over ten years, surrounding it with considerable mystique. "It has given us some unique personal insights into attitudes to pressing social issues such as drug abuse," said Jeff Banks, Y&R's forty-one-year-old chairman in London. "It gives us an edge over our competitors." CCCC replaced the conventional categories used by most researchers with more sophisticated groupings. The main category, making up 40 percent of the population, consisted of "belongers": patriotic, home-loving family men and women with a sense of duty, which was the group that had voted for Mrs. Thatcher twice already.

When Jeff Banks showed the study to Mrs. Thatcher and gave her his breakdown of the British voter, she was immediately taken by it. It did not necessarily present a more cheerful picture than the Saatchi findings at the time, but it did appear to offer an explanation for Mrs. Thatcher's low ratings as well as a few possible solutions.

She had further sessions in March and April with Y&R, each time without telling Tebbit. Then on Sunday, April 13, 1986, Mrs. Thatcher for the first time turned her full attention to Saatchi & Saatchi. The brothers at the time were moving into the final stages in their negotiations with Robert Jacoby at Bates and wrapping up their takeover of Backer & Spielvogel. Heading the Saatchi team—the new Tim Bell on the account, in effect—was John Sharkey, although as the election approached, the team coordinator would increasingly become Maurice himself, with Jeremy Sinclair.

The April 13 meeting was at Chequers, where Mrs. Thatcher preferred to handle party political briefings, as opposed to Downing Street, where the week was fully occupied with affairs of state. At center stage was the man who would play a significant role in the Saatchi story over the following eighteen months: Michael Dobbs. Dobbs, with his relaxed, slightly hesitant manner, was still in his thirties. He had worked for a while as a journalist at the *Boston Globe*, then returned to Britain in 1975 to work at Central Office just as Mrs. Thatcher took over as leader of the opposition. For two years Dobbs was in the research department at Central Office, then he was promoted to the private office of Mrs. Thatcher, helping to prepare material for questions and for major parliamentary debates. He continued in this role for another two years, then to his disappointment Mrs. Thatcher did not offer him a job at Downing Street after the 1979 election. Dobbs, although regarded by his colleagues as one of the brightest young people in the Tory party, reluctantly had to accept that the chemistry between Mrs. Thatcher and himself was wrong. Just as Mrs. Thatcher loved to have Tim Bell and Gordon Reece around her, so she seemed to dislike having Dobbs around.

Bell had come to know Dobbs during the 1979 campaign and afterward gave him a job as his assistant. Encouraged by Bell, Dobbs retained his interest in politics and acted as adviser to Norman Tebbit. When Tebbit took over as party chairman, he proposed that Dobbs become joint deputy chairman, alongside the novelist Jeffrey Archer, but Thatcher refused to allow it, and Dobbs had to settle for chief of staff. Saatchi agreed to let him move to the party, although there was no guarantee that Dobbs could return to Saatchi.

The Saatchi team had been working up to the Chequers meeting for three months, aided by a research program called "Life in Britain," which the Tories had used successfully in the 1983 campaign. "Life in Britain" was the result of detailed market research and analysis and contained some bad news for Mrs. Thatcher. Sharkey for Saatchi and Dobbs for Central Office, using videos and boards, presented their findings. They showed that much had altered since the 1983 election.

The message in 1983 had been clear and positive, but now the public image of the Tories was confused. A majority of the public wanted "Calvinism," a word the researchers used to mean a return to the work ethic and self-sufficiency, but Calvinism was no longer clearly associated with the Tories. Both Dobbs and Sharkey were careful not to personalize Thatcher's image and her role in the poor public support, but she still interpreted their findings personally, believing that what they were saying to her was that she was now seen as an extremist with no sense of direction or purpose and incapable of handling the major problems faced by the country: unemployment, education, the health service. Afterward Dobbs ruefully reported back to his staff: "We went in there knowing what we wanted to say and came out thinking we had told it too well." From that moment on Mrs. Thatcher wanted nothing more to do with either Dobbs or Sharkey—or, for that matter, with Saatchi & Saatchi.

One piece of research, presented by Dobbs, went down particularly badly: it showed that on three of the qualities of leadership, strength, confidence, and intelligence, Mrs. Thatcher rated highly, but on "forward-looking" she was below the other leaders. That revelation was the low point of what was a highly uncomfortable day. Perhaps Tim Bell, with his special rapport with Thatcher and his highly humorous asides, might have gotten away more lightly, but Thatcher that day did not want any more bad news, certainly not from Dobbs and Sharkey—or from Tebbit. At each point the researchers made, she intervened to snap, "Yes, we know that already," and by lunchtime the meeting had gone well off-track. In the afternoon it got worse, and when they finally broke for tea at four the representatives from Central Office and from Saatchi felt like wet rags. It was the day that would go down in legend as the first time Mrs. Thatcher heard the phrase "TBW" ("that bloody woman"), which was not used by either Dobbs or Sharkey but which was widely whispered behind her back.

The rumors of that awful day at Chequers soon spread. They became worse for Saatchi when the news leaked that Mrs. Thatcher had been seeing Young & Rubicam. Now, it was said, Saatchi & Saatchi was to lose the Tory party account, a move that had minimal commercial significance but would be damaging for the agency's reputation, particularly when it was trying to recover from the trauma of the New York fallout. In fact there was never a serious possibility that Y&R would replace Saatchi as the Tory party's agency. For a start, Young & Rubicam is an American-owned agency, which almost certainly ruled it out; second, it did not, on principle, go in for political advertising: some months earlier a couple of its executives in Austria had helped Kurt Waldheim with his campaign for the presidency and had been told by the agency to do it on their own time; third, Mrs. Thatcher knew she could not get rid of Saatchi, even if she had wanted to, without a major confrontation with Tebbit, who bluntly indicated that the agency reported to him in his capacity as party chairman, not to the prime minister, and if it went he would have to go too, since his whole position would have been compromised. After losing two cabinet ministers so quickly Mrs. Thatcher had no intention of losing a third.

Charles and Maurice Saatchi had thought seriously about resigning the Tory party account several times, particularly after the election victories. After 1979 it seemed unlikely they could ever achieve the same triumphant publicity again and everything that followed would therefore be an anticlimax. Why not go out on the crest of the wave? After the 1983 election that consideration seemed even more pertinent, particularly as the rift between the brothers and Tim Bell had steadily widened. Again they decided, after much agonizing, to stay with the Conservative party account. "The time never seemed to be right to resign the account, although we always wanted to," says one Saatchi employee.

From the summer of 1986 stories that Saatchi & Saatchi was about to be sacked began to appear, and the Tory party account switched from being a business winner to a liability. Somehow the future of Saatchi & Saatchi as the Tory party agency was inextricably caught up in the break in the relationship between Thatcher and Tebbit. At one point Dobbs wrote to Tebbit and offered to resign from Central Office if the chairman thought that might remove one of the areas of "angst"; Tebbit said no.

At the height of his estrangement from the prime minister, when the press and the political world were openly speculating on Tebbit's political future, I spent several hours with the Tory party chairman, preparing a *Sunday Times* "Focus" article on the conflict between Thatcher and Tebbit. Tebbit was preparing to depart the next day for France for a holiday with his wife, a tricky job that required special planes and ambulances. He was also moving to a new home in London, meanwhile accommodating his wife in a Belgrave house lent to him by the Duke of Westminster and fitted with elevators, widened doors, and special bathrooms. Unlike many of his cabinet colleagues, Tebbit was not a rich man (he had been an airline pilot before entering politics) and could not have afforded such a home himself. But his wife needed twenty-four-hour-a-day treatment, and he was finding the long night hours, which he insisted on covering himself, exhausting. Normally thin, he was now cadaverous, his face gray and wan. He had spent the morning putting up curtains, moving furniture, and generally trying to make the house livable for his wife. Although no stranger to battles and controversy, being at odds with his own prime minister, the person to whom he had devoted so much emotional energy, was deeply upsetting for Tebbit.

That morning he sat in the chairman's office at Central Office under a photograph of Mrs. Thatcher and carefully sifted the truth as he saw it from the gossip of recent months. He did not blame Mrs. Thatcher, even by inference, although he was hurt by a number of incidents, especially her decision to allow American planes to use British bases to bomb Libya without telling him. He had also been irritated by stories that Mrs. Thatcher was to bring back Cecil Parkinson to counter him.

Tebbit had no idea what his political future might be but indicated that he was willing to do whatever the prime minister asked him, including step down. He would still be loyal, still work hard for her, whatever *she* did. "He is probably her stoutest and truest supporter," said a leading Tory that day. "And it's not on the basis of trying to get to power either. He really believes in her, even now."

Her attitude toward him had clearly been colored by her continued low rating in the polls. In April the Conservatives lost a by-election and were trounced in that year's local elections, losing 789 seats and gaining just

62. As things got worse, Thatcher blamed Tebbit. Tebbit himself was philosophical: "When you lose by-elections, you start asking questions of the chairman of the party and the party machine. Nobody looks in the mirror." But that was limited consolation.

On August 9, Mrs. Thatcher rang Tebbit, the first time they had talked in weeks. She was as concerned as he was by the press reports of their growing rift and the gossip that was whirling around them. She was about to leave for Cornwall for her annual holiday, and Tebbit put back his French trip for a day as they talked on for twenty minutes. She had no intention of removing him as party chairman—she very much wanted him to stay on. She was sorry they had not been seeing more of each other and wanted to put that right from now on. She accepted his assurances of loyalty, and the conversation, leaked by Downing Street to the press that afternoon, settled any immediate suggestion that Saatchi would be fired. The agency was safe, at least while Tebbit was chairman, which meant until the next election.

Saatchi had been an innocent party in the Thatcher-Tebbit falling-out, unable to intervene but feeling the backlash. The Tory party rumors coincided with the beginnings of the account losses from Bates, and the fall in the share price throughout that summer did little for Saatchi's image back home either. It was yet more pain for Charles.

Just before Christmas in 1986, her party headquarters presented Mrs. Thatcher with a blue ring-binder file. Known internally as "the blue book," it went a good deal further than previous early campaign plans. Saatchi & Saatchi had submitted its proposals, which were incorporated into the 100-page strategy document by Dobbs, who pulled the plan together. Only half a dozen copies were made, carefully numbered and recorded: this was to be the blueprint for the election campaign. The blue book laid out a strategy that the Tories would soon diverge from as they entered their worst-run campaign of the Thatcher era. The document spotted many of Labour's strengths—Neil Kinnock's image, it said, would "doubtless be professionally presented," and his campaign would "emphasize his youth and family image and engage in 'razzmatazz' rather than detailed policies." The Labour leader must be put on the defensive and kept there by the Tories, who should concentrate on defense, tax, trade-union reform, and Labour's long list of extremist party candidates. "We must put as much personal pressure as possible on Mr. Kinnock," said the document, reflecting Tebbit's view, which was to prove wrong, that the inexperienced Kinnock could be pressured into a series of calamitous mistakes in a campaign.

Once a year Jeremy Sinclair takes himself off for a week entirely by himself, just to think about life in general. During that week he protects his privacy fiercely—even his wife and Charles Saatchi know better than to disturb him. He reads no newspapers, watches no news, and tries not to answer the telephone. In April 1987 Maurice broke Sinclair's golden rule and tracked him down in Oxfordshire. It was a year after Sinclair's last uncomfortable meeting with the prime minister at Chequers, and there was considerable speculation that Thatcher was about to call a June election—which meant that she would make an announcement during the next two weeks. "We're summoned to Downing Street," Maurice told Sinclair. "And they've asked for *you*." Sinclair had not seen Thatcher since the last campaign, and then only briefly. "I thought she would have forgotten who I was," he told Maurice; clearly she had not.

Back in London, Sinclair and Maurice prepared themselves; they wanted no repeat of the previous year's debacle and were determined to impress the prime minister with their readiness. But what did she want from them? A full presentation of the ads they had ready or just a run-through on the general theme of the campaign? They checked with an aide. Was she expecting a full presentation? Should they bring all their ads down? "No," said the aide. "Just come." Both men were wily enough to know how Thatcher liked to catch people off guard, and they decided they would compromise: they would not bring the ads, but they would take their presentation with its charts and strategy laid out in portable form so they would have something to show her should she change her mind and ask. Norman Tebbit, who was to accompany them to Downing Street, had already been through the presentation and approved it, and they were confident she would like it too.

Once again, it was not a comfortable session. As she entered the room Mrs. Thatcher began, "Well, what have you got for me?" and looked around for the ads she clearly seemed to expect. At that point Maurice and Sinclair were very pleased indeed that they had brought the presentation, which Maurice now began to show her. Its theme was how she could increase her already huge majority. Thatcher was incredulous—how could she possibly do that? "At least that's a challenge," said Maurice. "You aim high." The next idea went down just as badly. Saatchi & Saatchi wanted to tell the public that socialism was an idea whose time had gone, that it had served its purpose and even the Chinese and the Russians were beginning to turn their backs on it. Mrs. Thatcher's own recent trip to the Soviet Union, hailed by everyone as a great success, fit in well with this theme, which emphasized support for *glasnost* and how the Russians were tailoring their system to admit more freedom and capitalism. Most people acknowledged that socialism had also done something for Britain, Maurice told her, but the concepts of state ownership, trade-union power, high taxation, and an overly protective welfare state were ideas of the past. The next campaign should show that however the socialist parties put it, they were essentially dressing up an old idea. The future lay with Thatcherism.

Maurice could scarcely have misjudged his client more. Mrs. Thatcher hated the plan. She refused to accept that socialism *ever* had anything to offer, and for Saatchi to suggest that it had now brought a withering blast from her. She did not want anything at all along those lines; they must start again. Within twenty minutes, Maurice and Sinclair began to be glad that they had not brought any ads, feeling that whatever they showed her in her current mood would be shredded. She was less harsh on their copy, which attacked the other parties, but she demanded more positive material on the government's achievements. She asked that the advertising work should maintain a balance of two-thirds positive to one-third negative copy. Maurice and Sinclair, seeing the whole strategy that they thought they had agreed upon disintegrating before their eyes, were appalled—and tried vainly to fight back. They made little headway.

Thatcher then brought up the subject of Tim Bell. Why wasn't he working on the account? She understood he was available, and Saatchi had him on contract to advise on this election; she had expected to see him, she said. The Saatchi team had the impression that she had been briefed already on their position on Bell, but she still made a plea for him. Maurice, however, was firm; Saatchi would not be using Bell during the campaign, he told her. Other people had been phased in to do what Bell once did, the company had moved on since he left, and it would be too disruptive to use him now. Thatcher, however, did not easily let the subject go. "It was Maurice's refusal to use Bell in the 1987 campaign that soured her relationship with the Saatchis," said one close observer later. In truth, the relationship had already gone sour, but that day it went sourer still.

For three hours Maurice and Jeremy Sinclair batted around ideas, with Mrs. Thatcher both critical and quarrelsome. Out on the street afterward Sinclair was furious. "For this they dragged me back from vacation!" he exclaimed before going back into seclusion. However, on May 1, a week after that awkward visit, the Saatchi team was back with the "more positive" approach the prime minister had requested, and by the weekend of May 2 and 3, Mrs. Thatcher had approved a campaign package, including the first party election broadcast.

Everything was in place, and the momentum building toward a June election was unstoppable. Thatcher had now allowed expectations to go so far that she had lost control of the timing. She finally made her decision over the weekend of May 9 and 10 at Chequers after a long round of meetings with her ministers and advisers. There was no one from Saatchi there; but there *was* someone else, whose presence was kept secret from the others and whose invitation to the house that weekend, had the brothers known of it, would have caused them as much anger and irritation as the loss of another major Bates account.

Tim Bell and his fiancée, Virginia Hornbrook, arrived at Chequers at 6:30 P.M. on the evening of Saturday, May 9. They were ushered briskly into a downstairs study, where they waited for half an hour. Upstairs Mrs. Thatcher was working on the Conservative party manifesto with a group that included Tebbit. At seven o'clock Mrs. Thatcher finally went down to greet her visitors, apologizing to Bell for having to keep him "hidden"; she did not want Tebbit or anyone other than a few trusted advisers to know that Bell was there.

That evening there was a dinner party given in honor of Denis Thatcher, who was to be seventy-two the next day. Mr. Thatcher, however, was late—he was at a rugby final at Twickenham, where the drink traditionally flows freely, and he arrived not only late but happy. Mrs. Thatcher didn't mind; the delay of the dinner party provided an excuse for her to get together with Tim Bell. Most of the evening was taken up with a discussion of the coming election. The press expected the prime minister to visit the Queen on Monday and formally set the election process in motion, and she had already made up her mind that that was what she was going to do. Bell had seen her several times since his departure from Saatchi, usually at receptions, but this was the first time he had the chance to give her his advice in detail.

Mrs. Thatcher took out a notepad and wrote at length while Bell expounded on how she should present herself, the tone of the campaign she should run, and the general question of communications. They talked for hours, running through the television programs on which Bell thought she should concentrate, how to handle the press side, and much else besides—advice, in effect, that she had come to expect from Bell in his role at Saatchi & Saatchi.

For several reasons Mrs. Thatcher wanted to keep Bell's presence at Chequers a secret. First, Tebbit had already told her that he did not want Bell working on the campaign; the *Mirror* newspapers were said to be preparing a story on Bell that would be potentially damaging. Second, Bell had had a peripheral involvement with Guinness in its bid for Distillers, which was boiling up into the financial scandal of the decade. Third, she knew the terms of Bell's contract with Saatchi, and she wanted no trouble from that camp, either.

The next day, when Lord Young, who was in on the secret, asked her in the presence of other ministers about her conversation with Bell the previous night, Mrs. Thatcher instantly shushed him, saying, "No one here must know about that!"

Bell, however, was already busy working for her, proposing a video that would include most of the senior members of the cabinet talking about their achievements. Thatcher that day gave her enthusiastic go-ahead for the video, and the filming took place around the corner from Central Office at the house of Lord Alastair McAlpine, the party treasurer. When Tebbit arrived to do his bit a few days later, Bell quietly absented himself. A major part of the promotional work was thus being done for the Tories without any input from Saatchi. That had not happened since the agency was appointed.

As the campaign opened, the Tories were ahead with 42 percent against Labour's 32 percent and the Alliance's 23 percent, and barring a catastrophic campaign or a series of monumental gaffes, there seemed no way Thatcher could lose the election. But the campaign soon began going astray. Mrs. Thatcher started the campaign in measured enough style but within days had strayed into her first mistake. In her first major television interview, she waxed euphoric, talking evangelically about the tasks still to be done that would take her through a third term and even into a fourth.

"Yes," she told the BBC's political editor John Cole, "I hope to go on and on." Over the next few days her opponents had much fun with this, adding a few *on*s of their own so that she was now said to be "going on— and on—and *on*" forever. In contrast, Neil Kinnock set off at a cracking pace and was showing no signs of slowing down. Worried MPs were soon ringing Tebbit to plead with him to schedule more appearances for Thatcher, who after that first gaffe had been almost invisible.

By the end of the second week of the campaign, waves of unease were spreading through Central Office. Had they begun too late after all? In the opening days there had been jokes in the Saatchi camp about how Labour had "troughed too soon," but those jokes soon changed as Labour picked up momentum and the Tory campaign, when it was finally launched a week later, sputtered uncertainly. The Labour party used film director Hugh Hudson, whose *Chariots of Fire* had won a number of Oscars, to present Kinnock in the first party election broadcast, and Hudson's commercial was a polished and professional job that broke new ground in British TV. It included the famous phrase, later plagiarized by Joseph Biden in the 1988 U.S. presidential race, that the Labour leader was the first Kinnock "in a thousand generations" to get to university because his forebears had no platform "upon which they could stand." The broadcast ended with no ringing evocative cry to vote Labour—just the one word "Kinnock."

The Labour party for the first time was out-Saatchi-ing Saatchi—or at least that was how the ad was perceived—and it seemed to be working. Thatcher's advisers that weekend found her tired and depressed by her own performance and that of the party so far. Her daughter Carol, trying to put new life into her, was confronted by a prime minister who suddenly felt that she could well lose the election. It was a mood familiar to those who had seen Mrs. Thatcher through previous elections, although totally unsuspected by those who saw her confident television appearances and campaign speeches. Tim Bell had certainly experienced her depressions before, and it was he and Lord Young who now came to her to show her the way out.

Bell had been impressed with the Hudson broadcast and told her so. He also pointed out, much to her indignation, that Labour at that point was winning the campaign, although it still had not dented the Tory lead in the polls, which remained at 12 percent. At one point Bell, after relating a series of unpalatable truths to her, snapped: "It's no good surrounding yourself with people who tell you that everything's fine— that way you'll miss the boat, Prime Minister." He urged a change of strategy, a break with the Saatchi–Central Office campaign. The Tories must attack, go for Labour's policies, their "iceberg manifesto—one-eighth visible, the rest beneath the surface." Without realizing it, Bell was urging a return to many of the points agreed upon in the "blue book."

From that day on Bell would play a significant yet still highly secret part in Mrs. Thatcher's campaign. By telephone Gordon Reece (now Sir Reece) also contributed advice and succor. Cecil Parkinson, who was still out of government because of his affair with his former secretary Sara Keays, was also one of Thatcher's unofficial advisers. The fact that this small group of advisers, who called themselves "the exiles," had the ear of Mrs. Thatcher caused both distress and concern at Central Office— particularly since the prime minister was now demanding a change of strategy. When Bell's involvement became known to Charles Saatchi, he boiled with rage but knew he could do nothing about it: the Saatchis had no one who could compete for the prime minister's favors. They had forfeited that position back in 1978, and there was no recovering now.

For Saatchi there was little of the excitement and exhilaration that had characterized the first two campaigns. Its advertising, once such a talking point, continued to draw more criticism than praise. The early posters in particular came in for considerable flak within the party itself, although Tebbit and the Central Office officials were pleased with them: the first featured three dogs, with a British bulldog towering over a German shepherd and a French poodle to emphasize how much stronger Britain's economy was than those of its competitors. Then there were three red books, with the titles: *Young, Gay, and Proud*; *Police: Out of School!*; and *The Playbook for Kids About Sex* under the headline: "IS THIS LABOUR'S IDEA OF A COMPREHENSIVE EDUCATION?" The most memorable poster in the first week was the simple slogan "Don't undo eight years' work in three seconds—Vote Conservative." Saatchi, despite the success of some of its television ads and the defense poster, gave the impression that it was struggling, and Mrs. Thatcher conveyed her view that she was unhappy with the firm.

At the beginning of the third week Kinnock made his first serious fumble, and the Tory and Saatchi machines clicked into gear at last. It was David Frost who prompted the blunder. Arriving at the TV-am studios at 7:15 on the morning of Sunday, May 24, Frost was looking forward to interviewing the chief guest on his program that morning,

Neil Kinnock. Frost had worked on his line of questioning all week and had stayed up most of the night reading the early editions of the Sunday papers in preparation for confronting Kinnock on a number of themes, particularly defense.

Kinnock set off on his well-rehearsed antinuclear policy, arguing, as he had done many times before, that the use of nuclear weapons meant genocide and national destruction. What would happen, asked Frost, if a nonnuclear Britain were confronted by a nuclear-armed enemy? Would it not be either unfair battle or surrender? "In those circumstances," said Kinnock, "the choice is exterminating everything you stand for . . . or using the resources that you have got to make any occupation untenable." In other words, Britain's best hope was to let the Russians land, then resort to guerrilla warfare. Kinnock left the studio, unaware of the significance of what he had said. The Tories were slow off the mark too— no one in the high command saw the Frost program that morning. It was only later in the day that a researcher, going through the transcripts, came across Kinnock's statement. He rushed down to Tebbit, who exclaimed, "We've struck gold!"

Within minutes Saatchi & Saatchi was working on a poster to take advantage of Kinnock's blunder. Sharkey's team, with Jeremy Sinclair and Charles watching over them from a slight distance, soon got the idea for the poster: a British soldier, unarmed, with his hands held aloft as though he was surrendering. The caption read: "Labour's policy on arms." An actor and a soldier's battle dress were quickly found, but it was a bank holiday, and the costume-rental suppliers were closed. Nowhere could Saatchi find a soldier's helmet. It was decided that the poster would have to show the soldier in a beret, but this weakened the visual impact. Finally, someone found the real thing; the helmet was suitably draped in camouflage netting, and the ad was shot. It would be the best of the campaign.

From that point on it should have been plain sailing. The fact that it was not was to a large extent Thatcher's own doing.

Before the election campaign began Lord McAlpine, the Tory treasurer, put a little squiggle against the date Thursday, June 4, on the calendar on his office wall. What did it mean, someone asked? That, forecast McAlpine, would be "wobble day," the day when a rogue poll and a couple of misfortunes combined to spread panic through the ranks. Wobble day was usually a week before the election, so he had picked that Thursday. Other battle-hardened people at Central Office had seen the panic happen too. Tebbit's secretary, who had worked for Thorneycroft in 1979 and Parkinson in 1983, kept a little notice on her wall showing the six phases of a general election, starting with enthusiasm and working its way through disillusionment, panic, search for the guilty, punishment for the wicked, and, finally, praise and honors for the nonparticipants. The party was about to hit phase three, panic.

McAlpine's forecast date for the wobble was dead accurate. On Tuesday night a poll done for the BBC by a journalist not renowned for his sympathies to the Thatcher government showed that Labour had closed the gap dramatically and was only 2.5 percentage points behind. The following day rumors began to circulate that the next day's Gallup poll in the *Daily Telegraph* would be even more disastrous. Stock prices fell sharply. Dobbs got word of the poll that night: the Tories had fallen to 40.5 percent, their lowest yet, and Labour had risen to 36 percent. The gap had halved in a week. When people were asked about the quality of the two campaigns, Kinnock scored 39 percent to Thatcher's 23 percent, a 16-percentage-point lead. The figures, if translated into actual votes, threatened a hung parliament and the biggest election upset since Labour defeated Winston Churchill in 1945.

When Tebbit heard the news he was unperturbed. All other polls showed the Tory lead holding steady, and he considered both the Gallup and the BBC polls suspect. But when the news reached Downing Street the reaction was seismic. Mrs. Thatcher's depression had been exacerbated by a series of late nights, a ferocious schedule, and her continued frustration at the increasing problems she felt the campaign was running into. The target for much of her wrath over the next twenty-four hours would be Saatchi.

Thatcher was suffering from a bad toothache. She had started the campaign with an infection in one of her teeth, and it had grown worse; she dared not take time off to have it properly treated. That night she was in pain, and those who were unfortunate enough to see her during this time all testify to her savage anger and whiplash tongue. Jeremy Sinclair went to Downing Street that evening with what he hoped would be the final party election broadcast. It consisted of cuttings from Mrs. Thatcher's best speeches: to the Conservative conference, incorporating brief reminders of the Falklands spirit and the Brighton bomb, and to other audiences, building up to a climax almost drowned out by the stirring music of "I Vow to Thee My Country." There was room for a five-minute talk from her, yet to be filmed, which would bring out the main themes of freedom, peace, and the economy, to be put over in her softest and most persuasive tone. Thatcher at first was far from convinced, and the others in the room were noncommittal, awaiting her reaction. Gradually Sinclair talked her into accepting the ad. At 8:30 she left to go to the dentist, and Sinclair went home, telling Maurice, "We've made a sale," adspeak for "the client likes the ad." Early the next morning Sinclair went to Paris for a meeting.

"Wobbly Thursday," as it became generally known, began when Mrs. Thatcher arrived at Central Office at 8:30 A.M. for her regular morning briefing with Tebbit and other senior Tory staff members. She refused to take any comfort from Tebbit's efforts to minimize the morning's polls and demanded major changes in the way the campaign was being run.

The day continued to produce bad news. First, Kinnock upstaged her by producing the case of a ten-year-old boy who had been waiting fifteen months for a hole-in-the-heart operation; then a few minutes later, at her morning press conference, Mrs. Thatcher was trapped into her worst mistake of the campaign, stating that she paid for her own private medical insurance "to enable me to go into hospital on the day I want, at the time I want, and with the doctor I want." That might be fine for her, said Labour, but what about all the millions, like little Martin Burgess, the hole-in-the-heart boy, who couldn't afford the same privilege?

Thatcher's full fury was unleashed a few minutes later when she again sat down with her advisers. No one escaped her wrath, not even Lord Young. She gestured at the proofs of the Saatchi ads that lined the walls and verbally shredded them. Lord Whitelaw defended the one of the soldier with his arms raised, and she was forced to agree that it was a good ad. The others, she said, were terrible. She wanted new ideas, new ads—by that afternoon.

Sinclair, in Paris, knew nothing of all this. Midway through the morning, he suddenly had doubts about his own broadcast. Had he sold Thatcher the wrong one? He rang Sharkey. "John, you know that broadcast I sold the prime minister last night?" Sinclair asked. "I want you to do some research on it. Would you do it now?" Sharkey was puzzled. "Don't worry about it," Sinclair told him. "Just get the research done." Research of the kind Sinclair was requesting is not uncommon in the advertising industry. It consists of showing the ad to carefully selected audiences around the country, getting their reaction, and then analyzing it—in effect, a form of polling.

Before she finally left for the Midlands, Thatcher laid down her requirements: entirely new newspaper and poster ads for the final week. She wanted something more positive and hard-hitting than those she had seen so far, ads that stressed the Tories' success and Labour's failure. That afternoon's meeting was yet another unpleasant one, and at one stage Lord Young wheeled upon Tebbit, whom until that point he had been treating with great care and diffidence, and declared that he had not devoted eight years to the Tories to go down with a sinking ship.

Meanwhile, Tim Bell, in his office in Knightsbridge, had two calls in quick succession. The first was from Young to tell him of the prime minister's demand for a change in advertising. The second was from Downing Street, summoning him to a 3:30 meeting to discuss the final week's party election broadcast. The prime minister, it was explained, had thrown out the Saatchi broadcast, and she wanted new ideas. Furthermore, Jeremy Sinclair was in Paris so Bell could come to Number 10 openly—no one wanted a confrontation between the two men. It would be the first time in the campaign that Bell would enter through the front door rather than sneak in the back—"past the dustbins," as he referred to it. There must be a real crisis, he reasoned.

Just before lunch a fresh set of rumors reached the City: a new poll by Marplan for the next day's *Guardian* would actually show Labour ahead by two points. Stock prices crashed—notably that of Saatchi & Saatchi, which was seen as a big loser if Thatcher went out—and panic began to spread through the Tory ranks. What was going wrong? Tebbit was heard quoting Kipling:

> If you can keep your head while all about you
> Are losing theirs and blaming it on you,
> If you can trust yourself when all men doubt you,
> But make allowance for their doubting too . . .

He couldn't quite remember the final words, but it was the sentiment that mattered: "You'll be a Man, my son."

At the Knightsbridge office of Lowe Howard-Spink & Bell, Tim Bell and his chairman, Frank Lowe, worked through lunch on ideas that Bell had been thinking about for some days. They prepared eight or nine lines of attack, all revolving around a slogan for the final week, one they thought would appeal to Thatcher's desire to be positive and to hit at Labour: "Britain is great again. Don't let Labour ruin it," which was a version of the slogan used by the Tories back in 1959, "Life's better with the Tories. Don't let Labour ruin it." The agency's art director, Alan Waldie, hastily drew them up on boards, and Bell left for Downing Street.

Young chaired the meeting to discuss the final week's party election broadcast. By the time Sinclair got back from Paris, an entire new broadcast was to be made, and Saatchi was working on a new script presenting a more "caring" Mrs. Thatcher, showing how the Tories really did "care" for people—the precise strategy the "blue book" had rejected.

At the same time that this strategy session was taking place at Number 10, another meeting was taking place on Downing Street. The Young & Rubicam executives had arrived an hour earlier at the offices of John Wakeham, the chief whip, whose office was two doors away at 12 Downing Street. Y&R had prepared an analysis of the trends in the campaign, and it was not a cheerful paper for the Tories. The trend, it warned, was "now dangerous." Y&R advised a change of strategy, which should "center all" on Thatcher herself and repitch the campaign in the final week along the line: "We have not been through all this together for nothing. Don't let Labour throw it all away." In just three weeks, said Y&R, the Tory vote had fallen from 48 percent to 42 percent; Labour had increased from 27 percent to 35 percent. Y&R's "mainstreamers," a big middle-class category, were shifting in droves to Labour, which was winning their hearts rather than their minds. "Lost mainstreamers believe Kinnock—emotionally," Y&R said. "They believe he can control the party. . . . Labour have stolen the mainstreamer highground hearts and minds. They have undermined Tory fiscal success and are seen as 'caring' for mainstreamers." There was much more along the same lines. By the time the presentation was over, Wakeham, deeply depressed, decided the message was important enough to go to Number 10, and he took the Y&R people with him to see Mrs. Thatcher.

The broadcast meeting ended at five, and as Bell came out he tackled Lord Young. He had some ads he would like to show him. Would he like to see them? Young said he would, very much—preferably before Mrs. Thatcher got back. The ads Bell showed him were, decided Young, much more in line with what Thatcher wanted; they were getting somewhere.

When the prime minister arrived, Young intercepted her on the stairs and dragged her into the room where the Bell ads had been set up on the bookshelves. She was impressed. They were direct and to the point. One that stated, "The Conservatives are spending three times as much on the Health Service as the last Labour Government. The only government to reduce spending on health was the last Labour Government" particularly pleased her.

The prime minister, however, needed to prepare urgently for a live TV interview. Saatchi's team was standing by ready to bring its material over. She had no time to see it and in the end left it to Young to handle, on the basis that regardless of whoever did what, Bell's were the sort of ads she wanted.

There are various and conflicting versions of what happened next. Maurice Saatchi and John Sharkey arrived at Number 10 at 6:30; Tebbit was stuck in traffic and arrived some minutes later. Maurice wanted to see the prime minister, but she was preparing for her TV interview, and he and Sharkey had to wait. When Tebbit arrived, Young told him that Thatcher wanted to run the Bell ads. After some harsh words, Tebbit and Young both looked through the new Saatchi ads, rejecting several but agreeing that a number of the others had picked up the theme insisted on by Thatcher that morning—and were not very different from what Y&R was urging or what Bell had recommended for that final week. With all respect to Bell, it did not take a genius to work out the message the Tories needed to hammer home. All over Fleet Street and at countless dinner parties others were arriving at very similar conclusions.

Maurice exploded when Tebbit showed him the Bell ads. There was no way, Maurice said, that he was going to make those—the Saatchi ads made similar points and were much more professional. They were still talking when Young, who had stayed behind upstairs, stuck his head in the door. He had just heard the news of the Marplan poll: the Tories were not behind at all. They were still 10 percentage points ahead. The pressure was off. Thatcher left for her interview smiling. Maurice left soon after, having seen Mrs. Thatcher for only a few minutes; he was still irritated by Bell's intervention and what he saw as some odd behavior on

6 PHASES OF AN ELECTION

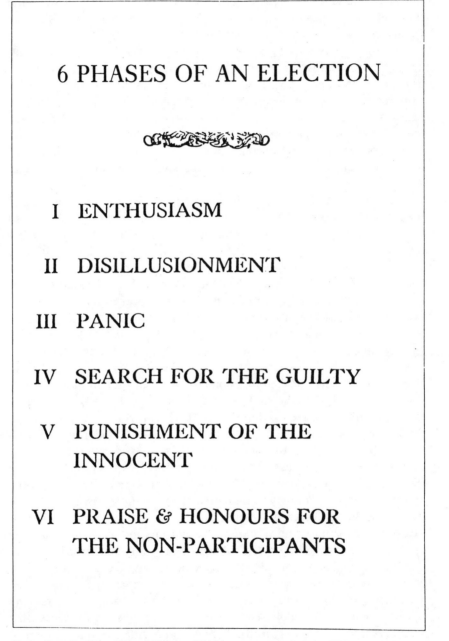

I   ENTHUSIASM

II   DISILLUSIONMENT

III   PANIC

IV   SEARCH FOR THE GUILTY

V   PUNISHMENT OF THE INNOCENT

VI   PRAISE & HONOURS FOR THE NON-PARTICIPANTS

From the wall of the office of Norman Tebbit's secretary during the 1987 campaign

the part of his client. The prime minister had not given in on her demand that Bell's ads be used—she wanted Saatchi to rework them. She also wanted a new party election broadcast.

The Tory party was breaking every rule in the book about client-agency relationships. Robert Townsend in his *Up the Organization* gave as his moral for dealing with advertising agencies: "Don't hire a master to paint you a masterpiece and then assign a room full of schoolboy artists to look over his shoulder and suggest improvements." Tim Bell and Frank Lowe could never be called "schoolboy artists"—they are both among the most professional and the best in the business—but their mere presence on the scene, second-guessing the Saatchi ads, makes Townsend's point.

The next day a new set of rumors spread, first through Whitehall and then into the City and Fleet Street: Saatchi & Saatchi had been sacked after a huge row with the prime minister. All sides denied the rumors, but there was no denying the conflict that was taking place. Jeremy Sinclair did his best to gloss matters over when one newspaper approached him. "Mrs. Thatcher's meeting with Maurice had an effect," he admitted. "It had everyone jumping up and down. But we remained in charge of the account." Lord Young insisted: "Our relations with Saatchi are as before. We are quite happy with the way things are going." Neither he nor Tebbit had any intention of downgrading the agency's role, Young added.

Sinclair meanwhile decided that he would not give up on his party election broadcast. The research done by Sharkey's team showed that it was even better than he had hoped; the broadcast had been highly effective with the audience that viewed it. He called Lord Young. Could they discuss the broadcast Thatcher had thrown out? Had Young himself seen it? Young agreed to come and look at it, and when he arrived Sinclair began with a classic advertising pitch—show the research before the client sees the ad. By the time Sinclair had taken him through the audience reaction, Young was intrigued. The broadcast itself left him of two minds: he had given the instruction to get rid of this ad, yet when he saw it and its supporting research, it was too good to lose. Finally he made up his mind: "This must go ahead." But how to convince Thatcher?

It was Young who came up with the idea of using Gordon Reece, who came around to see the broadcast the next morning, to persuade Thatcher to change her mind. Again Sinclair started his pitch by playing up the research and followed with the broadcast itself, and Reece, like Young, was impressed. That day Reece and Young showed it again to Thatcher, who by this time was in a more relaxed mood. Denis Thatcher was also in the room, and the consensus was favorable. Sinclair got his broadcast reinstated, and it would end the Tory party campaign.

That weekend papers ran ads of a more controversial nature: the results of the combined efforts of Bell and Saatchi—and goodness knows who else—placed at a cost of some £2 million. It was the biggest press advertising campaign in British history. Bell's line, "Britain is a success again—don't let Labour ruin it," came out as "Britain is great again—don't let Labour wreck it." Some of the ads bore more than a passing resemblance to the work produced by Bell, but this again may be due to similar minds arriving at the same conclusion. "We were given three sets of ads to make that day," said Sharkey wearily at the end of the week. "We ended up making the one we intended to all along."

As for the Young & Rubicam work, its proposal remedies to pull back the "mainstreamers" were at first incorporated into a draft of a Thatcher speech; when the Marplan poll came through, they were ripped out again. By the weekend all the polls were showing the Tories with a 10- to 12-percentage-point lead.

On June 11, that was how it ended—where in fact it had started before all the campaigning, all the battles and infighting. The Tories had started 12 percentage points ahead in the polls, and they finished that way. Mrs. Thatcher was back on Downing Street with a majority of 101, and the Saatchi brothers were left to brood on their future as advertising agents to a difficult client. At the low point of the campaign Saatchi had been blamed for all that went wrong, and the brothers hated being used as the scapegoat. "The Tory party went from being the best client in the world to being the most difficult over a space of eight years," said a former Saatchi employee later. This was a big shift from the days back in 1979 when Saatchi & Saatchi stood acclaimed by Tories and reviled by the opposition as the agency that had ushered in Thatcherism. Perhaps it was time for Saatchi to move on.

18

"LET'S BUY A BANK"

T he election campaign of 1987 may have ended on June 11, but the
battle between Tim Bell and the brothers did not. Once more the
Saatchis found themselves making front-page headlines day after
day, this time in a way that left them far from happy. The election itself
had been bad enough, with the criticism of the lackluster Conservative
campaign focusing particularly on the Saatchi ads. For the Conservative
leadership to be asked by the press if Saatchi had been sacked in mid-
campaign was humiliating. And for the Tories—and Tim Bell—to
interfere with the agency's carefully crafted work was intolerable. One
senior Tory was quoted as saying sympathetically that "if the advertising
is not up to scratch, then that is a reflection, not on the agency, but on the
client." The Saatchis in their more bitter moments might have felt that,
too, but the agency was scarcely blameless. The brothers had enjoyed the
benefits of the Conservative party account when Tim Bell ran it successfully. They could have used Bell again in 1987 and probably have
avoided most of the problems, but they had been too proud to do so.
Bell's replacements, Sharkey and Dobbs, grated on Thatcher. To an
extent at least the ad campaign was not *all* the problem of the client—the
agency had to shoulder some of the blame too.

In any case, one thing was clear: Mrs. Thatcher had no confidence in
Saatchi as her party's agency, and in those circumstances there was not
much point in going on. Saatchi had always contended that it treated the
Tory party account just like any other, but that was never entirely true,
simply because the account was not like any other. Working for the
Tories was high-profile stuff, with instant feedback and a unique level of
analysis from all sides. It could be very exciting, but it could also ruin the
agency's morale when the going got rough. It was worth little in terms of
direct reimbursement, yet it sharply affected the Saatchi stock price and
its financial shape.

All this made the celebrations of the Tory victory a subdued affair in
the Saatchi camp. I had a long postmortem with Maurice, Sharkey, and
Dobbs in Tebbit's office on the day after the election, when all three
defended the ads they had created and the campaign they had worked
out. They would not criticize the client, but they were grim-faced and
clearly very annoyed. It had not been a happy experience. The stock
recovered 30 to 600 pence on the day after the election, but the rumors

274

that Saatchi & Saatchi and the Tories would soon part had not gone away.

On the Saturday after the election *The Times* devoted the top of its front page and most of the back page to a story headed: "How Project Blue Rescued the Tory Campaign." The article was an account of how Young & Rubicam had purportedly stepped in to replace Saatchi and save Mrs. Thatcher from electoral defeat. It infuriated Bell and the Saatchis, who both claimed the report in *The Times* bore no resemblance to what had happened. That weekend there were more infuriating stories in the press. "The future of Saatchi as the Tory party's agents would now appear to be in the balance," said the *Observer* (June 14, 1987). "Speculation had it last week that a parting was nigh."

Saturday was the day Mrs. Thatcher was due to announce her round of cabinet changes. Norman Tebbit had already decided that he would not serve another term as a cabinet minister and had told her so several months before. Tebbit's decision had been a closely kept secret before the election but now had leaked, and this was widely expected to be his final day. Mrs. Thatcher had spent three hours with him on election day, but Tebbit remained adamant; he was going. By nightfall he would be out of government.

I went to see him in his rooms at the Cabinet Office that Saturday morning; it was a strange scene. In other circumstances there should have been an almost carnival atmosphere. It was a beautiful midsummer day in London, and all the windows overlooking Horse Guards Parade were open. From below, the swelling, uplifting music of the annual Trooping the Colour contrasted oddly with the somber, wakelike atmosphere in the offices. Wives and children gathered with the husbands who had worked through the past frenetic month with Tebbit, now come to watch the Queen. Margaret Tebbit sat at a window in her wheelchair, with perhaps the best view of anyone in the square of the ceremony below. There was drink and food, and from adjoining offices the sound of other parties uninhibitedly enjoying one of the privileges of government. Here even the children knew that something was amiss, and they talked in the same hushed tones as the adults.

I found Tebbit himself sitting at his desk in another room, his head down, redrafting a typed letter with a pen. He apologized when he saw me. Could I go through to the others? He was, he said, writing to the prime minister. I didn't have to ask why. Although it would not be officially announced for some hours, Tebbit was working on his letter of resignation. By the following day this fine suite of offices and all the trappings and privileges that went with the position of the Chancellor of the Duchy of Lancaster would be someone else's.

Tebbit's resignation was another factor militating against the Saatchis. Tebbit still retained the position of chairman of the party and therefore, nominally at least, was in charge of appointing its advertising agents; but even that role was looking increasingly vulnerable, and the wisdom among the political pundits and in the party hierarchy was that Tebbit would quit Central Office within six months. Lord Young had gained in power and stature right through the campaign in his roles as chief executive of Central Office and also head of the secret kitchen cabinet at Number 10. Now Mrs. Thatcher moved him from Employment Secretary to Secretary of State for Trade and Industry, the role once occupied by Tebbit. There were strong rumors that Young would also take over as chairman of the party, but that move was killed by strong opposition from the rest of the cabinet, and Young had to retreat later in the autumn. Saatchi was losing a powerful friend in the cabinet with Tebbit and found it hard to look on Young's rise with enthusiasm. Young had hardly shown himself to be a Saatchi supporter during the election, and he had far too close a friendship with Bell for the firm's liking.

Tebbit, however, had not lost his zest for a battle. That weekend he went to bat on behalf of his advertising agency. At a press conference he hit out at some of the wilder speculation about who had or had not written the ads. "There were two or three battles going on during the general election," he said. One was "the battle between an American advertising agency"—which Tebbit delicately refused to name but which everyone present knew was Young & Rubicam—"who were sore at Saatchi's success and who thought the best way to get back at them was to make a pitch at the account which was the most prestigious account they had—the Conservative party."

He went on: "After they failed [to get the Tory party account] quite clearly they set out to say that it was Saatchi's campaign that lost us the election. Since we won, they started again and said it had nothing to do with them [Saatchi & Saatchi]. They were saying it was their agency behind the scenes. That is the big bad world of business."

Tebbit's speech helped the Saatchi stock price again when the market opened on Monday. That morning, however, the ire of the brothers had been increased by another press item. On Sunday *Daily Mail* diarist Nigel Dempster had been phoned by Frank Lowe, an old friend of his. Tim Bell's considerable efforts on Mrs. Thatcher's behalf, Lowe complained, were being ignored. The success at the end of the campaign was not due to Saatchi, nor was it due to Young & Rubicam. The slogan "Britain is great again—don't let Labour wreck it" was a Tim Bell–Frank Lowe creation. Dempster duly obliged Lowe the next day with a lead item in his well-read and influential diary: "Privately Mrs. Thatcher is congratulating Tim Bell" for her victory, said Dempster.

Lowe, in contrast to his partner Bell, was no enemy of the Saatchis. On the contrary he was—and is—one of Charles's closest friends; they regularly play poker and tennis together and have similar ideas about the world of advertising, and both resented finding themselves on opposite sides in this public way. As a fresh row erupted, Lowe discovered that he had entered into a minefield from which it was not going to be easy to extricate himself. He blamed Bell for causing the events, as did the Saatchis. For his part Bell had his invariably good humor stretched that weekend as he found himself caught up in an increasingly messy situation that he also felt was not of his making. And the messiness seemed to be escalating by the hour.

That evening the BBC "Panorama" program, recapping the events of the election, reported that on "Wobbly Thursday," June 4, Mrs. Thatcher "had effectively dispensed with Saatchi & Saatchi and handed her campaign over to advisers from another agency." Maurice and Charles were incensed. Saatchi may not have finished the campaign in good shape, but the agency had finished it still writing ads for the Tory party, and there had been no sacking. The BBC was over the line.

It was time to hit back. The Saatchis, as Tim Bell avers, are good friends but bitter enemies. Brian Basham, the leading public-relations consultant in the City and a man who had acted for them for many years—but refused to be taken over by them despite offers that became larger each year as Basham's business prospered—was brought in to plan a countercampaign. So were the agency's lawyers. The brothers went into a huddle. Maurice and Charles wrote a statement that Basham issued to the press. Saatchi & Saatchi had not been sacked but were still employed by the Tory party, the statement said. Young & Rubicam's much-talked-about special research techniques with their "mainstreamers" and "belongers" were, said the press release, "completely useless" in the election. Both Y&R and Bell's agency were indulging in a "campaign of disinformation." Saatchi & Saatchi intended to sue for libel. Central Office issued a supporting statement saying that the "Panorama" reference was a "total fabrication" and that the agency was "at no time fired, nor did the question of firing arise."

In the days that followed, the heat suddenly turned off the Saatchis and on to Lowe Howard-Spink & Bell. There were rumors that Bell and Frank Lowe had fallen out, that key people were leaving, and that the tabloids were about to publish damaging allegations about Bell's personal life. Bell accused the Saatchis and Basham of spreading the rumors, and the Saatchis denied doing so. By midweek the situation had gotten out of hand. In the City of 1987, a year after the Big Bang when the markets had been deregulated, there were dealers who specialized in acting on just such rumors, and it soon turned into a classic bear raid. On Wednesday the shares of Lowe Howard–Spink & Bell fell over £6, wiping £12 million off the value of the company. The story was on the front pages of most papers the next day, linked to the row over the campaign ads. The situation was not funny for Frank Lowe. "I regret ever writing those ads now," said Lowe later. "I never should have got the agency involved."

Nor was the situation funny for the prime minister. Sir Gordon Reece called her on Wednesday. She was seething. "It really is unseemly," she said. "I've just won an election by 100 seats, and all anyone can talk about is which advertising agency wrote which ad in the campaign." Couldn't Reece do something? "You know the Saatchis and Tim Bell and Frank Lowe and all the others. Can't you stop it, Gordon?" Reece agreed the whole thing was absurd and would do what he could to "knock a few heads together."

Both sides felt the other was to blame. The Saatchis were bitter about Bell's interference, while Bell accused the Saatchis of using his ads and presenting them as their own. The stories of the row were being picked up in New York, Canada, Australia, and everywhere else Saatchi & Saatchi was known and they were damaging both to it and to Lowe's company, but neither side could let well enough alone, particularly the Saatchis. Bell must be made to back down.

Downing Street was getting alarmed by the growing clamor. That day calls went out to Tebbit, Lord Young, Lord Whitelaw, and others to see what they could do to "cool it." Meanwhile both sides were already briefing journalists for what promised to be yet another round. Lowe, Bell, and their finance director, Julian Seymour, went to the offices of Peter Carter-Ruck, a solicitor who specializes in libel, to talk about bringing suit against the Saatchis.

In the end a peacemaker appeared in the unlikely person of Lord Hanson, chairman of the giant conglomerate Hanson Trust. The saying about Hanson was that he loved "Mrs. Thatcher, free enterprise, and the United States—in no particular order." He did not like the damage this public squabble was doing to two of those three loves, and he was in a position to intervene to stop it.

Hanson had just completed his biggest-ever flurry of takeover bids, including the takeover of SCM Corporation for $920 million, pushing his company to number forty-eight on the Fortune 500 list in the United States and making it the fifth biggest in Britain. He now owned the Imperial Group, Britain's biggest cigarette company, which was a major client of Saatchi & Saatchi, while Lowe Howard-Spink & Bell also had a number of Hanson accounts.

Hanson called Lowe on Friday morning and suggested he come to see him. Lowe walked across from his own office in Bowater House to the 1960s office block on Hyde Park Corner, overlooking the gardens of Buckingham Palace, where Hanson had his headquarters. The Saatchis, still furious with the rumors about them, didn't want peace talks. They were intent on having their side of the story fully heard, establishing beyond all reasonable doubt that the advertisements used during the election had come from their team and their copywriters and artists, not from Bell, Lowe, Young & Rubicam or anyone else.

Hanson is a persuasive, calm, intelligent man who found Lowe only too willing to make peace. He could, he agreed, silence Tim Bell. But how to persuade the Saatchis to desist? The battle was damaging the shares of both companies.

Hanson called Maurice Saatchi and told him he had Frank Lowe in the office on the conference phone. Lowe was keen to resolve this silly matter between them, and Hanson thought it must stop too, if only to protect the prime minister, whose election victory should not be sullied in this way. What did it matter who had written those ads? What did matter was that Thatcher had won. Now, could there be peace?

Both Maurice and Charles spoke on the phone. They were reluctant to drop the argument there but could scarcely cross Hanson so blatantly. They finally agreed to a truce.

Later that morning an extraordinary press release was issued under the heading: "ALL SMILES AT LOWE AND SAATCHI." Both sides, it said, wished to end the rift. Frank Lowe formally congratulated the Saatchis "on their great success with the Tory election campaign," and the Saatchis thanked Lowe for his "valuable contribution."

The press the next day missed the key point of the statement: the Saatchis thanked Lowe for *his* contribution. Surely the contribution from the agency Lowe Howard-Spink & Bell owed something to Tim Bell? Yet there was no mention of Bell in the press release. Lowe later insisted that this was because the Saatchis would not have agreed to let Bell's name appear in a joint statement. "They really seemed to hate him," Lowe said. The Saatchi camp, on the other hand, told a different story. Lowe had been embarrassed by Bell's behavior, and it was he who insisted the latter's name not be mentioned. Bell, wisely perhaps, stayed mum (but later vehemently denied the Saatchi version of the press release).

The battle of the election advertising was over, at least for a time. The Saatchis settled their libel case against the BBC for a grudging retraction and a modest £1,000 paid to charity. The BBC had been tempted to fight but was still recovering from another bruising battle with the Conservative party that had cost it £500,000, savagely damaged publicity, and lost the director-general his job. It didn't help that the reporter, Michael Cockerill, was the same reporter in both cases. Saatchi issued a statement claiming victory, but at the BBC the message given to reporters was depicted by *The Times* the next morning as the "collapse of stout Saatchi." A BBC executive was quoted as saying: "With all the Tebbit pressure on the BBC there has been a certain loss of nerve. Once we would have fought a thing like this on principle but now we would rather wriggle out of it quietly." The BBC version, although not correct, had not been a million miles from the truth.

For Saatchi & Saatchi, it was time for more serious business ventures.

In New York the merging of the agencies into Simonds-Gooding's carefully worked-out structure was almost complete. The global gospel may have had holes in it, but it was holding together reasonably well as the brothers moved rapidly on, impatiently putting behind them complaints about conflicts of interest, size, demotions, and even mass firings—over 1,000 people were let go from the agencies acquired in the United States that summer.

Other problems too kept emerging: the British pharmaceutical group Beecham sued Saatchi in the United States over what it claimed was an absurdly optimistic projection made by the Saatchi market-research subsidiary, Yankelovich Clancy Shulman. The firm had claimed that by spending $18 million on advertising a new laundry powder, Beecham would get a 45 to 52 percent market share. Beecham had duly spent the money through a Saatchi advertising agency, but it had achieved only 25 percent at the peak. Its share soon lapsed back to between 15 and 20 percent. This was not a good advertisement for the powers of the multi-service approach. But in the overall picture it was a tiny sideshow.

The brothers wanted to move on to the next phase, one they had been considering in a vague way but that they now wanted to pull off the back burner and activate. It was time to move into financial services; time, in short, to buy a bank.

In August Maurice went to the south of France with Josephine and the two children, Adam and Edward. It had become an important place to him, where he could rest away from what had been a bruising year. He had bounced back quickly from the battering of the election and the fights over the American acquisitions and reorganization. Although Saatchi & Saatchi now employed over 14,000 people around the world, the management structure was designed so that little of the day-to-day load fell on the brothers. In their sixth-floor offices, they could plan their bold gestures and keep the adrenaline flowing. However, Maurice, after his marriage to Josephine, had begun to enjoy his holidays too, particularly in the beautiful house on Cap Ferrat. From there he kept in touch with the preparations going on for the biggest move the Saatchi group had ever attempted.

Back in London in the first week of September, Maurice joined Charles to review the progress on the financial-services plan. It was in the hands of the City merchant bankers Kleinwort Benson, but Maurice had asked Michael Dobbs, who had left the Conservative Central Office and rejoined Saatchi, to coordinate it on the company front.

Saatchi & Saatchi had changed a great deal in the two years that Dobbs had been away. Bill Muirhead was chairman of the agency, and Paul Bainsfair and John Sharkey (who later left to join Blue Arrow, the British employment agency that bought out Manpower Services, the biggest employment agency in the United States) were joint managing directors. Sinclair, Roy Warman, and Terry Bannister had all been moved into the international division, and Jennifer Laing, wooed back with the red Ferrari by Bell, was on the point of leaving again, this time to join a small agency where she felt she would welcome the challenge of building it up. In any case Maurice had another job in mind. Dobbs was given an office in the new Regent Street building, a floor below the spacious rooms occupied by the brothers, and Charles and Maurice briefed him at length on their plan to buy a bank.

As a prelude to the move the brothers had commissioned a study of the financial-service industry from Touche Ross, one of the top seven accounting firms. They had both become enthusiastic about the logic of it all, Charles in his typical straight-to-the-heart analysis picturing banking as an industry almost identical in structure and diversity to advertising as it had been in the 1970s. No bank, however big, had a large market share. Both brothers had seen uncanny echoes of their own thoughts—and those of Ted Levitt—on the subject of globalization. The financial columns were full of articles discussing the global-versus-niche argument taking place throughout the banking world as technology and deregulation had turned financial markets into one large international marketplace.

London's Big Bang, the equivalent of Wall Street's May Day a decade before, had brought the biggest changes in the financial-services industry the City of London had ever seen. Americans, Japanese, and Europeans had swept in to take positions in the securities markets, and all but a tiny handful of London's once proud stockbroking and jobbing houses had surrendered their independence, swallowed up in the financial combines that insisted that to survive in the new world you either had to have the capacity—and the capital—to distribute securities around the world or look for a specialized niche to make your profit.

To the brothers the prospect of moving into the banking industry was irresistible. The Saatchis had persuaded many, including themselves, that they had discovered the concept of globalization, at least insofar as putting it into practice in a service industry. Now everyone was jumping on the bandwagon. In a matter of weeks the trauma of the election had been forgotten. Here was a new challenge, many times bigger even than the Bates deal. By widening their field of activity beyond advertising to include consulting, marketing, sales promotion, corporate image, public relations, design, and the other areas, the brothers had increased the size of the market they were operating in—and intended to have a 10 percent share of—from the $40 billion a year of advertising expenditure to a market four times that size. By 1990 they estimated the consulting market alone would be worth $230 billion. Their management-consultancy business ranked twelfth in the world, but acquisitions already well

advanced would soon place it higher and by the early 1990s they planned
to have as much revenue from that area as they had from advertising.
There were other areas, such as specialist computer-based research for
the legal industry, where Saatchi now ranked first.

Saatchi & Saatchi was no longer just an advertising agency nor even a
communications company. It was a "multiservice" company. This would
be the brothers' approach to the financial-services industry, which would
widen their horizons much, much more. Dobbs was already drafting the
argument they would deploy. "Saatchi has brought together leading
companies in the management-service fields, each with independent
objectives but common standards of excellence and cultural values," he
wrote. "Its aim is to provide clients with a professional range, quality, and
coordination of services that allows them to pursue their goals effectively." There was more along these lines, material that would later make
City bankers look away, muttering disgustedly, "What's this got to do
with Mexican debt?" But Maurice was pleased with Dobb's assessment.

Now was the time to settle on the target. The professional adviser on
the deal was David Clementi, a merchant banker in the corporate finance
department of Kleinwort Benson, who was busily organizing the resources Saatchi would need. The British banking market was in turmoil,
with no less than five banks "in play" in the sense that someone had
announced a share stake or an actual bid for them, and it was only a
matter of time before those five banks were taken over.

Of these prospects one stood out above the others: Midland Bank,
once, thirty years before, the biggest in the world, now not even in the top
twenty after its disastrous takeover—and disposal—of the Crocker Bank
of California, which had run into major problems over South American
debt. Midland that summer had cleaned itself up, making a provision of
over £1 billion against its loans to Third World countries and at the same
time selling two British subsidiary banks, Clydesdale and Northern. Its
balance sheet suddenly looked much healthier, but Sir Kit McMahon,
the chairman of Midland and a former deputy governor of the Bank of
England, privately warned his board of something else: while Midland
was burdened with its bad Third World debt, no predator would dare bid
for it. Before the provision, it had been, in effect, the perfect "poison pill,"
something so unpalatable that no one would swallow it. That status was
now gone, and the world could see that Midland had a long-term future.
That made it very vulnerable. "Once we do this," said McMahon, "we
will become interesting. We will be a bank that is still weak but is
showing that it is prepared to do something and is now, in ratio terms,
tolerable."

Someone else saw Midland in the same light. Within three days of
Midland's major announcement, Lord Hanson began buying shares.
Early in September speculation heightened when Hanson let it be known

that he now owned between 5 and 7 percent of Midland. It was, he said, just "an investment." McMahon went to see him, and Hanson assured him that his intentions were "friendly." The City was skeptical, but McMahon believed him. Hanson, he reckoned, had made the same calculation he had; he had recognized the key moment when Midland had moved out of its trouble into the vulnerable period before the benefits of the reorganization begun by McMahon had come through. Someone, Hanson reasoned, would make a bid; and when that bid was made, he wanted a slice of the action. McMahon believed Hanson was a "punter" rather than a serious bidder, he reported back to his board. He might push the price up higher and be a "destabilizer," but the Midland chairman thought Hanson's objective was to put the bank "in play," persuading another bidder to come in. McMahon was right; taking over an industrial company held no terrors for Hanson. Taking over a clearing bank was another matter, and even he shied away from it, knowing that he would almost certainly not get away with it, even if he wanted to. There were too many regulators and vested interests to make it worthwhile even to attempt it. He had bought the shares as a speculation.

If Midland would have been an enormous leap for Hanson, whose company was capitalized at more than £6 billion, it was an even bigger leap for the Saatchis, valued on the stock market at less than £1 billion. But then Garland-Compton had also been a huge leap a dozen years before, and so had the big bids in the United States. The brothers were never afraid to try. If they did the planning right, taking over Midland would be no more difficult, they reasoned. But would the numbers work?

David Clementi calculated that they would. Midland was capitalized on the stock market at £2 billion. To win it, Saatchi needed to offer more than the current share price, so it would cost nearly £3 billion. There would have to be a capital injection as well, to have any hope of gaining the support of the Midland board and also of turning Midland back into a world-class bank. Clementi estimated that amount would have to be another £1 billion—£4 billion in all. Could Saatchi raise that much money? Clementi emerged a few days later with the answer: it could. He had made tentative arrangements for £3 billion of new Saatchi shares to be underwritten plus a standby credit line of another £1 billion. The City was awash with cash; Saatchi's credit stood high; and there was no problem raising money to buy an organization as distinguished as Midland, which still had huge assets and an excellent income stream from its domestic operations. Midland was a serious runner. Even if the takeover attempt failed, it would serve notice on the world that Saatchi was ready for its biggest move yet and was far more than just an advertising agency.

Maurice had been greatly impressed with a piece in the *Economist* that summer that mentioned the "commonly agreed view that the money industry will have room only for, at best, 25 global financial intermediaries." On the basis of what was happening in other industries, most of these would be Japanese or American. Why shouldn't there be another British one?

After the election Charles in particular wanted to regain the impetus of the business, and that, he felt, required the biggest, boldest move yet, something even those who thought they knew Saatchi could never envision. Acquiring Midland would be that move. Midland and its sister clearing banks, Barclay's, NatWest, and Lloyd's, were more than just companies: they were almost national institutions, a species as protected as the golden eagle.

However, just at that particular time there was a window, one that might never open again. The Bank of England, guardian of the banking sector, had allowed a number of bids in recent months. A new banking act was about to come into force that meant the Bank of England could limit any shareholding to 15 percent and could decide that anyone who dared to go above that limit without its approval was not a "fit and proper person" to control a bank. Although the Bank of England's powers would be retroactive, a number of bidders felt the time was ripe to move. Saatchi should launch quickly.

Maurice's first call was to an old Saatchi friend, Sir Donald Barron, a former Midland Bank chairman and now a semiretired City figure, whom the brothers had known for years. Maurice met with him a few days later and explained to an astonished Barron what the brothers proposed to do. Would Barron with his Midland connections act as an intermediary? Barron liked Maurice but was reluctant to get caught in the middle of a bid for his old bank. For a start, he thought a bid was a bad idea and told Maurice so. Secondly, he was a member of the supervisory board of the Bank of England, with responsibility for monitoring Britain's banking community, and this bid was bound to come before that board. He would not help the Saatchis in this bid, but he proffered some advice: they must approach the Bank of England and the Treasury before they did anything else.

Maurice took Barron's advice and a few days later found himself in the Whitehall office of Sir Peter Middleton, the Treasury's permanent secretary, who listened politely as the younger Saatchi outlined a well-rehearsed and reasoned summary of Saatchi's case for being allowed into the City's inner circle. Midland still had 15 percent of the U.K. domestic market, but that in turn was only 5 percent of the world banking market, so in global terms it was not large. Midland was too small to compete with the big players, and even retreating into a "niche" role was no answer: competitor banks with access to world markets would sweep it aside there, too. In the City, Midland had closed down its equity market-making side, Greenwell's, a casualty of the Big Bang.

Middleton, an unorthodox, ascetic fifty-six-year-old civil servant much respected both by his chancellor, Nigel Lawson, and by Mrs. Thatcher, listened with polite but noncommittal interest as Maurice talked for about twenty minutes, interjecting keenly when Maurice mentioned that in the past year the number of British-owned "market-makers" in U.K. government securities had shrunk from thirteen to ten out of a total of twenty-seven. That affected the Treasury, as Maurice had known it would. "I wasn't aware of that," Middleton said.

A few days later Maurice was at the Bank of England for a similar conversation with George Blunden, the deputy governor, and Rodney Galpin, the director in charge of the banking sector. Blunden and Galpin were also polite but noncommittal, careful to play it absolutely straight. They would give neither approval nor disapproval to Saatchi & Saatchi but suggested it was time Maurice talk directly to Midland. Much would depend on Midland's attitude. The Bank of England did not want a hostile takeover battle and would be unlikely to approve the Saatchi's move if it could not get an agreed bid. Blunden and Galpin also formally pointed out that their powers under the new banking act to prevent anyone going above a 15 percent shareholding would be retroactive. The brothers already knew that without Midland approval their bid was going nowhere, but the warnings were beginning to get heavy.

Seeking that approval was the obvious next move, and Maurice had his presentation all typed up and ready to present to Midland. The man he would meet at Midland was not an ordinary bank chairman. Sir Kit McMahon is an Australian who started his career as an English don before joining the Bank of England, where at one stage he was strongly tipped as the next governor. But he had never been a favorite of Mrs. Thatcher and finally left the Bank to join Midland, where he had made the difficult but necessary decision to retrench. After two years of McMahon's management Midland was smaller, but it was rapidly emerging from its problems.

McMahon already knew what the Saatchis intended before Maurice made his approach. The Bank of England had told Maurice that it was its duty to inform Midland of any takeover bid, and an official made a phone call to an astonished McMahon. The Bank's position, said the official, was that Midland's attitude to a Saatchi & Saatchi bid was "an overwhelming consideration," and that position had been made clear to Mr. Saatchi.

The Midland chairman had already decided he would not support a Saatchi bid before he had even met Maurice, but he still felt he must see him when Maurice rang for an appointment. The name Saatchi & Saatchi was so closely associated with the Thatcher government that McMahon was by no means certain of what forces Maurice could muster against him. Nor did he want the brothers to be able to say, as he confided to a colleague, that "this stick-in-the-mud can't do lateral thinking." He also had to be careful not to give the impression that

Midland was for sale, which could easily happen if he had a series of meetings with Maurice and his advisers. He made his own battle plans: one meeting with the Saatchi chairman, just the two of them; hear what he had to say; put it to a board meeting, which by chance happened to be scheduled two days later; get the board's unanimous backing (which he was certain he would do); and call off any further negotiations. He must end the speculation cleanly and quickly.

On Wednesday, September 9, Maurice traveled into the City. His car drew up outside the splendid portals of Midland's headquarters in Poultry, just a stone's throw from the Bank of England. Instead of entering the elegant banking hall, one of the finest in Britain, he took a small, anonymous elevator to the right of the entrance hall and ascended four floors. The flunkies were waiting as he stepped out, and a few minutes later he was sitting opposite McMahon. Both men, who had not met before, were courteous and elaborately polite, and no outsider would have guessed from their tones the keen verbal battle that was going on.

Maurice began his pitch cautiously and carefully, building his case brick upon brick. McMahon was not unfamiliar with the globalization arguments and embraced them himself as enthusiastically as most, so that bit was fine. Much of what Maurice said was neither surprising nor disagreeable to the Midland chief. The prospect of £1 billion of new capital made the banker catch his breath—Saatchi & Saatchi's proposed takeover was certainly tempting for a bank desperately short of capital and having trouble raising it anywhere else. (McMahon later got most of the capital he needed when the Hong Kong & Shanghai Banking Corporation bought a stake in Midland.) Also tempting was Maurice's assurance that the Saatchis wanted him, Kit McMahon, to continue running Midland, and they proposed no reductions in staff. This was more interesting than McMahon had thought. He listened attentively to the full exposition, already given, in varied form, to the Treasury and to the Bank of England; much of it made sense, and he could see some attractions in what Maurice proposed.

But he had some objections too—major ones. "You know, we depend for a great deal of business on a lot of people who don't want us to be livened up or made more exciting," McMahon told Maurice. "Our lifeblood is our deposit base, which comes from Swiss bankers and other very conservative people; we depend on the interbank market, and as far as they're concerned, the duller we are the better. If that deposit base goes, everything goes." That was why, he went on, Midland was different from all the other businesses the Saatchis were in: "We can't get out of that part of our business. We can diversify from it, but that's basically what we are." He repeated this argument several times, not certain that Maurice understood the complex nature of a deposit base, how important—and vulnerable—it was.

He made other points too: "My managers and customers would not

find it easy to understand why they were part of an advertising agency."
NatWest and the other clearers, he reckoned, could have great fun with
an advertising campaign built around that. He found Maurice responsive
and well prepared on the broader arguments but not so certain on the
more detailed ones. Maurice did not know where Midland's deposits
came from or how the treasury function worked and was ignorant about
other banking matters.

McMahon then delivered what he believed to be his clincher. "What
happens when things go to pot in Latin America and you have to put up
another billion?" Maurice visibly started. "I thought you'd taken care of
that," he muttered. McMahon was astonished. Maurice, he felt, obviously knew a lot about controlling the risk in his own business but had
not thought through the type of risk faced by banks. Midland had indeed
provided £1 billion against bad Latin American debt; but if the situation
in Latin America deteriorated again, Midland might have to provide
another slug of reserves. After two hours Maurice left, still clinging to a
hope that he could persuade McMahon to join him but uncomfortably
aware of the deep waters he had entered. Despite all his preparation, he
had been outargued by a man who knew as much about international
banking and globalization as anyone in the world. Saatchi & Saatchi
would never even get close to landing Midland.

On Friday, September 11, McMahon informed his board of the
Saatchi offer. The board reacted in precisely the manner he had predicted. Becoming part of a worldwide advertising agency, however
broadly based and go-ahead, would not do anything for Midland's
problems. It needed a tie-up with another international bank, and the
board was already talking to several prospects. The answer was "no."

Maurice, desperately disappointed, tried to set up another meeting
with McMahon. The Midland chairman had enjoyed the talk but decided that if he and Maurice met again, rumors would start and be
misinterpreted. He declined. The brothers had to accept defeat on the
Midland front.

Even before the final decision had come through from McMahon's
office, the brothers were already focusing on target number two. On the
morning of Friday, September 11, Sir Robert Clark, chairman of the
London-based merchant bank Hill Samuel, received a phone call. His
secretary passed him the message. Maurice Saatchi, chairman of Saatchi
& Saatchi, wanted to see him on a matter of urgency. Could he possibly
have an appointment that afternoon? Clark, irritated, told his secretary
to pass back a message that Hill Samuel was quite happy with its
arrangements for advertising and public relations, and he didn't think he
and Maurice had anything to talk about.

The news of the abortive bid for Midland had not yet leaked, and
Clark, together with David Davies, Hill Samuel's chief executive, had
been in meetings attempting to resolve some pressing problems of their

own. Hill Samuel was one of London's larger merchant banks, which like every other group in the City was going through the same strategic thinking process as Midland: whether to go "global" or "niche." Hill Samuel had chosen "global" and held months of detailed talks with the Union Bank of Switzerland, so much against the views of the chief executive, Christopher Castleman, that he had resigned. Then out of the blue the Union Bank pulled out, leaving Hill Samuel feeling foolish and exposed. Further catastrophe struck when Hill Samuel had been forced to fire the heads of the corporate finance division, who had been discovered negotiating to sell off a whole division of the bank without even telling the main board. In the first week of September, when the Saatchi approach came, Hill Samuel was spending all its time trying to find a way out of its problems. Clark did not want to be bothered with advertising proposals.

Half an hour later Davies got a call, this time from David Clementi at Kleinwort Benson. He was speaking, Clementi said, on behalf of his client Saatchi & Saatchi, whose chairman wanted to come and talk, not about advertising, but about taking the bank over. "There was pandemonium for a few hours," says one Hill Samuel executive. Clementi and Kleinwort Benson indicated that Saatchi & Saatchi was proposing a serious bid, and Davies knew Clementi well enough to know he meant it.

At four that afternoon Maurice appeared at Hill Samuel on his own. He was escorted into Davies's office since it was the chief executive rather than the chairman who would handle the matter of a takeover bid. Davies had Clark with him, but no one else. Unknown to Davies, Maurice already knew all about Davies. He had asked a headhunter to find someone to run the financial-services venture. High on the list was Davies, who had recently returned to London after three years in Hong Kong sorting out the problems of Hong Kong Land.

That same afternoon Davies was booked on a flight to Dublin, where he intended to spend the weekend at his house in Wicklow. He missed two planes as he listened in fascination while Maurice spelled out the case for a merger with Saatchi & Saatchi. Davies, he understood, wanted to keep Hill Samuel together rather than break it up, which most solutions now proposed would have done. Fine—Saatchi wanted that too. Maurice said he wanted to keep all of Hill Samuel's management. He was offering to open doors for Hill Samuel around the world: Saatchi had 150 offices in forty countries and a client base of 10,000 corporate customers. It worked with 280 of the Fortune 500 and with 300 of Europe's biggest companies. There was a clincher: Hill Samuel needed an injection of capital. Saatchi was prepared to put in £200 million, which would double Hill Samuel's existing capital.

When Davies finally caught his plane to Ireland, he didn't see how he or his colleagues could say no to Maurice's proposal. Every objection raised had been countered. Only the price had not been settled, and on that score too Davies was reasonably happy: Maurice assured him that Saatchi would pay a "substantial" premium, and when Davies pointed out that in banking parlance "substantial" meant 20 percent, Maurice nodded in agreement.

Over the next few days Davies talked to all his senior management colleagues. The most serious opposition to accepting Saatchi & Saatchi's bid came from John Chiene, a Scottish stockbroker who had built Wood Mackenzie into one of the most respected stock-brokerage firms in London as well as in Edinburgh. A year earlier, as part of the City's Big Bang, Wood Mackenzie had been taken over by Hill Samuel, and Chiene in turn took charge of the enlarged group's securities business. Chiene was dismissive of Saatchi, arguing that it had no place in the world of banking and financial securities markets.

However, by Monday Chiene had come around. That afternoon Davies reported to his chairman. The management was in favor of the bid, he told Clark. He had checked with Clementi at Kleinwort Benson and had established that the premium on the share price would indeed be "substantial," so that part of the deal looked good too. It seemed a wonderful way out of Hill Samuel's difficulties.

"Well, if the management thinks it's OK, we better put it to the board," said Clark. He arranged a meeting for Wednesday, when Maurice Saatchi would again appear to present his bid formally.

Outside in the City, events were moving against Saatchi & Saatchi. The controversy during the election campaign and the open battle with Tim Bell afterward had done the agency more damage than it realized. So too had reports that it was losing clients and that it was not able to manage the huge group the brothers had created. Worst of all, the news of the abortive Midland deal leaked that weekend, and the City hated it. The *Financial Times* commented that the proposed takeover was a move that would not "strike terror in the boardrooms of American Express, Citibank, and Nomura," three of the biggest international banking houses, and added that Saatchi "smacked of a firm which had run out of ideas." The *Economist* said that no one in the City believed that "the firm which polished Mrs. Thatcher's image can add much glamour to the Brazilian debt business." The word *megalomania* was to be heard in the City that week, and Saatchi, it was said, was being "carried away by its own self-importance." The Midland Bank deal was roundly condemned everywhere, and with some justification, as the most ill-judged deal the brothers had ever dreamed of.

As the storm broke, the price of Saatchi shares fell sharply, reducing the value of the offer the agency could make to Hill Samuel, which was still a secret. When Maurice redid his sums before going to the boardroom, they no longer looked so good. When he got to Hill Samuel, he was able to offer the "substantial" premium on the share price: £7.50, well above the current market price. That was fine. What about a cash alternative? asked Davies. Normally bidders in Britain make offers in two forms: in their own shares, which would have meant in this case that shareholders in Hill Samuel would exchange their shares for those of Saatchi & Saatchi, a paper-for-paper offer; and in a cash offer, or "cash alternative," which is usually around 5 percent below the paper offer.

Because of the fall in Saatchi & Saatchi's share price Maurice was not able to raise the cash he needed without future damage to Saatchi's profits. The best he could do was £6.40, an 18 percent discount on his paper offer. Hill Samuel shares stood at £6.60, and its assets were probably worth, if the company were broken up, around £8.50 a share. The board knew that if Hill Samuel accepted the cash alternative, two of its biggest shareholders, the Australians Kerry Packer and Larry Adler, would instantly make a higher cash bid and dismember the company.

The board could not accept Maurice's offer. There would be no Saatchi & Saatchi move into financial services—at least not for some time. A month later Hill Samuel was taken over by Trustee Savings Bank, much to Davies's relief. He, at least, has little doubt how near he was to joining the Saatchi empire. "If they had made their move just a couple of months earlier when their shares were high," Davies says now, "it would have worked out very well. It would have suited us perfectly."

On October 21, 1987, Maurice Saatchi wrote a letter to Margaret Thatcher. This letter marked the end of an era, both for Saatchi & Saatchi and for the Conservative party, which Thatcher had led since 1975.

The previous week, on the night of October 16, a freak hurricane had swept southern England, bringing devastation to the garden at Old Hall. Maurice had spent the weekend mournfully examining the 200-year-old oaks and beeches that had been uprooted, but within hours he had the bulldozers at work, tearing out the roots and planting new trees. After the man-made setbacks he had suffered, Maurice was not going to be put off by a mere act of nature.

On Monday, October 19, the stock market suffered the biggest one-day drop in its history, and Saatchi shares fell by one-third in a period of twenty-four hours. It was no consolation that every other share had gone down too or that if the Hill Samuel deal had gone ahead, Saatchi & Saatchi would now have had an £800 million stock issue in the market, placed at twice the current price. The brothers were much more concerned that Saatchi's ability to grow by takeover, financed through new stock issues, was being severely blunted. But even that fact could not be allowed to stand in the way of tidying up one loose end. Maurice carefully composed his letter.

"Dear Prime Minister," he began formally. She had always been "kind enough," he reminded her, to take a close interest in the development of Saatchi & Saatchi "and the success we have enjoyed in recent years." Now the company was widening its range of activities—it would become involved in direct satellite broadcasting (in competition with Simonds-Gooding) and in financial services, both fields heavily regulated by the government and thus potential areas of conflict with the Tory party account. The advertising business was also operating for more and more government departments. "We are conscious that this might open the company, public authorities, and ministers to misrepresentation," he added, and the commercial links between Saatchi and the Conservative party could "only complicate the task of all concerned." Saatchi was therefore "with the greatest regret" resigning the Tory party account. The agency had worked for the party for a decade, seen Mrs. Thatcher through three election victories, and also "benefited from your revolution in enterprise"—profits had grown from under £2 million to £125 million in those ten years. "Charles and I remain deeply committed to you and your cause and shall remain your most enthusiastic supporters," Maurice concluded.

Mrs. Thatcher sent back a courteous reply. Maurice had addressed his letter to 10 Downing Street, the official residence of the prime minister, rather than to the leader of the Conservative party. But this was party business, not an affair of state, and she observed the correct protocol when she wrote back on Conservative Central Office stationery. She shared Maurice's regret, was grateful for his and Charles's efforts and enthusiasm, which she would never forget, and wished Saatchi & Saatchi "every success in the years ahead."

It was over at last, an association that had had a dramatic impact on the business and personal lives of Charles and Maurice Saatchi and that also had some importance for Thatcher and her party, particularly in the first election campaign. No other account could ever have the same impact on the agency again; and probably no other agency would have such an effect on party politics in Britain.

19
FALL OF THE UNIVERSITY OF ADVERTISING

T he brothers now entered one of the very few times in their careers when they decided that the best thing to do was to consolidate—a word scarcely in their vocabulary until then. From New York came pleas from Milt Gossett and Carl Spielvogel to "do nothing" for a while and let the businesses there sort themselves out in a time of relative tranquility; the Midland Bank and Hill Samuel bids had both astonished and dismayed the Saatchis' followers in the investment community, and in the postcrash atmosphere much reassurance was needed. From now on the bid for Midland would be dismissed as an aberration, almost as something that never happened. "We are not interested in buying an investment bank," Andrew Woods, Saatchi's newly appointed group deputy chairman, told *Management Today* from New York in April 1988, "even though there are investment banking activities, such as human resources, which interest us." Jeremy Sinclair was even more dismissive. The Midland affair, he told the magazine, had been blown out of all proportion: "We were not interested in High Street banking. It was unfortunate that it came out as a major change of strategy." Saatchi & Saatchi, he added, now had no "great aspirations" in financial services.

By that stage, he meant it. The investment community, however, would not forget the Saatchis' attempt to take over Midland so easily. "Their ill-fated and ill-timed announcement of their move into financial services was probably the most glaring example of poor strategy on their part that we've seen," says Charlie Crane of Prudential-Bache. "It must have crossed the minds of so many clients to think: 'Here's this company, which is supposed to be an expert marketer and disseminator of information and presenter of an image, and then they bungle their own PR in this way. How can they do that?' And I think that is a legitimate gripe."

Unlike the advertising world, which thought the Saatchis had gone out of their minds, Crane and other Wall Street analysts could see some sense in the Hill Samuel deal as a business opportunity in its own right. The bid for Midland, however, baffled them, not least because if it had gone through, all the advertising analysts would, in the words of Greg Ostroff of Goldman Sachs, "have turned the stock over to the bank analysts." Saatchi & Saatchi would have ceased to be an advertising company with financial ambitions and become instead a bank with advertising interests. What would the analysts have told the clients they had persuaded to invest in Saatchi in the first place? "I'd have said, 'I don't know what they're trying to prove but it beats the hell out of me,' " says Ostroff. "If you want to own a bank, I would have told them, stock with the shares. If you want to own an advertising agency, I've got a couple of better investments for you. The communications in the company were so convoluted, so directionless, that I had no clue as to what was happening until they finally went for Hill Samuel."

Gradually the analysts resumed some of their old interest in Saatchi, but it would be some time before a bruised Charlie Crane would begin to recommend the shares as a buy again. The analysts' renewed interest in the shares reflected the fact that after the savage fall they represented good value, as opposed to reflecting the old positive view that Saatchi was a good growth company. The stock market glamour had gone and with it the Saatchis' ability to raise money from the stock market. They did not know it yet, but already the brothers had lost their most powerful weapon, the very engine of their expansion. "We pushed our luck very hard for years in the City and Wall Street," said a senior Saatchi executive in the spring of 1988. "Now the luck's turned against us. They don't realize what a good deal Bates *is* for us."

Nor did anyone seem interested in realizing it. On Madison Avenue— or what corresponds to it these days—the Saatchis, megamergers, and British takeovers remained the main topics of conversation whenever advertising people got together. So much had changed in a year, and Saatchi was seen as the catalyst for the changes. The criticism of the price Saatchi & Saatchi had paid for Bates and the argument about advertising people making too much money from the merger boom was further fueled when Saatchi took two-page spreads to advertise its seventeen-year unbroken record of rising profits. This attempt at self-promotion was Charles's idea, and he designed the ad basically to prove that financial success transcended all the nitpicking and petty criticism he felt the firm was being subjected to. The ad misfired badly. Now Saatchi & Saatchi stood accused of making *too* much money—clients' money. Alex Kroll, chairman of Young & Rubicam, commented acidly that "we go to consumers for our capital; our competitors go to Wall Street for theirs," making the point that Y&R, a private company with 900 stockholders, was an advertising business first, a financial group only incidentally.

The controversy surrounding the Saatchis and the megamerger trend continued to nag at Bob Jacoby, who felt that the criticisms were aimed at him personally and that he must have the final word. On January 18, 1988, Jacoby issued a 617-word statement from his Saddle River, New Jersey, house under the headline: "Did I Make Too Much Money?"

Jacoby's press release is a curious document, rambling and bitter, directed more at his former peers in the big agencies than at the Saatchis, whom he now, for want of anyone else, claimed as allies. He accused the rival agency bosses of being "little people" who "relished my bloody firing from Bates." None of them, he said, had contacted him since he had left Bates, although these same people "used to call me for personal favors every day when I was CEO at Bates." The jealousy of these same people when they heard of his $110 million fortune was "disgusting."

There had been much talk, said Jacoby, that the $507.4 million paid by Saatchi for Bates (the Saatchis still publicly insisted that the correct sum was $450 million) "caused a ground swell of indignation on the part of clients and has led to a rush to cut agency compensation." He had stayed clear of the debate, Jacoby continued, because "the ruckus was being raised mostly by self-serving hypocrites at ad agencies." He pointed out that the chief executives who were most vociferous in condemning mergers were those who had bought and sold agencies themselves. *Their* criticisms he would disregard: "But the emotional issue with clients persists. Clients consider their agencies to be servants and have for many years. When your servant gets rich and you don't, the blood boils." He and John Hoyne, he went on, had negotiated with Maurice Saatchi for two years and had convinced him that Ted Bates was worth $507.4 million. "Of course it was worth $507.4 million: a year later JWT was sold for $566 million even though it barely made a profit. This just shows that Hoyne and I are good negotiators and that Maurice Saatchi is smart."

This wasn't what he had said just a few weeks earlier to the *New York Times* when he accused the brothers of being "amateurs." But now Jacoby brought in Maurice in defense of his own argument. Several times in the statement Jacoby came back to the "emotional issue" with clients, which he defined as, "Why should all those agency people get rich, and particularly, why should Jacoby get $110 million?" This had been raised by "some client types" but his answer was very simple: "I must be smarter than they are."

Nor was it clients' money "we were getting." The money paid by the Saatchis belonged to U.K. stockholders. (There were a few American stockholders in there too, but Jacoby ignored them.) "Then our clients said, 'Yes, but they wouldn't have paid all that money if Bates wasn't making a lot of money, and that was our money.' These clients don't understand that the Saatchis didn't care what Bates's profit was. They just wanted to be the biggest agency in the world. We knew that, we capitalized on that, and we made the Bates shareholders—and there were a lot of Bates shareholders—a lot of money."

In the middle of his statement, Jacoby made some good points: "The main issue clients must understand is that agencies must run themselves as businesses. They have obligations to their own shareholders, not just to the client. It amuses me to read that Ogilvy discovered recently that 'profit margins' are important. We at Bates knew that twenty years ago. Agency managers had not been good businessmen, before Bates sold to the Saatchis and woke up every agency president."

Bates was certainly a highly profitable agency, with profit margins around twice the average; that part of Jacoby's statement is certainly right. But had he been responsible for waking up the other presidents by selling out to the Saatchis? Some at least had been awake before, although some were still sleepy. Marion Harper at McCann-Erickson created the first advertising holding company in 1960, and there had been another wave of mergers in the 1970s when the top U.S. agencies sought to maintain their status as the biggest. Maurice had been doing his rounds for most of the 1980s and in the last two years had intensively lobbied just about every advertising house worth the effort. There may have been some who did not get the message before the spring of 1986, but the megamerger phase had made every agency boss the world over think about his organization and position in the industry. The Saatchi-style thoughts on globalization, which came some years after JWT, Interpublic, Ogilvy, and others were already building global networks, were not familiar stuff.

Even after all that, however, there were big New York agencies still available to a hungry predator long after Jacoby had shuffled off the stage. In the summer of 1987 Madison Avenue saw a classic example of Saatchi training and philosophy in action as the greatest name in the business—indeed, one of the great corporate symbols of America—was carried off in one of the most spectacular takeover coups the corporate world has ever seen. Martin Sorrell took over J. Walter Thompson.

The Saatchis watched Sorrell's hostile bid for the company generally regarded as "the university of advertising" with a mixture of emotions. On the one hand, they were proud that a protégé of theirs, even one for whom they no longer had much affection, should attempt such a daring bid. On the other hand, they still had a lingering regret that they themselves had never managed to take over JWT, which had loomed so large in their careers from the beginning and which occupied such a special position in the annals of advertising.

Even in the 1980s, when J. Walter Thompson was no longer what it had been, most children in America, asked to name an advertising agency, could name only J. Walter Thompson. As Maurice had trawled Madison Avenue before doing the Bates deal, the brothers had several times crossed JWT off their lists of takeover prospects only to put it back and think again a few weeks later. Its reputation for looking after clients and producing good ads was as high as any in the industry, but its profits were desperately low. In 1980 J. Walter Thompson had lost its position as the biggest agency in the world to Young & Rubicam, and other agencies, including Saatchi itself, had since galloped past it. It still employed some

10,000 people, but since 1982 revenues from international operations had stuck fast in the $160–170 million range, and JWT's profit margins were only 4 percent, a third of Bates's. In 1985 earnings dropped again, this time from $20.5 million to $18.5 million, and seemed headed even lower. The biggest name in the advertising industry was heading into financial problems; more importantly in terms of the events about to take place, it was also heading into a management battle that would mark the end of JWT as an independent company.

Several times in the early and mid-1980s Maurice Saatchi had spent time with Don Johnston, the chairman both of JWT Group, which he had expanded through acquisitions well beyond advertising, and of J. Walter Thompson Company, the advertising agency. As he did with so many agency chiefs in that period, Maurice went through Saatchi & Saatchi's merger options with Johnston, carefully examining the potential for a deal. Johnston was not interested in selling but heard him out, and each time, Maurice and Charles had been forced to accept that there was no way Saatchi & Saatchi could ever take over the JWT business because of the many conflicts of interest. Procter & Gamble would not stand for a merger (JWT worked for its archrival, Unilever), nor would several of the other leading accounts, and there was no fit with the Saatchi group. Nonetheless, the idea nagged at Charles.

JWT was vulnerable to a takeover bid, that much was clear, but even the Saatchis shied away from a hostile bid. Nevertheless, they watched with fascination as the rumors of trouble inside the JWT Group continued to spread. Johnston was now fifty-nine, approaching the age at which J. Walter Thompson executives were obliged to retire. His career had been as distinguished as might be expected for the head of such an important agency, and he had dutifully served as chairman of the American Association of Advertising Agencies. He now stood as one of the more respected elder statesmen of the industry.

Internally, however, everything was far from well. In mid-1985 Johnston began a complicated series of management changes designed to put in place his own replacement as head of the $3 billion advertising agency but not to disturb his own position as chairman of the parent group. Johnston, in short, had no intention of retiring at the normal retirement age of sixty. He was the first person to occupy the job of chairman of JWT Group, largely because that position had not existed before he had created it. He could therefore set whatever retirement age he wanted.

There were two candidates in particular for the head of the agency: Burt Manning, creative chief and chairman of the U.S. company, then in his mid-fifties; and Wally O'Brien, five years Manning's junior, who was president and chief operating officer of the U.S. company. Manning and O'Brien worked uneasily but well together; *Adweek* made JWT Agency of the Year, and billings and profits both increased. Both men, however, had problems as far as Johnston was concerned. Manning, he felt, although one of the best creative people in the industry, had personality and image trouble—he was said to be "too egotistical" in his dealings with clients. His shaggy beard and disordered clothing were also not appropriate for the senior role, at least in Johnston's eyes. More importantly, Johnston did not see Manning as a great thinker on a global basis. And at fifty-four he was just that crucial few years too old. O'Brien, on the other hand, was a first-class account executive, described by his colleagues as "terribly ambitious," but from Johnston's point of view probably too independent—O'Brien was not the sort of person who would easily accept Johnston's plan to stay on as chairman of the group.

In the summer of 1985 Johnston secretly began to groom a third man for the job as JWT's next agency head. Joe O'Donnell was only forty-three and for the past three years had run the $500-million-a-year Chicago office with considerable success. Without telling either Manning or O'Brien, Johnston offered O'Donnell the job of chief executive and chairman-elect of the whole agency (Johnston, of course, would stay on as chairman of the group), and O'Donnell accepted on the condition that he could make the key decisions as to who would be on his team.

O'Donnell and Johnston began to meet on weekends in Johnston's house in Connecticut, with the older man adopting the role of mentor and teacher. Both men said later that they became close friends. Although O'Donnell remained in Chicago, rumors of his visits east began to circulate, and the speculation began. Soon there were rumors in Chicago that O'Donnell was moving to New York, and although he denied them at first—even jokingly putting a "not for sale" sign outside his house and sending the pictures to the trade press—it soon became obvious that New York was where he was headed.

O'Donnell's ideas for his team soon crystallized. He wanted to keep Manning, whom he respected, in his existing role and promote John E. Peters, president and chief operating officer of the U.S. company. He also envisaged more senior roles for W. Lee Preschel, president of the Latin American and Central Pacific operation, and Jeremy Bullmore, the thoughtful and successful head of the British subsidiary. But in this scheme of things, there was no place for O'Brien; O'Donnell had little time for him or for the expensive system of centralized management for the big multinational accounts such as Kodak, Pepsi, and Kraft that O'Brien was setting up.

Early in 1986 Johnston finally told O'Brien of his decision to install O'Donnell as JWT's next chief executive. Not only would O'Brien not get the position of chairman, but the new appointee wanted him to go—and reluctantly Johnston agreed with this condition. A few days later, O'Brien's resignation was announced. Then on February 19 came the second stage of Johnston's operation: Burt Manning, it was announced, was nominated to the holding-company board. This position was an obvious consolation prize, and in case there was any misunderstanding, Johnston followed up this news with an interview in which he said that Manning would not be getting the chairmanship of the worldwide agency because he was too old—Johnston wanted the new chief executive to be able to commit a good ten years to the job. Manning at the time made the best of the situation, putting out his own supportive statement to the effect that "becoming a director of the JWT Group board will allow me to provide a creative/business perspective that will be useful to all of the JWT Group companies." Six months later, on August 14, 1986, Manning resigned. He had been with JWT for twenty years.

By then O'Donnell was installed as chairman, where he encountered a more fundamental problem. Johnston had never been much interested in the financial side of things. He had averaged one financial officer a year in his six years as chairman of the advertising business and had ignored the growing crescendo of complaint from the financial community. As the Saatchis wooed Wall Street and the investment analysts, Johnston was freezing them out. O'Donnell found waste and extravagance everywhere; a new computer compound in Florida seemed to have no logic to it, and O'Donnell soon reckoned that profits had been overstated in previous years. There had also been acquisitions that defied common sense, notably the purchase of Grey & Company Public Communications, which was merged into Hill & Knowlton.

For the next year O'Donnell had a rough time as JWT lost some key accounts, at least partially as a result of the departures of O'Brien and Manning. In October 1986 Kraft, which had been with J. Walter Thompson for sixty-four years, pulled $75 million of billings out of JWT's Chicago office, in this case because Kraft didn't much care for the man who had succeeded O'Donnell. The Wall Street analysts began to produce some even more gloomy estimate forecasts, now reckoning that JWT would be lucky to make $10.5 million in 1986, down nearly 50 percent on the year.

In January 1987, six months after Saatchi had completed its Bates deal, a bizarre management conflict suddenly put JWT "in play." O'Donnell, no longer enjoying the role of protégé, decided that he had to get rid of Johnston. The catalyst was the date, February 3, 1987, when O'Donnell was due to take his seat on the main JWT board. He was not, he decided, willing to accept "moral and legal responsibility" for the decisions that the board, under Johnston, was making for the company. The board was not a group of people "I desired to serve with," he said afterward. According to financial specialists O'Donnell had consulted, JWT, properly run, could make a good profit. But under its present management it was headed for disaster.

Before facing Johnston, O'Donnell first arranged to meet on an individual basis with five outside directors and a series of key managers. To each of them he made the same case: JWT was being disastrously run, Johnston intended to defy all past precedent by remaining at his post past the age of sixty, and by keeping the position of chairman of the holding-company board he was neutralizing O'Donnell's efforts. Financially the company was headed into crisis, and something had to be done rapidly.

On Tuesday, January 20, O'Donnell faced Johnston to tell him that things had to change "or I can't be party to them." Johnston, he said, had lost the confidence of the executives of the company; he could have a five-year contract, but he must abandon all line management. He could keep his role of senior statesman, but he had to hand over the executive reins. O'Donnell had had the investment company, Claremont Group, prepare a report on JWT, and he passed Johnston a copy. One of the report's key proposals was that the JWT senior staff should take the company private through a management buyout—but only on the basis that O'Donnell was in executive charge.

O'Donnell seemed to assume that Johnston, faced by the damning indictment of his colleagues and the disloyalty of his former protégé, would quietly move aside. O'Donnell misjudged his man badly. Johnston called a board meeting for the following Friday, three days later, where both the Claremont proposal and a letter, signed by O'Donnell and a group of senior executives, making ten "charges" against Johnston, were to be considered. The "charges" mostly related to lack of financial controls and to alleged irregularities in the running of JWT's foreign companies.

The directors listened as O'Donnell made his case. At one stage he referred to Bob Jacoby's "obscene" payment, adding that there were too many sixty-year-old managers leaving the business with large capital sums, not caring what sort of industry they left behind. At the end of his presentation, O'Donnell left and an hour later the news was out: the board of JWT had fired him. His ally Jack Peters was also asked to leave. Johnston, still two months short of his sixtieth birthday, was reappointed chairman and chief executive of J. Walter Thompson, and he was soon giving interviews from O'Donnell's old office saying he was doing his best to "stabilize the company." But the damage had been done; it was only a matter of time before somebody made a bid for JWT.

For a while it looked as if the somebody might be Bob Jacoby and his old Bates team of Hoyne and Nichols. They were rumored to be buying shares. Salomon Brothers, the big Wall Street house, were big buyers. The Saatchis took another longing look to see if there were not some way they could get hold of JWT but wisely decided it was not for them. Venture-capital groups all over Wall Street were approached by long-serving JWT executives with plans for management buyouts.

Martin Sorrell had been watching JWT closely since the previous August when one of his old Wall Street analyst friends, appalled by JWT's poor performance, took him along to meet a former (and discontented) JWT executive. Now, with Johnston in big trouble and rumors of more client defections following the departures of O'Donnell and Jack Peters, Sorrell decided to make his move. He had a vehicle at hand ready for just such a bid. In the spring of 1985, while still working at Saatchi, he had bought a stake in a tiny company called Wire & Plastic Products, or WPP. Based in Kent, WPP made supermarket baskets and was valued at a minuscule £1.4 million; it was no more than a "shell," a company with a stock-market listing into which Sorrell planned to inject other businesses. He then went to Maurice to tell him about his plan to use WPP to acquire J. Walter Thompson, expecting an explosion. Instead, Maurice pulled out a copy of the *Financial Times* and said, "Gosh, we were thinking about doing something similar—taking a stake in a public company and developing it."

Although he did not formally step down as Saatchi & Saatchi's finance director until March 17, 1986, from that moment on Sorrell was disengaging himself from the agency. At first the brothers seemed to accept Sorrell's sideline and even took a stake in WPP, but they gradually realized that there was a conflict and they would not be able to hold Sorrell. "I wanted to do my own thing in my own time," says Sorrell. Emotionally the brothers found it difficult to accept the idea of Sorrell's leaving, but after a year they gave in. "It put them in a little bit of a difficult position," admits Sorrell. "First, the financial director had a stake in another company; and second, there was the question of what the long term was going to be." Sorrell, both sides agreed, would have to leave Saatchi.

Sorrell stayed long enough to ensure that he had a good successor, but relations between him and the brothers were not good at the end. At one stage there had been talk that Sorrell, rather than Bell, was really "the third brother," but his role was never that. Charles and Maurice acknowledge him to be a first-class finance director, and all who worked with him support that view; but they also point out that Sorrell was not quite the innovative and creative corporate genius that he would later be given credit for, at least not at Saatchi. This can probably be put down to the Saatchis' irritation first at losing him and then at his rapid success outside their orbit. Sorrell had contributed a great deal to the success of Saatchi & Saatchi but had also taken something with him: Ken Gill remembers Sorrell watching Maurice and "soaking it all in like a sponge." Sorrell refined and perfected the Saatchi systems for forecasting cash flow, but it was Maurice who originally installed them. (Today they are so sophisticated that on $9 billion of billings in 1987, the projection was less than half a percent off.) Sorrell himself acknowledges how much he learned from Maurice, but he is also very much his own person.

The Saatchis would later argue that their history is to have the right person for each different stage of their agency's development, but that argument implies that the organization outgrew people like Bell and Sorrell. That suggestion is possibly unfair to Bell; it is certainly unfair to Sorrell, who could handle the big capital-raising operations in the City and the analysts on Wall Street probably better than Maurice—and who could also, as he proved over the next few years, handle a world-scale business as well as, if not better than, most, including the Saatchis. The *Wall Street Journal* would later write about the securities analysts "who have been infatuated with Mr. Sorrell," which is not a compliment anyone ever paid the brothers. Sorrell might not have had the charm of Maurice, but he could communicate better than either of the brothers with the financial community, and others would note that after his departure the Saatchi share performance was never the same (although that would probably have been the case with or without Sorrell).

In two years after striking out on his own in 1985 Sorrell made fifteen takeover bids and took the market value of his WPP Group to £134 million, which was still far short of JWT's. The company, he says, although constantly being voted "best agency" by one magazine or another, had always disappointed the Wall Street analysts and disenchanted both them and the institutional investors. In both New York and London JWT was staging a creative revival, but financially its margins were disappearing. Although in London it was back at either number one or number two—depending on which list you believed—if all the Saatchi businesses, including Dorland, were added together, there was no contest: Saatchi & Saatchi was still bigger. In the final quarter of 1986 JWT began losing money, and it opened up 1987 with another loss—and its boardroom row. Johnston foiled the buyout arrangement of O'Donnell, Peters, and half a dozen other executives, but JWT's chances of remaining independent were nonexistent. "Low profit margins and management upheaval put JWT Group in play," said *Advertising Age.*

A week after the annual meeting came the final factor that clinched it for Sorrell: Burger King, one of JWT's biggest and most prestigious accounts, put its account up for review, and it was clear to Sorrell that JWT was going to lose Burger King. From a peak of $40.50 in March 1986, the JWT share price fell to $27. Quietly he began buying a stake and then made his first gentle approach to Johnston. This approach was rudely rebuffed, Johnston sending back a message that he did not even consider it was worth talking about. Soon Sorrell realized that he was going to have to do what Saatchi had never done: make a hostile bid.

By coincidence Sorrell used some of the same financial people who had put together the money for the £2.7 billion bid for Distillers made by his old mentor, James Gulliver: Rupert Faure-Walker and Ian MacIntosh at

Samuel Montagu and the stockbrokers Panmure Gordon. In New York they brought in Bruce Wasserstein and his team at First Boston, then probably the hottest mergers-and-acquisitions team in the business. Sorrell had figured out early on that he couldn't afford to pay the expenses of the bid unless he could make a profit from JWT shares, which he would expect to rise after the bid was announced.

At JWT's annual meeting on May 5, 1987, Johnston told his stockholders that the company was not for sale—nor were any of its subsidiaries. The past year, he admitted, had been a bad time, but "professional strength and resilience are built into the fiber of this company, and they give me the confidence to look forward to a better 1987." He also took the opportunity to get in his own little homily about the megamerger trend. The Thompson company, he said, had no intention of participating "in this mating of giants." It didn't need to—it had grown over the course of 122 years "one account at a time, one office at a time, one country at a time." JWT would not grow by megamerger but intended to keep its identity as "advertising's leading brand with all that means in terms of coherent professional philosophy and a distinct corporate culture."

In truth, at that particular moment it didn't mean very much. Sorrell and his team were now working day and night, rechecking their figures and getting their financing into place. Their bid for J. Walter Thompson would be financed in the special British way the Saatchis had used to pay for Bates: a stock issue, or the offer of new shares to existing WPP shareholders at a discount. The issue would be underwritten by the big London banks, so that, whatever happened, Sorrell would get his cash.

By early June he had just under 5 percent of JWT's shares, and the rumors that somebody was going to bid for JWT were everywhere. On June 8 Johnston called another board meeting and swiftly put through a package of "golden parachutes" for more than twenty executives, giving them 2.9 times their annual salary if they left the company within two years of a change of control. Johnston himself agreed to accept a lesser multiple: he would only get twice his $700,000 salary.

Two days later a letter from Sorrell arrived, offering $45 a share, or $460 million, in cash. Sorrell added that he had engaged Jack Peters, who had worked for J. Walter Thompson for thirty years, "to come back to JWT in a senior management capacity following the consummation of our proposed merger." That news went down very badly indeed in the JWT camp. When Johnston failed to respond, Sorrell launched a full-scale $45-a-share tender offer for the whole of JWT. Adland had just entered its first major hostile takeover bid.

Johnston's defense was feeble. He hired Morgan Stanley, but JWT's poor financial record and Johnston's disdain for Wall Street over the years meant that there was never much of a contest. Sorrell's plans had been well laid, and he kept the initiative. Johnston tried to revive

O'Brien's plan for a management buyout but now found that he could not get the money. JWT simply did not have the credit to finance it. Whichever way the analysts added up the sums, they could not get them to work. Johnston would have had to sell almost all of the subsidiaries, just keeping the J. Walter Thompson agency. But that would still have left JWT with borrowings of $350 million, which would require a cash flow of $60 million to service it—money the company didn't have. There were a couple of weeks of frantic deal making while JWT sought out various "white knights" in a last-minute attempt to get backing to go private: Jacoby was still in the offing and was rumored to be supporting a Lazard Frères consortium that included John Hoyne (who insisted that Jacoby was not involved).

Sorrell was prepared to go as high as $60 a share if he needed to, but in the end a $55.50-a-share offer was enough. Finally, after a series of legal exchanges, Johnston capitulated, and at 9:30 A.M. on June 26 at the offices of Sullivan & Cromwell, JWT's New York law firm, the two sides signed a "definitive agreement." All lawsuits were dropped, and Sorrell agreed not to bring back O'Donnell or Peters to JWT unless the JWT management agreed to their reinstatement. (Peters already was—and still is—a consultant to WPP.) Sorrell had won, and one of the world's largest agencies—it had slipped to seventh in the United States—a name that symbolized the heart of American business to outsiders, had fallen to the British.

Where were the brothers during this time? There were all sorts of suspicions that they stood right behind their old finance director. "Saatchi owns 7 percent of WPP, and some observers believe this investment was designed to keep Mr. Sorrell from doing what he's doing—becoming a competitor in the ad agency arena," wrote *Advertising Age* on June 29. "Other industry observers believe Mr. Sorrell is acting as a 'front man' for the Saatchis." This allegation was nonsense, of course, as soon became apparent when the Saatchis sold their shares in JWT. Sorrell had not needed the brothers; he had accomplished the takeover of J. Walter Thompson on his own.

The brothers would later observe that Sorrell had broken all of the rules they had taught him, rules they had used in their careful move into New York. "Maybe you don't need to woo people for years and sign them up with long-term contracts," Charles remarked wonderingly to Maurice. "Maybe we didn't have to put all the work we did into our U.S. acquisitions. Maybe we should just have done what Martin did." Charles did not mean this literally, of course. The Saatchis have never made a hostile takeover bid. Even if they had to wait several years, pay a higher price, or even lose a good deal, they have always either made an agreement with the management or walked away. The reason is a purely practical one. Advertising is a "people business" where hostile bids are anathema; by getting an agreed deal with Compton and even with Bates, the Saatchis were able to tie up the senior managers on long-term contracts and keep most of the people they wanted. With the takeover of Bates they had been forced to rush and had abandoned one of their cardinal rules—the "earn out" deal whereby the Bates management would only have received a portion of its buyout—and had come to regret it bitterly. Although agreement with the Bates board had not helped much, on the whole the Saatchis had kept most of Bates's senior staff.

Now they watched with keen interest to see how Sorrell would fare. Within weeks their forecasts seemed to be confirmed. JWT lost some of its biggest clients, including Burger King (which would have gone anyway), PepsiCo's Slice brand, and Sears Roebuck's Discover card. Goodyear, the tire company, withdrew its account in disgust at the British takeover—Goodyear had recently fended off a bid from Sir James Goldsmith and had developed a strong attack of xenophobia that Sorrell now caught the brunt of. Ford withdrew its European business, and before the tide turned, JWT had lost $450 million of billings and had gained only $300 million.

The effect on the company, already reeling from the events leading up to the takeover, was dramatic. Losing so many accounts so quickly had caused "a shock wave," said a former employee, Pamela Maythenyi. "It's never good for morale and never good for an agency to have your concentration divided." By the end of the year 200 people at JWT had been laid off, and morale had plummeted. One employee was quoted in the *Wall Street Journal* as saying, "There's a bunker mentality taking hold." WPP's stock fell more than 50 percent in the October crash, dropping the value of the company to £147 million—less than half the $566 million paid for JWT.

Martin Sorrell, however, was far from written off in the Wall Street community, where his reputation still stood him in good stead. "Here is a company," said Greg Ostroff, "which was top of the charts for service and account handling and bottom of the charts for profits. The key question is: can Martin change this entire culture?" The commonly held view seemed to be that he could, and Sorrell was proving it right. He replaced Johnston with Burt Manning, the former chief executive of JWT's U.S. operation, in a move widely hailed as a clever one; he confirmed in their existing roles three other chief executives, Robert Dilenschneider (head of the public-relations division Hill & Knowlton), Dick Lord (head of the specialist agency Lord, Geller, Federico, Einstein), and Frank Stanton (head of the MRB market-research organization). For the rest Sorrell went slowly, carrying out what he called a "mild reorganization," which abolished the old JWT structure under which advertising executives had been imposed on nonadvertising businesses; now both divisions reported directly to WPP.

In March 1988 Sorrell announced profits of £14.1 million, £1 million better than even his analyst fans had expected, and showed that despite the account losses JWT's revenues were up 8.5 percent. "Things have bottomed out and are starting to rebuild," said Emma Hill, an analyst at Wertheim Schroder, who was among Sorrell's leading Wall Street admirers. Within a matter of days, however, the worst problem yet arrived: six top executives of the JWT subsidiary Lord, Geller, Federico, Einstein walked out, complaining that Sorrell, worried by possible conflicts with JWT's Ford account, had stopped them from trying to win business from General Motors. The six men also complained that Sorrell withheld staff bonuses as a means of trying to get them to sign employment contracts. More than forty other Lord, Geller employees joined them in a new agency, Lord Einstein O'Neill & Partners. Lord, Geller, although a small agency, had been important to JWT's image; it was regarded as one of the most creative in the industry, and it nurtured one client in particular: IBM, which accounted for half its revenues. There were strong rumors that IBM would pull out, with devastating results for the JWT subsidiary. "Without IBM, this agency would close," said an account executive gloomily. A few months afterward IBM duly departed, and Lord, Geller's billings plummeted to $35 million.

Lord, Geller had never accounted for more than 5 percent of JWT's earnings, but Sorrell determinedly pursued the executives through the courts. "They're wrong, and there's nothing else we can do but sue," he said, charging the former executives with conspiracy to sabotage the agency. The Lord, Geller affair made the headlines for months, with Sorrell replacing the Saatchis as the most controversial figure on Madison Avenue.

On other fronts, however, Sorrell fared much better. He set out, with Saatchi-style ambition, to make WPP into the world's largest marketing-services company. By the spring of 1989 it was fourth, behind Saatchi (with $11 billion), Interpublic Group, and Omnicon. WPP's profits in 1988 nearly trebled from the $23.7 million total for 1987, and operating margins were over 9 percent, on target for Sorrell's 10 percent by 1990 and vastly improved over the low point of 1986. Sorrell brought in even tighter financial controls at WPP than he had instituted at Saatchi. At the New York headquarters of WPP, for instance, Sorrell closed Johnston's extravagant dining room and leased it to a law firm, thereby cutting $1.7 million from overhead. He sold the Tokyo office to reduce debt, which at the end of 1988 had dropped to below £60 million.

The return of Burt Manning to JWT began to pay off too. In 1988 Manning's creative reputation was at least partly responsible for attracting $500 million of new business, including clients such as Bell Atlantic and Southland, while Ford and Kodak, both existing clients, gave JWT new accounts. In Johnston's last years, JWT had acquired a reputation for being so distracted by its management and financial problems that the agency's creative reputation had begun to suffer. Now clients began to report that they were getting quality service from JWT again.

Even while Sorrell was planning still bigger moves, there were still many unanswered questions, notably about his concept of a marketing-services empire in which the various WPP subsidiaries cross-refer clients. Sorrell introduced financial incentives for WPP managers who referred clients to other parts of the empire, but these incentives had mixed success. "We should recommend the best company for the job, whether or not it's WPP," said one executive, while Sorrell himself admitted that it was not going to be easy.

Sorrell also ran into the worst of the backlash of the anti-Saatchi and anti-megamerger feeling. His bid had been even more of a financial deal than anything the Saatchis had accomplished, although Sorrell soon showed that he was interested not in "stripping" the company but in running it as a profitable and well-balanced agency.

Oddly enough, while the brothers watched every detail of Sorrell's maneuvers with fascination, in Washington their own representative seemed wholly uninterested. The *New York Times* interviewed Victor Millar, head of both the advertising agencies and the management-consultancy division, in the middle of the Lord, Geller dispute and asked him what he thought about it. Millar "said he was unaware of it," the paper reported with some astonishment. Millar, it surmised, was "clearly detached from the world of advertising. In fact his appointment [as head of communications at Saatchi] seemed so incongruous there were rumors that it was temporary."

The Saatchis had high hopes for Millar, detached or not. On him rested their plans for doing to the consulting industry what they had done to advertising. Simonds-Gooding had brought order to the great splurge of takeovers, and by the time the Lord, Geller issue surfaced, Millar could afford to leave the advertising industry to others to worry about.

"Victor Millar has one of the best track records and one of the best strategic brains of anyone in the business-service sector," said Michael Dobbs, acting as Saatchi spokesperson when the *New York Times* rang for a reaction to what it perceived as Millar's *faux pas*. "We already had the best advertising brains."

Born in California in 1935, Millar (pronounced Mill-*arr*) joined Arthur Andersen straight out of graduate school as an accountant. He transferred to the consulting division in San Francisco, then moved rapidly up through the ranks to become senior managing director at the top of Andersen's worldwide consultancy practice, which he helped propel into the position of the world's biggest management consultancy, a business that Maurice Saatchi coveted. In 1983 Millar took charge of all Andersen's practices, including accountancy, audit, and tax, and was second-in-command to its worldwide chief executive, Duane Kullberg. In January 1987 Millar joined Saatchi & Saatchi, where he is said to be paid $1 million a year.

Saatchi had moved seriously into the business of consulting with the takeover of Hay in 1984, but the brothers had not been able to devote much time to it. Millar, based in Washington, was charged with making Saatchi as big in consulting as it was in advertising—a formidable task. In his 1987 chairman's statement Maurice spelled out this goal in greater detail. In Britain between 1980 and 1987, he said, advertising expenditure grew by 126 percent, twice as fast as "real" investment in the economy as a whole. In the same period management-consultancy fees grew by 443 percent. Companies, he argued, were investing in "know-how" at a far faster rate than they were in machinery, buildings, or other tangible assets. This movement toward consultancy was a process that could only speed up; by 1990 Saatchi & Saatchi estimated the total consulting market would be worth $230 billion worldwide, and Saatchi, with its Hay subsidiary, only had a tiny fraction of the market.

Maurice would later talk about his ideal conglomerate as being a combination of Saatchi & Saatchi's advertising skills, the consulting business of McKinsey, the accounting skills of Arthur Andersen, and the financial clout of Goldman Sachs. He could mention those latter names with confidence, because none of those firms was for sale, but it gave a clear enough idea of the size of the mountain still to be climbed. To advance toward the summit, however, the Saatchis needed to be able to raise money for more bids. And after the Bates, Midland, and Thatcher reelection fights Saatchi & Saatchi's stock-market rating did not allow it. "The City and Wall Street are no longer in love with us," said a senior Saatchi executive, "and it may take some time to get that right." In March 1989, when Saatchi & Saatchi announced a fall in profits for the first time in its history, this ambition to create Maurice's ideal conglomerate disappeared completely, perhaps to be revived in the 1990s but not before then.

But for a time the cash flow from the advertising agencies and another—and highly unpopular—stock issue for £176.5 million allowed Millar to begin a series of small- to medium-sized takeovers in the consulting field. In the autumn of 1988 he pulled off perhaps his most interesting deal yet: the backing of a four-person breakaway from Arthur Andersen to form a new company, Information Consulting Group. The London stockbrokers James Capel reckoned that "the move should go some way to allaying fears in the market that Saatchi's development strategy in consulting centers around major acquisitions." But the price of Saatchi's stock continued to fall, and its collapse removed the possibility of a single great stroke in the management-consultancy field.

Ask the brothers whether they regret taking over Bates because of all the fallout, and their reply is an emphatic "no." In terms of total world billings, Young & Rubicam was still ranked as the number one advertising agency in the world, but close behind it were the two Saatchi agencies, Saatchi & Saatchi DFS and Backer Spielvogel Bates. Taken together, the two Saatchi agencies were well ahead of Young & Rubicam.

"If you've got two of the top five agencies in the world you will always do well, just so long as you put some decent people into place and mind the accounts," says a Saatchi executive. "And Charles and Maurice have always been pretty good at finding, motivating, and keeping good people—and at minding the accounts. So really they don't have to concern themselves too much with advertising. That's all in place now and in good shape."

The central parts of the Saatchi empire continued to perform well. In Britain in the spring of 1988 figures published by the *Media Register* for the year ending March 1988 showed that the Charlotte Street–based agency, Saatchi & Saatchi Advertising, still seesawing with JWT for first place in 1987, had moved clearly into top place with the biggest increase in new business ever seen by an agency in Britain. Behind Saatchi & Saatchi Advertising was a new agency created by merging Ted Bates with Dorland, which jumped into second place above JWT. And still a third Saatchi agency, KHBB, boasted third place in the new business league. That was a jubilant moment for the brothers, giving them an unprecedented position in the market that still matters most to them psychologically. By the end of the year the Saatchi & Saatchi agency in London by itself had pulled in nearly three times as much new business as any other agency. The same tables a year later, however, showed JWT once again closing in on the Charlotte Street agency.

But early in 1988 the brothers could boast of something else. As *Campaign* remarked in February 1988, "Saatchi's dominated most awards ceremonies" during the previous year, although neither Collett Dickenson Pearce nor Boase Massimi Pollitt was too far behind. At the 1987 Cannes Festival, the big prize-giving event of the year, Saatchi's international network won more awards than any other agency in the world. In five years, *Campaign* estimated, Saatchi had won 12.6 percent of the principal European awards for creativity, more than any other group. It led the field for two of the five years and was in second place for the other three. The bigger Saatchi & Saatchi got, the harder it worked at keeping its creative image. Jeremy Sinclair, who had been responsible for so much of the good creative material produced by the agency over the years, had now moved into an even more senior role at Regent Street— joint deputy chairman of the group—which the brothers hoped would spread some of the Saatchi culture through the empire and also would help the City image. Behind him Sinclair left a creative department of over 100 strong at Charlotte Street with no less than four creative directors to run it.

To Charles in particular but also to Jeremy Sinclair, new business and awards for creativity had lost none of their importance. In the early days they associated "small" with "good" in the creative sense— and big meant bad. How could Saatchi & Saatchi marry the two as it got larger?

"When we started, the big agencies, the Thompsons and Masiuses, didn't get an award from one end of the year to the other," says a Saatchi employee. "One of the enormous achievements of Saatchi is that the bigger we've got, the more awards we've won. We've defied gravity." Others would say that by single-mindedly chasing awards, of which there are so many in the advertising industry, any agency could do well, and that awards by themselves mean little. But they still meant something to Charles, and if the new business kept coming in at the rate it did through most of 1988, he was happy. In 1989, however, the influx of new business began to slow, and the brothers began to feel a new kind of pain.

20
SWEET ARE THE USES
OF ADVERSITY

At noon on March 21, 1989, Maurice Saatchi rose to address Saatchi & Saatchi's shareholders. It was annual-meeting time, and the large City shareholders and a smattering of private stockholders had gathered to hear what the chairman of Saatchi & Saatchi had to say. Beside him were Jeremy Sinclair and the other main board directors. Charles, as always, was not present. In previous years Maurice had used the occasion to talk about the Saatchi philosophy, convinced that constant reiteration would be effective now, as it had been a decade before, in getting his message across. The previous year he had preached that in the future the big global companies would want *all* their services around the world from the same company: not just advertising, but banking and management help as well. "Thirty great companies now work with us across five or more types of service," Maurice had said, "and a fifth of all new business projects now arise from existing clients of one member of the group beginning to work with another."

On the occasion of this annual meeting, however, Maurice was in no mood to philosophize. He had the worst news he had ever had to deliver: Saatchi profits had faltered. Just weeks before, he had still been able to sound cautiously optimistic in his chairman's statement in the annual report. After all, Saatchi had been through some slow starts to its financial years in the past, and Christmas Eve had more than once been a bad time for the brothers as they added up the figures for the coming year and decided that this would be the one that was at last going to break their record of continuous growth. But this time, for the first time in nineteen years, business had not picked up. Maurice began his speech with a look at the wider picture: uncertain outlook in the United States because of a "wait and see" policy in the Bush administration; the budget deficit and higher interest rates; major clients postponing expenditures, although this was expected to recover later in the year; communications profits "broadly similar" to those of the previous year but problems in consulting. Soon Maurice got to the point: "Total group profits will be below those of last year."

There was a stunned silence in the room. Had people heard him correctly? In the City where analysts were receiving the statement at the same time, there was equal consternation; then Saatchi's share price started to fall. Within an hour it had dropped 60p to £3.20, back to a level it had not seen for five years. The rest of Maurice's statement attempted to explain what was happening, but by then no one was very interested.

The advertising agencies acquired in New York had been through a major period of reorganization and consolidation. Everyone at Saatchi had spent the past two years "engaged in a successful management drive" to mold and streamline the new structure. Seventeen units had been merged into two, which were now the second and third biggest advertising agencies in the world.

The marketing-services activities had been consolidated into "worldwide service lines" under unified brand names, such as Rowland in public relations, Siegel & Gale in design, and Kobs and Draft in direct marketing. But during this period of restructuring, Maurice explained, "we had to give up a large amount of revenue due to conflict." Saatchi & Saatchi had shown its loyalty to its major clients in 1987 "by clearing a large amount of conflict revenue out of the system." That revenue had since been replaced, but the new business had not yet "begun to contribute to profits growth."

Maurice went to some trouble to insist that the advertising businesses had "settled down well" and were in "good shape and in good heart." The era of large-scale acquisition was over, he emphasized. So was the restructuring. Now there was a "new era" when the number one advertising business in the world could "win more and more business from satisfied clients—the qualities that built the business from scratch eighteen years ago."

In effect, he said, there was little wrong with the advertising side of the business—it was just moving a bit slower than expected. But there *was* something wrong in consulting. Maurice chose his words carefully here. He had expected revenues to be sharply up (his own private estimate had been 80 percent), and the company had geared up its costs on that basis. But revenues were only 30 percent higher. The Washington-based Hay consulting business, the cornerstone of the Saatchi move into consulting, had "disappeared." Saatchi now had £250 million of revenues from consulting, but it was proving fairly profitless as costs got out of hand. The Saatchis had never learned how to control consultancy businesses in the way they had learned to control advertising, but Maurice had only come to accept that realization a month before. Now there was a major cost-cutting exercise right across the group. A quarter of the million square feet of office space occupied in New York had been released, Saatchi's separate Manhattan office abandoned, and Andrew Woods and most of the others brought home to London. And there would be disposals of some "noncore" businesses, something totally opposed to the Saatchi philosophy as it had been understood up to that point.

The news was one of the major items in the financial world all week.

The *Wall Street Journal* featured it on the front page under the heading "Fast Global Expansion of Saatchi & Saatchi Now Hobbles Profits," with the subheading "Iraqi Brothers, Boy Wonders of Advertising Business, Face Management Test." Analysts and industry experts were quoted widely, most with a similar message. According to the *New York Times*, "Analysts say the seeds of Saatchi's current troubles were sown at the time of its greatest triumph, in 1986, when the company purchased Ted Bates Worldwide." Scott Black, president of Delphi Management of Boston, which owned 321,000 Saatchi shares, reckoned the brothers "had got too big for their own good. They've lost control." From another analyst, Richard Dale of James Capel in London, came the view that "They've pared costs, merged agencies, reduced the number of employees, but the problem is they have not driven revenue back up. You can't just go in and cut costs."

There were many more comments along the same lines. Emma Hill of Schroder Wertheim, an old Saatchi fan, voiced the disillusionment of the Wall Street community: "There is a real credibility problem here. These figures show that management has no control over the destiny of the company. And it didn't just happen overnight."

It hadn't, of course, happened overnight. But the loss of control had happened fast, and the brothers had only been aware of the full extent of the problem for a matter of weeks. Only four months earlier Maurice had publicly predicted "rapid growth" in the consulting group, which had accounted for 19.7 percent of profits in 1988. Now that division was "significantly underperforming." There had been storm signals that the brothers had failed to acknowledge—and perhaps also a lapse in the famous Saatchi financial controls. Early in March David Newlands, a forty-two-year-old accountant hired to replace Martin Sorrell, departed to join Lord Weinstock's General Electric Company (no relation to the American GE) as finance director. Maurice carefully explained that this event was entirely due to the fact that Newlands, in his capacity as a partner at Touche Ross, one of the Big Eight accounting firms, had audited GEC for years and regarded the number one financial spot as the role he most wanted. When it became available, he seized it. This explanation for Newlands's departure may well have been true, but there was some skepticism around the industry. From New York came word from Carl Spielvogel that he was "surprised" by Newlands's departure, adding that "We had a very good working relationship." Newlands was replaced by Andrew Woods, who was forty-five, but in the City, analysts began to total up the number of finance people who had left Saatchi since Sorrell's departure. They could name at least half a dozen, most of them unimportant but still adding up to what many interpreted as a significant list.

A week after Newlands left, there was another indication that all was not well at Saatchi & Saatchi. Carl Spielvogel was upset and was saying as much in public. Spielvogel and Ed Wax, who were running the two agencies in New York, had been through the trauma of the mergers and the move to new offices. Ed Wax could cheerfully talk of the past eighteen months being "sheer hell," adding "but now we're in pretty good shape." Spielvogel, however, was still touchy about working for anyone else, including the Saatchis, and the brothers had to treat him carefully. On this occasion they failed. Spielvogel had been trying to persuade the brothers to grant stock options to his senior management in the way that the old Ted Bates management had. From Regent Street came the reply that there was "no stock available," and disgruntledly Spielvogel had accepted that answer. Then an early copy of the annual report confirmed that twelve directors of Saatchi's had granted themselves an additional 1.26 million options—and that the brothers themselves had increased their salaries again, this time to $1.1 million a year each.

"I'm trying to protect the interest of our key people," Spielvogel told *Advertising Age* in New York. Receiving stock, he added, was important because "we've thrown in with the worldwide parent company. There is supposed to be synergy, and you get that by everyone working to increase the value of the stock." Later he was even more outspoken to the *Wall Street Journal*: "Stock options were granted to the directors and corporate staff at a time when I have been trying unsuccessfully, for two years, to get stock options for my key operating people."

Spielvogel was the one person in the group whom the brothers could not afford to irritate. His bargaining power was now considerable, because the recovery of Bates and the merger with Backer Spielvogel had been accomplished by him; he was the man with the credibility and the relationship with clients, and the Saatchis could simply not afford to lose him. His "earn out" agreement still had several years to run, so to an extent he was tied in. But the brothers could not risk disillusionment on the part of a man responsible for so much of their business, and Spielvogel was far from happy.

According to *Adweek*, "Since selling his agency in 1986, [Spielvogel] has been dis-Saatchified not only about some pumped-up billing figures his new owners tried to impose on him, but also about having to spin off his AdCom acquisition in Chicago." Spielvogel had spoken out strongly when the brothers decided to sell off AdCom, which had previously been the captive shop of the Quaker Oats account. The brothers had assured Spielvogel that they would help him hang on to the Quaker Oats business, then had suddenly decided that it was in conflict with the General Mills cereal business inherited with Dancer Fitzgerald Sample. Backer Spielvogel had to give up its Quaker Oats account, much to the annoyance of its chairman.

Spielvogel flew to London in late March 1989 to join all the other senior executives of the Saatchi & Saatchi group; the brothers had decided to bring them up to date on the profits news. Maurice briefed them on the position as it now stood. The group had made £138 million the previous year, including about £11 million in exchange gains. Nearly six months into the new financial year, it was not clear that the group's eighteen-year profits growth was over, at least for that year. In the first half of 1989 Saatchi & Saatchi would be lucky to make £20 million, and Maurice's best guess was for a figure below £100 million, possibly closer to £95 million. Spielvogel was suddenly less eager to have stock options.

When the brothers first realized that they were heading for a sharp profits fall, they were, in the words of one close associate, "flat on the floor." This was something far more than one indifferent year in nineteen: 1989 marked a major turning point in the Saatchi & Saatchi success story, and the brothers knew it. With a few accounting tricks, such as showing currency gains above the line, Saatchi & Saatchi had been able to present their figures in the best possible light—and had broadcast them in a two-page advertising spread in newspapers around the world. Now that self-confident gesture was rebounding on the brothers. They had enough enemies in the industry to rub their noses in their miscalculation. Their one consolation in the week leading up to the annual meeting and Maurice's announcement was that the news didn't leak—when it came, it was a surprise to the markets. A leak, on top of everything else, would have been intolerable.

Even senior executives of the group wondered how the brothers would cope with a setback that was easily the most serious in their career. Would they withdraw even more, letting others sort out the situation? Or would they regain their old drive, respond to the biggest challenge they had yet faced by deciding to tackle it with everything they knew? Even if the brothers did become more involved, could they reverse this new downtrend in the company, turn it into no more than a blip that in three or four years' time would be forgotten? Or was Saatchi & Saatchi entering the same type of decline that had destroyed JWT and so many others?

Both brothers were aware that they had been taking life easier than they used to. They had both, in their different ways, been affected by the breakup of their marriages. Maurice, who for years had not taken a holiday, had fallen into the habit of taking longer and longer vacations—and of spending more and more time in his garden. There were those who would later measure the beginning of the fall in Saatchi & Saatchi's share price from the moment Maurice married Josephine Hart. His private life was happier than it had ever been; but it seemed to his own executives and friends to be distracting him from running the company in the way he once had, anticipating trends and trouble before they became apparent to anyone else (such, at least, was the legend inside Saatchi) and somehow producing cost savings and extra profits from areas most of the others did not even understand.

Charles had not remarried, but both he and Doris took their breakup hard. Some of Charles's legendary drive and bounce seemed to have left him. The long period of restructuring had bored him. He was frustrated by the fall in the share price and the constraints it placed upon him. He did not understand the consultancy business in the way he did the advertising industry and had no clear idea how to sort out the management problems Saatchi & Saatchi encountered through that year.

As they read the comments that the "Saatchi magic is gone" or "the game is over," both brothers made a clear decision: they were going to become more involved in the business than they had been in years. They could now see what the *Wall Street Journal* pointed out that week: "Saatchi . . . has a basic problem: Investors simply don't trust the company the way they used to. The importance of that mistrust can't be underestimated; it is largely to blame for Saatchi's poor stock-market performance and many of the difficulties that have followed." The brothers now set out on the long, hard haul to counter the view that Saatchi & Saatchi's best days were behind it and that there was something structurally wrong with the company.

Jerry Della Femina, one of the leading gurus of the advertising industry, was asked that weekend for his views on the profits fall. He replied by sounding a warning that would echo around the industry: "I don't understand why anyone is surprised by what has happened," he said. "It is very clear that you cannot just acquire and never build up those businesses. This is a very serious failure. They [the Saatchis] haven't been able to get any real new big accounts and I don't see how they will."

One could, Della Femina believed, trace Saatchi's problems back to the crash of October 19, 1987. "There simply are no more acquisitions they can make," he went on to say. "They are not able to buy their way into the business in the U.S. any more, and if you look at all the agencies they acquired over here, they are mostly filled with people who were ready to retire and didn't have much interest in building their businesses any more. They don't have a reputation in this country that is good enough for them to win any big accounts. The coverage that they have had over this [profits] problem is not going to help them either. They were on the front page of the *Wall Street Journal* on Thursday and you can bet that every CEO in America read that and will see Saatchi & Saatchi as a sick agency. *They're* not going to give them any new business."

The brothers could counter much of Della Femina's prediction by pointing out that they had already bought all the agencies they wanted, that there were plenty of younger people coming along to replace the retiring ones, and that they *were* winning new accounts. But even if they could pick the holes in Della Femina's analysis, the brothers still had to deal with the message. "Sick" agency? No one had ever said that before about Saatchi & Saatchi. Reputation not good enough to win new accounts? The Saatchis' reputation had always been their biggest selling point. These were serious matters indeed.

Over the next few weeks the brothers and their inner team did some hard thinking. If they were going to fight back, they needed a clear strategy. Overall, despite what Della Femina and others might say, they concluded that the advertising and communications part of the business was, as Maurice had said, in "good shape." True, it was worrisome that so many of their big clients had postponed campaigns when others, like Philip H. Geier, Jr., chairman and chief executive of the Interpublic Group of Companies, could say, "We do not see in our agencies a switch in budgets from the first half [of the year] to the second." But even in their more pessimistic projections, profits from Saatchi & Saatchi's communications side in 1989 seemed to be running level with those of the previous year.

Maurice in his analysis for his senior executives pointed out that economic growth in all the Western countries had approximately halved in 1989—and advertising revenue growth had slowed even more. Yet Saatchi was still geared up to recent levels of growth. For years Saatchi & Saatchi had outperformed the industry but in the past two had come through a huge restructuring process that would have set back any company. It was a time, he emphasized, of "unprecedented upheaval." But Saatchi had now achieved the optimum shape: two global networks that ranked number two and three in the world. In 1987 there had been twenty-four profit centers. Now there were five, "all truly global in the way they are run." The pain of the past few years—and both brothers that week talked a lot about "pain"—had been justified by what had emerged. If Saatchi had not gone global, had not taken over agencies in New York, Maurice concluded, "then I would be most uncomfortable about the future of this company." With Europe heading toward its Big Bang of 1992, Saatchi was ideally placed with the first and second agencies—and that placement was beginning to pay off. Earlier that same week Johnson & Johnson had awarded Saatchi & Saatchi the campaign to relaunch its OB tampon across Europe—the biggest pan-European account yet won. Roy Warman and Terry Bannister had now assumed Simonds-Gooding's old role and were getting hold of the communications business worldwide.

Saatchi & Saatchi was still the largest and most profitable advertising business in the world, with the highest margins—its 12 to 13 percent, Maurice pointed out, looked very good when other agencies were struggling for 10 percent. Furthermore, globalization and cross-fertilization were working at a faster and faster rate. Sixty-five percent of new clients were interested in three or more Saatchi services. Two years before, fifty clients had used three or more of Saatchi & Saatchi services; now the figure was 276. Saatchi & Saatchi had launched the new Zenith media-buying operation, whereby in Britain all the agencies in the group pooled their buying of media space under a single roof—and that too was working. The problem lay in management consulting. Maurice openly confessed that he had not been able to install in that division the same type of financial controls as he had in the advertising agencies. He had, he admitted, expected consulting profits to double in 1989, but costs had risen abruptly, and revenues were disappointing.

The task was to generate the same margins from consulting as the group did from advertising—or get out. But retreat would mark the end of his "supermarket" dream, and his intention, avowed Maurice, was to succeed in consulting. "We have to make ourselves certain we can manage the margins," he declared. "I'm convinced we can."

All that week Maurice tried to hammer home one key message: this setback could be the best thing that had ever happened to the brothers and to the company. They had had it too easy for too long, and they needed this jolt of adversity. "Adversity" became another favorite word, which by the end of the week allowed Maurice "to see good in every-thing." The brothers felt better for it, he insisted. They *were* better for it. The company would be better for it too. They were being forged in "fire and pain," and they would emerge stronger. They were *grateful* for the experience.

Events that week had a particular poignancy for Martin Sorrell. His shares were now handsomely outperforming Saatchi's as the view spread that he was the one who had got it right and that it was his departure from Saatchi & Saatchi that had started the slide. Sorrell refused to join in the general savaging of his old firm that week. He had recently announced that WPP's profits had gone up from £14 million to £40.3 million and that its shares had risen from 305p postcrash to 686p. From this comfortable cushion Sorrell could allow himself a degree of magnanimity. He felt that the Saatchi setback was no more than a "temporary blip." Charles and Maurice "have built a vast organization and a good structure in a relatively short space of time," Sorrell said. They would, he forecast, soon be back on course.

Earlier that spring Sorrell had been busy on another front. He was now planning a move that in a single bound would take him within spitting distance of the Saatchis, turn Madison Avenue on its head once more, and reopen all the savage antimerger phobia that had gripped the industry three years before. He was stalking no less a company than

Ogilvy Group, parent of the Ogilvy & Mather agency and the business founded by the great David Ogilvy himself. Having toppled one of the great pillars of American advertising, Sorrell was now after another.

Sorrell's tactics were the by now well-rehearsed ones he had used for J. Walter Thompson; he used the same team, the same financing techniques, and the same approach to the company. Sorrell's bid for JWT had broken new ground as the first hostile takeover the advertising industry had known. Now he was preparing to go hostile again, although as with JWT he would first try the friendly route.

In 1989 Ogilvy Group was one of the last refuges of the old-style advertisers, one of the few groups that had stood aside from the merger frenzy of 1986. Its chairman, Kenneth Roman, talked proudly about its being the "length and breadth of one man." David Ogilvy's picture hung in the firm's reception area alongside a poster that read: "How to run an advertising agency, by David Ogilvy." Ogilvy himself, now seventy-seven, had retired fourteen years earlier and lived in a twelfth-century château south of Paris, but he was in regular touch. "He still peppers us with memos and inquiries. His spirit is felt all over the place," remarked one Ogilvy Group executive. Ogilvy still regarded it as *his* firm, and he was determined to keep it independent.

Sorrell met Kenneth Roman in the middle of 1988 to discuss a possible media-buying joint venture of the type that was suddenly becoming popular in the industry, but nothing came of this discussion. They continued in desultory contact until February 1989, when Sorrell invited the Ogilvy chief to lunch in New York. He had a proposal to make: why didn't the two companies merge? They were both about the same size, there would not be too much conflict of accounts (although there would be some), and the two agencies together could quickly outdistance the newly sluggish Saatchi. Roman was not as enthusiastic as Sorrell, however. There was no deal.

Then in April, Roman, in London for a few days, received a telephone call from Sorrell. He would like to pursue the merger idea. Roman again repeated that he wanted to keep Ogilvy independent and that a merger with WPP had no attractions. By now rumors that Sorrell was interested had got around the market and the Ogilvy shares had started to rise, but it seemed unlikely Sorrell would make such a huge move so soon after his JWT takeover. In the City, however, Sorrell had already laid his plans and had his cash organized.

At the end of April, the WPP chief decided to do what he had done with J. Walter Thompson—make a formal offer. He wrote to Roman, offering to buy the entire Ogilvy Group for $45 a share, valuing the company at $720 million—$150 million more than he paid for JWT and $200 million more than the Saatchis had paid for Bates. Sorrell still intended it as a friendly bid, arguing that WPP and Ogilvy shared a common philosophy and approach to the advertising business, stressing the development of nonmedia areas such as consulting, direct marketing, and public relations. The two companies fit well internationally too, he argued.

Roman, who had worked for Ogilvy most of his career, reacted fiercely. To Sorrell's consternation he chose to go public over the weekend of May 1, releasing both Sorrell's letter, which Roman described as a "sales pitch," and his own scathing reply. "My conversations with you over the past several months have been the direct result of your persistence and not my interest in your grand scheme," he wrote to Sorrell. "I have repeatedly and consistently said to you, it has been the Ogilvy board's policy to maintain Ogilvy as an independent company." There was more along the same lines, but Roman was polite in comparison to his old boss. From France David Ogilvy lashed out savagely. "It took me 40 years to build this damn thing up. I *got* my clients but this little jerk *buys* them." Over the next few days the invective continued to flow from France. By Tuesday, Sorrell was a "megalomaniac" and even worse. "God, the idea of being taken over by that odious little jerk really gives me the creeps," Ogilvy spat. "He's never written an advertisement in his life."

Roman and Ogilvy, however, had made a critical mistake. By going public they had put Ogilvy Group in play, and as the share price roared from $32 up to $49, Wall Street's short-term speculators, known as arbitrageuers or "arbs," clambered aboard. More than half the shares moved from longer-term investors into the hands of the arbs in just forty-eight hours. Now even if Sorrell didn't accomplish the takeover Ogilvy's chances of remaining independent had declined sharply. It was just a question of who could offer the highest price.

A few days later Sorrell raised his offer to $50 a share. Quietly, he opened up negotiations with individual members of the board, but by now he was dealing with another problem: the storm of personal abuse his offer had attracted. The other agency chiefs were now all too keenly aware that if the bid succeeded, four of the world's six biggest agencies would be British-owned, two each by Saatchi and by WPP, who would be almost neck and neck with worldwide billings of $11 billion—nearly twice the next biggest, Interpublic, with Omnicon trailing a poor fourth. The great names, and the power, of the industry would indeed pass from New York to London. As the *Wall Street Journal* remarked of Sorrell: "He, along with two fellow Britons named Saatchi, is hammering the final nail in the coffin of the country-clubbing, martini-drinking Man in the Grey Flannel Suit."

The same article, headed "Agency Ogre," called Sorrell "the most hated man on Madison Avenue." Polished ad executives, it said, "quaked when he called." All of them "dread Mr. Sorrell because he is almost singlehandedly changing the ad business" with his hostile bids, the battles he had fought with the Lord, Geller defectors, and his ability to pick off the most august names in the industry. Phil Geier of Interpublic almost spat the worst insults he could think of: Sorrell was a "predator" and a "manipulator," commonplace words on Wall Street, but anathema here in the less commercial world of Madison Avenue.

But it was all to no avail. Sorrell had one final trick up his sleeve that clinched the deal for him: he offered David Ogilvy the role of non-executive chairman of the WPP group that would own both JWT and Ogilvy—and with some misgivings, Ogilvy flew to New York and accepted. The board soon followed.

Sorrell's WPP group and Saatchi between them now owned four of the six biggest advertising agencies in the world. They were almost the same size in revenue terms, well ahead of Interpublic and Omnicon. The difference between the two British rivals is that, at this time of writing, Sorrell's fortunes are rising, while Saatchi's are in decline.

21
FROM MINIMAL TO MAJOR

M any of the residents in London NW8, near Regent's Park, are quite unaware of the extraordinary art gallery hidden in their midst behind a row of shops on Boundary Road. Even those who live on the street may have passed the anonymous gray steel door a thousand times without noticing it; the sole hint of what lies inside is the button and the tiny sign beside it, readable only from a few feet away: "Saatchi Collection." Behind the door is a newly surfaced asphalt yard, leading to a building that from the outside still resembles what it once was: a motor-repair shop, later converted into a paint-distribution depot. Once inside the building, the impression is stunning.

Here is one of the biggest private galleries of its kind—30,000 square feet of exhibition space, three times as big as the Whitechapel in London's East End and ten times the size of the Serpentine. The reception area, once a loading dock, is seventy feet long and leads into five other large exhibition spaces—huge, roomy, and starkly bare areas, purpose-designed to display the owners' taste in art.

Charles and Doris bought the building in the early 1980s and commissioned the architect Max Gordon to convert it into what one critic called "the handsomest of London's new galleries." The renovation was an expensive operation. Within the old factory Gordon fitted a new skin of white plaster walls to form a background for artworks that would overpower many galleries. The original sawtooth factory roof and exposed steelwork were left as they were, and the floors are clean, simple, and bare. The whole space is cleverly lit by reflected light from fluorescent tubes carried by hidden metal trays in the roof structure, giving the feeling of perpetual sunlight. The effect is of great, bright, uncluttered, almost cavernous space, ideally suited for the works the gallery houses.

Big as the gallery is, at any given time only a fraction of the more than 800 pieces in the Saatchi collection can be shown there. The other works are held in storage, adorn the walls of Charles's and Doris's (now separate) houses or the offices of the brothers, or are on loan for other shows. They are exhibited on Boundary Road on a rotational basis with no fixed pattern: Charles may decide it is time for a change, and out go the Schnabels and Kiefers and in come the Warhols and Serras. In the spring of 1988, for instance, the Saatchi collection show was called "NY Art Now" and featured the work of a new school of art that Charles and

Doris were buying keenly and that had suddenly become fashionable: New York East Village art, particularly that of Jeff Koons, a sculptor then given to putting vacuum cleaners in Plexiglas cases; it included outsize sinks, one of them partially buried in earth, by Robert Gober; huge oil and wax canvases by Ross Bleckner; and moving-light structures by Jonathan Kessler. The catalog to the show acknowledged that the art, although of recent vintage, had already "elicited numerous cries of 'Fraud!' and 'Foul play!' from within the New York and international art communities." In fact, it went on, all of the works in the exhibit had been "dismissed as cynical, derivative, repetitive, market-oriented, superficial, antihumanist, cold, obvious, overhyped, and/or a case of the emperor's new clothes." On the other hand, the "NY Art Now" show had "held up, for the world to see, something which the world would prefer to see concealed (or suppressed) indefinitely."

In other words, Charles Saatchi had, in the art world as in the advertising world, exposed a nerve. In March 1988, when Maurice (on his own) made the cover of *Newsweek*, the magazine included a section on the art collection that began:

> A visitor to the Saatchi Collection could be forgiven these days for thinking he has taken a wrong turn and walked into a somewhat quirky appliance store. There . . . is a display case containing two shiny new vacuum cleaners. Let's be clear about this. We're not talking about paintings or sculptures of vacuum cleaners but the real thing: honest-to-goodness Hoovers, straight out of the box, lovingly arranged by Jeff Koons.

Koons, a great favorite with Charles and Doris, dominated the show. One of Koons's pieces, a blow-up toy rabbit cast in stainless steel and reflecting the other works, was even more striking than the Hoovers. So perhaps was a series of basketballs in various stages of suspension in glass tanks. The experts were divided in their opinions of the exhibit's worth. One London art critic dismissed Koons and the other East Village artists as "designed to appeal to the dealers, who know that the Saatchis and the followers of the Saatchis are likely to plump for the latest, the quickest, the most fun; in their parlance, the 'sexiest' works marketable." *Newsweek* found that such criticism was exacerbated "by the fact that Charles has been no more willing to talk to journalists about his burgeoning art collection than he is about his advertising business."

In fact Charles does not talk to many people, journalists or not, about his collection. This is the private collection that he and Doris have put together, essentially for their own enjoyment; they love others to see it but not when they're around. Some of their pleasure in it seems to disappear when they are asked to explain it. Charles is an intuitive art collector who does not much enjoy the intellectualizing that so many in the art community feel obliged to employ. That is not to say that he cannot—or does not—talk about it in private. When he wants, Charles can be a forceful, witty, and eloquent conversationalist. The one recorded occasion when he did talk to a journalist about his collection was in May 1985 when he agreed to discuss it (over the phone and on the strict basis that he was not to be directly quoted) with Don Hawthorne of *ArtNews*. Hawthorne reported that as soon as the conversation turned to art, Charles became "animated, sometimes passionate. Contemporary art could find no more sincere endorsement than Saatchi's boundless enthusiasm."

The gallery itself is an extension of the Saatchi collection, the anonymous industrial building almost a modern sculpture in its own right. Here Charles and Doris can come whenever they wish (except for the two days a week when it is open to the public, a time they avoid) and see their artworks displayed as they should be: the huge, empty plywood boxes of Donald Judd, so large (one is twelve feet high and eighty feet long) that a wall had to be knocked down to get them in; the firebricks of Carl André that once caused a sensation in the Tate Gallery in London; or the immense steel plates of Richard Serra, which dwarf the person standing beneath them.

Although the Saatchis share their collection with the public, that was not Charles and Doris's intention when they began. They set off to buy works that pleased them and soon discovered they had a collection too important to be kept just for themselves. Like other collectors before them, Doris and Charles found that no art can be "owned" by any individual but has a life of its own. Every week the gallery gets requests from all over the world, but particularly from the United States, to borrow works for exhibitions. Without some of the Saatchi pieces it is difficult to assemble a genuinely representative exhibition of contemporary art anywhere in the world. "The Saatchi gallery is now a stopping point," says Marina Vaizey, art critic of the *Sunday Times*. "I get a lot of telephone calls from abroad, from Americans, from Europeans, saying: 'Where is the Saatchi collection? When is it open?' It's considered the showplace for art made in the last fifteen years, because it's exclusively devoted to that, unlike museums which have a mixed, historical collection." The London magazine *Modern Painters* took a different view, arguing that the Saatchi collection exemplified "a tacky preference for the novel and the fashionable" and that a recent exhibition, of the painter Ron Kitaj, "clearly demonstrated American art, today, is aesthetically bankrupt."

From his earliest days Charles has been a collector. His elder brother David was surprised to discover that instead of throwing away his Superman comics Charles was saving them—and building a collection.

Soon it seemed that all the other children were collecting Superman comics too; they were not necessarily influenced by Charles—old Superman comics had suddenly become a vogue. Charles just seemed to be the first.

Later Charles took to collecting jukeboxes; he introduced one into his father's house when he was still a teenager, and soon the whole house seemed to be filled with them. Six months later, recalls David, it became a "terrific craze" to collect jukeboxes. Others who grew up with Charles also remember his finely tuned antenna for picking up new fashions before they were even recognized as such. Charles did not consciously spot new trends from reading magazines or watching television, although he did a great deal of both; he just seemed in tune with changes going on in his generation. He did it to please himself, and more often than not what pleased him one day would please others months later. The appealing subject could be pop music or films or even clothes: his family was appalled when he first sported jeans in the late 1950s, but within a year or two jeans were being worn by everyone, even middle-aged men.

There are people like Charles in every field—market or commodity traders who see a price trend emerging before anyone else does, more by "nose" or feel than by anything more tangible; fashion designers, architects, artists, writers. All of us know someone who has this ability to predict trends. David Saatchi is positive about his brother's almost extrasensory ability throughout his life to anticipate emerging trends and fashions and "to live his life three months ahead of the present time." David, a successful commodity trader himself, feels Charles would have excelled in any occupation. His father must have had some of the same instinct too, anticipating the Iraqi diaspora as he did before almost all his generation. Maurice has it in a business sense, with his proven record of being able to see and exploit major commercial trends—going for a high rating on the stock market, for international agencies, globalization, consultancy, and so on, the key decisions that singled out Saatchi & Saatchi from other agencies.

Charles combines his ability with an interest in collecting that goes far beyond the norm. He continued to collect Superman comics well past the time he could have been interested in reading them. In the early 1970s, when Charles was in his mid-twenties, Ron Collins recalls going into his room in Golden Square one lunchtime to show him some artwork. Charles was on the phone, so Collins waited outside; but in that tiny office he could overhear Charles's conversation. Collins had never heard of anyone collecting Superman comics, so it took him some time to work out what it was about. Charles was bargaining with a dealer: "No, I've got that one; how much are you asking for the train one? Thirty bob? Too much—make it a pound. . . ."

When he had finished and realized Collins had overheard him, Charles was unembarrassed, complaining about the way prices of Superman comics were rising. But Charles was not collecting comics to make a profit—it was the collecting that interested him.

From his teenage years on Charles collected cars too—an enthusiasm he shared with Maurice. At times the basement garage of Saatchi & Saatchi's Charlotte Street office would be half-filled with the brothers' machines. When Jaguar announced it was closing down the E-type production line, Charles bought one of the last three E-type cars produced, which he still drives. Maurice bought an old AC Cobra and had its aluminum body restored by one of the two living panel beaters in Britain with the skill to do it. Maurice drove the Cobra sparingly, taking it for a ritual spin on Sunday mornings. He once told me how, as he was approaching his home, he met a post office van in a narrow lane. Maurice arrived at his garage with a nasty dent. He was so upset that he wept.

Maurice, however, never had the true collector's mania that Charles has—nor, as time went on and more and more of the running of Saatchi & Saatchi's business fell to him, the time to indulge that mania. The art collection was something the brothers would not share. Maurice shows little interest in it, saying deprecatingly, "You can call me Phil E. Stein" when asked about modern art. This declaration was never entirely true, and Maurice was appreciative enough to decorate his own office with art—and enjoy it; and, as we have already seen, he was a keen theater-goer from his late teens. But the art collection is something Charles shared only with Doris, who is as avid a collector as he is. Doris too has always been a collector. For years before she married Charles she had specialized in what is called "whitework," white embroidered tablecloths, nightgowns, and so on, a kind of specialist, almost minimal area of textiles in its own right. She showed her collection of whitework in a tiny gallery in Regent's Park, but, like Charles's comics, this collection was primarily for her own pleasure.

Together Doris and Charles have built a collection of modern art that is regarded today as perhaps the most important of its kind in the world in private hands. Charles at peak times has probably spent a third of his time (including weekends and evenings) and most of his money on it.

Charles Saatchi first discovered modern art when Doris took him to Paris for a weekend in the late 1960s. Doris, who often went to exhibitions, caught sight of a poster for an exhibition of photorealists. "We walked into this gallery, and I think it took us a while to realize you could just acquire something off the wall," Doris recalls. "It was just amazing to us that we had enough money to actually buy something."

There was no blinding flash that converted Charles to a love of modern American art. But the Saatchi collection began that day in Paris when Charles and Doris suddenly realized they could actually afford to buy it. "At the time it seemed like some wonderful adventure we were sailing off on together," says Doris. They quickly concluded that they could not afford to buy the established artists. "The only way we're going to be able to afford to buy art and enjoy it as well is to buy the work of our contemporaries," Doris argued. They would concentrate particularly on the American Minimalists, ignored at the time by all but a few European collectors. "What used to give us a real thrill time and again was to walk into a gallery or an auction house like Sotheby's and circle the room and come back again agreed on the same painting as what we wanted. And that happened a lot."

In 1969 Doris and Charles bought their first work by Sol LeWitt, a New York Minimalist who came to the fore with his wall-drawing ideas: literally, sets of written instructions capable of being executed by anyone who had a wall big enough. For instance, there are pieces by LeWitt in the Saatchi collection that consist of no more than the following: "Within 6 in. (15.2 cm) squares, draw straight lines from edge to edge, using yellow, red and blue pencils. Each square should contain at least one line. Graphite and coloured pencils."

LeWitt sculptures are modular structures or incomplete open cubes constructed in stove enamel on aluminum. Many sneer, but for devotees of Minimalist art LeWitt is one of the movement's great figures. "Le-Witt's understanding of art as activity, as an unreasonable course of action pursued reasonably, is the very soul, as opposed to the theory, of mainstream Minimalism," says Peter Schjeldahl in his introduction to the first exhibition of the Saatchi collection, "Art of Our Time." LeWitt would become one of the central artists in the Saatchi collection, which now contains twenty-one examples of his work.

In 1969 Charles was a casual collector, with no particular knowledge of the Minimalist movement then beginning to take root in New York with Andy Warhol, Frank Stella, and Carl André, who by the mid-1960s was exhibiting his neat rows of bricks. Warhol was already expensive, but most Minimalist art could be bought cheaply, and Charles began acquiring at a few thousand dollars a time some of the best and most characteristic works of the period. At this stage he had no interest in British or European art—all the work he acquired was American photorealist or Minimalist art. Nor was Charles interested in drawings, although Doris tried to convince him that drawings could be instructive of how an artist worked and what he or she was aiming at.

In London Charles had a friend named Alain Merten who ran not only a clothing store in the King's Road but also a print gallery, and Charles would often drop in to see what was happening in Merten's gallery. But it was his discovery of the Lisson Gallery in Marylebone that was to have the greatest influence on Charles. From the late 1960s, the Lisson specialized in American Minimalist art even before it had been discovered by many galleries in New York. Charles bought many of his early paintings and sculptures there very cheaply and developed a relationship with the gallery that still lasts. Like everything else he did, Charles was single-minded about assembling his art collection from the beginning; having discovered American Minimalist art, he bought only that. There was some photorealist art in his early collection too, such as Malcolm Morley's wonderfully detailed paintings of ships (Morley is an English painter who now lives in America and paints in an entirely different style), but Charles regarded photorealism as just another form of Minimalist art. It was at the Lisson that he bought his first Carl Andrés and LeWitts for tiny fractions of their contemporary values.

In New York, then setting the pace for the rest of the world in contemporary art, the late sixties was a time when new vogues came and went rapidly—"pattern" paintings, for instance—which Charles dabbled in briefly and then got out of. On the whole he avoided most of the short-lived trends, keeping to what he regarded as mainstream contemporary art. He had his own definite and distinct taste and interest, which by the mid-1970s, long before he had emerged from the closed circle of the London advertising world, had already made Charles Saatchi well known among the galleries and studios of New York's SoHo where all the main galleries then were. (The East Village galleries did not emerge until 1983.) Charles's interest broadened to include examples of American figurative art (Susan Rothenburg and Eric Fischl in particular). There would be mistakes and wrong turns along the way, and Charles could lose interest in an artist as quickly as he had gained it; what he regards as his mistakes do not feature in the Saatchi collection today. (Most of those "mistakes" have probably been sold to make way for other work.) Doris sometimes accused him of "playing safe," of sometimes buying art that was no more than refined graphic design—"refined to cocktail conversation." But overall his eye was a remarkably certain one, and works Charles bought then for a few thousand dollars are now seen as classic examples of the period, worth a hundred times what he paid for them.

After Saatchi & Saatchi became a public company in 1975, Charles had both more money and more time to spare for what had now become a passion. He and Doris bought many works by Julian Schnabel, the man regarded by some art critics as among the best living artists in the world today (and by others, such as the critic Robert Hughes, as "talentless, cackhanded . . . [whose] development has been smothered by his own self-esteem") before Schnabel even exhibited in a proper gallery in New York. Charles and Doris were now regular visitors to New York, visiting the artists in their studios and often buying directly from them rather than through galleries. They were frequently accompanied by Michael Green, head of Carlton Communications and probably one of Charles's closest friends, and Green's wife Janet, the daughter of Lord Wolfson, one of Britain's wealthiest men. Janet Green became almost as passionate about contemporary art as Charles, and her collection is second only to his in Britain. Michael Green recalls Charles dragging them all off to an attic somewhere and glowing with excitement when he found something that caught his eye. Sometimes the object of Charles's enthusiasm would just be an old art magazine that he hadn't seen before in which he might find an early article on LeWitt or Warhol; sometimes it was a new artist or one he had passed over the first time around.

The gallery owners in New York soon learned to respect this young Londoner and his American wife when they appeared at previews. Charles and Doris read everything written on the contemporary art scene, becoming deeply interested in every detail about the artists they followed even if they were not represented in the Saatchi collection. Career updates, photographs of new work, catalogs, and insider's information about art available on the market were collected assiduously by Charles and Doris. New York gallery owner Leo Castelli, at whose gallery the Saatchis have bought many works, says that before Charles ever appeared in Castelli's gallery "he knew exactly what he wanted. You may think he comes in, looks around, decides to buy something. It's not that way at all. He reads the magazines, he goes to exhibitions, he comes in interested in certain pieces. Being a collector like that is a full-time business." Others independently bear out Castelli's assessment. Janelle Reiring of Metro Pictures says that the Saatchis "are incredibly well informed on the artists they deal with. They're able to spot things fast, make quick decisions, and go for the best pieces."

The curator of the Saatchi collection, Julia Ernst, was working for the Sperone Westwater Gallery in New York when she first came across Charles and Doris. "One thing I noticed from day one," Ernst says, "was that they had a very specific, discriminating taste, a specific sense of connoisseurship."

Those who know the Saatchi collection well and have followed its creation over the past fifteen years divide it into separate collecting periods. The first was Charles's discovery of Minimalism, which ran from roughly 1970 to 1976. "That was what he and Doris were most effective in, and that was what they were known for," says a friend. "At the time nobody in America was buying Minimal art, and there were two very big collectors in Europe—and the Saatchis. The Germans all fell in love with pop art, but for some reason the Americans just ignored it, and it is an extraordinary fact that the great collections on American pop art ended up in Europe."

From 1976 to 1980, as they grew richer and more confident, Charles and Doris bought more adventurously, still keeping to American art but now shopping directly among the generation of young New York artists who were emerging at the time, seldom paying more than a few thousand dollars even for Schnabels (which may be worth $150,000 each today) and buying them in large numbers. That was the Saatchi collection's second phase.

In 1981 the Saatchis began to buy a number of works by artists they had previously ignored, particularly European ones. Nick Serota, the director of the Tate Gallery, and Norman Rosenthal, exhibitions director of the Royal Academy (both close Saatchi collection followers), dated this change to an exhibition they were involved in called "The New Spirit of Painting," which was put on at the Royal Academy in London in January 1981. The Saatchis lent several works to the exhibition and took a keen interest in it, but Charles was not impressed with some of the paintings Rosenthal and Serota had chosen. "I remember him being extremely critical of an Anselm Kiefer [a major German artist]," says Serota. "It was in part an unfamiliarity with the work."

Doris, however, loved Kiefer. She wrote a review of the show for the *Royal Academy Year Book* and singled out Kiefer as one of the most exciting painters exhibited. Under Doris's influence, Charles changed his mind six months later. He not only began buying Kiefer, but visitors to his house were astonished to find a huge, gloomy Kiefer landscape hanging above his bed.

"After that show he changed course and began to go for a different type of collection in which he decided if an artist was worth representing he was worth representing in depth," says Serota of Charles's change of heart. "And he began a very determined pursuit of major works by those emerging artists." Serota is not strictly correct here; to a large extent, that had already happened. The Saatchi collection of Minimal art had already been formed before the Royal Academy show, with ten, twelve, or fifteen works by most of the big-name artists. The Saatchis had decided that the way they wanted to collect was to buy certain artists in depth. But Serota is absolutely correct when he identifies that show as a watershed for the Saatchis. "Until that show, they were very blinkered in what they were doing," says one of the Saatchis' art friends. "They were only looking at New York Minimal art, and then these other people emerged who they thought had found a way out of Minimal art but were still very influenced by it, and they began buying them. Then this new show arrived on the scene, and they began to look at art that was being done in Europe and Britain for the first time."

In the mid-1970s Doris and Charles had bought artists such as Jennifer Bartlett (who did the tiles in the Saatchis' St. John's Wood house), Elisabeth Murray, Joel Shapiro, Neil Jenney, and, in the late 1970s, David Salle—all of them American artists who were emerging from the age of Minimalism and beginning to paint again. Minimal art, of course, tends to be just that: blank sculptures or blank paintings in which not very much activity is visible. "In the late 1970s there was a cry around that painting was dead and that contemporary artists had painted themselves into a corner, and no one could find anywhere else to go, because Minimal art had closed all the doors," says the Saatchis' art friend. "The rather avant-garde view was that it had all been done and said, and that Minimal art was the final step with all painting. I suppose that sort of sentiment happens every so often, but it was very strong at that time. And then this group of people suddenly emerged in the mid-1970s who found that there were things they could do with paint, and then there was a gigantic explosion of paint, signaled by that Royal Academy show, which had a tremendous worldwide influence. It was a show that proved that artists were painting again. And it opened a lot of people's eyes to work that was being done all over Europe."

It certainly opened Charles Saatchi's eyes. Says Rosenthal: "That was the time of the real explosion of his potential, and he began to become more significant, and the art market began to boom. In the seventies the art market of the Minimalists was rather esoteric and quiet. When suddenly grand painting seemed to begin again internationally, particularly in Germany, Italy, and America, then prices started booming and the market took off. Charles Saatchi emerged as one of the leading collectors."

In her review of the Royal Academy exhibition Doris identified three artists as particularly impressive: two British figure painters, Frank Auerbach and Lucien Freud—and one German, Kiefer. Freud was already a big name and was in any case a decade or two ahead of the others. But Charles did begin buying works by both Auerbach and Kiefer. He bought other European artists too for the first time: Georg Baselitz (known as "Mr. Upside-Down" because many of his paintings are done that way), Sigmar Polke, and Francesco Clemente (two Germans and an Italian) in particular. Within a few years Charles had a serious group of work by the European school—twenty-four Clementes and twenty-three Kiefers, for example. He was also buying British artists at the same time, and not just the new and emerging artists: besides Auerbach, he bought works by Leon Kossoff and Victor Willing, both veteran painters, and Howard Hodgkin, a British painter who had been very influenced by his early visits to the Museum of Modern Art in New York. The Lisson Gallery was still important to Charles, and it was there that he spotted three new sculptors: Richard Deacon, Tony Cragg, and Bill Woodrow.

Friends at this stage found Charles excited and passionate about his art. The discovery of the European and British artists, both old and young, had been a revelation for him. But he could barely contain himself when he came across another new movement emerging in New York at the same time, a movement that would attract a variety of labels: Neo-Geo, Neo-Futurism, Neo-Conceptualism, Smart Art, or New Abstraction. This group of artists emerged in the East Village in the early 1980s in a range of new galleries that Charles and Doris now began to haunt. "He became terribly involved in these Neo-Geo people in the East Village," says the Saatchis' art friend. As with the Minimalists a decade earlier, no one wanted the Neo-Geos, and the Saatchis bought in bulk, paying very little for them. It was some of these artists, including Jeff Koons, who made up the show in the Saatchi gallery in the winter of 1988.

By now the Saatchi & Saatchi stock was booming, dividends were flowing, and Charles's earnings were rising. He could afford to buy both the Europeans and the East Village artists—and what he had missed out on earlier. He began to fill in some of the gaps in the collection. He bought his first Warhols in 1982, largely because he saw Warhol as the progenitor of many other artists in the collection.

By the mid-1980s Charles and Doris Saatchi were spending at least $1 million a year on new works, much to the puzzlement of outside observers. Where did they get that sort of money? In 1984 Charles's dividends were about £400,000 before taxes—and unless he had a very clever tax scheme (which he probably had), he would have had to pay 60 percent tax on that amount. His salary was £225,000, again before taxes. The company would provide his cars and other expenses, but even so there was a large gap between Charles's aftertax income and the money he was spending on art.

All the works shown in the Saatchi gallery are part of the Saatchi collection; when works are lent out, they are accompanied by a discreet little card that reads: "From the Saatchi collection." But not all of the items in the Saatchi collection are owned by Charles and Doris—Saatchi & Saatchi also owns some (not many). Before Saatchi & Saatchi reversed into Garland-Compton and became a public company, some—possibly all—of the art collection was owned by a subsidiary of Saatchi & Saatchi called Brogan Developers, based in the Isle of Man for tax reasons. Charles bought out Brogan Developers. The accounts of Saatchi & Saatchi PLC contain an item under "fixed assets" called "Furniture, equipment, and works of art" (amended in the latest accounts to "Other, including works of art") valued at £13 million. Furniture and fittings are depreciated in the accounts—works of art are not, although it is unclear if they are revalued. This confirms that some company money has been used to buy art, which is neither unusual nor indeed a bad investment— the sixth floor of the Lower Regent Street building is full of contemporary work, much of it worth many times what was paid for it. And in New York the landlord of the new Saatchi & Saatchi headquarters on Hudson Street in Lower Manhattan proposed giving the mezzanine floor over as an art gallery specifically to house art owned by the company, thereby improving the prestige of the building.

But the bulk of the Saatchi collection belongs to Doris and Charles, with perhaps a fifth of it owned by the company. Yet the question of how Charles pays for his art is one constantly debated in the art world.

It is actually less of a mystery than it seems. For a start, most of the works in the Saatchi collection were bought at remarkably low prices; some of them have been sold later and the money used to finance new purchases. Charles hates selling, but he will do so—and has done so— when an artist does not fit the collection any more or if he feels the money can be better used elsewhere. His lifestyle is far from lavish; other than his art, he has no expensive hobbies, and most of his money for the past fifteen years has gone into art.

Refurbishing the art gallery and buying the flurry of Warhols and other established artists, however, needed other financing. Charles found it from an obvious source: the stock market. It had been used to finance Saatchi & Saatchi's expansion; now it was used to finance Charles's art collection. In 1981 he and Maurice each sold several million pounds' worth of Saatchi & Saatchi shares (they bought nearly £5 million again in 1987 when the stock price fell), a move that went largely unnoticed because there was a split, and the accounts published at the end of the year showed the brothers owning more shares than at the start.

Apart from the art itself, which is controversial enough, the Saatchis' reticence and unwillingness to explain has led to distrust and misunderstanding of Charles's motives. The explanation for his collecting mania, commented one critic, "is a powerful desire on the Saatchis' part to be important on the art scene and known as such." Art, he added, conferred status, power, "even intimations of immortality" on the collector.

There are many who dislike the new policy of buying up large numbers of pieces by a single artist. There are more trenchant criticisms that the Saatchis lend and exhibit basically to hype the values of the works they already own, an argument that came to a head at the Tate Gallery in 1982. It was then that Charles, keen to promote the cause of contemporary art, agreed to join Patrons of New Art, a group of rich and influential people who would, in the words of the exhibition catalog, "enable the Gallery to show and collect very contemporary art." The first show the group organized in 1982 included eleven Schnabel paintings, nine of them from the Saatchi collection. The next exhibition contained six works by Jennifer Bartlett, one of them lent by the Saatchis. Charles at the same time had also become involved with the new publicly funded Whitechapel Gallery, which he lent a number of paintings; one exhibition, Clemente's *Stations of the Cross*, included twelve Saatchi-owned works.

The visibility of these works obviously increased interest in these particular artists—a fact that was frequently commented on in art circles in London at that time. The Saatchis were so big and so influential that merely by adding an artist to their collection the value of all the artist's work went up. "What collectors like the Saatchis do has a tremendous influence on what other people do, and also the market," said Leo Castelli. The disquiet over their role increased with the second Thatcher victory in 1983—Thatcher was hated by much of the art establishment in Britain, which on the whole prefers its support to be state-directed. When it was also discovered that Saatchi & Saatchi had the advertising account for the Tate and a number of other art institutions, the critics' anger boiled over.

It erupted in a curious way. Initially Charles got on well with Alan Bowness, the Tate director, and offered to help him when a Schnabel show was first proposed. He had, Charles explained, fifteen Schnabels then in the Saatchi collection, which he was already lending to museums all over the world. "The Tate can have access to any of this work," he told Bowness. "Any time you want to borrow anything, your curators can just crawl all over it and borrow whatever they want for any shows they want."

According to his friends, it never occurred to Charles that this gesture would be misinterpreted in the way it eventually was. "He just thought that the artists would be very happy to be shown, and that he could help the Tate show the highlights of what was happening around the world," one friend says, "but he was a bit naive not to recognize the jealousies that exist in the art world. It never occurred to him that there was going to be a lot of resentment at this young thirty-year-old American [Schnabel] coming along and getting a Tate show when there are plenty of young struggling British artists who couldn't."

The Tate made no real attempt to explain why it was showing Schnabel, or more specifically, why most of the works had come from the Saatchi collection. Soon Bowness was being accused of giving in to the powerful Charles Saatchi, who was using the Tate for the purpose of hyping his own favorite artist, thereby increasing the value of his collection, which, it was hinted, he would then begin selling at inflated prices. "The Tate did an enormous disservice to Doris and Charles Saatchi," says Marina Vaizey. "They got a lot of personal abuse for lending their Schnabels and their Bartletts and then having these little notices saying that these works had been lent by the Saatchi collection. People attacked the Tate for validating the Saatchi collection by showing their work, and they attacked the Saatchis for using the Tate to give the museum's blessing to their collection. That was terribly unfair, because it was a public-relations failure on the part of the Tate as much as anything else. If the Tate had made a big fanfare of it and said, 'We have one of the greatest collections of contemporary art and amazingly enough it happens to live in London, and we are going to show some of this work to a wider public,' then there would never have been that negative publicity which caused Charles Saatchi to withdraw from active participation in the Patrons of New Art and as a potential major supporter and sponsor of the Tate."

Others agree with Vaizey's conclusion. "The Tate just bunged up the Schnabels and let all the little bitternesses that were being muttered build up into a real political storm," says the Saatchis' art friend. "And Charles thought that he wasn't going to put the artists through that sort of mess again. . . . In any event he and Doris had decided it would be nice if they could find their own place to show their collection."

There was another and more public Tate incident, which curiously irritated Charles and Doris far less than the acrimonious publicity over the Schnabels. The German artist Hans Haacke likes to expose what he calls the unethical and morally dubious involvements of art-world figures and institutions. Nonetheless, in early 1984 when the Tate offered him an exhibition, Haacke jumped at the opportunity. "For an artist like me," he said, "who has a somewhat tenuous relationship with Establishment institutions like the Tate Gallery, it is almost a question of survival, in terms of principle, to stay aloof, to not embrace the institution just because it gives you a show."

Haacke deliberately set out to expose what he felt was the Tate's weakest point: the influence of Charles Saatchi and, through him, of Thatcher and the Conservative party.

Haacke's show included a work called *Taking Stock*, which was an attack on the Saatchis, on their advertising empire, and on Mrs. Thatcher. It was a picture of the prime minister painted in mock Victorian style; behind her Haacke painted bookshelves whose volumes contained on their spines the names of major Saatchi clients: from Allied Lyons to Wrangler jeans, passing in alphabetical order through the Conservative party, the National Gallery, the National Portrait Gallery, and the South Africa Nationalist Party. The painting even showed a paper on the desk with details of Brogan Developers, the company that once held the Saatchi collections, and figures from the Saatchi & Saatchi PLC accounts relating to the valuation of the artwork. On the top shelf of the bookcase were two cracked plates, a reference to some of Schnabel's broken-plate paintings exhibited a few years before, containing pictures of Charles and Maurice Saatchi and their initials.

The painting epitomized, in Haacke's own words, the painter's view that in Charles the Tory party had "gained a powerful foothold inside the hallowed halls of the Tate." The same painting was later shown at the new Museum of Contemporary Art in New York in 1987, with accompanying text by Haacke, which read: "In July 1982, Julian Schnabel, who is known for his paintings incorporating broken plates, had an exhibit at the Tate Gallery. Nine of the 11 paintings in the show were owned by Doris and Charles Saatchi. It was the first exhibition the museum organized in collaboration with the Patrons of New Art of the Tate

Gallery, a group that had been established the same year. Charles Saatchi was a driving force behind its establishment and an influential member of its steering committee." Haacke then went on to make the same point about the Jennifer Bartlett show and related it to a very contemporary New York theme: insider trading. Charles, accused Haacke, had bought Clementes and Morleys in bulk just before an exhibition of their work at the Whitechapel Gallery in February 1984. He was, Haacke said, a member of the board at the Whitechapel at that time: "It is suspected that he profited from insider information about the gallery's exhibition plans, which allowed him to buy works at a favorable moment."

Haacke's Tate painting created a minor sensation, as he hoped it would. His research had been meticulous, but he had overlooked several key points: the first is that Charles had never spoken to Mrs. Thatcher in his life and had no desire or intention of carrying her influence into any hallowed halls other than Downing Street. More fundamentally, Haacke's text misrepresented Charles's whole approach to the art world. He had no more intention of engaging in the politics of the Tate or any other art gallery than he had of involving himself with the internal workings of the Conservative party. To do so would be completely against his nature.

Charles and Doris were philosophical about the Haacke critique; they had been warned in advance and were also familiar with Haacke's regular attacks on sponsors and the business establishment. However, the row that followed over the Schnabels finished Charles's relationship with the Tate—though that may change again now that Nick Serota has arrived there. Charles opened his own gallery, where he could display his work in the way he wanted to: people who wanted to see it did so on his terms. "All the great British collectors of this century have received similar treatment to the Saatchis," says Norman Rosenthal of the Royal Academy. "They all ended up not leaving their collections to the Tate. We're about to do the same for Mr. Saatchi. They've alienated him, and in twenty or thirty years time there'll be great regret."

There was another reason for opening their own gallery: by 1985 the Saatchi collection was attracting worldwide interest, and Doris found herself giving tours through her house. "We felt we owed it to the artists to let people see the paintings, but we had strangers continually walking through our bedroom, and I began to have a feeling of deep embarrassment," says Doris. When the gallery opened, the collection contained eleven Donald Judds, twenty-one LeWitts, twenty-three Kiefers, twenty-four Clementes, twenty-seven Schnabels, seventeen Warhols, and many others—an extraordinary range of contemporary art by any standards. "The Saatchi collection is one of the most complete and impressive records of the art activity of the past 20 years in private hands, or, for that matter, in any hands," commented the magazine *Art News*. Norman Rosenthal echoes that assessment: "The Saatchis are probably the most important living collectors of modern art anywhere in the world." The critic David Sylvester says the Saatchi collection is only comparable in British collections with that of Ted Powers, who collected Impressionists in the 1950s: "the Saatchis and Powers are easily the two most distinguished collectors of modern art that have been produced in Britain this century."

The New York dealer Leo Castelli reckons the Saatchis are unique among collectors; there are few "precedents," he says. Count Giuseppe Panza di Buomo, an Italian collector, worked in a similar way; and there is Dr. Peter Ludwig, a German chocolate manufacturer far richer than Charles Saatchi, who is seen as his only other rival anywhere in the world. Ludwig probably has a larger collection, but it is different from the Saatchis'. The Saatchis follow individual artists in depth, while Ludwig collects eclectically. According to Castelli, Ludwig "has a little bit of everything. He is, you know, omnivorous."

There are plenty of people who see obvious links between Charles's drive to run the biggest advertising agency in the world and his desire to collect art. In both cases, they say, it is his "Napoleonic drive," the need to be bigger and better than anyone else at whatever he does. There may be something to that theory; but the Saatchi collection—any decent collection—is a far more complex affair than simply buying up everything produced by a couple of dozen modern artists. "Charles is mad about art—absolutely crazy about it," says Rosenthal. "Obviously, he doesn't discover things completely by himself by seeing thousands and thousands of studios, but he knows how to find good things, and he works hard at it. He's a very good collector of modern art. It's very easy to collect Old Masters and antique furniture if you've the money, much more difficult to collect contemporary art."

During 1987 there was another concern voiced about the Saatchi collection: the marriage of Doris and Charles had finally broken down, and they had decided to live their own separate lives. They moved from the chapel into their own individual houses in the West End, Doris into a little mews behind Park Lane and Charles just around the corner. So who owned what in the collection? It will not be split; that much seems certain. Both of them agreed that whatever happened neither wanted the collection broken up or "diminished in any way"; it had a life of its own. Doris, however, has become less involved with it; at one stage she and Charles talked about her becoming the curator of the new museum in New York, but that never happened. She still calls Charles when she has spotted a new artist or a work she thinks the collection should have, and Charles responds. But as time goes on, the collection is likely to become more and more that of Charles Saatchi rather than that of Charles and Doris. Whether that will make it better or worse, only time will tell.

22
"THE MOST IMPORTANT COMPANY"

W hen I first told Maurice Saatchi I was planning this book, he was appalled. Apart from the desire to protect his and his brother's privacy, he had a basic objection. Books are written about people at the end of their careers, not at the beginning, Maurice argued; the brothers were just entering their forties. "Give us another few years at least. We haven't *done* anything yet." From anyone else that statement would seem excessive modesty, but Maurice meant it. At that point the brothers had not taken over any big American agencies other than Compton, and Saatchi & Saatchi was still some way from being the world's largest advertising business. Even so, the brothers' achievements were considerable. Maurice seemed to be measuring their performance against plans—and performance was at that stage some way behind.

As events turned out, this book took more than three years to write, during which time Saatchi & Saatchi bought Bates, moved into consultancy, had its battle with Bell, and gave up the Tory party account. Maurice's objections to my writing this book, however, have not changed. The book, he still insists, would be better written ten or preferably twenty years hence when he and Charles have achieved what they have in mind, when they are nearer to the end of their corporate lives than to the beginning. When he came upon me in the Saatchi building interviewing one of his staff, Maurice threw up his hands in mock horror: surely I must be bored by now. After I had returned from interviewing in New York, Charles asked me how the book was going. I replied that I was finding it "very interesting." He appeared startled. What could I find that was "interesting"? Had I unearthed something he did not know about? He went away shaking his head.

Maurice gave me many hours of interviews and also arranged for me to see anyone in his organization I wanted. The only restriction he imposed was that I would not quote either him or any Saatchi staff member directly—the same rule the brothers have always applied to journalists. I have tried to observe that rule, and this explains why at various times I have felt obliged to attribute a quote to "a senior Saatchi executive" or "one of the Saatchi team." I recorded all my interviews and have worked from transcripts of them.

In the weeks leading up to the publication of the first edition of this book in Britain in the autumn of 1988, I learned that the brothers were far from pleased with what they had heard about it. They had never talked to me about their Iraqi background and were disturbed at its public airing. They also hated the thought of the Bell battle becoming as public as this book would inevitably make it. Nor were they entirely pleased with the way they themselves might emerge. After reading an early manuscript I sent to him for his comments, Charles remarked to a colleague that one of the central characters in this book is so horrible "I wouldn't want to be in the same room as him."

Before I began this book I knew Maurice reasonably well, Charles barely at all. As I got into the research, I found the reverse was true: the character and personality of Charles appeared more and more clearly from the interviews I did and the material I collected. Maurice, on the other hand, became more shadowy, a person more complex and more important to the story than I had initially imagined. Like most observers I had half-believed the myths: of the brilliantly creative but semireclusive Charles, whose gargantuan ambitions were interpreted to the world by his brother Maurice, who was the clever technocrat. It was never quite like that.

In many ways Maurice is more important than Charles. The cool and self-disciplined young man who joined Lindsay Masters and Michael Heseltine in 1967 has matured into one of the major figures in the British corporate world today. Yet he is so reticent, so disdainful of anything that even borders on boastfulness, that even those who have grown up with the business see Charles as the key brother.

The reality, as both brothers confirm, is that from the beginning Maurice was just as ambitious as Charles, just as determined that whatever he did he was going to be the best at it. It did not have to be advertising. From his earliest days in school, right through the London School of Economics and then during his tenure as personal assistant to Masters and Heseltine, Maurice has always done exceptionally well. He has the ability to analyze the most complicated of problems, reduce it to a simple form, find a solution to it, then apply that solution. He learned some of his techniques from watching Professor Cohen at LSE, but he picked up much more afterward.

From Masters he learned the systems that made Haymarket, then a small concern, into one of the publishing successes of the past twenty years; from Heseltine he picked up the shotgun approach both to take-overs and to getting new business; from Procter & Gamble he learned proper business systems; today he soaks up the experience and ideas of running a global company from Victor Millar. Maurice never stops learning.

That is not to say there are no gaps in their talents—there are. And they are huge ones. Maurice learned to use the investment community cleverly, persuading it that advertising companies deserved a decent investment rating and that Saatchi & Saatchi stock should sell at a premium. But when the market turned against both the company and the industry, Maurice floundered. Saatchi pulled up the whole sector and then dragged it down again, with Maurice trying first another blitz on the analysts and financial press, then a period of aloofness, then another period of wooing. None of it worked, and Saatchi's engine of progress slowed to a crawl. In January 1989 the London *Times* remarked: "The Saatchi brothers have put themselves on probation, to see if a period of hard work and no playing with major acquisitions will put the share price back into line with those who make their money by simple toil." It marked about the fourth or fifth different and conflicting strategy since Saatchi & Saatchi's share price began to collapse—and was dramatically overtaken in March 1989 when Maurice was forced to reveal that profits for the year would be dramatically lower.

Until this latter period, both brothers had always taken great pleasure in seeing theory worked out in their sixth-floor offices become reality; but the rigorous intellectual process of producing a workable doctrine and then executing it always fell largely to Maurice. Charles acknowledges this—and is keenly aware that his own special skills, creative copywriting and an extraordinary eye for anticipating trends—are not so valuable at higher levels of management. As Saatchi's share price has fallen even lower, Charles's frustration has mounted. But other than taking his frustration out on Maurice, he can offer no contribution. Years of abstinence from the financial community make it impossible for Charles to involve himself directly now, even if he knew how.

There is a danger that one may underestimate Charles too. His contribution in the Golden Square days and up to the time of the takeover of Compton in New York is obvious enough. If one takes away the "guru" element, Charles's value to a worldwide group that is only partly an advertising business becomes less clear; yet all who work in the higher reaches of Saatchi today regard Charles's importance as considerable. Maurice, for all his growing self-confidence and public persona, has never made a major move without the agreement and support of his brother—and would not dream of doing so now. The same, of course, is as true of the disastrous moves, such as the bid for Midland Bank, as it is of the good ones.

The brothers may argue, but in the end they agree; on the whole, they have respect for each other's judgment, and when events turn against them, as happened after the Bates takeover and even more so in the spring of 1989, they also have the strength of each other's support. Charles has lost none of his ability to drive those around him, nor has he moderated his demands for *more* and *better*, and Maurice responds to these demands, as everyone else does. Relations with the financial community may be Maurice's area of responsibility, but that is so only because Charles refused to have anything to do with financial matters. He may vent his frustrations on his younger brother and on Jeremy Sinclair, who is assigned to improve the corporate image, but this frustration is as much with his own inability to find a solution to the problems the company has suddenly found itself in as it is with what he regards as the blindness of the City and Wall Street.

In many ways Charles is an enigma. It would be a mistake to believe that because of his dismal academic record he is any less bright than Maurice. Tim Bell, no fool himself, talks about the "mind games" that Charles plays. Others tell of meetings with Charles when he needs no more than minutes to understand the most complicated problems. His taste in art is not universally shared, but his love of contemporary art is deep and long-lasting, not just a passing worship of whatever is fashionable. His friends are successful, self-made men in business, the arts, and entertainment; he became a friend of David Puttnam when they were both unknown copywriters at Collett Dickenson Pearce and now almost daily the two share their thoughts on the battles of Hollywood and Madison Avenue.

Charles's friends from the world of business are men like Michael Green, who in a few short years has built Carlton Communications into a bigger company than Saatchi & Saatchi, and Gerald Ratner, who says that Charles had a huge impact on him as he developed his jewelry-retailing business into the biggest in the world.

In the arts Charles's relationships are with leading figures such as Nick Serota, the new director of the Tate, Norman Rosenthal of the Royal Academy, and a few gallery owners in London and New York—as well as a small selection of the artists themselves. He does not discuss art at quite their level, but they respect his knowledge and his "eye." Charles's response to art is more intuitive than academic, not dissimilar to his approach to advertising.

How does one equate all this with his miserable time at school? There are those who see in Charles the classic signs, better recognized today than they were thirty years ago, of a specific learning difficulty that marks a person whose formal written and examination work falls well short of his obvious mental ability. The short attention span, the over-powering impatience and frustration, the quick bursts of anger, the unwillingness to read long reports or sit through long meetings, combined with an outstanding visual ability—all these might well be interpreted today as a form of dyslexia. Thirty years ago, no one in Britain knew much about that disorder (the United States was—and is—miles ahead in understanding dyslexia), and there are many successful people in public life today who only recognize their own symptoms when they are diagnosed in their children. Charles would probably be appalled at the suggestion that he ever had any such difficulty. How could he become the best copywriter of his generation if he had suffered some form of learning disability? Any remedial teacher, however, could give him the answer to that.

Maurice has less of his brother's pent-up energy; his great virtue is an extraordinary degree of self-discipline, remarked on by all who know him. He has a clinical, academic approach to problem-solving, best demonstrated by his achievement in improving the stock rating of Saatchi when the brothers decided they needed to use the City to finance the agency's expansion. Problem: Saatchi needed money to expand by acquisition. Difficulty: investors despise the advertising industry and rate it so low that the stock market is a prohibitively expensive source of new capital. Solution: change investors' views of the advertising industry. Action: public-relations blitz on City and financial press, getting across the message that the advertising industry is historically stable, is fast-growing, and contains bright and financially astute young people. Result: Saatchi shares rise one-hundredfold, there are multimillion-pound placings of new shares, and companies are bought all around the world. Advertising becomes a respectable sector for the City and Wall Street (at least for a time), and dozens of other advertising groups go public too.

In the election campaign of 1979 it was Maurice, rather than any of the whiz kids in the Tory party, who first put down on paper precisely what Thatcherism stood for. His disciplined approach to problem solving extends even into his gardening: before the first shovel was put into the ground of his present home, Maurice had read dozens of books on roses and carefully worked out where each variety and each color would go. As he had with the growth of the company, he took as much pleasure in seeing his ideas translated into reality as he took in the roses themselves. For Maurice gardening is not the physical therapy it is for the amateur; it is not his style to come home from the office, put on his gardening clothes, and get out the spade. Other people do that work under his direction. His pleasure is in the planning and design—and in seeing it work. Josephine teases him about being a "checkbook" gardener, but he is more of an executive garden organizer than a green-thumb gardener.

Maurice also relies on another strength: his charm. Charles, who can turn on his own charm when he wants to, acknowledges without jealousy that Maurice has a better way with people than he does. Anthony Simonds-Gooding, who had been sitting comfortably in the role of chief executive of Whitbread, remarks wonderingly that he gave up this pleasant and secure position to move to Saatchi when "the most charming man in the world called Maurice Saatchi climbed in my window with a rose between his teeth." Talented people joined Saatchi as much because of Maurice's sales job on them as they did because of Charles's creative reputation.

Both brothers had a natural instinct for surrounding themselves with good people. Jeremy Sinclair wandered in off the street with a portfolio typed on a sheet of paper and one ad that Charles liked; Sinclair was given a test, then a job. The brothers chose Tim Bell, with his remarkable range of talents, and Martin Sorrell; they chose John Hegarty, now established in his own right as one of the most respected agency heads in Britain, and they found Collins, Warman, Bannister, Muirhead, and many others. As Maurice would say, the brothers have always tried to put together the best management and creative talent they could find: "To do that you have to have the resources to get them, motivate them, and incentivize them in order to get them to do their best work." The brothers in the early days did not have the resources, at least as measured in money terms, but they still managed to motivate; money alone would never have produced the devotion that Bell in particular gave them. Today the brothers have all the resources they need—and ironically they find it more difficult to motivate, except perhaps in their Charlotte Street agency, which still remains the core of the company and is watched over personally by Charles.

Over and above these attributes, probably the most potent force in the Saatchis' drive to the top was their clear single-mindedness. Their ambition has always been of a different order than that of anyone else in the advertising industry. Ogilvy tried his hand at half a dozen different jobs before he strayed into advertising; the great figures of Bates and Bernbach never had the same early devotion to the business that Charles had—nor the management skills of Maurice.

Where did these business instincts come from? I have argued to them that they probably have in their genes generations of the bazaar, of Middle Eastern traders who almost invented the world of commerce thousands of years ago. The brothers don't like to be reminded of Baghdad—it is something they left behind as infants and they claim no inheritance from it. If they ever had any of the insecurity of the immigrant, no one, not even their wives, ever glimpsed it; yet they are inheritors of a culture that may have given them an advantage over the less highly motivated society into which they settled.

If Nathan Saatchi had moved to New York rather than London, Charles and Maurice would probably still have done well. But there would have been many like them, from similar backgrounds and with the same underlying need to succeed. From that base, they would never have built the biggest advertising business in the world. In Britain they stood out, newcomers in a mature society. And by the time they entered the world of Madison Avenue, it too was a mature and stagnant business, ready for the immigrant predator bred on a different culture and armed with London stock-market money denied to New York agencies. In many ways Madison Avenue in the early 1980s was a microcosm of Britain in the 1950s and 1960s: well-established, self-satisfied, and in decline. It was as ripe for reorganization and megamergers as rust-belt America had been five years earlier. The only surprise is that Madison Avenue waited around for a couple of young Brits to effect those changes.

There is also the fact that the two brothers, middle brothers at that, are so close that they operate almost as a single person. David is eight years older than Charles, Maurice eight years older than Philip, so in effect the three years that separate Maurice and Charles—they were both born in June, both Geminis—make them the closest. Neither can ever remember disagreeing about a major decision, at least for more than a week. Again, their background may partly explain this: family in Baghdad tended to mean something more than it does to most modern-day European families. Philip, launching himself in the world of pop music, refused to accept the help of his elder brothers but was greatly touched by their interest: "They have both been incredibly supportive, but we live separate lives; we are separate people linked by blood and bound by unconditional love," he says. As Tim Bell found, blood and unconditional love between Charles and Maurice left no room for him.

The original *Sunday Times* ad of 1970 made the point that there was a number of small bright agencies, and there were big firms that were a bit dull; wouldn't it be nice, the brothers thought, if we could combine the two? That objective has never changed. The challenge for them has been to create what would inevitably become a large company but would also remain dynamic. They both become agitated at the suggestion that they keep a tight control on everything in the organization, insisting that the reverse is true. Maurice's "tight-loose" principle best describes the Saatchis' system of control: with a tight financial structure but with considerable creative autonomy for the subsidiaries. Even in Golden Square, where Charles was writing the advertisements and Maurice telephoned potential clients and made presentations, they were consciously planning how they would "work ourselves out of a job." But in the spring of 1989 they suddenly became aware that they might have overdone it—and started to work themselves back in again.

From the beginning, say the Saatchis, they saw the company "as an institution" from which they could stand back rather than as a personal operation. Others will find that concept strange, since their name is above the door and it is their absolute insistence that no other name join it. Their line of reasoning on this matter also strikes one as a neat way of reconciling their working lives with their preferred work style. Because they get bored so easily, they insist on keeping themselves stimulated. And that is only accomplished by fresh challenges: creative, financial, or intellectual. It is torture for them to stand still and do nothing. In this sense—and this sense only—the crisis of 1989 almost came as a relief.

As *Campaign* remarked in September 1970, "each is caught up in the infectious enthusiasm of the other. If they become aware that you are accusing them of oversimplification or platitudes, they are sure that you will still accept that what they are saying is true and unique to their thinking." *Campaign* remarked wonderingly on the "self-confidence, conviction, and innocence" with which the brothers launched their agency and their seemingly impossible ambition to make the agency a public company within three years. In the end the realization of that ambition took longer—five years.

Whatever the target, the brothers have applied the same method: define the objective, work out a way of achieving it, then set out and do it. Ask them how, and they reply simply that "if you want something enough, you will get it." There is a chilly single-mindedness about that statement, because they mean it. They wanted a public company and they got one; they wanted to be number one in Britain and they got there. They wanted a major American advertising company and they got one. Then they set out to become the world's number one and they got there too. There are dangers of overconfidence, of course: they made a clumsy run on the Midland Bank and fell flat on their faces. For the first time, simply wanting something wasn't necessarily enough to get it. Their shock upon discovering that profits in 1989 were going to be substantially lower was profound, but nothing in comparison to their reaction when in June 1989 they finally took their biggest setback on the chin: they decided to pull out of management consulting and to sell that whole business.

Looking back, one has to ask: just what *have* they achieved? How important are the Saatchi brothers? Have they really changed an industry, influenced or developed new philosophies? Has their effect on the American advertising industry, undoubtedly considerable in corporate terms, been good or bad? Are they anything more than just another couple of young entrepreneurs who have done well for their shareholders and made a bit of money along the way?

In *Confessions of an Advertising Man*, David Ogilvy quotes Frances Cairncross of *The Economist*: "The common characteristic of success is the deliberate creation of a corporate culture." Ogilvy claims that the factor that differentiates Ogilvy & Mather from any of its competitors is that it is the only agency in the world with a real corporate culture. That is simply not true. Ogilvy may not like Saatchi's corporate culture, but it is clearly defined, stated, and *understood* throughout the group, even among the new arrivals. Indeed, the brothers have deliberately created and fostered it, even at the expense of losing some of the identity of agencies they have taken over. In terms of Ogilvy's criterion, then, the Saatchis are without doubt a success.

As for their importance and impact on the industry, there is not much doubt about that either. In London advertising circles it is fashionable now to talk about the "second"- and "third"-wave agencies; Saatchi, along with Collett Dickenson Pearce and Boase Massimi Pollitt, is "first" wave; agencies such as WCRS, Bartle Bogle Hegarty, and Lowe Howard-Spink & Bell are "second"—meaning that they were founded mostly by people who left the "first" wave to go it alone. In the last five years a "third" wave has come along, created by refugees from the "second"—which makes Saatchi & Saatchi a grandfather agency. These successive waves have made London a considerable center of creative and imaginative advertising. Even Ogilvy, in his updated version of *Confessions*, acknowledges it. When he originally wrote his book twenty-five years ago, he says, "advertising people still looked to Madison Avenue as Muslims look to Mecca." And today? Now, says Ogilvy, they look to London: "They hire British copywriters and have their television commercials produced in England." Ogilvy does not like what the Saatchis stand for, but he cannot ignore them. And his book is still required reading for every budding advertising executive, who now learns that London is the creative Mecca. Before the Saatchis led the charge across the Atlantic, British advertising was generally regarded as irrelevant in New York. If New York agencies did look to London occasionally for ideas, who had the creative reputation in the 1970s? In Saatchi & Saatchi's early days even Charles Saatchi sought his inspiration 3,000 miles west of London.

Fashions in advertising, as in all other industries, come and go, and Madison Avenue in its time has seen plenty of new trends. The Saatchi agencies in America operate autonomously and are as American as any other. Already the fashion is changing as new, creative American advertising comes forward, most of it from agencies other than the Saatchi ones. But the Saatchis have had a deeper and more fundamental impact on America that will not be forgotten so easily. Bob Jacoby argues that the Saatchi takeovers were what made every agency in New York more profit-conscious and efficient—which may be a good thing for the shareholders but not necessarily for the clients. There are also plenty of advertising people, as we have seen, who blame the Saatchis for the greater megamerger phase that reshaped the American advertising industry in a space of a few months, with large numbers of employees laid off and a shrinkage in competition. Time may possibly show that these were changes for the good, but right now the argument is still, what does it do for the client? It may take longer to persuade customers that the marketing "supermarket" is good for them than it does to actually make that "supermarket" work to the customers' advantage. It is also not clear what it does for the shareholder—those benefits too are far from proven.

In the meantime the Saatchis remain the major talk of the industry. As I write this in March 1989, I have the latest issue of *Campaign* in front of me. On page one there is a story that Saatchi & Saatchi has become the first British agency to break the £300 million billings barrier, which means that the Charlotte Street agency—and remember, Saatchi has three other agencies in London—has tripled in size since 1981. According to *Campaign*'s figures, the Charlotte Street agency is £60 million ahead of its nearest rival, which is still J. Walter Thompson; BSB Dorland, a merger of Dorland and the British end of Ted Bates, was the third biggest British agency. There are more stories about Saatchi & Saatchi on pages two, three, and four. On page five there is a picture of Roy Warman and Terry Bannister, now appointed to the main board of the holding company, and an analysis of the breakup value of Saatchi, putting it at £1.5 billion—more than twice the current market value. There is another story about Saatchi on page eight, one on page nine, a mention on page twelve and page thirteen—and so on. It is a typical week.

But the spring of 1989 found the brothers in a box, the sides of which seemed to become ever tighter. Saatchi's stock price at less than half its former heights effectively ruled out acquisitions. Its infallibility as the group that could produce higher profits year after year had collapsed. The brothers no longer had access to the stock market because at the current low price of Saatchi stock, raising money through a new offering would have been prohibitively expensive. Nor could they borrow because the debt market is largely closed to advertising agencies due to their lack of assets.

The London magazine *Financial Weekly* commented that it would not be difficult "to put together a theory about Saatchi that says it has reached a strategic impasse, consisting of an over-dependence on the patronage of a City that is no longer indulgent and too slavish an adherence to theories that Saatchi's own experience has demonstrated to be invalid." There were plenty who were putting together that very thesis, while the brothers now spent much of their time trying to find a way out. They investigated the possibility of a leveraged buyout but found that specialists such as Kohlberg Kravis Roberts in New York were unenthusiastic. The LBO merchants don't like advertising agencies either, for the same reason banks don't: there are no assets to sell off. The brothers sought advice from investment bankers on both sides of the Atlantic and considered a variety of schemes, such as reversing Saatchi & Saatchi into an already quoted American company. None of these possibilities would get them out of the box.

Most of the advice the Saatchis got was along the same lines: they would have to work their way out over a period of years, persuading the markets that everything they had talked about for the past fifteen years was more than rhetoric and that globalization and size actually meant something in reality. The decision to sell out of consulting ended the period of probation. The argument had been lost, at least by the Saatchis.

Charles and Maurice pressed on with new ideas, notably the launch of

Saatchi's centralized media-buying operation called Zenith, under which all the media buying in the various agencies owned by the group would be handled by a single organization. Initially, the idea was launched for the British agencies, but the brothers indicated that it would soon go to Europe—and then worldwide. "At present top advertisers are dwarfed by the size of revenues of the top media groups," said John Perriss, the Saatchi board member charged with putting Zenith into operation. It would alter the balance back, he argued. Zenith met a mixed reception, but in effect it was the logical extension of Charles's original passion for offering something different in the media-buying division. It also served to show the world that Saatchi was still radical and innovative—and controversial.

There were other events that kept the brothers in the headlines through the autumn of 1988 and early 1989. In October 1988 Victor Millar in Washington announced that Saatchi & Saatchi was backing a new consulting group set up by a number of his old colleagues from Arthur Andersen. Maurice still longed to take over the consultancy business of Andersen, but having failed at that the next best thing was to bring in as many senior Andersen staff members as possible.

The new company, called Information Consulting Group, aimed to specialize in systems integration, part of the information-systems area Millar and Maurice had decided was central to their consultancy operations. They had already paid $90 million for the U.S. information-technology specialist Gartner Group. The Andersen team, led by Gresham Brebach, the former head of its U.S. consultancy side who earlier in 1988 had fallen out with his old firm, agreed to give Saatchi an option (for $8 million) to buy out the Gartner Group after five years. This was seen as a move of some significance: Saatchi now had both Millar and Brebach, two very senior Andersen people, in its camp. But the Hay Group consultancy subsidiary, still only accounting for 20 percent of group profits against Maurice's stated target of 50 percent, was well below expectations. Months later, it would all be for sale.

The brothers also got Saatchi's shares listed on the booming Tokyo stock market, although doing so had no measurable impact on the share price. Saatchi signed a deal with Gostelradio, Moscow's state radio and television service, to advise on its modernization, a move that gave the press some fun along the lines of "Thatcher's favorite agency defects to the Russians." When the British Bar Council, the heart of the British legal establishment, found itself threatened by Thatcherite reforms, it called in Saatchi; when British Rail, attempting to drive a new high-speed rail link through the Kent countryside (solid Conservative territory) to connect with the new Channel tunnel, ran up against savage demonstrations, it too sent for Saatchi. The Saatchi business was as much at the center of British life as ever.

In June 1989 Saatchi & Saatchi also moved its office again, this time to grander quarters than anything the agency had ever enjoyed before: a new building in Berkeley Square in Mayfair, paying the highest rent in the West End.

Some of these moves were designed deliberately to show the world that there was life in the company still. But the stock price responded only when headlines of a different kind started to circulate: Bob Jacoby was back in the brothers' lives. In mid-February the New York advertising industry was suddenly alive with news. Jacoby was said to be putting together a consortium, with Arab backing, to take his revenge by making a bid for Saatchi & Saatchi. "Some industry observers suggest Jacoby is prepared to risk the massive client and staff fallout which would inevitably result from his hostile bid, so great is his desire to seek vengeance on the Saatchis for what he sees as his earlier ill-treatment," reported *Campaign* on February 17, 1989.

In London the brothers responded to the rumors about Jacoby's new venture with a mixture of horror and amusement. They had been unable to raise the money for a buyout—how could Jacoby succeed where they could not? But at the same time they took the precaution of running the numbers again. What was Saatchi worth in a breakup? Nearly three times the current stock value, they concluded. So why didn't the market register that? Their frustration became all the greater.

Martin Sorrell sympathized. Although neither he nor the Saatchis acknowledged any great rivalry between them, there was little doubt among outside observers that this rivalry existed and was intense. Saatchi's stated intention was to be the world's "foremost global know-how company," while WPP wanted to be "the major multinational marketing-services company." There is little fundamental difference between the two objectives. Sorrell, however, had fared much better in terms of the stock market. By February 1989 WPP's shares had climbed back to their postcrash high and had outperformed the rest of the market by 50 percent. Sorrell was well ahead of schedule with his debt-reduction program, and his object of getting margins up to 10 percent was in sight. Even the Lord, Geller subsidiary was beginning to show signs of new life. From this background Sorrell could afford to be generous in analyzing his old company.

Saatchi, he says, succeeded famously in reaching its first objective: to become the largest advertising agency. The next target, to become the largest consultancy company, was still a possibility. The move into financial services was the right strategy, Sorrell argued—but Saatchi's timing was wrong. But none of this, he said, would ever satisfy the insatiable investment analysts. "It doesn't matter how well you do," Sorrell concluded; "they still ask you what you are going to do for an encore." Maybe, he added, there was an argument that you should be in financial services once you dominated marketing services and consulting:

"There are linkages there; whether they are financially viable or advisable is another issue." But by then it was academic to the brothers—the drop in profits had indefinitely killed any idea they had of going into financial services. Sorrell had gone a long way down the road toward convincing the investment community that his strategy was right. In that he was ahead of the Saatchis. In terms of size, he was now level pegging.

On one point, however, Martin Sorrell is insistent: no one should ever underestimate the Saatchi brothers. Their greatest talent, he says, is "persistence."

"In ten years time, Saatchi & Saatchi could be the most important company in Britain," Maurice told Sir Kit McMahon during the course of their two-hour meeting to discuss the takeover of Midland Bank. McMahon was puzzled. "Why," he asked Maurice, "do you want to be the most important company? I can see it if it were the biggest, the most profitable, the smartest, the most interesting—but the most important? What does that mean?"

McMahon saw Maurice's projection as "marketing thinking," the view that the image mattered more than the substance. Maurice would see matters differently. Only by becoming all those things—biggest, most profitable, smartest, most interesting—would Saatchi become "the most important." That is the logical extension of the targets the brothers have so far set themselves—and for a while actually hit.

It was George Orwell who remarked that one cannot "succeed" at life. The Saatchis have had a good shot at it.

APPENDIX A
SAATCHI & SAATCHI COMPANY PLC ACQUISITIONS

1973   Public-Synthese (Belgium)
Ricardo Slesian (Holland)
E. J. Dawes
Optadragon (France)
1974   Netleys
George G. Smith
1975   Garland-Compton
1977   Halls Advertising
O'Kennedy Brindley (80 percent acquired)
1981   Age Synergy Ltd.
Garrott Dorland Crawford Holdings Ltd.
O'Kennedy Brindley Ltd. (20 percent acquired)
1982   Compton Communications Inc.
1983   McCaffrey & McCall Inc.
Hunter Advertising Ltd.
Kohua Pty. (trading as Gough Waterhouse)
1984   R.J.A. Holdings BV
Harrison Cowley (Holdings) PLC
Cochrane Chase Livingstone Inc.
Yankelovich, Skelly and White Inc.
McBer Inc.
Way Associates
Wedger Mitchell Stark
1985   Infocom Group Ltd.
Wong Lam

The Rowland Company
Siegel and Gale
Marlboro Marketing Inc.
Sharps Advertising Ltd.
MC-Croupe 7
Clancy, Shulman and Co.
McCaffrey McCall
Kingsway
D&H Agentur (Germany)
1986   Humphries Bull Barker
R.C.P. (Spain)
Grandfield Rork Collins
Backer and Spielvogel Inc.
Chow Lang
Ted Bates
MVL
Sallingbury-Casey
Dancer Fitsgerald Sample
Grupo Alas
1987   Patterson Minority
Cleveland
Straiton Pearson
Type Edition
SSC—Denmark
Arellano-Bates
Campaign Palace
Litigation Sciences Inc.
Grody Tellem
Mann Wardle
Ottesan Bates
Peterson
Neilson McCarthy
Bond International

1988   Gaynor Associates
        Laurent
        Trucolour Transparencies
        Syllogistics
        Knoth and Meads
        Cross Associates
        National Research Group
        Creative Displays
        Corporate Planners and Co-
            ordinators
        Ted Bates New Zealand
            Minority
        Gartner Group
        Allied Advertising
        Ray Morgan and Partners
        M.H.I.

        MacKay King
        FDBP SA
        Turner Spurrier
        Graphic Evidence
        Information Consulting
            Group Option
        D.F.S. Australia
        Comark
        Cash Plus (minority)
1989   Adaptus
        Jahnsson & Sjogren
        Smith Marketing
        Diamond Advertising (10
            percent)
        Taylor Tarpay

Appendix B
Saatchi & Saatchi Company PLC Financial Record

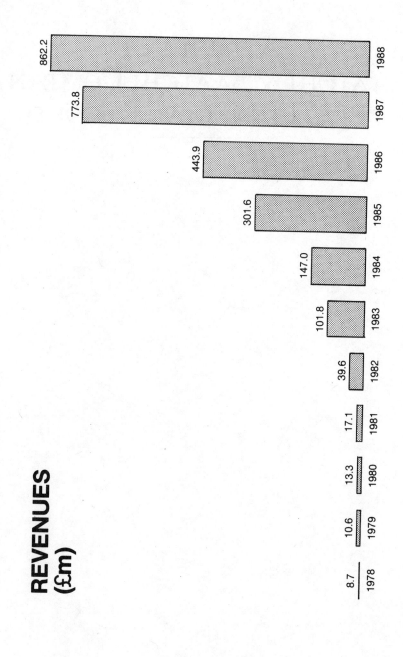

REVENUES
(£m)

862.2 — 1988
773.8 — 1987
443.9 — 1986
301.6 — 1985
147.0 — 1984
101.8 — 1983
39.6 — 1982
17.1 — 1981
13.3 — 1980
10.6 — 1979
8.7 — 1978

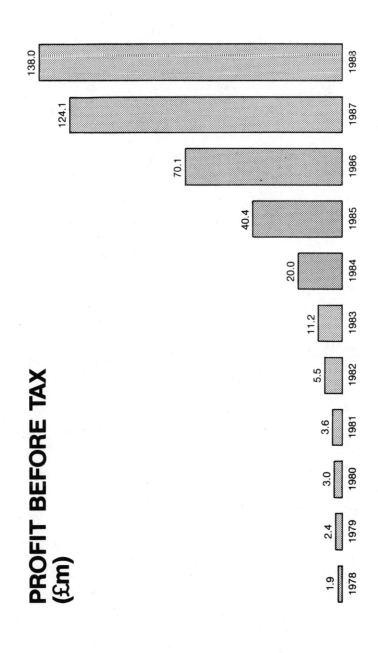

PROFIT BEFORE TAX
(£m)

Year	Profit
1978	1.9
1979	2.4
1980	3.0
1981	3.6
1982	5.5
1983	11.2
1984	20.0
1985	40.4
1986	70.1
1987	124.1
1988	138.0

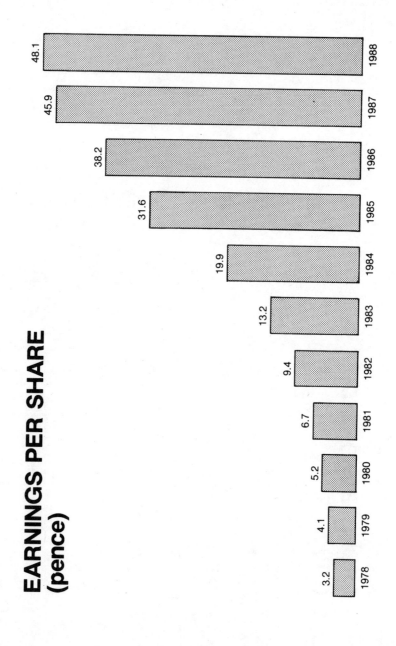

EARNINGS PER SHARE
(pence)

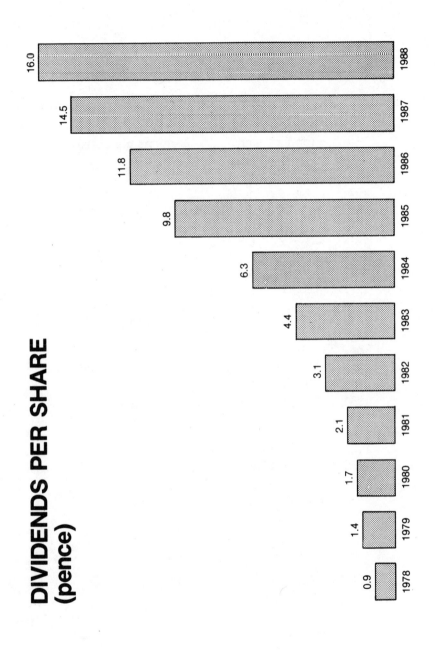

DIVIDENDS PER SHARE (pence)

Year	Pence
1978	0.9
1979	1.4
1980	1.7
1981	2.1
1982	3.1
1983	4.4
1984	6.3
1985	9.8
1986	11.8
1987	14.5
1988	16.0

Pretax Profits and Earnings per Share
Year Ending September 30

	Pretax profits (pounds sterling, millions)	Earnings per share (pence)
1971	£ .1	
1972	£ .4	
1973	£ .6	
1974	£ .6	
1975	£ .8	
1976	£ 1.0	2.6p
1977	£ 1.2	3.0p
1978	£ 1.9	3.2p
1979	£ 2.4	4.1p
1980	£ 3.0	5.2p
1981	£ 3.6	6.7p
1982	£ 5.5	9.4p
1983	£ 11.2	13.2p
1984	£ 18.3	19.9p
1985	£ 40.4	31.6p
1986	£ 70.1	38.2p
1987	£124.1	45.9p
1988	£138.0	48.1p

Bibliography

Barnet, Richard, and Ronald Muller. *Global Reach: The Power of the Multinational Corporations.* New York: Simon and Schuster, 1975.

Birmingham, Stephen. *Our Crowd.* New York: Harper and Row, 1975.

Brittan, Samuel. *The Economic Consequences of Democracy.* Brookfield, VT: Gower Publishing Co., 1988.

Butler, David, and Dennis Kavanagh. *The British General Election of 1979.* New York: Holmes and Meier, 1980.

———. *The British General Election of 1983.* New York: Macmillan, 1984.

———. *The British General Election of 1987.* New York: St. Martin's, 1988.

Central Office of Information. *Advertising and Public Relations in Britain.*

Clark, Eric. *The Want Makers.* Kent, Eng.: Hodder and Stoughton, 1988.

Corina, Maurice. *Trust in Tobacco.* London: Michael Joseph, 1975.

Davis, William. *The Innovators: The World's 200 Most Original Business Thinkers.* New York: AMACOM, 1987.

Della Femina, Jerry. *From Those Wonderful Folks Who Gave You Pearl Harbor.* London: Pitman, 1971.

Drucker, Peter F. *Management: Tasks, Practices, Responsibilities.* New York: Harper and Row, 1974.

———. *The Age of Discontinuity.* New York: Harper and Row, 1978.

Fallon, Ivan, and James Srodes. *Takeovers.* London: Hamish Hamilton, 1987.

Galbraith, John Kenneth. *Annals of an Abiding Liberal.* New York: Houghton Mifflin, 1979.

———. *The Nature of Mass Poverty.* Boston: Harvard University Press, 1979.

Heller, Robert. *The Supermarketers: Marketing for Success, Rules of the Master Marketers, the Naked Marketplace.* New York: Dutton, 1987.

Henry, Brian, ed. *British Television Advertising: The First Thirty Years.* London: Century Hutchinson, 1987.

Kleinman, Philip. *Advertising Inside Out.* London: W. H. Allen, 1977.

———. *The Saatchi & Saatchi Story.* London: Weidenfeld and Nicholson, 1987.

Levitt, Theodore. *The Marketing Imagination.* New York: The Free Press, 1983.

MacGregor, Ian, with Rodney Tyler. *The Enemies Within.* San Francisco: Collins, 1986.

Mayer, Martin. *Madison Avenue U.S.A.* New York: Penguin, 1958.

McMillan, James, and Bernard Harris. *The American Takeover of Britain.* London: Leslie Frewin, 1968.

Millman, Nancy. *Emperors of Adland.* New York: Warner Books, 1989.

Naisbitt, John. *Megatrends.* London: Macdonald and Co., 1984.

Nevett, T. R. *Advertising in Britain.* London: Heinemann, 1982.

Ogilvy, David. *Confessions of an Advertising Man.* New York: Atheneum, 1980.

———. *Ogilvy on Advertising.* New York: Random House, 1985.

———. *The Unpublished David Ogilvy.* New York: Crown, 1987.

Packard, Vance. *The Hidden Persuaders.* New York: Pocket Books, 1981.

Pearson, John, and Graham Turner. *The Persuasion Industry.* Hampshire, Eng.: Eyre and Spottiswoode, 1965.

Piggott, Stanley. *OBM 125 Years.* (Pamphlet), 1975.

Reeves, Rosser. *Reality in Advertising.* New York: Alfred A. Knopf, 1961.

Rejwan, Nissim. *The Jews of Iraq.* Boulder, CO: Westview, 1986.

Schjeldahl, Peter. *Art of Our Time: The Saatchi Collection.* London: Lund Humphries, 1984.

Townsend, Robert. *Up the Organization.* New York: Alfred A. Knopf, 1970.

Turner, Graham. *The Leyland Papers.* Hampshire, Eng.: Eyre and Spottiswoode, 1971.

Tyler, Rodney. *Campaign.* London: Grafton Books, 1987.

Worcester, Robert, and Martin Harrop. *Political Communications.* Winchester, MA: Allen and Unwin, 1982.

Articles and Periodicals

Day, Barry. "100 Great Advertisements." Times Newspapers Ltd., Mirror Group and *Campaign* magazine, 1978.

Levitt, Theodore. "Marketing Myopia." *Harvard Business Review,* 1984.

———. "The Globalization of Markets." *Harvard Business Review,* 1983.

Sheth, Jagdish N. "The Future of the Advertising Agency."

West, Douglas C. "The London Office of the J. Walter Thompson Advertising Agency 1919–1970." *Business History,* vol. 29, 1987.

INDEX